Praise for *Lost Kingdom*

"In Siler's second book (after *The House of Mondavi: The Rise and Fall of an American Wine Dynasty*), she brings to life the story of America's annexation of the sovereign Hawaiian Islands. . . . Siler gives readers a sweeping tale of tragedy, greed, betrayal, and imperialism. The depth of her research shines through the narrative, and the lush prose and quick pace make for engaging reading. Anyone interested in Hawaiian history or American imperialism will find this an absorbing read."   —*Library Journal* (starred review)

"Too many Americans forget (if they ever knew) that our 'island paradise' was acquired via a cynical, imperious land grab . . . Siler skillfully places her account within the context of late nineteenth-century power rivalry, as France, Britain, and the United States sought dominant position in the Pacific. . . . The missionary-educated queen [Lili'uokalani] is seen as an admirable, tragic figure whose efforts to straddle both the modern and traditional Hawaiian worlds proved futile. This is a well-written, fast-moving saga that explores a seamy aspect of our territorial growth."   —*Booklist*

"Siler rehearses the dark imperial history of how Americans first arrived in the islands, how they rose in power and how they deposed the queen and took everything. . . . But this is mostly the story of white entrepreneurs and missionaries who came and conquered. . . . Eventually, white economic interests trumped all else, and the queen struggled and failed to retain authority. A well-rendered narrative of paradise and imperialism."   —*Kirkus Reviews*

"It's easy to think of Hawaii as a relatively untouched paradise. . . . But author Julia Flynn Siler shows another side of Hawaii that many tend to forget . . . before it was annexed into the United States, Hawaii was ruled for generations by a thriving monarchy. And before that, it existed in blissful isolation until Polynesian islanders first settled. . . . What happened to the islands is known as one of the most aggressive takeovers of the Gilded Age. And Siler, a contributing writer for *The Wall Street Journal*, gives us a riveting and intimate look at the rise and tragic fall of Hawaii's royal family using historical documents, letters (many of which had never been published), and diary entries."   —*Fortune*

"Julia Flynn Siler's *Lost Kingdom* is a well-told history of the U.S. acquisition of Hawaii. The central figure is Lili'uokalani, who had the misfortune of being queen when Uncle Sam closed his grasp on the islands. . . . But by the time she took the throne, those who had gone before her had given away most of the store. . . . Her well-told history with its photos and glossary of Hawaiian terms comes at a time when sovereign rights are being considered for native Hawaiians and debate continues over ownership of land seized from the monarchy, now worth billions."   —*The Seattle Times*

"Queen Liliʻuokalani is the focus but not the sole subject of *Lost Kingdom*, journalist Julia Flynn Siler's well-researched, nicely contextualized history of events leading to the U.S. annexation of Hawaii in 1898. . . . Siler is balanced, if hardly impartial, in chronicling the tense two years leading to that moment . . . indeed, as Siler characterizes it, 'one of the most audacious land grabs of the Gilded Age,' so blatant that even the U.S. government was embarrassed by it."   —*Los Angeles Times*

"Richly and diversely sourced . . . [Siler is] able to color in many figures who had heretofore existed largely in outline or black and white . . . a solidly researched account of an important chapter in our national history, one that most Americans don't know but should."   —*The New York Times Book Review*

"Behind the modern bustle of the nation's only island state lies this sad, sobering tale of decline, betrayal, and imperialism. It centers on the admirable last monarch of the Hawaiians, Queen Liliʻuokalani, who struggled against palace intrigue, American sugar barons, and eventually cynical American military diplomacy before losing her throne in 1893, a few years before the United States simply annexed the Hawaiian islands as American territory. *Wall Street Journal* contributing writer Siler skillfully weaves the tangled threads of this story into a satisfying tapestry about the late nineteenth-century death of a small nation."   —*Publishers Weekly*

"In Julia Flynn Siler's new book, *Lost Kingdom*, we get a close look at how foreigners from Germany, Britain, and the United States jockeyed for influence and schemed to take over the government during Hawaii's last few decades of independence. Siler's experience as a reporter for *The Wall Street Journal* serves her well as she depicts the figures who brought down the islands' monarchy. . . . Siler paints an engaging portrait of Hawaii's ruling class under fire and desperate to keep the monarchy together. She tells the complicated story of Hawaii's last king, Kalakaua, and his sister who succeeded him, Queen Liliʻuokalani, whom she calls 'Liliʻu.' . . . With new access to diaries and writings by Liliʻu, Siler is able to reveal the queen's fragile state of mind as she is brought down by her enemies."   —*The Washington Post*

"This imperious slice of American history hasn't exactly been hiding under a rock for the past 125 years, but Siler, a *Wall Street Journal* reporter based in San Francisco, retells it with agitating freshness. . . . Though Siler coaxes out a cultural, personal, or geopolitical context for most every event that comes onstage, it is with the greater setting, the diorama, where she excels. Throughout the story, Siler, the author of *The House of Mondavi*, fashions a sense of intimacy in mood and atmosphere. It might be in the way she fluently describes a Hawaiian night, so easefully accomplished and seemingly innocuous, but in truth it is a powerful act of transport."   —*San Francisco Chronicle*

Lost Kingdom

Lost Kingdom

*Hawaii's Last Queen, the Sugar Kings,
and America's First Imperial Adventure*

JULIA FLYNN SILER

Grove Press
New York

Endpaper map by Dorling Kindersley/Getty Images

Published simultaneously in Canada
Printed in the United States of America

FIRST EDITION

ISBN: 978-0-8021-2070-0

Grove Press
an imprint of Grove/Atlantic, Inc.
841 Broadway
New York, NY 10003

Distributed by Publishers Group West

www.groveatlantic.com

13 14 15   10 9 8 7 6 5 4 3 2 1

TABLE OF CONTENTS

CAST OF CHARACTERS   vii

GLOSSARY   xi

INTRODUCTION   xvii

PREFACE   xxv

PART I: ISLAND KINGDOM

CHAPTER ONE: *Born in Paradise*   3

CHAPTER TWO: *Progress and Liberty*   18

CHAPTER THREE: *Aloha*   38

CHAPTER FOUR: *High Chiefs of Sugardom*   53

CHAPTER FIVE: *Pele's Wrath*   74

PART II: THE HOUSE OF KALĀKAUA

CHAPTER SIX: *Merrie Monarch*   97

CHAPTER SEVEN: *To England*   113

CHAPTER EIGHT: *Bayonet Constitution*   131

CHAPTER NINE: *Be Not Deceived* 148

CHAPTER TEN: *Enemies in the Household* 177

PART III: MANIFEST DESTINY

CHAPTER ELEVEN: *Pious Adventurers* 199

CHAPTER TWELVE: *Crime of the Century* 220

CHAPTER THIRTEEN: *Secrets of the Flower Beds* 245

CHAPTER FOURTEEN: *Kingdom Come* 261

CHAPTER FIFTEEN: *Born Under an Unlucky Star* 274

EPILOGUE 289

A NOTE ON LANGUAGE AND SOURCES 297

ACKNOWLEDGMENTS 303

BIBLIOGRAPHY 309

ENDNOTES 325

INDEX 397

CAST OF CHARACTERS
(in order of appearance)

King Kamehameha I The warrior chief who united the eight inhabited islands of Hawai'i into a kingdom by 1810, using Western weapons and advisors. He founded the Kamehameha dynasty.

Queen Lili'uokalani Born in a grass house in 1838 and adopted by Hawai'i's then ruling Kamehameha dynasty, Lili'u (pronounced *Lee-lee-ooh*), as she was known by intimates, was a fervent patriot and the last queen of Hawai'i.

Claus Spreckels This German immigrant to the United States was a driven entrepreneur who, on his periodic trips to the islands, carved out a Hawaiian sugar empire from former royal lands and became known as the uncrowned king of Hawai'i.

Lorrin Andrews Thurston A grandson of New England missionaries to the islands, Thurston was a fiery orator, lawyer, and entrepreneur who led Lili'u's overthrow and, afterward, became the publisher of what is now the *Honolulu Star-Advertiser*.

Amos Starr Cooke Amos and his wife, Juliette, were missionaries who ran the Chiefs' Children's School and taught Lili'u and other royal children there. After retiring in 1850, Amos went on to found Castle & Cooke, which became one of the "Big Five" sugar firms.

Bernice Pauahi Bishop Lili'u's *hānai*, or foster who married the American banker Charles R. Bishop and inherited the largest share of the Kamehameha dynasty's royal lands from Princess Ruth, making her the islands' largest landholder.

King David Kalākaua Lili'u's older brother, born in 1836, David ascended to the throne in 1874 and was the first ruling monarch to circumnavigate the globe. A man of large appetites and even larger ambitions, he became deeply indebted to American sugar planters.

Lord George Paulet A renegade commander of a British frigate, he forced the first cession of the islands to a foreign power in 1843—a move his superiors quickly reversed—in what became known as the "Paulet Affair."

John Owen Dominis This American-born son of a ship captain married Lili'u and became prince consort when she ascended to Hawai'i's throne in 1891. Their sometimes difficult marriage produced no biological children.

Queen Emma Rooke An anglophile *ali'i* who married Kamehameha IV in 1856. As a widow, Emma sought the throne in a bitter contest in 1874 with David Kalākaua and warned against rising influence of American planters and merchants.

Sanford Ballard Dole A missionary's son and cousin of the Dole Food Company (Hawaiian Pineapple Co.) founder who described himself as "of American blood but Hawaiian milk," he was the first president of the newly formed Republic of Hawai'i and played a key role in Lili'u's overthrow, though afterward he privately expressed remorse.

Princess Miriam Likelike Lili'u and David Kalākaua's fun-loving sister, she was the mother of Princess Ka'iulani and wife of Scotsman Archibald Cleghorn. Miriam Likelike was Lili'u's closest friend and confidant until her early death.

Archibald Cleghorn Miriam Likelike's husband, a Scotsman, was O'ahu's governor and a royalist who sought to protect his daughter's interests. Like King Kalākaua he, too, became deeply indebted to sugar interests, although British instead of American.

Princess Ka'iulani Niece to Queen Lili'uokalani and heir to the throne, this lovely half Scottish, half Hawaiian princess captivated the author Robert

Louis Stevenson and died in 1899 shortly after America's annexation of Hawai'i in 1898.

Walter Murray Gibson A white adventurer with a murky past, Gibson came to Hawai'i to preach the Gospel as a Mormon missionary. After being excommunicated he became King Kalākaua's prime minister and a supporter of sugar interests.

Princess Ruth Ke'elikōlani A member of the Kamehameha dynasty, Ruth sold her stake in the crown lands to the American sugar baron Claus Spreckels in a questionable deal. Upon her death, Ruth willed her remaining lands to Bernice Pauahi Bishop.

Joseph Nāwahī This missionary-educated Hawaiian who was a journalist, legislator, landscape painter, and one of the leaders of an uprising in support of the monarchy. He opposed a treaty leasing Pearl Harbor to the Americans, calling it a "nation-snatching" agreement.

Robert William Wilcox A Native Hawaiian who led two insurrections, six years apart, in support of the monarchy. Wilcox fashioned himself after the Italian revolutionary Garibaldi, leading a team of red-shirted revolutionaries and marrying an Italian contessa; he was twice tried for treason.

Colonel Sam Parker Descended from Kamehameha I, he was a cabinet minister and a member of the family that owned the vast Parker Ranch on the island of Hawai'i. Like others in the royal circle he, too, succumbed to sugar fever.

Charles Wilson A tall, powerfully built, half Tahitian, Wilson stepped into the role as Lili'u's protector after her husband's death. He was Marshal of the Kingdom at the time of the overthrow and was married to the former Eveline "Kitty" Townsend, Lili'u's "particular personal friend."

John Leavitt Stevens He was the U.S. minister to Hawai'i who supported the overthrow of the monarchy. A former Universalist pastor, newspaperman, and state Republican party leader, he authorized the landing of U.S. troops.

Albert Francis Judd Longtime Chief Justice of Hawai'i's Supreme Court, he presided over Lili'u's trial in 1895. His father, Gerritt P. Judd, an early medical missionary, served as a royal advisor and legislator and was one of the founders of what became the Punahou School.

GLOSSARY

What follows is a selection of the most frequently used Hawaiian terms in the book. Definitions are adapted from the *Hawaiian Dictionary* by Mary Kawena Pukui and Samuel H. Elbert, which is available online at www. wehewehe.org.

ahupua'a Traditional Hawaiian land division, in which wedge-shaped parcels stretch from their broadest points at the fertile land near the sea to the uplands at their tip. They often followed the paths of streams, giving each family group that worked them access to fish, arable land, timber, and fresh water.

'āina Land or earth.

ali'i Chief, ruler, noble or monarch, depending on the context. Traditionally, the term *ali'i nui* was used to denote the highest rank of chiefs, who were treated like gods and in turn, had obligations to fulfill to the commoners, with *ali'i* signifying a chief of secondary rank.

aloha A word with many meanings, including love, affection, compassion and charity, often said as a friendly greeting or farewell.

'awa The kava (*Piper methysticum*) plant, which is native to the Pacific islands, as well as the name of the narcotic drink made from the plant's root. The drink was used as a traditional Hawaiian medicinal tonic and for ceremonial purposes.

'awapuhi   Wild ginger (*Zingiber zerumbet*), whose root was used to dye and impart a fragrance to *tapa*. *'Awapuhi ke'o ke'o*, white ginger (*Hedychium coronarium*), features fragrant white flowers popular for *lei*. Both varieties are originally from India but grow in the wild and in cultivation in Hawai'i.

haku mele   Poet or composer.

hānai   Literally a foster or adopted child, the term refers to a Hawaiian tradition whereby newborns were sometimes given to close friends and relatives for adoption, as a means of strengthening bonds among families.

haole   In modern parlance, the word means a white person or Caucasian, and is sometimes used disparagingly. Originally, *haole* merely signified any foreigner, or could be used to describe anything of foreign origin, such as plants or animals.

hapa haole   A person of part-Caucasian origins. The term can also be used to describe a thing, such as a song, that is part Hawaiian, such as a *mele hapa haole*, a song with a mix of English and Hawaiian words.

heiau   A traditional Hawaiian place of worship, a temple or shrine; some *heiau* were simple raised earthen terraces, while others were built of stone.

heluhelu   To read or count, or to learn to read; a reader (both in the sense of an instructional book and a person who reads).

holokū   A loose, form-concealing dress with a yoke and, sometimes, a train, patterned after the Mother Hubbard gowns worn by the early Christian missionaries to the islands.

ho'okupu   A tribute or tax; a ceremonial offering to a chief as a sign of respect; a church offering.

hula   A traditional Hawaiian form of storytelling through dance, using graceful hand gestures and sinuous movements of the hips.

hula ku'i   Literally meaning "a joining hula" or "to join old and new steps," the *hula ku'i* was introduced during the reign of Kalākaua and incorporated traditional Hawaiian chants and movement in combination with Western-influenced music and costumes.

hula ma'i   A *hula* celebrating the chiefs and their sacred genitalia and procreative vigor. With rapid hip revolutions, the dance is lively, sexually erotic and provocative.

'iolani   Literally, soaring hawk—an image associated with royalty due to the towering height of a hawk's flight. Derived from the word *'iolana*, which means to soar.

kāhili   A feathered standard used to mark royalty.

kāhuna   Literally meaning a priest, magician, minister, or expert in any profession, the term came to refer to practitioners of traditional Hawaiian religion and/or healing rites.

Kanaka maoli   A full-blooded Hawaiian person.

kapu   Literally, a taboo or prohibition; sacred, holy, or forbidden; in modern times, the word means "no trespassing" or "keep out." A system of *kapu* regulated traditional Hawaiian life.

kaukau   Food or snack. The word is a pidgin English/Hawaiian term, derived from the Chinese term "chow chow."

kipi   Rebel, traitor; to revolt, plot, or resist authority; to ram, like a goat.

kuleana   A multifaceted word meaning right, privilege, responsibility, title, ownership; a reason or justification; or a small piece of property.

lei   A garland or wreath; a necklace of flowers, leaves, shells, feathers and/or other ornaments, usually given as a symbol of affection.

limu   The general term for plants living underwater as well as algae, mosses, and lichens; soft coral; seaweed.

lū'au   Originally a term for young taro tops, the word came to be used for Hawaiian feasts, at which the delicacy of tender taro tops was traditionally served.

luna   A foreman, boss or overseer; the term was used for plantation supervisors.

mahalo Thanks, gratitude; to thank.

mahele Literally, a portion, division, unit, or share; the word refers to the division of Hawaiian lands by Kamehameha III in 1848.

makaʻāinana Commoner; the populace or people in general; a citizen or subject.

makai A directional indication meaning toward the sea, as opposed to *mauka* (see below).

mamo Black Hawaiian honey creeper (*Drepanis pacifica*), whose yellow feathers above and below the tail were used in traditional featherwork. Presumed extinct since the 1880s.

mauka A directional indication meaning toward the mountains or inland.

mele Song or chant; poem. *Mele hapa haole* means a hymn or religious song.

mele hoāla Song or chant to wake someone who is sleeping.

oli A chant that is not danced to, characterized by long phrases chanted in one breath.

ʻonipaʻa Fixed, immovable, steadfast, motionless. This was Liliʻuokalani's personal motto.

ōʻō The extinct black honey eater (*Moho mobilis*), with yellow feathers in a tuft under each wing which were prized for use in traditional Hawaiian featherwork.

pau Finished, ended; final; completely consumed, possessed, or destroyed.

pīkake Peacocks, peafowl (*Pavo cristata*), introduced to Hawaiʻi around 1860; also Arabian jasmine from India (*Jasminum sambac*), with small, fragrant flowers used for leis. Since Princess Kaʻiulani liked both the flowers and the birds, she used the same name for them.

poi A Hawaiian food made from cooked taro or sometimes breadfruit, which is then pounded into a purplish paste and thinned with water.

pono A word with dozens of meanings, including goodness, righteousness, morality; prosperity, well-being.

tapa   A variant of *kapa,* which literally means "the beaten thing." Cloth made from beaten bark, which was then boldly decorated with plant dyes in traditional Hawaiian culture.

wai   Water, liquor, or liquid of any kind other than seawater; to flow like water; fluid.

INTRODUCTION

The story of Hawai'i begins millions of years ago, long before the green folds of its mountains were creased by cataracts foaming into the sea. Two enormous plates struck each other, creating a crack that reached the earth's liquid core. Plumes of molten rock shot up, piercing the black depths of the sea. Hissing steam burst into the air.

Hardened black rock grew mound by mound, forming a range of cone-shaped peaks which surfaced at around the same time the first mammals roamed the African plains. At first, only the tips of this underwater mountain range jutted above the ocean swells. But as lava accumulated, the range rose. A host of creatures made new homes on these harsh outcroppings: grubs, coral polyps, sea urchins, mother-of-pearl, conch shells, seaweed, ferns, and finally man and woman.

Thus began the world, as told in the *Kumulipo*, the Hawaiian chant which some scholars have compared to the Greek creation myths and Hebrew Genesis. In more than two thousand lines, it describes a world born in "deep darkness" advancing toward the light, expressing both the geological beginnings of the islands as well as the experience of a human emerging from a womb into the world.

The people who memorized this long chant were descendants of intrepid voyagers. Navigating by the stars and by observing subtle shifts in the wind, the flight paths of migrating birds, and even the changing color of the air, they accomplished an extraordinary feat. They found their way from Tahiti or the Marquesas to one of the most remote chains of islands in the world, some 2,400 miles from the nearest continent.

Setting off around the time that Constantine ruled the Roman Empire, perhaps as early as 200 A.D., they travelled thousands of miles before reaching the Hawaiian islands, paddling through the windless doldrums of the north Pacific and surviving its unpredictable squalls, gales, thunderstorms, and cyclones.

It's uncertain how many people made the trip or why they left their homes. Were they pulled to sea, drawn by the hope of new lands to settle? Or pushed onto the waves by drought, hunger, or warfare? Or maybe they were just adventurers, eager to discover what lay beyond the horizon's edge.

Whatever the reason, they prepared for a long journey. They brought gourds filled with fresh water, dried fruits, as well as dogs and pigs. They also brought cuttings of foods they hoped to plant, including tiny shoots of sugar cane—a crop that would come to shape the Hawai'i's destiny as much as the arrival of the first people who introduced it.

Once these voyagers reached the islands, they found an untouched Eden: a world with no four-legged predators, no serpents or snakes, and few biting insects. The seas teamed with fish and swaying underwater gardens. The forests rang with trills and flashed with the yellow brilliance of birds that had tumbled out of the jet stream. The islands were home to flightless birds and other defenseless creatures.

The highest peaks of this volcanic chain soared more than thirteen thousand feet and were often covered with snow. When the volcanoes erupted, they'd spew orange-red lava, which sped down the slopes of the mountains, releasing clouds of steam when they hit the cooling waters of the Pacific. Beyond the shores lay a separate underwater world of fluorescent coral reefs.

Hawai'i may have looked like a gentle paradise, but the ancient Hawaiians knew its terrors. A volcanic eruption, the fury of the goddess Pele, might destroy villages of grass houses and bury carefully tended fields of sugar cane and sweet potatoes beneath ash. Jagged deserts of sharp, black lava could appear overnight, creating new land where there had once been sea.

Pele, on a whim, might send pungent swirls of sulfur dioxide into the atmosphere, infusing the air and the mountain streams with its rotten-egg scent, or she might hurl flames down the slopes. The goddess was a force to be worshipped and placated with small offerings: taro root, dried fish, or mountain berries left near the edge of the crater. Sometimes larger offerings were necessary. Early visitors described criminals thrown into the volcano's depths as sacrifices to appease her.

The Polynesians who arrived in Hawai'i brought beliefs with them, including their long genealogies, memorized in the form of chants, and taboos, known as *kapu*. Like other South Sea Islanders, they believed in many gods. To worship them, they built stone temples, *heiau*, overseen by priests. They would lay offerings at fields and fish ponds, in hopes of the gods granting them good harvests. Priests, or *kāhuna*, would perform ceremonies seeking prosperity by offering up a black pig.

Some chiefs ruled with the imperiousness of Pele. They'd order lawbreakers put to death in fearsome ritualized killings that took place in a *heiau*, accompanied by beating drums and chants. Carved wooden statues of *Kū*, the god of war, bore silent witness to strangulations, followed by their practice of scorching the human skins over fire.

Afterward, these fierce people would pile coconuts and bananas next to the blackened skins of the victims—the stink of burned human flesh mingling with the sweet fragrance of fruit.

Perhaps because they lived with the unpredictability of the earth and the seas, the ancient Hawaiians adopted strict rules governing nearly every aspect of life. Their world was hierarchical and status depended on blood rank. At the top were the high chiefs, or *ali'i nui*, who were treated like gods but, in turn, had obligations to the commoners. Below them were the lesser chiefs, known simply as the *ali'i*, followed by such honored posts as the *haku mele*, or master of song, who composed and memorized the long genealogical chants by which a family would extol its nobility. At the bottom were a small group of slaves and outcasts.

The high chiefs literally towered above the commoners: tall in stature and with majestic physical prowess, the *ali'i* almost seemed like a distinct race. They commanded absolute obeisance. Commoners who failed to heed the cry of "*E noho e!*" or "Squat down!" as chiefs walked past risked instant death. Anyone who allowed his shadow to cross over that of the very highest chief faced having his throat slashed with a shark-toothed knife.

Is it any surprise that the Hawaiian creation chant, the *Kumulipo*, expresses awe at the world's beginnings as well as a deep sense of dread and fear? The life of the ancient Hawaiian, particularly among commoners and slaves, was one of strict rules, harsh punishments, and the volatile uncertainty of life on a volcanic island. Chant seven begins,

O kau ke anoano, ia'u kualono	Fear falls upon me on the mountaintop
He ano no ka po hane'e aku	Fear of the passing night
He ano no ka po hane'e mai	Fear of the night approaching
He ano no ka po pihapiha	Fear of the pregnant night
He ano no ka ha'iha'i	Fear of the breach of law

The lives and livelihoods of the commoners depended on the *ali'i*. Each of the eight populated islands was ruled by one or more chiefs. The ruling chief controlled the land, allocating arable sections to his followers, who, in turn, owed the chief his due, in the form of his share of their crops. In that sense, it was feudal. The chiefs also conscripted the commoners into armies and for countless years, warfare periodically erupted among rival *ali'i*, who fought over land, fishing rights, and perceived insults. But much of their time was spent in peaceful pursuits.

The ancient Hawaiians were ingenious in finding ways to use stones, plants, and bounty from the sea. They had no metal and had not discovered the wheel; instead, they used stone, shells, and hardened lava for tools. For this reason, later visitors would describe them as living in the Stone Age and in a sense they were.

With great care they cultivated taro, yams, and sweet potatoes planted in wedge-shaped sections of land that stretched from the mountains to the sea at their widest. Known as *ahupua'a*, these parcels of land often followed the paths of streams, giving each family group that worked them access to fish, arable land, timber, and fresh water.

To irrigate their fields, the Hawaiians built intricate stone aqueducts, some soaring twenty feet tall. They also dug extensive fish ponds, which allowed them to stockpile food. With limited resources, they found ways to make beautiful things, such as by weaving blades of dried grass into intricately patterned mats and dying them subtle shades of red from dyes derived from plants. They lived in framed houses lashed together with fiber and thatched with *pili* grass and covered their floors with finely woven sleeping mats.

Because commoners worked in the fields and tended the fish ponds, the *ali'i* could devote themselves to sports. Their favorite pastime was surfing and they rode the waves on enormous, carved wood boards—some more than eighteen feet long and weighing 150 pounds. Both male and female chiefs also excelled at related sports such as canoe-leaping, in which the surfer would jump from a canoe carrying his or her board into a cresting ocean swell, and then ride the wave to the shore.

When the surf was high, entire villages rushed to the beach. Men, women, and children would paddle out to ride the rolling waves. While Tahitians and other Pacific Islanders also surfed, the Hawaiians took the sport to a higher level—standing fearlessly on their massive boards, often three times as long as those used elsewhere in Polynesia.

The Hawaiians were magnificent athletes. Some excelled at cliff-diving into the sea, from heights of many hundreds of feet. Even young women would strip naked and leap from the summit of high cliffs, diving headlong into the foaming water and bobbing up afterward. One can only imagine their dark hair streaming down their shoulders and their faces beaming with delight.

Then came Captain Cook. Two ships, the *Discovery* and the *Resolution*, sailed into Kealakekua Bay on the island of Hawai'i in January, 1778, as Britain was fighting to regain control over its rebellious American colonies. The Hawaiians first spotted Cook arriving on what they believed was a floating *heiau*, or temple.

Was he the god Lono, who was prophesied to return during this season? A chief and a priest rowed out and boarded one of the strange ships. What they saw were men with fair skin, bright eyes, sharp noses, and deep-set eyes. At first, the Hawaiians didn't recognize what the foreigners were wearing: their odd cocked hats seemed to be part of their heads and their clothing wrinkled skin. Upon reporting back, they concluded "This is indeed Lono, and this is his heiau come across the sea . . . !"

Cook and his men arrived at a time when the vast wealth generated from sugar plantations in the West Indies was fueling the expansion of the British Empire. Yet Cook wasn't searching for sugarcane: he came in search of the elusive Northwest Passage—a fabled sea route between Europe and Asia.

When they landed, Cook and his men found fields flush with yams and taro nourished from cleverly-constructed aqueducts. They also found sugar—a plant brought to the islands by its original Polynesian settlers, who chewed stalks of cane to release the sweet juices inside. Although estimates vary, the islands supported a large and thriving population of people who farmed the coastal lowlands and fished the abundant sea.

To Cook's surprise, the Hawaiians welcomed him and his men with lavish hospitality, offering hogs, sweet potatoes, feather capes, and cloth of *tapa*. They landed during the season when the Hawaiians worshipped the benevolent fertility god Lono and Cook was venerated as the god himself, or at least his emissary.

To honor the Earl of Sandwich, who was then First Lord of Britain's Admiralty, Cook named the islands after him. For decades afterward, they were known in the English-speaking world as the Sandwich Islands. He never found the Northwest Passage, but his discovery of the islands would open up the Hawaiians—who had remained isolated from the rest of the world for thousands of years—to the expanding economies and empires of the West.

The English sailors also brought fleas, infection, and fearsome new weapons to the islands. When Hawaiians stole metal objects from the foreigners, the English sailors fired muskets to scare them off. Soon, there were other confrontations and the Hawaiians came to learn the power of what they called the "death-dealing thing which the white men used and which squirted out like the gushing forth of water." Recognizing their value, the Hawaiians avidly sought to trade for weapons by offering the English sailors hogs, chickens, and other items.

One young chief who visited Captain Cook aboard ship was Kamehameha, who was then in his mid-twenties. He approached the British vessel in a large, double canoe, paddled by about twenty-five men. A powerfully built man standing over six feet tall, he wore "a reserved, forbidding countenance" and a "keen, penetrating eye," according to the ship's surgeon. Within minutes of climbing aboard, Kamehameha was examining every part of it. The surgeon, who asked Kamehameha if he'd like him to explain how a compass worked, came to regret his offer because the chief questioned him "continually until he learned it." Two decades later, with the aid of Western advisors and guns, Kamehameha would unite the island and found Hawai'i's first ruling dynasty.

Although Cook forbade sexual intimacy between the sailors and the Hawaiians, the crews of the *Discovery* and the *Resolution* ignored his orders, as did the Hawaiian women, who swam out to the boats, offering themselves up freely in exchange for clothing, mirrors, scissors, knives, and metal hooks they could bend into fishhooks. The fevered pox of venereal disease soon spread rapidly across the islands, eventually leading to infertility and death among Hawaiians.

It wasn't long before the Hawaiians and English sailors clashed. After sailing more than 200,000 miles and exploring from Newfoundland to the Antarctic, Captain Cook met a swift and bloody end on February 14, 1779. In a dispute over a stolen boat, Cook shot one of the Hawaiians. In turn, a group of them attacked a landing party of Cook's men at the water's edge. In the melee, one Hawaiian clubbed Cook, another stabbed him in the back. He fell face-first on a shelf of black lava in knee-deep water, where they continued to pummel him until he died.

The fatal skirmish touched off a burst of violence from the British. They fired the ships' cannons into the crowd onshore and then shot six dead for throwing stones at a group of sailors who had gone ashore to find fresh water. They then set fire to 150 homes, and shot at the fleeing Hawaiians, bayoneting those who stayed behind.

Yet such bloodshed did not dissuade the Hawaiians that Cook deserved a chief's deathly due: funeral rites including skinning and disemboweling the corpse. Perhaps as a gesture intended to end the hostilities, the Hawaiians returned a grisly package to the crew of the *Discovery*. Wrapped in a feather cloak, it contained scorched limbs, a scalp with the ears still attached, and, apparently to preserve them, two hands that had been scored and salted.

The British sailors, more horrified than honored by the return of Cook's remains, lowered the Union Jack on both ships to half-mast, fired a ten-gun salute from the *Resolution* and tolled the ship's bell before committing the great explorer's remains to the deep. The ships left Kealakekua Bay shortly thereafter.

Although Cook didn't make it back to Britain alive, dozens of his sailors did. While they told of the famous explorer's gruesome end, they also told tantalizing stories of an archipelago of tropical islands, bursting with fruit and erotically swaying *hula* dancers. That brought a new wave of visitors to the islands. Some were drawn by the lure of trade and opportunity. Others were searching for an unspoiled paradise.

PREFACE

She walked down the palace steps toward a horse-drawn carriage. Four footmen in white knee breeches carried the train of her lavender silk gown. She was fifty-four years old and strands of silver ran through her black hair. Despite her many sorrows, Hawai'i's queen walked with dignity. On that January day in 1893, she was determined to right a wrong.

Lili'uokalani, the reigning monarch of the Hawaiian kingdom, belonged to an ancient line of chiefs. Long before her birth, perhaps around the time Constantine ruled the Roman empire, her ancestors had paddled double-hulled canoes from Polynesian settlements thousands of miles across the heaving swells of the Pacific. Using the stars to navigate, they settled on a remote chain of volcanic islands they called Hawai'i.

For more than fifteen hundred years they lived there unbeknownst to Westerners, passing along their understanding of the world through chants, *hula,* a form of storytelling. But on January 18, 1778, when the queen's great-great-grandfather was a high chief, two sloops from the British navy appeared on the horizon. Commanded by the explorer James Cook, the ships' sailors shattered the splendid isolation of the Hawaiians, bringing deadly diseases, liquor, and firearms.

A few decades later Christian missionaries arrived, bringing the word of a new god and the printing presses to spread it. Wood frame houses arose alongside grass huts: the once languid capital Honolulu became a riotous port town, filled with whalers, roustabouts, and sailors of every nationality. By the time Lili'uokalani reached adolescence Hawai'i had adopted a declaration of rights, a constitution, a national legislature, and a public education system and had accepted the Western concept of private property.

The world rushed into Honolulu through its harbor. Newcomers founded the kingdom's banks, its steamship lines, and many of its newspapers. Some former missionaries and their descendants became businessmen and soon began demanding greater say in the kingdom's government. Foreigners brought the wider world to Hawai'i. But they also threatened to subsume the traditional livelihood, language, and culture of native Hawaiians.

Lili'uokalani herself spanned the worlds of both ancient Hawai'i and the West. Born in a grass house, she lived as queen in an ornate palace illuminated by electric lights, installed four years before the White House's in Washington, D.C. Educated by missionaries alongside other high chiefs' children, she spoke and wrote fluent English and Hawaiian, along with a smattering of French, German, and Latin. She also had traveled across the United States and halfway around the globe to England.

She ruled over a kingdom that was independent but tiny. Just eight inhabited islands surrounded by thousands of miles of Pacific Ocean, Hawai'i was one of the most remote places on earth. When Cook arrived the native Hawaiians numbered 300,000 to 400,000. In the 1890 census, the kingdom's entire population was 89,990, less than a third of San Francisco's, which at nearly 300,000 people was the largest city on America's west coast. As the mighty nations of the day surged west in search of new markets, Lili'uokalani's island kingdom was isolated and virtually defenseless. It became a stopover where traders provisioned their ships on their way between North America and Asia.

As she left the palace to step into her carriage, Lili'uokalani cast off the subservience that she had learned as a sweet-faced girl from her missionary teachers. On that day, Saturday, January 14, 1893, Hawai'i's queen planned to substitute a new constitution for the one forced upon her brother several years earlier, which had turned Hawai'i's monarch into a mere figurehead. Now she aimed to reclaim power for the throne and her people.

Beneath cloudless skies she left the palace. Cannons boomed as the royal carriage rolled toward the legislature. She expected the day to be one of the most triumphant in her two-year-reign, if all went as planned.

But that very morning the USS *Boston*, a warship based in the islands with special orders to protect U.S. interests, steamed into Honolulu harbor. Aboard was the United States envoy to the islands, a tireless advocate of American expansionism. Unbeknownst to Hawai'i's queen, a small group of conspirators, backed by the envoy, was plotting to wrest her away from the throne.

With its fragrant ginger blossoms and mist-swathed mountains, the independent nation of Hawai'i was the reluctant bride in a contest among three suitors—America, Great Britain, and France. During the nineteenth century each at times had sought to expand its influence in the Pacific by controlling the islands, a key stopover in the trade route between North America and Asia.

By 1893 a mounting threat to Hawai'i's independence had also come from within: powerful white sugar planters and merchants sought relief from an economic depression by pushing to annex the islands to the United States, the primary market for Hawaiian sugar. Already, they'd almost completely transformed Hawai'i's economy. For decades, vast sugar plantations had been subsuming the patchwork of taro fields and fish ponds that had long sustained native Hawaiians. This chain of verdant volcanic islands had been harnessed into a sugar-producing powerhouse, in which a small group of white planters controlled four-fifths of the islands' arable land.

A German-American named Claus Spreckels was the most aggressive of those sugar barons. Unlike the missionary descendants turned businessmen, Spreckels was loyal to profits above God or country. He dominated Hawai'i's sugar industry and became the kingdom's chief moneylender, entangling Lili'uokalani's predecessor, her brother, King Kalākaua, in many of his schemes.

Spreckels, who was known as the Sugar King, was just one of a long line of entrepreneurs and adventurers who sought their fortunes in Hawai'i. He favored the islands' continued independence to protect its planter-friendly labor laws. On the mainland he was not involved when a zealous group of white lawyers and businessmen took the next step. They formed a secret Annexation Club a year earlier, which hoped to push Hawai'i into America's arms. These machinations set the stage for a brutal clash between a relentlessly expanding capitalist empire and a vulnerable Polynesian island kingdom.

Packed into a one-story armory in downtown Honolulu two days after the queen's attempt to introduce a new constitution, a crowd of roughly a thousand white men were electrified by Lorrin Thurston, a passionate, dark-eyed lawyer who's grandparents had arrived with the first company of missionaries to the islands. As a founder of the Annexation Club, he spoke in a booming voice that reached the back of the hall, asking, "Has the tropic sun cooled and thinned our blood, or have we flowing in our veins the warm, rich blood which makes men love liberty and die for it?"

Thurston sought out the American minister, who had already sent a message to the commanding officer of the USS *Boston*. A few hours later at 5 p.m. on January 16 the warship's commander ordered the landing of 162 American sailors and marines onto the nearly deserted streets of Honolulu. The queen was then at the palace, just a few blocks from the Honolulu harbor. Hearing the beat of the American military drums, she stepped onto the veranda and watched from above as the troops marched from the harbor. As they kicked up dust in the unpaved streets, she could see they were heavily weighed down with double belts of cartridges.

The sun sank and the skies over Honolulu darkened. The blue-jacketed sailors approached the palace. Beneath the town's newly installed electric streetlamps, Lili'uokalani could see them pushing a revolving cannon and a fearsome Gatling gun, equipped with 14,000 rounds of ammunition that could rip through a large crowd. Following their movements in the streets she was frightened. Why had the troops landed when everything seemed at peace?

The air was heavy with the scent of gardenias. Mosquitoes were drawn to the sweat of the blue-jacketed sailors. As the troops marched past the palace grounds, accompanied by drum rolls, they hoisted their rifles to their shoulders and seemed to point them in the queen's direction.

Were their weapons drawn and ready to fire, as Lili'uokalani later recalled? Or were they merely signaling their respect for Hawai'i's queen by marching past and beating the drums in a royal salute, as one of their commanding officers later insisted?

Whatever their intention, this brash display of military power ignited a crisis that would alter the course of American history.

The landing of U.S. Marines in 1893 came after decades of tension between Hawaiians and the West. The events leading up to it are passionately debated even today among legal scholars, Hawaiian rights activists, and historians. It is the crux of the story of how Hawai'i became part of the United States and it is at the heart of the racial conflict that still tears at the state that bore America's forty-fourth president.

Until recently, American history textbooks have largely overlooked how a small group of businessmen, many of whom were descendants of early Christian missionaries to the islands, managed to overthrow a sovereign kingdom. Most tourist guidebooks simply note the historical curiosity that Hawai'i was once an independent nation, boasting the only former royal palace on American soil.

Yet a glance at the state's newspapers today makes clear that many of the families and firms behind Queen Lili'uokalani's overthrow more than a century ago still wield power in Hawai'i. Vast fortunes accrued to some of them in the years after the overthrow. What happened to the Kingdom of Hawai'i was one of the most audacious land grabs of the Gilded Age, in which 1.8 million acres of land now worth billions of dollars was seized from native Hawaiians and claimed by American businessmen.

It was also the first major gust in a brewing storm of American imperialism, occurring just before U.S. troops took control of Cuba during the Spanish-American War, conquered the Philippines, and turned Guam and Puerto Rico into U.S. territorial possessions. As Americans gained a new belief in their manifest destiny around the globe, Hawaiians lost their country, the first sovereign nation to become a casualty of America's imperial outreach.

The queen stood watching the troops, facing an impossible dilemma. Should she remain "civil," risking her overthrow and the surrender of native Hawaiian culture and sovereignty? Or should she order the troops under her command—outnumbering the *Boston*'s force by nearly four to one—to fight back?

To do so risked inciting the slaughter of a race of people that was already disappearing, decimated over the years by smallpox, syphilis, and measles. Epidemics had carried away tens of thousands of native Hawaiians, who had little resistance to the deadly viruses that swept regularly through the islands. If her people fought off the Americans, would the British, French, or possibly even the Japanese swoop in to replace them?

What should she do?

PART I
ISLAND KINGDOM

CHAPTER ONE

Born in Paradise, 1820–1843

On April 4, 1820, a small merchant vessel, the *Thaddeus*, carrying a group of Christian missionaries, arrived off the coast of the Hawaiian archipelago's biggest island, Hawai'i. The New Englanders' unwavering belief in the righteousness of their mission gave them the courage to undertake a dangerous, 164-day voyage from Boston.

The brig made its way through the treacherous Atlantic during the winter storm season, navigated the southernmost tip of South America, and then fought winds and high seas to make its way back up into the north Pacific. Fourteen members of missionary families were on board, including the Reverends Hiram Bingham and Reverend Asa Thurston, as well as four Hawaiian youths.

Before setting off on this 18,000 mile journey, the missionaries gathered at the Park Street Church in Boston to receive their public instructions. Warned by one of the leaders of the American Board of Commissioners for Foreign Missions that they were headed to a pagan "land of darkness as darkness itself," their orders were clear. "You are to aim at nothing short of covering those Islands with fruitful fields, pleasant dwellings, schools, and churches."

The Americans hoped to bring what they considered progress to the islands while reaping the souls of the Sandwich Islanders. When they arrived, they were horrified by what they saw.

"The appearance of destitution, degradation, and barbarism among the chattering, almost naked savages, whose heads and feet and much of their sunburnt swarthy skin were bare, was appalling," wrote the Rev. Bingham. "Some of our numbers, with gushing tears, turned away from the spectacle. Others with firmer nerves continued their gaze, but were ready to exclaim: 'Can these be human beings?'" They soon overcame their disgust and sought and received permission from the chiefs to move into thatched houses, living alongside the natives.

Just a few months before their arrival, two powerful chiefesses had overthrown the *kapu*, the system of rules regulating Hawaiian life, by overtly disregarding the ancient law against women eating with men. At a feast in November, 1819, Alexander Liholiho, the young king who had assumed the throne as Kamehameha II after the death of his father, Kamehameha I, broke the ancient law against women eating with men by sitting down at their table. "The guests, astonished at this act, clapped their hands and cried out, '*Ai noa*,—the eating tabu is broken.'"

That was just the first of the radical changes that Kamehameha II made. After the meal was over, he ordered the *heiau*, the places for worshipping the many gods of the old Hawaiian religion, destroyed. It seemed sudden, but this revolution within Hawaiian society had fomented long before that fateful meal. Cook's arrival had ended the islands' long isolation and, inevitably, Hawaiians began to see themselves differently. They had watched as foreigners disregarded the *kapu* with no ill effects. And they had observed that Pele did not unleash her fury on Hawaiians who dared to break the rules surreptitiously.

Thus, the Reverand Thurston and the other missionaries arrived just in time to fill a void in the Hawaiians' belief system. As Congregationalists who practiced an austere, Calvinist form of Christianity, they quickly spread out, settling initially on the islands of Hawai'i and O'ahu. They also brought *heluhelu* (reading and writing) to the islands for the first time.

Within a year and nine months of arriving, they'd given the Hawaiian language a seventeen-letter alphabet, later reduced to twelve (all the vowels—*a e i o u*—and a handful of consonants—*h k l m n p w*), introducing writing to an oral culture. Compared to the visiting whale men, who first arrived a year before the missionaries, in 1819, and only wanted pleasure from the Hawaiians after months at sea, the missionaries opened a wider world to them through education. By 1839 they had published the first complete Hawaiian-language Bible.

The first company of missionaries was soon joined by many more, including such passionate evangelists as Titus Coan, who began preaching in Hawaiian in the Hilo district on the island of Hawai'i, reducing hundreds of natives to crying, shouting and weeping at his descriptions of hellfire and promises of redemption. In short order, missionaries had established more than a dozen churches in the islands and won thousands of converts; even Kamehameha II himself became a Christian.

Was there ever a stranger match than that between the New England missionaries, dressed in tightly buttoned black, and the barely clad Polynesians? Did the missionaries fully grasp the fierce history of the Hawaiians or did they lump them in with the African slaves they encountered on the streets of Boston because of the dark color of their skin? Did they realize that the king was a descendant of people who had conquered the seas in canoes, and that his father was the great warrior who had unified the far-flung Hawaiian archipelago?

One missionary who grew close to the chiefs was Asa Thurston, who was assigned to head the mission at Kailua on Hawai'i Island, about ten miles from the site of Captain Cook's death. There, he instructed the king and his brother on Christianity until the itinerant court moved on to Lahaina on the island of Maui and then to Honolulu on O'ahu. Like the other missionaries, Thurston and his family lived a life far removed from the relative comforts of New England, struggling to make ends meet. The family, for instance, went without butter so they could afford to buy a dictionary. Their plan backfired, though, for when the authorities of the missions discovered how they'd obtained the dictionary, they deducted its cost from Thurston's salary.

The missionaries may not have understood much about the Hawaiians when they first arrived, but they saw an opportunity for spiritual harvest. Sometime in late 1820 or early 1821, Thurston wrote to the mainland urging other missionaries to join the cause if they possessed a single-minded devotion to God: "We want men and women who have *souls* . . . who have their eyes and their hearts fixed on the glory of God in the salvation of the heathen—who will be willing to sacrifice every interest but Christ's."

Such purity of purpose wouldn't last long in Hawai'i, however, especially among Thurston's own descendants.

Looming over Honolulu lies a geological oddity known as the Punchbowl, an extinct volcanic crater whose brilliant red soil stands out from the green skirts of the mountains. New England sailors gave the crater this nickname because its rounded shape reminded them of punch bowls they remembered from home. But to Hawaiians it was a sacred site known as Pūowaina, "the hill of human sacrifices."

In a compound of grass houses at the base of the Punchbowl, where some of Hawai'i's ali'i, or high chiefs, lived, a baby was born on September 2, 1838. As the mother labored inside the windowless home, lying on mats braided from the bladelike leaves of the pandanus tree, men and women waited outside, reciting chants, *oli*, which traced the family's genealogy and described their ancestors' feats.

The infant emerged and began to cry. A midwife wrapped her in a soft blanket made from tree bark. The hut was filled with sweet and musky fragrances, including the coconut oil and turmeric that were often sprinkled on such cloth to give it a soft golden color.

The baby was a girl, later named Lili'u. Soon after the cries of the child were heard, gasps of a different sort were made. A few drops of rain had fallen from an otherwise cloudless sky and a rainbow had spanned the horizon. "*Aliʻi! Aliʻi!* That is the sign of our *Aliʻi!*" the men cried out. Nature was signaling a propitious birth.

She was born during the time of year some islanders called Māhoe Hope, meaning "the time when the plumes of the sugarcane begin to unfurl from their sheaths." It was a significant coincidence, since Liliʻu's life would be inextricably bound to the fortunes of Hawaiʻi's sugar trade.

Although Liliʻu was born a high chiefess, with lineage that reached back to the high chiefs under Kamehameha the Great, at the time of her birth it would never have seemed possible she would someday become queen. And despite the appearance of a rainbow shortly after she was born, the full name she acquired foretold not a blessed life but one filled with pain. As was the tradition, she was named by the highest chiefess who, unfortunately, was suffering at the time from an eye infection. Marking the birth with her own complaint, the chiefess named her Liliʻu (smarting) Loloku (tearful) Walania (a burning pain) Kamakaʻeha (the sore eye.)

Bloodlines were crucial to Hawaiian society and elders scrutinized genealogy closely before a marriage to make sure that a partner of high rank was marrying an equal. Liliʻu's social position rose soon after her birth, when she was adopted by chiefs of a higher rank than her own: Konia, a granddaughter of Kamehameha I, became her foster mother and Pākī, a high chief and adviser to Kamehameha III, became her foster father. The couple's only daughter, Bernice Pauahi, became Liliʻu's foster sister.

Liliʻu was welcomed by Pākī and Konia as part of a Hawaiian custom known as *hānai*. To strengthen family ties, newborns were sometimes given to close friends and relatives for adoption. The birth parents could not reclaim their child, except in the event of a death or serious illness on the part of the adoptive, or *hānai*, parents. They could, however, maintain a connection with the child by visiting and conferring with the adoptive parents over the child's welfare.

Liliʻu adored her foster parents, particularly Pākī. An imposing man at six foot four and three hundred pounds, Pākī was a gentle giant, with a light complexion and reddish hair. In the early 1850s, a photographer captured an image of the enormous chief, looking somewhat uncomfortable in a dark, Western-style suit. Perhaps to display his wealth, a watch chain is looped from his vest and he holds out in front of him a walking stick topped with an ornamental knobbed handle.

Lili'u's feelings toward her adoptive father were much warmer than those for her biological parents. She recalled climbing on Pākī's knees and putting her small arms around his neck, kissing and hugging him. He returned her affections and "caressed me as a father would his child," she later wrote. Yet when she met her biological parents, "it was with perhaps more interest, yet always with the demeanor I would have shown to any strangers who noticed me."

The practice of *hānai* was abhorrent to the New England missionaries, who discouraged it. But it continued anyway, reflecting not only a communal attitude toward child rearing but also a practical response to the rising incidence of infertility on the part of native Hawaiians.

It was a time when old Hawaiian customs were being swept away and new ones emerging to replace them. One sign of the changes was a flurry of activity on Punchbowl Street, not far from where Lili'u was born. Rising above the few square blocks of storefronts, taverns, and grog shops that then made up downtown Honolulu, an extraordinary structure, Kawaiaha'o church, arose out of blocks of buff-colored coral rock, weighing 200 to 1,200 pounds each. Native divers had quarried them from an offshore reef and then dragged them from the sea to the site of an ancient freshwater spring. Soaring above the palace and every other building in town was the first large Christian church to be built on O'ahu.

The child Lili'u was swept up in the Christian fervor. She was baptized at two and given the Christian name Lydia. She spent her earliest years with Konia and Pākī in Lahaina on the island of Maui, the Hawaiian capital until the court moved permanently to Honolulu in 1845. Looked after by a Hawaiian nursemaid there, Lili'u as a toddler wandered one afternoon out of her hut, where she was supposed to be napping, and climbed onto a morning glory vine to swing. Losing her grip, she fell off, and her howls of pain sent her nursemaid running. Lili'u lay on the ground, writhing. She had broken a leg, which left her with a mild limp all her life.

Perhaps believing Lili'u needed closer supervision, her parents sent her to a boarding school on the neighboring island of O'ahu just before her fourth birthday. At the school, near the palace and the stone church at the eastern edge of Honolulu, American missionaries educated *ali'i* children, with the support of Kamehameha III and the chiefs.

Known as the Chiefs' Children's School, later renamed the Royal School, it was founded by Amos Starr Cooke and his wife, Juliette, in 1839. The rooms of the modest mud-brick building ringed a central courtyard. As the unlit streets of Honolulu grew dark in the evenings, the Cookes kept a lamp burning in the courtyard, setting out a beacon of light against what they saw as the sins and temptations of the rollicking port town.

The Cookes sought to protect their royal charges from bad influences by keeping them away from the rougher elements of Honolulu, as well as from their own people, whom they were allowed to visit for only short periods in the spring and fall. Honolulu, along with the port of Lahaina on the island of Maui, had become the Pacific base for the hundreds of ships that made up the American whaling fleet. As the kingdom's exports to China trailed off, trade with whalers took its place.

The first thing the land-sick sailors would hear after their ship entered Honolulu harbor was the eerie blow of the conch shell announcing their arrival. At the height of the whaling season, up to five hundred ships would anchor in the harbor at any one time and ships so crowded the port that it was possible to cross the harbor by jumping from one ship's deck to the next. A Hawaiian composed a song describing Honolulu's harbor crowded with masts, calling it "*Ka Ulu La au o Kai*," or "Forest Trees of the Sea."

As the ships disgorged hundreds of sailors onto the streets of the town, the languid port would roar to life with merchants hawking their wares and large groups of horseback riders kicking up dust. Merchants' tills clattered with English guineas, French double Louis, American eagles, Spanish doubloons, and even Russian ducats. The sailors' appetites drew them not only to taverns and shops but also to a special red-light district near the harbor, named Cape Horn.

But prostitution was not the only way lusty sailors found pleasure. Some were happily surprised to find that native women offered themselves up freely. The islanders even had a lighthearted word for this practice: *moekolohe*, or "mischievous sleeping." The result was a growing number of half Hawaiian, half white children, known as *hapa haole*. In Honolulu's schools, the skin colors of the students were often not just dark or light but somewhere in between.

Missionaries such as the Cookes and the Thurstons sought to counter the sexual exuberance of native Hawaiians by instilling modesty. Lucy Thurston joined with Hawai'i's dowager queen to start a sewing circle, stitching modest calico dresses for native women to wear. That and other efforts led to the adoption of the *holokū*, the form-concealing dresses (patterned on the Mother Hubbard gowns worn by the missionaries that native women began to wear in the 1820s.) That replaced *tapa* cloth wrapped around the hips and gathered at the waist, which left the breasts uncovered—a shocking state of undress, at least to some foreigners.

The aesthetics of the West also reached the draftsman's table. Honolulu and Hawai'i's other ports absorbed the West's culture and architectural styles, as tidy wood frame houses with white clapboard fronts rose alongside the Hawaiians' grass houses. Even the Chiefs' Children's School, where the missionaries were educating the next generation of chiefs, became a blend of the two cultures. The Cookes filled their parlor with furniture and knickknacks from New England, along with goods imported from China, within whitewashed adobe brick walls and beneath a thatched roof.

Literacy flowered in the kingdom. As the *ali'i* children learned from the Cookes, thousands of Hawaiian adults and children attended other schools, learning to read and write in Hawaiian and sometimes also in

English. Lahainaluna, a high school on the island of Maui, produced the first generation of native Hawaiian journalists and historians working in the written word. This thirst for learning began with the king and the chiefs. Within two decades of the missionaries' arrival, Hawai'i had achieved one of the highest literacy rates in the world.

The routine of Lili'u's school days followed the pattern set by schools in New England. She and the other Hawaiian students started their day at 5 a.m. with morning devotions, receiving their instruction in English and attending Kawaiaha'o church every Sunday, sitting in a straight-backed pew near the king's. All of the students were required to take a temperance pledge, which the older boys, in particular, had difficulty keeping as drinking alcohol was pervasive among Hawaiians and *haole* alike. As well as studying from English textbooks, the students had more than sixty books that the missionaries had translated into Hawaiian, most of which had moral or practical lessons to impart, such as *Pilgrim's Progress, Animals of the Earth, Geometry for Children,* and tracts on marriage and intemperance.

Some of the girls, including Lili'u's *hānai* sister Pauahi, played the pianoforte, and the boys rode horses. Every evening the children would write in the journals they were required to keep. The parents who enrolled their children in the school hoped that they would bond as a group and become better rulers resisting the urge to fight among themselves, an admirable but elusive goal. Their Congregationalist teachers seemed more focused on saving what they considered their heathen souls than in grooming the kingdom's next generation of rulers.

Attending the Chiefs' Children's School was a miserable experience for Lili'u, who'd arrived kicking and screaming. But it was there that she first came to know her biological brother David Kalākaua, who had been adopted by a different family. The first time she was brought from her home to the school's entrance, she clung tearfully to the family attendant who delivered her. Food rations were meager, especially compared with the generous portions *ali'i* children enjoyed at home. "I recall the instances in which we were sent hungry to bed, it seems to me that they failed to remember that we were growing children," she wrote in her memoir, years later. "A thick slice of bread covered with molasses was usually the sole article of our supper."

Lili'u's childhood was Dickensian in another sense. Illness was a frequent visitor, as the young royals were routinely threatened by chicken pox, smallpox, fevers, typhoid, influenza, measles, and other ailments of modern Western civilization, brought to the islands by travelers. Carts covered with yellowish cloth regularly rattled through the streets of the town, hauling away the dead.

The strict discipline from their headmaster was a far cry from the indulgence they received at home. In their own homes, it was traditionally *kapu*, forbidden, to discipline a young noble. But not at the Cookes'. Lili'u's brother David endured beatings from the stern taskmaster Amos Cooke for bad behavior. Cooke once even slapped him in the face for talking during a church service.

Young Kalākaua also witnessed firsthand the kingdom's sometimes harsh justice when he saw his own grandfather's hanging. Not five years old at the time, and a rebellious student who loved to sing and fight, Kalākaua received word that his paternal grandfather by blood, Kamanawa, a former high chief, wanted him to visit while he was bound in irons and awaiting execution. He had been found guilty of murdering his wife with poisoned '*awa*, a medicinal tonic used by native Hawaiians to induce drowsiness.

Six days later, a crowd gathered as the convicted man was marched up the scaffold at the old fort, near the harbor, to face his punishment. Some of the royal children witnessed the execution, including Kalākaua himself, who was said to have saved a piece of the hangman's rope to remind him of that dreadful experience. In later years, perhaps remembering the day of his grandfather's hanging, Kalākaua grew embittered and cynical toward those who preached Christian mercy.

As the sixteen *ali'i* children sat in the schoolroom, learning to read, write, and do their sums, they were living in a time that would later be viewed as the golden age of the Hawaiian kingdom. The nation's longest-ruling monarch, Kamehameha III, had introduced a declaration of rights in 1839, followed by a written constitution in 1840. He gave, for the first time, some measure of political power to the common people through the creation of a house of representatives. He also established a supreme court.

With a constitutional monarchy firmly in place, the king sent a pair of emissaries to Washington, D.C., London, and Paris, seeking formal recognition of his island nation's sovereignty. The United States recognized Hawai'i's independence in writing in late 1842. Great Britain followed on April 1, 1843. France expressed a verbal assurance soon after.

But as the Hawaiian emissaries were crossing the English Channel in an effort to convince the French to commit to writing what they had pledged in words, news of an astonishing coup in the islands reached Europe. In what would come to be known as the Paulet Affair, a triumvirate of Englishmen living in Honolulu staged a takeover of the islands, turning Hawai'i, at least temporarily, into a British protectorate. This odd but important episode gave the young Lili'u her first glimpse of how attractive and vulnerable Hawai'i was to foreign powers.

In 1843 Kamehameha III was entering the final decade of his thirty-year reign. Five years earlier, wracked with grief over the death of the sister who was also his bride, Nāhi'ena'ena, he had moved his court to Lahaina, on the island of Maui, subsuming his sorrows with alcohol.

The king's private struggles allowed ambitious Westerners to accumulate power in the newly formed government, and several became royal advisers—most notably an American medical missionary named Gerrit P. Judd, who held a succession of posts over two decades, including minister of foreign affairs.

Other Americans and Europeans also made their way into court, drawn by its brilliant pageants and lavish *lū'au*, or feasts. Herman Melville arrived in Honolulu aboard a whaling ship in 1843 and worked for a time as a clerk and a pin setter in a bowling alley. Unimpressed with the quality of the Westerners who became courtiers, he described the royal entourage as "a junta of ignorant and designing Methodist elders in the council of a half civilized king ruling with absolute sway over a nation just poised between barbarism and civilization." Surely Melville was indulging in hyperbole, but his description of "designing" Westerners would prove all too accurate.

The roots of the Paulet Affair lay less in court intrigue than in the intricate courtship dance being performed by three rivals for Hawai'i— Britain, France, and the United States. In the years prior to Kamehameha III's rule there were strong ties between the British empire and the islands. But by the 1840s British power in the islands had begun to wane as trading with American whaling ships accelerated.

A scheming Englishman named Alexander Simpson, who had come to the islands in 1839 as superintendent of operations for the Hudson Bay Company, hoped to change that. Very quickly, he concluded that Hawai'i should become a British possession. It wasn't long before he convinced Lord George Paulet, the commander of the British frigate *Carysfort*, to demand that the Hawaiian king address a long list of British grievances, backed up by the force of the *Carysfort*'s guns. Compounding matters, a French ship had recently entered Honolulu harbor, leading to talk that the islands would soon be claimed by a foreign power—perhaps by Catholic France, at that.

Rumors began swirling that the British frigate moored in Honolulu harbor would bombard the town, sending the townsfolk into a panic. Facing this threat, the king decided to yield to the British demands "under protest," knowing that his emissaries, at that very moment, were in Europe and, when they heard the news, would be able to personally press his case. Instead of turning for aid to either France or the United States, he "decided to throw himself into the arms of England, trusting in the justice of his cause, and hoping still for independence." After all, many islanders already considered themselves under Britain's protection, often referring to themselves as *kanaka no Beritane*, or "men of Britain."

Nonetheless, the scene the children from the Chiefs' Children's School witnessed a few days later, on February 25, 1843, was a mournful one. Standing in the fort near the harbor, addressing a group of both

Hawaiians and white foreigners in English, King Kamehameha III said, "Hear ye! I make known to you that I am in perplexity by reason of difficulties into which I have been brought without cause; therefore, I have given away the life of our land, hear ye! But my rule over you, my people, and your privileges, will continue, for I have hope that the life of the land will be restored when my conduct is justified."

The Hawaiian flag was lowered and the Union Jack hoisted in its place. Introduced by Kamehameha I in the opening years of the century, the island nation's flag reflected the swirl of national influences: the top-left quarter contained a Union Jack, while the rest of the flag consisted of eight horizontal stripes, repeating in a pattern of white, red, and blue, one for each of the major islands. The design and color scheme called to mind not only the British flag but those of France and the United States, too, whose flag displayed twenty-six stars at the time.

As the Union Jack took its place, troops from the fort and the *Carysfort* fired twenty-one-gun salutes. It was a moment that reflected a painful truth for the island kingdom: it was merely an afterthought in the grand plans of that century's superpowers, as easily snatched up without much thought as put back down again and permitted—for the moment at least—its independence.

The *ali'i* children watched sorrowfully as the Hawaiian flag was lowered and the last notes of the ship's band died away. It was a brutal, public humbling of their once all-powerful king. As Amos Cooke wrote in a letter a few days afterward, "Our children feel very bad & many of the foreigners have expressed much sympathy for them. They feel as if their glory had departed. On Sabbath morning they all [the boys] took their gold bands off from their caps saying they were no longer Chiefs."

One of Lili'u's fellow students wrote later that the children held many "indignation meetings" at the school, "laying plans for revenge on Great Britain." Lili'u and the other children from the Chiefs' Children's School glared at the occupying soldiers "with scorn whenever we met [them] on the street." They also took delight in calling the red-uniformed British officers "lobster backs."

While the event must have shocked and saddened the schoolchildren, some Hawaiians had already foreseen the demise of their tiny kingdom at the hands of a great Western power. Writing in 1837, more than two decades before Charles Darwin published *On the Origin of Species*, the native historian David Malo had warned of "the small" being gobbled up by "the large" and made a prediction:

> The ships of the whitemen have come, and smart people have arrived from the Great Countries which you have never seen before, they know our people are few in number and living in a small country; they will eat us up, such has always been the case with large countries, the small ones have been gobbled up.

Just as the scheming Englishmen Paulet and Simpson rushed to send their version of events to London on the first boat they could commandeer, so did the king's advisers prepare their own plea for justice.

To prevent the British from discovering their plan, the dispatches and documents were composed in top secrecy by Judd within the darkness of the royal tomb, using the coffin of the late widow of Kamehameha I as a writing desk. Kamehameha III, who had again retreated to Lahaina after the cession ceremony, was spirited back to Honolulu by "express" canoe at night so he could sign the protest documents without Paulet's knowledge.

The intrigue didn't stop with the secret signing ceremony. The ship that the British commandeered belonged to an American concern, Ladd & Company, which insisted that one of its own agents travel with the British. Nicknamed the "Pious Traders" because one of its founding partners was educated at Yale's School of Divinity, Ladd & Co. supported the Hawaiian king. Its agent became his emissary, carrying the documents with him. The king hastily appointed Ladd & Co.'s agent as his "envoy extraordinary and minister plenipotentiary"—a title as grand as the Hawaiian kingdom was small—and dispatched him to plead Hawai'i's case in London and Washington.

After months at sea, both sets of documents reached London, where the Hawaiian kingdom's plea prevailed—coming as it did at a time when England was preoccupied with far more important matters, having just extended its empire beyond India to Hong Kong and South Africa as well. Lord Richard Thomas, admiral of Great Britain's Pacific fleet, concluded that the coup was an embarrassing diplomatic blunder. So he left Valparaiso, where he was stationed, and sailed to Honolulu. With the simple stroke of a pen, he then restored power to the Hawaiian monarchy.

The last day of July in 1843 dawned clear and cloudless. The children from the Chiefs' Children's School, along with most of Honolulu's residents, made their way to a plain east of town. At ten that morning the children witnessed the formidable sight of several hundred English marines marching toward the plain carrying flags and banners, while Admiral Thomas and the Hawaiian king rode together in a royal carriage.

The dignitaries arrived at the site of the ceremony and standard-bearers unfurled over the king's head a broad Hawaiian banner decorated with a crown and an olive branch. The royal children and the large crowd of onlookers cheered as soldiers hoisted the Hawaiian flag.

A thanksgiving service followed in Kawaiahaʻo and the king spoke the words that were later to become the motto of Hawaiʻi: *Ua mau ke ea o ka aina i ka pono,* "the life of the land is perpetuated in righteousness." He then proclaimed a ten-day Restoration Day celebration. Tables laid for a celebratory feast were decorated with miniature flags of Hawaiʻi, along with the flags of its trading partners America, France, and England. Overall, the British had ruled Hawaiʻi for just five months.

With the end of the short-lived takeover of the islands, the small kingdom seemed secure. But ships from the larger nations prowled its seas. While economists and philosophers in Europe would soon debate Darwinism, with its suggestion—at least to some—that only the fittest would survive, the vulnerable Kingdom of Hawaiʻi was facing an economic Darwinism that would prove swift and brutal.

CHAPTER TWO
Progress and Liberty, 1843–1861

Despite this unfortunate incident, the affinity between Hawaiian *aliʻi* and the British remained strong through most of Liliʻuʻs youth. Her contemporary, the part-British Emma Rooke, who later married Kamehameha IV, was said to have spoken with a pronounced English accent all her life. Hawaiian royals continued to use English and Hawaiian names. Great Britain's Queen Victoria remained the model for Hawaiʻi's monarchs and was revered as much as Admiral Thomas for restoring Hawaiʻi's independence.

Perhaps most important, British ships carried new ideas and novel technology to the islands. Three years after the Paulet episode, in 1846, Liliʻu and the other students from the newly renamed Royal School climbed aboard the first ship to use steam power to reach the islands, Britain's *Cormorant*, and were entertained with mild shocks from its newfangled "electrical machine." Precisely what kind of device was aboard is not clear, but whatever it was it amused the children.

Back in the classroom they were reciting their nation's recently adopted

Declaration of Rights. These rights were just one part of the sweeping changes Kamehameha III had introduced to the kingdom.

Land reform was one of the most profound, with far-reaching and ultimately destructive consequences. Land previously had been vested in the *mōʻī aliʻi*, or king, who granted to the chiefs lands that commoners farmed in a communal tenure system. Each wedge-shaped land section, called an *ahupuaʻa*, stretched from the tip of a mountain down to the sea, containing a swath of mountainous terrain and springs, arable midlands, and access to fishing grounds.

In what became known as the *mahele*, Kamehameha III had planned to give outright ownership of just over 4 million acres of land to three groups: the king, the chiefs, and the commoners. He was advised by Gerrit Judd, among others. When enacted, however, the division of lands was more complex and less egalitarian. The king retained a portion of just under a million acres that came to be known as the crown or royal lands; a new category, known as the government lands and totaling about 1.5 million acres, were also set aside, "for the good of the Hawaiian government" and "to promote the dignity of the Hawaiian crown." The lands granted to the chiefs totaled about 1.6 million acres.

The problem was that no lands were specifically set aside for the commoners. The idea was that they would claim deeds to the individual properties they had farmed, and it was understood that the king and the chiefs would grant these requests so that the commoners would end up owning "one-third or at least one-fourth" of the lands.

But after the *aliʻi* had received their awards, many commoners were unable to obtain legal possession of the lands that they'd traditionally occupied. One reason may be that the concept of private ownership of land was foreign to the Hawaiians, who lacked a word in their language for it. The *aliʻi* were also required to pay a commutation fee equaling one-third of the value of the land in order to receive their deeds. But because they were cash poor and land rich, many preferred instead to sell off the lands they had been awarded. In turn, since the commoners' rights remained tied to the owners of the property, if the new owners didn't permit the commoners to stay the commoners effectively became homeless. Many commoners simply weren't aware that they needed to file a formal petition to keep their lands, so foreign was the mercantile mind-set of the West.

To address this problem, in 1850 the legislature enacted the Kuleana Act, which encouraged commoners to file claims for land, specifically the acreage they were currently cultivating plus an additional quarter acre for a house. Kuleana is an important but hard to translate value in Hawaiian culture. It is often defined as a person's rights and privileges, but it reflects a far broader meaning, extending to spiritual and family responsibilities as well. Few natives, however, actually took advantage of the act to petition for their deeds; only 14,195 claims were filed and 8,421 awards approved, averaging under three acres each. In the end, only 28,658 acres, or less than 1 percent of the kingdom's land, went to the commoners.

The new system, whereby Hawaiians held private title to lands that could be bought or sold, was a drastic shift from the society that preceded it. Perhaps most significantly, as of 1850, a separate act permitted foreigners, for the first time, to own Hawaiian land. More accustomed to notions of private ownership than were the native Hawaiians, Westerners quickly snapped up much of what had been designated government or chieftains' lands, often for pittances. In one example, the eighty or so acres that would become the heart of Kaua'i's Grove Farm Plantation were bought by an American in 1850, just after the *mahele* land reform. The first owner sold it the same year to another white foreigner for $3,000, who then sold it six years later to yet another for $8,000. Thus, those clever enough to spot the opportunity for profit often did very well indeed.

There was some discussion of adding legal protections to help guard against the native Hawaiians' lack of experience. But the king and his foreign advisers did not enact them. As a result, much of the most valuable land quickly slipped away from native Hawaiians and into the hands of foreigners. As Ralph S. Kuykendall, author of the three-volume history *The Hawaiian Kingdom*, wrote in the 1930s, "The door was thus left open for the evil that afterwards crept in."

Lili'u's fondest memory as a schoolgirl was of savoring Hawaiian sweets at a neighboring home. Otherwise, her life was overshadowed by Western diseases that struck even the king, queen, and *ali'i*. In 1848, when Lili'u was ten, a particularly virulent strain of measles led to the deaths not only of one of her former schoolmates but of a younger biological sister who had been given in *hānai* to King Kamehameha III.

Some Hawaiians tried to shake the disease with a "cold water" cure, which seemed only to hasten their deaths, and the king declared a national day of fasting and prayer. The official government journal, the *Polynesian*, in turn, ran an editorial beseeching foreign residents to help pay for new hospitals to help the natives. "We should like to see white men more generally engaged in relieving sufferings which white men have introduced," it stated in an editorial, asking for $100 donations apiece from the foreign community.

Deaths from the epidemic steadily climbed: in October of 1848, the count in Honolulu was 117. The next month it jumped to 562 and included Lili'u's former schoolmate Moses, who had rebelled from the Cookes' strict rules by sneaking off school grounds at night to carouse. When Moses died on November 24, 1848, Mrs. Cooke wrote unforgivingly of the disgrace he had brought to the school, suggesting it might serve as a lesson to the other students: "We hope his vicious course and sudden death will be a beacon . . ."

The epidemic made a deep impression on Lili'u. Decades later she recalled how the "relatives and companions of my youth died and were buried on the same day, the coffin of the last-named resting on that of the others." While immediate burial might have helped bring the epidemic to a swifter end, it violated the Hawaiians' tradition of allowing their dead to lie in state for weeks; the shock of death was compounded by this break with custom. Moses's own funeral was delayed due to the illness sweeping the capital, and it was not until December 30, about five weeks after his death, that a service for him was held.

The terrible measles epidemic of 1848 killed thousands, if not tens of thousands, of Hawaiians, possibly as much as one-tenth of the kingdom's entire native population. Between it and a smallpox epidemic that began in 1853, the native population of the islands fell to just over 71,000 people—half what it had been just three decades earlier and a quarter of the total at the time of Captain Cook's arrival only seventy-five years previously. Local publications voiced grave concerns about the future of native Hawaiians and some commentators suggested that extinction—or near extinction—was inevitable. A table published in 1850 in the *Polynesian* showing "the probable future decrease of the Hawaiian Race," suggested there would be fewer than one hundred Hawaiians surviving in the year 1930.

At the same time, unions between Hawaiians and *haole*, that is, whites or foreigners, including those born in Hawai'i to foreign-born parents, had been acknowledged in marriage laws enacted during Kamehameha III's long reign and were becoming more common. As Western diseases decimated the native population the Hawaiians continued to intermarry. The old ways began to disappear, as native Hawaiians died off and mixed-race children were born into families that often adopted Western customs.

Perhaps the most striking example of the growing number of marriages between Hawaiians and *haole* was the union of Pauahi, Lili'u's *hānai* sister. Her light complexion and "Grecian" features, which were considered strikingly lovely by both Hawaiians and whites, attracted many admirers, among them the American Charles Bishop. A former clerk from Glens Falls, New York, Bishop had made his way to Hawai'i almost accidentally and become the kingdom's customs collector. Pauahi had been expected from childhood to marry Prince Lot, a grandson of Kamehameha I. But Bishop began courting her while she was still at the Royal School. Sometimes they would sit together in the Cookes' parlor—Pauahi quietly stitching while Charles read aloud passages from *The Life of Hannah More*, a biography of the popular moralist playwright. At other times they would both take part in school excursions and horseback riding.

Juliette Cooke favored the match, despite the wide age difference between the eighteen-year-old Pauahi and Bishop, who was a decade older. But Pākī and Konia strongly objected to their daughter marrying anyone but another *aliʻi* and refused to attend the eventual wedding ceremony, which took place in the parlor of the Royal School on the evening of June 4, 1850. With only a few witnesses, almost certainly one of them being Liliʻu, Pauahi wore a gown of white muslin and a jasmine wreath around her head. Then the small wedding party sat down together for tea and the entire event was concluded in an hour.

Pauahi had been warned by her parents that if she married Charles she would have to look to the Cookes for all her *pono*—a word with many meanings, but in this instance "welfare," "prosperity," and "well-being." In other words, Pākī and Konia had threatened to stop supporting her if she married a *haole*. But Pauahi was by no means the first *aliʻi* to wed a Westerner. Well before their wedding day other Hawaiian-*haole* couples had begun producing mixed-race children.

Soon, the white children of missionaries and other foreign settlers in the islands began to be educated alongside the *aliʻi*. A small number were admitted to the high chiefs' school as day students, forming a new island elite.

One such young man was John Owen Dominis, who would grow up alongside the *aliʻi* and eventually play a major role in the kingdom. His father, a naturalized American citizen, had been a Dalmatian sea captain and his mother was an American. In the late 1830s, the Dominis family moved to Honolulu. In 1842 they began building a large home in the Greek revival style, near the Royal School. But John's father was lost at sea in 1846, and when the house was completed a year later his mother began taking in boarders to help make ends meet. One of the first tenants, the United States representative to the islands, suggested naming the home in honor of George Washington's birthday, and Kamehameha III himself decreed the home to be known as Washington Place.

Doted on by his widowed mother, young John did not enjoy the same indulgences at school as he'd come to expect at home. Within a few months the Cookes expelled him from the Royal School for bad behavior, despite his mother's protests. Yet Dominis's expulsion would not impede the long and successful political career he would later enjoy, nor would it stand in the way of his marrying into royal circles.

In 1850, the Cookes retired from their missionary work as teachers, and the Royal School eventually became a part of the public school system. The following year, the Cookes went into business with another missionary family, the Castles. Both had been sent to Honolulu by the American Board of Missions, the agency founded at the start of the nineteenth century in the swelling of evangelic fervor known as the Second Great Awakening.

Castle & Cooke started as a general store selling tools, sewing equipment, and medicine. Over the next few decades the firm jumped into Hawai'i's surging sugar industry, operating plantations on O'ahu and Maui. As former missionaries, the Cookes' conversion from church-sponsored altruism to brisk mercantilism traced a pattern the young Lili'u would see over and over again, giving rise to the local saying "they came to do good and did well."

After the closing of the Royal School, Lili'u continued her education by becoming a student at a day school that was also run by American missionaries. She lived with Konia and Pākī in Honolulu at a gracious two-story home named Haleakalā. Wrapped by deep porches, its large garden included a tamarind tree planted at her sister Pauahi's birth. As Lili'u matured, the home became a hub for social visits and impromptu dances. In contrast to the unbridled sexuality near Honolulu's wharves, an early photograph of Lydia Pākī, as she was called by the Christian missionaries at this time, shows a solemn young woman dressed modestly in a dark, high-necked gown. Her hair is parted in the middle and plaited down her back and her face still retains some of the roundness of childhood. She stands erect, staring directly at the camera, a proud high chiefess whose austere Victorian gown would not have looked out of place on Louisa May Alcott, who was born in America just a few years before her.

Yet death again brought sorrow to this period in Lili'u's life. In 1853 another epidemic ravaged the town, this time smallpox, bringing with it wide-scale devastation. The town had barely recovered when, on December 15, 1854, King Kamehameha III died at age forty-one, not of smallpox, but of a sudden illness. He had reigned for nearly three decades as sovereign, beginning as a child with a regent ruling in his stead. He ruled longer than any single Hawaiian monarch beginning shortly after the arrival of the missionaries; the king presided over nothing less than a total upheaval of his country's laws, from adoption of the kingdom's first constitution to the *mahele*, and foreign land ownership. And after the Paulet incident, Hawai'i had won recognition as an independent nation from the great powers of Europe as well as the United States.

The Hawaiian king's death came at a time when the United States was roiled by struggles between pro-slavery and abolitionist forces, leading to the founding of the antislavery Republican Party. Just a few months before Kamehameha III's death a young Illinois lawyer named Abraham Lincoln called for the gradual emancipation of southern slaves.

Hawai'i's *ali'i* were aware of the rising tensions over slaveholding in America and that young nation's divided views on race. Princes Alexander Liholiho and Lot Kamehameha, Lili'u's onetime schoolmates who would become Kamehameha IV and Kamehameha V, respectively, had traveled to the United States with the American royal counselor Gerrit Judd. They experienced the country's racial prejudices firsthand when a conductor asked them to leave their seats on a train because of the color of their skin. As Prince Liholiho wrote in the diary he kept during the trip, "A conductor had taken me for somebodys servant, just because I had a darker skin than he had. Confounded fool. The first time that I ever received such treatment, not in England or France, or anywhere else. But in this country I must be treated like a dog to go & come at an Americans bidding."

Almost certainly as a result of that humiliating experience, which took place before Kamehameha III died, Lot and Liholiho argued forcefully against American annexation of Hawai'i, an idea which was starting to gain supporters in Honolulu and elsewhere. They pointed to a political climate poisoned by the "evils of slavery, race prejudice, hatred of aristocracy, crime and corruption, vigilantes, and lynch laws."

Yet the economic pull of the American mainland proved impossible for Hawai'i to resist. The rapid population growth of the U.S. West Coast in the early years of the Gold Rush caused a food shortage there, creating strong demand for Hawaiian sugar. As competition from other sugar-producing countries surged, Hawai'i lost its advantage and fell into a depression in 1851 and 1852. Following failed attempts at negotiating a reciprocity treaty that would have lowered tariffs on trade between Hawai'i and the United States, Kamehameha III consented to draft an annexation treaty—a cause for jubilation among the Americans who lived in the islands.

Eager to celebrate even before the treaty was signed, the Americans organized a Fourth of July parade. In a cart decorated with greenery rode thirty-two lovely American girls, all dressed in white and wreathed in flowers. Across their breasts, each wore a sash with the name of an American state plus Hawai'i, spelled out in large gold letters. Behind them marched "Young America"—a company of young men in uniform. And following them, in tow, was a boat on wheels representing "Young Hawai'i" carrying eight young native Hawaiians, all chewing sugarcane.

This vision of Hawai'i as America's young cousin in tow—a possible thirty-second state—was derailed by the king's sudden death. The new king was the twenty-one-year-old Alexander Liholiho, the young prince who had been asked to change cars in the American train because of his dark complexion. Upon his accession to the throne he became known as Kamehameha IV and was soon renowned for his "brilliant talents and winning manners." The day after his predecessor was laid to rest, Liholiho praised the late king.

The age of Kamehameha III was that of progress and of liberty—of schools and of civilization. He gave us a Constitution and fixed laws; he secured the people in the title to their lands, and removed the last chain of oppression. He gave them a voice in his councils and in the making of the laws by which they are governed. He was a great national benefactor, and has left the impress of his mild and amiable disposition on the age for which he was born.

Yet the flowering of Hawai'i's constitutional monarchy would not last. The boom in trade across the Pacific was drawing foreigners to Honolulu's narrow streets by droves, to its coral-stone royal palace and to its shanty town across from the harbor, where the odors of rotting vegetables and dead fish mingled with the sweet fragrance of freshly strung *lei*, sold by native women near the quay. Commerce was flourishing in the kingdom and the rising merchant class was made up largely of *haole* rather than Hawaiians. They'd brought with them to the islands a Protestant work ethic, equating godliness with hard work, and the resulting accumulation of wealth as a sign of personal salvation. But they also benefited from easier access to loans from mainland banks and a growing population that seemed impervious to the epidemics that continued to decimate native Hawaiian households.

Illustrating the point is a story that was told for years afterward. Parke, the marshal of the kingdom, was put in charge of collecting money from Honolulu's residents to pay for Kamehameha III's funeral. After receiving the donations he put the money into a wheelbarrow, which he pushed through the dusty streets of the town, paying off the merchants who had supplied food, flowers, and other goods for the fortnight of mourning. Since there was no Hawaiian currency in circulation, the wheelbarrow was loaded with American coins.

On a June morning in 1856 thousands of guests poured into Kawaiaha'o, filling the pews and the balconies of Honolulu's Westminster Abbey. They had come to see twenty-year-old Emma Rooke, the part British, part Hawaiian *ali'i*, marry her childhood sweetheart. Her groom was twenty-two-year-old Alexander Liholiho, who two years prior had taken Hawai'i's throne as Kamehameha IV.

The palace had declared the day a public holiday, so most offices and businesses were closed. Native Hawaiians, white merchants, and foreign dignitaries waited in the Protestant stone church, whose stark walls were softened by decorations of flowering vines and delicate greenery. The pews at the front were reserved for *ali'i*. At 11:30 a.m., the graceful Emma, renowned in Honolulu for her fearless horseback riding, walked slowly up the aisle, accompanied by her British *hānai* father. She wore a wreath of white roses and delicate orange blossoms in her hair as she approached the altar.

The marriage of Emma and Liholiho was the island nation's most important social event of the year—and its first-ever royal wedding in the Western fashion. Yet despite the strong European influences, glimpses of the old Hawai'i could be seen. As the royal couple's horse-drawn carriage rolled toward the palace, spectators had prostrated themselves along the route "until their foreheads touched the ground"—a traditional gesture of respect to *ali'i* that would soon become obsolete.

The wedding also marked a collision of the old Hawaiian ways and new Western ideas about whom the king should wed. Some native chiefs—including Lili'u's biological father—had advised Liholiho that he should marry the highest-born *ali'i* maiden. That was Lili'u, whose biological parents were both native Hawaiian and whose ancestors had been closely allied with Kamehameha the Great. But Liholiho, with all the impetuousness of a young *ali'i* newly bestowed with power, refused. He insisted on marrying for love.

A week after his public declaration, the volcano called Mauna Loa on the island of Hawai'i erupted, threatening to destroy the town of Hilo. The impending catastrophe was viewed as a sign from the gods that they were displeased with Liholiho's break from tradition, and he temporarily postponed the nuptials. According to one account, it was only after the lava stopped short of the town months later that Liholiho proceeded with his plans.

When Emma finished her walk down the aisle she stood beside her groom. A tall, slender man who had suffered from asthma all his life, Liholiho had taken boxing lessons with a fighter named "Yankee" Sullivan as a way to improve his stamina and conditioning. That day, he wore a "Windsor" uniform, his blue coat richly embroidered with gold lace and a plumed hat. He also forgot the ring, so he dispatched a messenger to hurry back to the palace to get it for him.

The couple knelt before the minister. At their request, the clergyman performed the wedding ceremony of the Church of England, reading the vows in both English and Hawaiian. (Emma was adopted in *hānai* by a half Hawaiian, half British mother who was married to a British doctor.) The new king Liholiho, perhaps because of his ugly experience in the United States, found more comfort in Anglican rites than in the Congregational churches of the American missionaries.

The year of the wedding was filled with uncertainty for the seventeen-year-old Lili'u. She left school in 1855, the same year that her father Pākī died at Haleakalā, the family home, in June. Because he died without a legal will, his estate went jointly to his widow Konia and his biological daughter, Bernice Pauahi Bishop. It was a surprising reversal, for Pauahi's decision to marry the *haole* Charles Bishop in 1850 had caused Pākī temporarily to disown her and declare Lili'u his only daughter and sole heir. But by the time Pākī died he had reconciled with Pauahi. Pauahi and Charles moved into Haleakalā with Konia, and Lili'u effectively became the guest of Konia and the Bishops.

The life they led there was slow and sociable. From the veranda, Lili'u could hear the cooing of the ring dove and the sounds of old native women sweeping the black sand walks of the estate with brooms made from the stems of coconut tree leaves. On either side of the home were wide lawns and long, low buildings divided into rooms occupied by the family's retainers. Konia sat for hours beneath Haleakalā's large tamarind tree, listening to rural folk who'd traveled to Honolulu to ask her advice and tell her their troubles. Even after

Pākī was gone, Konia observed the responsibility of the *ali'i* toward the commoners.

Whatever sorrow or confusion Lili'u must have felt over Pākī's death and the sudden arrival of new heads of the household, she revealed none of it in her memoirs, written many years later. Instead, she recounted how Emma and Liholiho's ceremony was followed by weeks of teas, *lū'au*, and balls lasting until dawn given by "each of the nations represented on the island, even the Chinese." One of the most spectacular took place the night after the ceremony, when the palace and grounds were lit up for a royal ball and supper for some five hundred guests, capped off by fireworks launched from the top of Punchbowl Hill.

Now nearly eighteen years old and her figure turned voluptuously round, Lili'u enjoyed the social delights of the season, including her un-expected reacquaintance with a man she'd first remembered seeing as a child: John Owen Dominis. He had been one of the "curious urchins," as Lili'u would later write, who many years earlier had climbed a high wall separating the Cookes' Royal School from a neighboring day school to catch a glimpse of the Hawaiian *ali'i* at play. The next time she encoun-tered him, John Dominis was an eligible bachelor in his mid-twenties who served as private secretary to Prince Lot, the brother of the king and next in line to the throne.

It was foolish chivalry on the part of the young *haole* that captured Lili'u's heart. John Dominis and Lili'u were riding side by side in a large cavalcade of two hundred or so riders accompanying the new king shortly after his wedding when a less skilled horseman forced his way between the pair. In the ensuing melee, John was thrown from his horse, breaking his leg. Yet he insisted on getting back up into his saddle and accompa-nying Lili'u home before riding back to Washington Place to attend to his painful injury. The young man was confined to his home at length, tended by his protective mother.

Lili'u passed from her teenage years into her early twenties as a member of the royal court, contributing her lovely voice to singing parties at the

Bishops' home and attending balls and state functions, where she danced quadrilles, waltzes, polkas, and mazurkas.

The court revolved around a couple of simple, wood-framed cottages where the king and queen lived, on the grounds of what would become 'Iolani Palace in downtown Honolulu. The palace was then a modest one-story building, constructed of coral blocks, with a deep veranda, a billiard table, a library, and oil portraits hanging on the walls. In earlier decades, under the rule of Kamehameha III, the royal family's informal manner of dress and deportment—often barefoot, with the king wearing a traditional *malo*, or loincloth, and the queen wearing only a *tapa*, a bark cloth skirt—startled some Western visitors. But Kamehameha IV and his wife, the part-English Emma, were Anglophiles who wore clothes from England and read the *Telegraph* and the *Illustrated London News*.

British decorum ruled. That was the case at the sumptuous formal dinners to honor visitors. One, held in 1861 in honor of a British aristocrat, was as well appointed as a similar occasion might have been in Mayfair. The table was festooned with silver candelabra and place settings included a bill of fare printed in gold on royal blue silk, including *Compote de pigeons* and *Pommes de terre Carolina*. Serving the guests was a genuine English butler, imported at great cost and vexation by the royal family, for their new servant, they soon discovered, possessed less than perfect manners.

Lili'u, who attended the dinner, impressed the visitors. One later wrote that "Miss Paki . . . speaks English very nicely, without a particle of American twang." The missionary education that gave her crisp diction also set her apart linguistically from both native Hawaiians and American English speakers.

The royal circle visited the other islands in a grand fashion. One memorable journey took place in 1859, on the verge of civil war erupting in the United States. Lili'u and a group of *haole* and *ali'i* journeyed to Hawai'i Island, whose population was far smaller than that of the capital island of O'ahu yet whose land mass was nearly twice as big as all the other Hawaiian islands combined.

The party trekked up some 4,000 feet through rain forests to peek over the rim of one of the island's five volcanoes, Kīlauea, which spewed lava from time to time, making it a highlight for some adventurous travelers to the islands. After peering into the crater, which ancient Hawaiians believed was the home of the volcano goddess Pele, the group headed back down thirty miles to the city of Hilo, where Lili'u and the others were joined by the king's entourage.

The combined group shared a large grass house—one room occupied by the women, another by the men, and, in the middle, a large space used for banquets and balls. When the *ali'i* traveled from their accommodations in Hilo they rode through a landscape fringed with grass huts, taro patches, and mullet ponds. Local people, who revered the royals and considered the king and queen as godlike, would pull their carriages themselves. Occasionally, the carriages would get stuck in mud or a ditch, requiring the *ali'i* to be rescued by horses.

It was a blissful period in Lili'u's young life. As she would later recall, "We were lighthearted, merry, and happy."

To foreigners, signs of rapid economic changes in the kingdom were impossible to miss, as the landscape Victorian visitors called a tropical jungle was tamed into straight rows of sugarcane. A decade earlier, after James Marshall, a foreman at Sutter's Mill, had discovered four pieces of the shiny metal in the American River, gold fever had swept through California. Fortune seekers flooded what would come to be known as the Golden State and demand for such basic commodities as flour, cloth, and sugar soared. Hawai'i's planters and businessmen soon realized that the islands' consistently mild climate and fertile soil were ideally suited to growing sugarcane.

At the same time, they discovered that they were in the perfect position to satisfy the sweet tooth of Americans, who, like their European counterparts, preferred to sweeten their tea and coffee with sugar rather than honey. By 1850, Hawai'i's sugar exports had more than doubled to 750,238 pounds from four years earlier. But sugar from the Philippines and China also flooded into the California market, driving down prices. When the gold rush–driven boom for sugar in California ended a year later, in 1851, sugar exports plunged to a mere 21,000 pounds, and Hawaiian sugar producers found themselves vulnerable to global forces they could not control.

When war erupted in the United States, however, the market for Hawaiian sugar once again exploded. Seven southern states seceded from the Union and Confederate troops fired on Fort Sumter in South Carolina. What became known as the War Between the States had begun. At that time, much of the nation's sugar came from vast plantations worked by black slaves in Louisiana and other southern states. The start of the American Civil War disrupted that supply, creating an opportunity for businessmen who bought their raw sugarcane from other countries.

The war electrified Hawai'i's once sleepy economy. From the time Captain Cook spotted the islands' sugarcane, which had been first brought there by the Polynesians around 200 A.D., to the founding of the first permanent sugar plantation by Ladd & Co. on leased land in Kaua'i in 1835, the islands began to grow cane for export. By 1860 there were a dozen plantations; five years later that number had multiplied to thirty-two. In 1861, the year the war began, Hawaiian sugar exports were double what they had been a decade earlier. By 1865, when the war ended, they had multiplied more than tenfold.

Sugar's success rippled through Hawai'i's economy. Honolulu was the biggest port and the biggest boom town. Huge building projects sprouted. On the south side of the Honolulu harbor work was roaring ahead to fill in sixteen acres of reef overlooked by an old fort and creaky, ancient cannons. Once owned by the royal family, the widow of Kamehameha III had sold it for $22,000. Soon after, the buyers demolished the fort, replacing it with a prison near the site of the old fort, a customhouse, and waterworks costing more than twice as much.

Sugar cultivation required laborers who were willing to do the backbreaking work of cutting cane by hand in the fields. In the plantations of the West Indies and South Carolina, African slaves were forced to perform these brutal jobs, with many perishing from the broiling heat, tropical diseases, and malnourishment. But although Hawai'i's 1852 constitution banned slavery in the kingdom, the work was still punishing. Using cane knives, or machetes, the workers would grab a stalk in one hand and swing the knife as close to the ground as possible to cut it at the thickest point in order to capture the plant's best juices. The work was hot and dangerous: aside from the peril of cutting themselves or a fellow worker with their cane knives, they risked needle-sharp splinters from the cane stalks, which got under their denim trousers and penetrated work shirts or stuck between the toes of their bare feet.

Finding free men willing to do this grueling work was difficult, especially since other opportunities beckoned. Although the gold rush created demand for Hawaiian sugar, it also created new opportunities for adventurous and enterprising Hawaiians, some of whom joined the frantic search for gold in the foothills of California's Sierra Nevadas. Others joined the crews of whaling ships, an industry that was then at its height. Between 1845 and 1847 alone, some two thousand Hawaiians left the islands to become sailors on foreign ships, never to return. By one estimate, the departure of around four thousand native Hawaiian men in 1850, as the whaling industry neared its peak, represented almost 12 percent of all Hawaiian males of working age. A powerful diaspora swept native Hawaiians from the islands as they sought opportunity elsewhere.

As the native population dropped, the Hawaiian legislature, comprised of both *haole* and Hawaiians, passed an act prohibiting native subjects of the king from immigrating to California or any other foreign country, except for certain specified reasons. That same year, the kingdom's lawmakers made another attempt to address the labor shortage by passing an "Act for the Government of Masters and Servants." The plantation owners organized themselves into the Royal Hawaiian Agricultural Society and immediately began contracting laborers from China.

The act drew sharp criticism. Opponents argued that it gave license to plantation owners to create a system of indentured servitude, under which laborers could be imprisoned for breaking their contracts, whatever the reason. The *Advertiser*, noting that the U.S. Senate in 1867 issued an official condemnation of the "coolie trade," thundered that the penal provisions of Hawai'i's act "can only be viewed as a relic of barbarism."

But the demands of the sugar planters for labor won out. The result was that Hawai'i's population of native Hawaiians dwindled while the number of part-Hawaiians and Caucasians soared. Hawai'i suddenly became home to Chinese and, later, Portuguese and Japanese workers. Most of these immigrants were desperately poor, single men.

On the plantations themselves, the owners would provide their contract laborers with housing, food, and clothing in exchange for long days and low pay. They treated their workers less cruelly than in other parts of the world, such as in the British West Indies, which had relied on slaves until the late 1830s, and in Louisiana, whose plantations used slaves until the end of the Civil War in 1865. Still Hawai'i's workers—though not enslaved by the plantation owners—labored under often dehumanizing conditions. Plantation supervisors, called *luna*, oversaw field workers on horseback and carried whips. Capital punishment was outlawed by the government but some plantation managers and luna still delivered lashings and other forms of abuse.

Members of the Royal Hawaiian Agricultural Society were, primarily, *haole* who had begun planting sugarcane after the land reforms following the *mahele* permitted them to own land. In 1851 they contracted with a merchant in Hong Kong to bring the first group of some two hundred Chinese "coolies" by boat to the islands to work in the sugar plantations. They arrived in early 1852. The planters paid for their transportation from China to the islands and paid each laborer $3 a month for five years, significantly less than the 25 cents a day wage paid a decade earlier.

Hawai'i's nascent sugar industry quickly swung from boom to bust after California, its largest market, became a state in 1850. Prodded by Louisiana's powerful sugar planters, the U.S. government imposed a tariff on Hawaiian sugar. Just as the kingdom's sugar industry was beginning to take off, the new, U.S.-imposed tariff drove down profits, causing several island plantations to fail.

Those who managed to hang on through the difficult times struggled to fund their businesses, particularly before Bishop & Co. opened the first locally owned bank in 1858. Sugar was a capital-intensive industry, requiring heavy investments in mills powered by steam engines and centrifugal machines designed to separate sugar from molasses. Much of the initial capital came from San Francisco, then the financial hub of the American West.

Getting water to the cane fields was also a challenge. The islands periodically suffered from drought, with vast differences in annual rainfall from one valley to the next. Cultivating crops on often thin volcanic soil was no mean feat, particularly considering that some locations were still subject to lava flow and others were buffeted by winds and Pacific storms. With growing zones typically located on the lower flanks of the volcanic rises, freshwater sources were often situated higher up in the mountains.

The first plantation to tackle the problem of irrigation was one on Kaua'i, the oldest island in the chain, whose high annual rainfall had carved lush, steep canyons into the volcanoes and made one of its high peaks, Mount Wai'ale'ale, among the wettest places on earth. In 1856, workers at the Līhu'e plantation dug a ten-mile ditch to bring water from mountain streams to the flat cane fields.

It was an enterprising but disruptive solution. But by diverting the course of streams and lowering the water table, these large-scale irrigation projects parched the surrounding lands and helped displace the taro fields and fish ponds that had long sustained native Hawaiians. Like the introduction by plantation owners of the mongoose to the islands to control rats in their cane fields irrigation, too, would have far-reaching consequences.

Hawai'i's sugar pioneers surely never imagined the damage they would wreak on the natural world of the islands, with its lack of four-legged predators and delicate balance of plants, insects, and birds. Just as church leaders had instructed the first company of missionaries in 1819 to cover the islands with "fruitful fields, pleasant dwellings, schools and churches," some plantation owners saw themselves as carrying forward this mission, which fulfilled both God's calling and the mandate to create wealth.

"A plantation is a means of civilization," reasoned the *Planters Monthly*, a publication for the burgeoning industry founded, in large part, by missionary families, such as the Alexanders and the Baldwins. "It has come in very many instances like a mission of progress into a barbarous region and stamped its character on the neighborhood for miles around."

This "mission of progress" also changed the kingdom's capital. Around the same time as planters dug the first irrigation on Kaua'i, sugar agents, known as factors, began setting up shop in Honolulu, providing capital and trading with customers in California and elsewhere. Castle & Cooke by then had branched out from its early days as grocer and merchant and moved into this potentially much more lucrative business. Members of the family of Lili'u's old headmaster Amos Cooke and his partner, Samuel Northrup Castle, would become powerful forces. In the island industry that would soon be known as Big Sugar, they poured their missionary zeal into the pursuit of profits.

CHAPTER THREE
Aloha, 1862–1873

F ar away from the fast-changing sugar fields, Lili'u matured into a cultured and conscientious young woman. She was a regular churchgoer who took to heart lessons on humility and obedience from her missionary teachers. She joined the king, queen, and other members of the royal court in knocking door to door in Honolulu to raise funds for Queen's Hospital, the first public hospital to serve Hawaiians. Unlike other young royal women, one of whom caused a scandal by her increasingly open love affair with a married white man, Lili'u's public behavior was irreproachable. She occupied the highest rank of any unmarried woman in the land.

In court, Lili'u became an attendant to the young Queen Emma, and she was present at Emma's bedside in May of 1858 when she bore a son. The birth was cause for an outpouring of joy in the kingdom, since a succession of stillborn children and infant fatalities had meant that no legitimate heir had survived into adulthood since the reign of Kamehameha I. Feeling strong loyalty to Britain, the royal couple wrote to Queen Victoria, asking her to be their son's godmother. The monarch agreed, sending an Anglican bishop to the islands to baptize the child, who was named Albert after Queen Victoria's consort, and establish an official presence of the Anglican Church in Hawai'i.

The gently civilized nature of Hawaiian court life during the 1860s surprised some foreign visitors, who had half expected Hawaiians to be dark-skinned savages. Instead, they found a society than included ladies' fancy fairs, moonlight rides on horseback, sea bathing at Waikīkī, balls and parties, an amateur musical society, and two sewing groups, which served as benevolent societies.

"This is no longer a nation of barbarians, any more than of cannibals; though you can hardly be any more prepared than we were to find them as advanced as they really are," wrote Sophia Cracroft, an unmarried woman from Lincolnshire who accompanied Lady Franklin, widow of a famous British explorer, to the islands for two months in 1861. Her writings reflect the belief in racial superiority on the part of whites that was prevalent at the time. In a series of condescending letters, Cracroft describes her meetings with Queen Emma and King Kamehameha IV, cautioning her readers to "drop all idea of savage life," for the "King and many of his people are highly educated and accomplished men . . . English in their habits and tastes."

Relating her first meeting with the king, she wrote that he "came in alone, looking the perfect gentleman, his manner very cordial and unaffected." He spoke with a British accent and "complete command of the language—and surrounded as he is by Americans, educated also as he has been by them it is truly marvelous that he should have totally avoided their odious intonation." Miss Cracroft reported in her letters home that the king regularly received a fine assortment of British publications, including the *Times,* the *Edinburgh Review,* and *Punch;* he also wished for his son to be educated at Eton and was an avid cricket fan.

Before he became Kamehameha IV, when he was sixteen years old, Alexander Liholiho had visited London, which was then the capital of the world's most powerful colonial empire, presided over by Queen Victoria. There he had met Lord Palmerston, the longtime foreign secretary, inspected the royal stables at Windsor Castle, and attended services at

Westminster Abbey, forging a lifelong bond to the Anglican Church. The English treated the Hawaiian prince with respect, a welcome contrast to his treatment in the United States.

One of the most striking figures Miss Cracroft encountered in the royal court was Liliʻu's brother, David Kalākaua, who had been a member of the House of Nobles since 1859. Then serving as the king's aide-de-camp, Kalākaua was reputed to be the best dancer in the kingdom and "lucky with the ladies." As Cracroft described him:

> He was a pure Hawaiian, excessively stout, but of most gentlemanlike manners and appearance, dressed exactly after the morning fashion of Englishmen in light grey . . . He is *very* dark brown (not black) with an aquiline nose and thick lips—whiskers and moustache and hair much more woolly in its crisp curliness than is usually seen among this people. Queen Victoria's Aide-de-Camp could not have acquitted himself better.

She went on to note his excellent English, "with the accent and intonation of a perfect gentleman."

The dashing David Kalākaua served as Miss Cracroft's guide on a trek to the Kīlauea volcano, organizing litters, saddle horses, and bulls for the luggage. Joining them was Lady Franklin, who brought an iron bedstead that was set up for her wherever the party settled for the night. Late in the trip, a timing mishap caused them to miss the boat back to Honolulu, and for several days they stayed in grass houses near the shore waiting for canoes—an arrangement that required the ladies to spend time with Kalākaua in close quarters.

Wearing a scarlet woolen shirt over his usual white one, black trousers, and a large, black waterproof hat festooned with a wreath of crimson and yellow Hawaiian flowers, the darkly handsome *aliʻi* was almost theatrically masculine in his riding attire, with his white buckskin gauntlet gloves and Mexican spurs. His masterful skills as an equestrian, perhaps evocative of matters best left to the bedchamber, seem to have thrilled the maiden traveler.

*　*　*

For a brief period, Liliʻu was engaged to William Lunalilo, a Hawaiian prince. But because of Lunalilo's increasing intemperance, it was an alliance of which Charles Bishop and his wife, Pauahi, Liliʻu's *hānai* sister, almost surely disapproved. Instead, the Bishops favored a match between Liliʻu and her childhood acquaintance John Dominis, since there were strong ties between the Bishop and Dominis families. Charles Bishop's banking partner was married to John Dominis's cousin, and the Bishops and many members of the royal circle had come to respect the forceful Mrs. Dominis, who ruled over Washington Place.

Liliʻu's letters to John during their courtship reveal a young woman pressing to spend time with her new suitor. She beseeched him to join her in Waikīkī (as the Bishops would be away and "I shall feel *so lonesome*") signing the letter, "Yours Affectionately, Lydia." During a trip to Lahaina, she admitted feeling uncertain about her grammar and spelling in English. On more than one occasion, she apologized for her errors: "Now don't laugh at the mistakes that I make, but correct them, and I expect when I get back to Honolulu you will show them to me."

Whether the strength of her feelings was reciprocated is unclear, since few of John's letters survive. But Liliʻu seemed eager to please those around her and in 1860 agreed to marry him. From existing photographs, Dominis seemed to have been a peculiarly unattractive man. But it may be that Liliʻu, with her growing sensitivity to rank, found the prospect of marrying into a prominent family with one of the biggest houses on the islands along with the lack of any other suitors within her circle reasons enough to agree to a match that the Bishops favored.

Liliʻu and John's engagement lasted a full two years. Even then, a tragedy delayed their wedding. The couple initially chose September 2, 1862, as the date of their wedding ceremony, since it would be Liliʻu's twenty-fourth birthday. The groom was thirty. But they were forced to push it back because of a death in the royal family: the four-year-old Prince Albert, the only child of King Kamehameha IV and Queen Emma, was believed at the time to have died of "brain fever," now known as meningitis, but probably appendicitis.

Weeks of public mourning ensued. As Lili'u later recalled in her memoir, the king "completely lost his interest in public life, living in the utmost possible retirement." In the months following the young prince's death, his father attempted to console himself by concentrating his efforts, begun before his child's fatal illness, on translating the Anglican Book of Common Prayer into Hawaiian.

When Lili'u and John finally did marry—a fortnight later, on September 16, 1862—they exchanged vows at a quiet ceremony in Charles and Pauahi Bishop's home. A Congregational minister officiated, as the grieving king and queen looked on. The Bishops hosted the couple's wedding reception, including a center table piled high with "a variety of elegant and costly bridal gifts."

After the wedding party at the Bishops, Lili'u and her groom made their way back to Washington Place, the residence that they would share with John's mother. Her new home was one of the most palatial in Honolulu, a large white mansion with pillars and porticos on all sides, set back far enough from the street to avoid dust and noise and shaded from the noonday heat by tamarind and mango trees. For Lili'u, who took special pleasure in arranging fragrant 'awapuhi or ginger blossoms cut from its gardens, Washington Place seemed like "a choice tropical retreat in the midst of the chief city of the Hawaiian Islands."

As a bride about to embark on her wedding night, Lili'u entered what would be her new home filled with aloha, the Hawaiian word for love, affection, and greeting. Little did she imagine how oppressive Washington Place would become.

Lili'u and John's wedding trip took them to Hawai'i Island, where, as part of a royal entourage, the local chiefs welcomed them to their houses and lands with outpourings of hospitality. The mahele, enacted in 1848, had begun sweeping away the system in which the ali'i provided for the common people and the royal lands were worked collectively. But the customs surrounding the old form of land ownership were still in place as the honeymooners enjoyed weeks of feasting and celebrations.

Had the newlyweds instead traveled to the smaller island of Kaua'i, they would have seen a whir of activity taking place at Līhu'e plantation, on the southeastern side of that island. Here had sprung up a sugar industry being replicated across the islands. Passing through a grove of *kukui* trees, with their silver-gray leaves, and then through a valley, they would have reached sugarcane fields, their stalks as tall as a man and densely clumped together. Fields with enough water would become a leafy, impenetrable jungle of jointed stalks, so dense that a man on horseback couldn't ride through them.

Eventually, they would come to a clutch of bamboo huts with sugarcane thatching, where the plantation workers slept in wooden bunks. At the edge of the valley stood a mill with a redbrick chimney, which was situated on a small pond. The air carried a faint sweet-and-sour odor of fermentation—the smell of molasses.

After fresh cane had been cut in the fields, workers would pile the stalks high onto carts pulled by oxen. Once the carts reached the mill, the workers would unload the stalks and feed them by hand, a few at a time, into enormous granite rollers—weighing three tons each— powered by pond water. The juice from the crushed cane stalks trickled out into a catch basin to be boiled off in a large vat along with powdered lime and water.

Then came the most delicate part of the process: sugar boiling at the nearby Līhu'e mill. The work took place in a big, barnlike room where five shallow pots, about six feet in diameter, were bolted together in a long row. A history of the plantation described it as a scene that a Dutch master might have painted.

> The pots, diminishing in size, were set in a brick oven. An enormous Hawaiian, naked except for a loincloth, his skin glistening with sweat, threw chunks of wood and cane trash into the fire to keep it going.
>
> The scene was like a painting by Rembrandt. In the late afternoon dusk, the flames threw weird, flickering shadows against the factory walls. The syrupy liquid in the pots bubbled and gurgled in violent agitation

throwing up clouds of steam. Muscular Chinese workmen, as naked as the Hawaiian, handled long, oar-like sweeps with which they skimmed off the frothy scum that kept coming to the surface of the boiling juice.

The technology of sugar production was advancing, though. By the 1860s the mill manager at Līhuʻe was using a centrifugal machine, a tub with a round, brass wire cage in the middle that separated the molasses from the sugar grains. It represented an improvement over the slower earlier process of simply letting the molasses run off. As the cage inside the tub began to revolve, powered by steam, the black molasses would stick to the walls of the tub, while the sugar crystals remained inside the wire mesh.

The last step in the process was to pack the granulated sugar for shipping. Workers loaded the wooden kegs onto steamers bound for Honolulu. From there, they'd be handled by sugar factors such as Ladd & Company and later Castle & Cooke, which would act as middlemen for the planters, finding customers in the United States and elsewhere, arranging transportation, and collecting payments.

But the sugar business was fraught with risks. Crops were vulnerable to storms, droughts, trade disputes, and competition from China, the Philippines, and the East Indies. And while the privileged world of the ali'i that Lili'u and John knew still existed, the island nation's economy was becoming increasingly tied to the fortunes of the sugar planters. Indeed, when Lili'u and John returned from their honeymoon, Honolulu's newspapers were filled with talk of the benefits of a reciprocity treaty between Hawai'i and the United States, its biggest market. Under such a treaty, Hawaiian goods would be admitted into California and elsewhere at the same duty rates as California goods were admitted into the islands. Efforts to ratify a treaty between the Kingdom of Hawai'i and the United States sputtered on for years, as Congress focused on more pressing matters, such as bringing an end to the bloody War Between the States.

*　　*　　*

Liliʻu's honeymoon was brief. The newlyweds were relegated to a first-floor bedroom next to that of Mrs. Dominis, who continued to occupy the larger master suite. Mary Dominis had furnished Washington Place as an outpost of America in the tropics, filling the front parlor with dark, ornately carved wooden furniture, with nothing to suggest that this was the new home of a revered island chiefess. In the back parlor was a dark wood settee, imported by Captain Dominis from China. Its arms were carved in the shape of dragons, as if to dare someone to sit down on it comfortably. Every night, Mary made sure to keep a light in the window, in case her missing husband returned home.

Although Liliʻu was living in one of the largest private homes in the kingdom, with a lush garden that flourished under her mother-in-law's care, it was an unhappy domestic arrangement. Explaining the awkward situation in her memoir, Liliʻu wrote "No man could be more devoted than was General Dominis to his mother. He was really an only child." And as her mother-in-law "felt that no one should step between her and her child, naturally I, as her son's wife, was considered an intruder; and I was forced to realize this from the beginning. My husband was extremely kind and considerate to me, yet he would not swerve to one side or to the other in any matter where there was danger of hurting his mother's feelings."

After the first year of their marriage, a musical evening was planned at the palace to mark the twentieth anniversary of the recognition by England and France of Hawaiʻi's independence. But the king never appeared, perhaps due to an asthma attack. His absence puzzled his guests, but unbeknownst to them Kamehameha IV lay on his deathbed. He died two days later, on November 30, 1863, at the age of twenty-nine, of poor health and chronic asthma. An old friend of the king wrote afterward, "It cannot be wrong to say that the death of the son hastened the death of the father. God grant that we may never again see so heartbroken a man."

Since the king left no heir, his brother Lot ascended to the throne as Kamehameha V. The new king was far different from the more polished Anglophile Liholiho, his predecessor. Darker in complexion, large and heavy compared to the late king's lithe boxer's physique, Lot also embraced the old Hawaiian ways, including the *kāhuna*, or priests, and the *hula*, a native dance tradition that the missionaries had prohibited because they thought it was obscene. Resembling his grandfather Kamehameha I more than any other successor to the Hawaiian throne, Kamehameha V was considered more intelligent than his predecessor and "the last great chief of the olden type."

Ruling at a time when the kingdom's economic power was shifting toward sugar planters and the kingdom's mostly white merchant class, Kamehameha V sought ways to regain more political power for himself, as monarch, and for his Hawaiian subjects. Although he convened a constitutional convention of sixteen nobles, twenty-seven representatives, and himself in 1864, it failed to reach agreement. So Kamehameha V declared a new constitution "on his own authority." The king believed "'the influence of the Crown ought to be seen pervading every function of the government,'" and accordingly his constitution greatly expanded executive power while combining the upper and lower chambers of the legislature into a single assembly.

Not surprisingly, expansion of royal prerogative and the curbing of power of Westerners drew strong criticism from the English-language press. But Lili'u, for one, celebrated it by composing a simple song for Hawaiian schoolchildren. Titled "'Onipa'a," or "Stand Firm," she wrote it in 1864, shortly after the king proclaimed the new constitution. The anthem fervently urged the students:

Do not abandon	*Mai noho a ha'alele*
This good work.	*I kēia hana maika'i.*
Steadfast, stand firm,	*'Onipa'a, 'onipa'a,*
For our constitution.	*Ko kākou kumukānāwai.*

Lili'u took 'Onipa'a as her motto. But her attempt, decades later, to return to Kamehameha V's constitution would invite powerful resistance.

The feeble state of Hawai'i's military forces was on the minds of some of the king's advisers, particularly Lili'u's brother Kalākaua, who served on Kamehameha V's privy council. Writing to the kingdom's foreign minister during the U.S. Civil War, Kalākaua saw the threat to the monarchy posed by Americans and reflected, presciently, "If in case we are called upon today or say tomorrow to put down and quell an excited and riotous mob, lead on by religious fanatics and the cry for a *popular government* (as many a secret heart is now most anxious to see this nation in) where? and who are the men to be called upon, to confide the vital trust? I see but a few."

The foreign-born minister dismissed Kalākaua's request for a stronger military on the grounds of tight funds, explaining that "as the next Legislature has to provide for so many extraordinary expenses of the Royal Family debts of the Crown etc. it is indispensable to keep the appropriations for the military as low as possible." He suggested instead raising a volunteer militia for the next two years. That was one of the first, but not the last, instances of Kalākaua bumping up against financial constraints imposed by *haole* advisers.

Kalākaua may have been frustrated in his efforts to build a paid military force for the kingdom, but he refused to be thwarted in matters of the heart. He fell in love with the widowed Julia Kapi'olani, an *ali'i* who spoke only Hawaiian all her life. He was determined to marry her and defied custom by doing so before the official mourning period for Kamehameha IV had passed, keeping the secret even from his parents and sisters.

Although Kalākaua faced some criticism for the timing of his secret nuptials, the king himself didn't seem to mind. But Lili'u was offended by having been excluded from her brother and new sister-in-law's secret. She said as much in a letter to her younger sister Likelike, which suggested an early schism between the siblings that would only grow wider through the years, writing, "To say the truth between ourselves, I don't think he ever cared as much for his own family as does for those who are no connections of his whatever."

Nonetheless, Lili'u and her brother remained part of the court's inner circle, as Kamehameha V chose John Dominis as one of his closest advisers and appointed him governor of O'ahu. Dominis would rely on the *ali'i* he'd first met at the Royal School for government positions throughout his working life. With this job, he could pursue his passion for guns, boats, and horses, earning his reputation as an avid sportsman.

Part of his duties as governor were to make an annual tour of the island, and Lili'u joined her husband on this trip. But she increasingly found reasons to spend time away from him, as well as from Mrs. Dominis. One day in 1865, Lili'u made her way to O'ahu College at the edge of the lush rain forests of the Mānoa Valley, which is today the elite Punahou school that Barack Obama attended. She met with a teacher there named Susan Mills and asked to become a student. Already far better educated than most Hawaiians and many of the missionaries' children, she soon began studying Greek, Latin, and French.

By the 1860s Lili'u had become a striking young woman, with a graceful way of moving and an inner light that drew men to her. Lili'u was as lovely to Westerners as she was to Hawaiians, moving fluidly between both cultures, perhaps with the exception of navigating her own difficult marriage. A young American from Boston, the journalist Julius A. Palmer, observed her in 1867 as a young married woman attending a ball on a French warship moored in Honolulu. Through the racially tinged lens of the time, he wrote:

> Of all the fair women who then moved through the dance on the great maindeck of the frigate, she is the one that, from that moment to the present, retains the strongest hold on my memory. Why?
>
> This element is not beauty, but it is grace. As Mrs. Dominis moved through the misty mazes of the waltz there was nothing but grace in

every movement, nought but the most bewitching attraction in every smile. She did not dance as the stately court lady: she threw her whole heart into the poetry of her motions; and, whosoever the partner opposite to her, you saw that she was in love with him—yes, at every glance of her flashing black eyes.

Liliʻu may have been lavishing attention on her dance partners in a way that was unusual to an observer used to the more staid manners of Boston society. Or she may have been longing for an approving male gaze, since it does not appear from her letters of the time that she was receiving much of her husband's attention. Perhaps she had simply harnessed the sensuality that *hula* dancers knew.

There is no indication Liliʻu was unfaithful to her husband. Indeed, her letters from this period reflect her missionary upbringing, which taught her to be subservient. In one, she advised her sister Likelike, who was then in school, to "*Practice humility . . .* "*Remember then duty before pleasure.*" In another letter to her younger sister, who already was starting to show a tendency toward flirtatiousness, Liliʻu urged her to "strive to control your feeling . . . if any harsh word begins to rise to your lips suppress it—do not let it escape and then when you succeed in doing so you will afterwards be happy to think you controled yourself." Whereas just a generation ago the *aliʻi* unapologetically celebrated the war exploits and fierceness of their ancestors, the values of humility, meekness, and obedience that Liliʻu absorbed from her missionary teachers undercut the traditional power of the *aliʻi*.

Meanwhile, her friendship with the king also gave her the perfect excuse to escape from her airless domestic arrangement. Intent on preserving Hawaiian culture, Kamehameha V had asked Abraham Fornander, a Swede who'd arrived in the islands on a whaling ship several decades earlier and had married a Hawaiian chiefess, to undertake an extensive study of Hawaiian history based on gleanings from the oral tradition. Liliʻu set to work assisting Fornander by translating *mele* and legends for him.

Besides strengthening her awareness of her people's history, the task deepened Lili'u's understanding of Hawaiian poetic expression, with its rich metaphors and secret meanings. It may also have bolstered her confidence as a composer; because she could understand both Hawaiian and Western music, she was able to blend the two in what was then an unusual style that came to be known as *hula ku'i* music. In her education and her marriage, Lili'u was herself a blend of the West and Polynesia and the music she would later become famous for delicately folded in musical elements from both cultures.

On one rainy day when Lili'u was feeling dejected, the king came to visit her at Washington Place and remarked that he was displeased that Hawai'i did not have its own national anthem. For state occasions, Hawai'i used Britain's "God Save the Queen." "Each nation," he told her, "but ours had its expression of patriotism and love of country in its music." To address this shortfall Kamehameha V asked Lili'u to compose a Hawaiian national anthem. In a week Lili'u had written the music and lyrics, in both Hawaiian and English, for a deeply Christian anthem, "He Mele Lahui Hawaii." As the new leader of the Kawaiaha'o choir, Lili'u led the performance of her anthem for the first time in the great stone church.

Beneath the broad balconies and before pews seating hundreds, Lili'u directed the members of the choir to sing the new national anthem she had composed with a simple but profound prayer embedded in its chorus.

Grant thy Peace thro'out the land	*Ma kou pono mau*
O'er these sunny, sea-girt Isles	*A ma kou mana nui*
Keep the nation's life, O Lord,	*E ola, e ola ka mō'ī*
And upon our sovereign smile.	*E mau ke ea o ka 'āina*

The storm clouds arrived sooner than expected. In December 1872, Kamehameha V lay in his bed. Struggling for many years with obesity and poor health, his doctors told him he was dying. The shock of learning that his condition was fatal wasn't all the king was struggling with: unmarried and childless, he had yet to name a successor or write a will.

He called John Dominis to his side to put his last wishes into writing. When Dominis urged him to name a successor, the king replied sharply that he needed time to consider such an important matter. He sent Dominis out to get his breakfast, telling him that when he returned they'd "sit down quietly by ourselves and arrange all these matters."

By the time Dominis returned the king's bedchamber was full of wellwishers and potential candidates for the throne. Lili'u and Pauahi stood at the head of the bed, while Kalākaua and others clustered at the foot of the bed and in the doorway. The king turned to a long-serving Hawaiian adviser and asked him to name the new *mō'ī*, but he declined, saying they were all his *ali'i*. The king then asked Pauahi to be his successor. She said, "No, no, not me; don't think of me, I do not need it."

It is unclear why Pauahi, who by then was a leader of Honolulu society, turned down the throne. Perhaps she felt that taking on such a role would strain her marriage, since the needs of the Hawaiian people were increasingly coming into conflict with those of the ascendant business class her husband, the banker Charles Bishop, led. Perhaps she truly believed she could better serve Hawai'i as a society matron wielding the Victorian values of charity and selflessness rather than political power.

Whatever the reason, the king died moments later without naming a successor. After a tumultuous few weeks, William Lunalilo, the closest relation of the Kamehameha dynasty to the late sovereign and the prince known as "Whiskey Bill," was overwhelmingly elected as the next king. Yet the Hawaiian royal family was soon struck again by misfortune.

Earning his nickname for his prodigious drinking, Lunalilo's health began to fail almost as soon as he took the throne. As the rainy season descended, the king took to his bed. Lili'u was one of the *ali'i* who kept a twenty-four-hour vigil over him. Despite Lunalilo's popularity and his commitment to democratic ideals, the ailing king's attachment to the bottle made him ineffectual and created a power vacuum in the kingdom. So lingering was the king's death that the marshals festooned the outer walls of the royal residence with black funeral crepe two days before the passing, mistakenly thinking he had already died.

On February 3, 1874, barely a year after beginning his reign and just after his thirty-ninth birthday, Lunalilo succumbed to tuberculosis and alcoholism. Grief-stricken Hawaiians mourned for weeks following his death. The sound of their wailing raised the hair on the backs of the necks of the white settlers who heard it. With the Kamehamehas dying out and no heir named to the throne, the menace of foreign intervention loomed large.

CHAPTER FOUR
High Chiefs of Sugardom, 1874–1876

With Lunalilo's death, the kingdom was forced to elect another monarch. This time, there were just two serious candidates: Queen Emma, who laid claim to the throne as the widow of Kamehameha IV, and Lili'u's brother, David Kalākaua. Neither was a direct descendant of Hawai'i's great conqueror Kamehameha I. But Kalākaua's supporters argued he was the more suitable candidate because he had held a series of government posts, spoke fluent English, and had studied the law. Emma's connection to the Kamehamehas was through marriage to her late husband, as well as distantly through blood. Thus Kalākaua's election would bring a resounding end to that family's dynastic reign.

Less than an hour after Lunalilo had died the cabinet met and set a date for a special meeting of the legislators a week and a half later. The Americans, who supported Kalākaua over the pro-British Emma, arranged for a steamer to pick up legislators from the other islands and bring them to Honolulu to vote. There were whispers for years afterward that the Americans had plied the politicians with alcohol to try to win votes for Kalākaua. Both candidates announced their intent soon after the king's death. Within days, hundreds of election placards and broad-sides, printed in both Hawaiian and English, papered the island capital. The newspapers ran banner headlines about the contest, with the *Pacific Commercial Advertiser* and the *Hawaiian Gazette*, which had replaced the *Polynesian* as the official government newspaper, strongly supporting Kalākaua. To one editorial writer, voters faced the choice of a "petticoat government" or "a pair of pants, with boots for the purpose of kicking people around."

Both the American and British ministers feared that violence would erupt. Three warships were then anchored in Honolulu's harbor, the USS *Tuscarora*, the USS *Portsmouth*, and the British gunboat *Tenedos*. They were each prepared to land an armed force to preserve order. In case a landing became necessary, the Americans had arranged a shore-to-ship signal.

Until this contest, Emma and Kalākaua had been friendly toward each other. When Emma went to Europe in 1865 shortly after her hus-band had died, she wrote letters to Kalākaua in which she addressed him as "Dear Taffy," a nickname derived apparently from the Welsh Dafydd for David. But that would soon change as the rivalry between the two turned bitter and even violent.

The succession crisis stemming from Lunalilo's failure to name an heir deepened the split between those in favor of Hawai'i drawing closer to the United States and those opposed to it. The Honolulu newspapers were filled with rumors of a reciprocity treaty with America, which would permit Hawaiian sugar and other goods to enter the United States duty free, and U.S. goods to enter Hawai'i without duty. There was also talk of allowing U.S. ships to anchor at the inlet now known as Pearl Harbor.

Indeed, during Lunalilo's reign, a secret mission had been undertaken by two representatives of the U.S. secretary of war to determine the mili-tary and strategic value of Hawai'i's ports. Henry M. Whitney, founder of the *Pacific Commercial Advertiser*, had suggested to the late king that he consider leasing what was then the Pearl River basin as a means to stave off annexation and sweeten the reciprocity deal for the United States. The chamber of commerce and the legislature both hotly debated the proposition, with the result that Hawai'i first offered, then withdrew, it as part of the proposed treaty. When Lunalilo died the issue remained unresolved.

Planters and merchants hoped to draw closer to the United States, while the pro-British camp, led by Queen Emma, feared the growing American influence. Although Kalākaua had stated his desire for independence, the Americans saw him as the less objectionable candidate than his pro-British rival, presenting a Hobson's choice, as one later put it. That fanned the suspicions of Queen Emma and her supporters, who viewed Kalākaua as an ambitious and dangerously flighty man who could be manipulated by the American merchants and planters. "The reciprocity treaty, giving away land, is much discussed these days," Queen Emma wrote. "There is a feeling of bitterness against these rude people who dwell on our land and have high handed ideas of giving away someone else's property as if it were theirs."

Sanford Ballard Dole, a missionary's son whose life would later intertwine with Lili'u's in fateful ways, jumped into the fray. Dole's father had left New England as a preacher bound for a religious mission to Hawai'i, arriving in 1841. But because he had difficulty learning the Hawaiian language, which was necessary if he hoped to convert the natives to Christianity, he was assigned to be the first principal of O'ahu College, then called the Punahou school, which was the newly established boarding school for missionaries' children.

Sanford was born in Honolulu on April 23, 1844. Because his mother died four days after childbirth he was taken from his biological father and adopted by white missionary parents who hired a Hawaiian nurse to care for him. Years later, Dole would describe himself as being someone raised in both cultures, explaining that "I am of American blood but Hawaiian milk."

Athletic and long-limbed, Sanford set off for Williams College in Massachusetts in early April of 1866, just before his twenty-second birthday. He sought out other students from Hawai'i, forming a group called the "Cannibals"—a name they chose as a humorous twist on the islands' fearsome reputation. Although his father had urged him to study for the ministry, Sanford decided instead to focus on the law, with the goal of starting a legal practice in Honolulu. As a law clerk in Boston, he enjoyed a busy social life, which included lectures, theater, dances, taffy-pulling parties, and debates over political and economic issues related to the islands with fellow Cannibal.

Sanford returned to Honolulu in late 1868 and began working as a lawyer. His practice started slowly so, during his spare time, the young man with the dark bushy beard and intent gaze penned anonymous articles in the *Punch Bowl*, a new monthly publication that he started with fellow Punahou classmate Alfred Castle and roommate Thomas Walker. Dole's idealism was revealed in this statement of editorial policy: "Our plan is to conduct a small journal which shall be in the interests of no Party, Church or State . . . The Right shall be supported whenever it may be found. Wrong shall be exposed whenever and wherever the public good can be advanced by so doing." But his youthful idealism soon succumbed to parental pressure; his father admonished him to pay more attention to business affairs, so Dole folded the *Punch Bowl*, with its last issue appearing in October of 1870.

By then Dole and a fellow bachelor had taken up quarters in a cottage on Emma Street in downtown Honolulu. Nicknamed the "Rookery," it quickly became a social hub for some of the town's white residents, with readings and gatherings of officers from visiting ships. In his diary, the young attorney recorded the boating excursions, dances, horseback riding, and many jolly parties involving the young ladies in his social set. In 1873, he married Anna Prentice Cate, a teacher from Maine whom Sanford had met two days after she'd arrived in Honolulu in 1870.

The Doles' honeymoon period was soon over. Anna had been a vivacious and sociable companion to her new husband until Christmas Day in 1873, when she fell while horseback riding. Soon after, she became despondent when she learned she could never have children. Like Liliʻu and John Dominis, Dole and Anna also would be childless. Sanford, who taught a Sunday school class at Kawaiahaʻo church for several years before Anna's accident, became enchanted by a half Hawaiian, half Tahitian child named Lizzie. Again, like Liliʻu, he would later adopt her as a *hānai* child of his own, over the tearful objections of his spouse, who may have feared that the unusually beautiful child would drain his affection for her.

Also like Liliʻu, Sanford harbored a passion for the natural world. A long sojourn on the island of Kauaʻi, where his family had moved from Punahou when Sanford was nine, had instilled in him a love for ornithology. While a law student in Boston, he penned a book on Hawaiian birds, a volume that was reprinted in Honolulu in 1878. In 1886 he would accompany Liliʻu on a trip to study endangered native birds on the island of Nihoa.

Another man whose life would be closely intertwined with both Liliʻu's and Dole's also embraced the kingdom's natural splendors, as well as its commerical opportunities. Lorrin Andrews Thurston, grandson of the missionary Asa Thurston, grew up on the island of Maui, where his widowed mother and uncle ran an industrial school for boys called the Haleakalā Boarding School. Situated just nine miles from the summit of the famous volcano, the school made a convenient trailhead for the enterprising young Lorrin, who would guide tourists to the summit; he made more than fifty ascents, along with nine trips into the mountain's volcanic crater. "A wild and tangled mass of rocks and lava flows lay toward the top, but I knew the country so well that I could follow the trail even on a dark and rainy night," Thurston would recall in his memoirs.

Later, when working as a plantation overseer on Hawaiʻi Island to earn money to attend Columbia University's law school, Thurston continued his study of Hawaiʻi's volcanoes. He and a friend took a side trip to the Kīlauea volcano in 1879 and amused themselves by ladling hot lava, from pools and dipping coins in it.

Lili'u shared with Dole and Thurston a reverence for Hawai'i's land-scape, where all three were born. In coming years, though, they would re-peatedly clash over who should control the land that each fiercely loved.

The morning of February 12, 1874, began with fair skies and a light breeze. But already tempers were rising among several hundred mostly native Hawaiian supporters of Queen Emma who gathered at her home and then moved, en masse, downtown to the courthouse on Queen Street, where the legislators were gathering to elect a new ruler. Although unarmed, the crowd was primed for physical conflict, with one Hawai-ian allegedly telling a reporter from a Hawaiian-language newspaper, "If the representatives do not do as we wish, we shall burn their bodies and strip their bones of their flesh."

The legislative assembly convened at noon. The spectator gallery was packed and the tense hush in the chamber contrasted with the rising furor of the crowd outside. Rumors were flying that Kalākaua's backers had plied native voters with alcohol and bribes to sway them to their side. The legislators quickly moved to the most important business of the day: casting their votes. Thirty-nine voted for Kalākaua and just six voted for Queen Emma, raising suspicions of ballot swaying on the part of Kalākaua's supporters. When a small committee of lawmakers left the courthouse that afternoon to inform Kalākaua that he had won election as the new king, they were confronted by an angry mob.

Trying to make their way to a waiting carriage, the legislators were attacked by liquor-fueled supporters of Queen Emma. They fled back into the building to escape the crowd while some of the Emmaites began demolishing the wooden carriage, tearing pieces from it to use as clubs. Then the mob turned to the courthouse, breaking windows and rushing in through an unguarded back door. Destroying furniture and ripping apart books and papers, some of Queen Emma's backers beat the law-makers and even tossed one out the second-story window of the build-ing. More than a dozen lawmakers were wounded; one died.

In the thick of what was effectively a race riot, pitting native Hawaiians against whites, was Sanford Dole. He barely noted the day in his diary, yet his young bride wrote a vivid, racially charged description of the scene in the courthouse in a letter to her mother.

> It seems as though he [Sanford] had been through something almost too dreadful to speak of . . . Sanford said that at one time during the fray, happening to go into the court room, he saw two of the Representatives who were the only ones then left there, assailed by eight or ten powerful natives who with their flashing eyes and dark skins looked the very personification of fury . . . Sanford said it looked so dreadful that he hesitated one moment, and then rushed in between them, throwing out his arms and talking, and for a moment making a diversion in their favor so that they escaped out the door and down the stairs followed by a part of their pursuers, while the rest gazed savagely at him and threatened to kill him if he interfered with their work.

During the riot, several people hurried to Queen Emma's residence, a two-story bungalow located near Washington Place, hoping to persuade her to address and calm her followers. But she turned them away, explaining that the riot "was no concern of hers." Dole himself called on Emma, only to find that her staff was in such a state of "hysterical excitement" that he could not gain an audience with her. Many of the rioters eventually made their way back from the government building to Emma's home and continued "hurrahing and making speeches."

Alarmed by the violence and the approach of nightfall, the king-elect, David Kalākaua, Liliʻu's husband, John Dominis, and others beseeched the American minister to land troops from the U.S. warship, since some of the police and Hawaiian guards had thrown their support behind Queen Emma. The prearranged signal was made. Tellingly, this call for assistance from the American government was the king-elect's first official act.

Soon, 150 or so marines landed and began marching through the streets of Honolulu, toward the courthouse. An additional force of 70 British troops landed from the *Tenedos*. As one white resident wrote afterward, "The Americans got there first, and when the British force arrived a few minutes after, the mob met them with cheers, showing that they expected them to aid their cause as it was well known all the Britishers were for Queen Emma, & they were much disappointed when they found that the British troops joined with the Americans to put the rioters down."

In a violent coda to the Kamehamehas' nearly seven-decade rule the House of Kalākaua was under siege from the first. Guards were posted that night at Kalākaua's residence, Washington Place, the palace, and other government buildings and munitions repositories. For eight days afterward, British and American troops remained on shore, patrolling the streets. Many of the rioters were arrested and about fifty later stood trial.

With this ill-boding backdrop to his accession as king, David Kalākaua took the oath required by the constitution, as legislators, foreign ministers, and some Hawaiians looked on. Taking place the day after the riot, the ceremony was held at the chamberlains' office, *Kinau Hale*, rather than at Kawaiahaʻo church, where other kings had been sworn in, and was marked by the deafening cracks of a twenty-one-gun salute. Queen Emma formally recognized Kalākaua as king only after the French and the British ministers did so, and then only grudgingly. From Liliʻuʻs perspective, "Queen Emma never recovered from her great disappointment, nor could she reconcile herself to the fact that our family had been chosen as the royal line to succeed that of the Kamehamehas."

Perhaps in a moment of bitterness toward the previous royal family, Kalākaua refused a request from Lunalilo's father. He had asked to have a royal salute fired from the government battery on Punchbowl Hill as the body of his son was carried from the royal mausoleum in the Nuʻuanu Valley to the tomb that had been built for him in the yard of Kawaiahaʻo church. Apparently, Kalākaua reasoned that Lunalilo had already had a state funeral and thus was not entitled to further honors.

The new king's decision was unpopular. A group of *haole* students from Punahou stood at the front gate of the churchyard as the funeral cortege arrived. One of them later recalled that the rain, which had been falling gently beforehand, had started coming down in torrents as the body arrived. Thunder boomed and the scene was lit up by a terrifying flash of lightning, a rarity in Honolulu. Some saw the storm as a sign that God had provided for Lunalilo's burial what Kalākaua had denied: thunderclaps.

Hawai'i's new king was a man of wide girth, in his physical presence as well as in his *mana*, an expression Hawaiians use to convey life force or power. In a black-and-white photograph from the time, he fixes his gaze slightly upward, to a distant horizon, and his strong, dark features are framed by the muttonchop whiskers favored in those days. His broad frame is complemented by an elaborate dress uniform, complete with epaulettes, metal stars, braided cord, high boots, and a feather-fringed metal helmet. He holds a long sword by the handle, tip down, in front of him, his love of military pageantry on full display.

Kalākaua's fascination with the military had begun during his adolescence. After attending the Royal School, he returned to live with his biological father, who was then commanding the Punchbowl Battery, a small militia based near where Lili'u had been born, and began training under a former Prussian captain then serving in Hawai'i's militia. At sixteen, Kalākaua became a first lieutenant in his father's unit of 240 men. Soon after, he began studying the law with an American lawyer, Charles Coffin Harris, who served in Hawai'i's legislature and who argued forcefully against what he saw as the gradual takeover of Hawai'i by foreigners. Among Kalākaua's first appointments in his new government was this American mentor, whom he named a justice of the Hawaiian supreme court. Since his predecessor Lunalilo had disbanded the household troops following a failed mutiny, leaving the kingdom without a regular organized military force, the new king quickly sought to reestablish one, particularly since the disaffected supporters of Queen Emma continued to vocally oppose him.

The British commissioner James Wodehouse, more Emma partisan than objective observer, wrote a letter to London a few months after Kalākaua's accession suggesting that Hawai'i's new monarch was being propped up by foreigners and lacked support from his own people. "The king is not popular in this Island, and were Honolulu left without the protection of a Ship-of-War, in my opinion, there would be a Revolution in which He would lose His Throne, and possibly His life. It is the fear of foreign intervention alone that keeps the Hawaiians quiet."

Soon after becoming king, Kalākaua and his queen, Kapi'olani, made a goodwill tour of the islands, continuing a tradition among the kingdom's new rulers. His goals, he proclaimed, were to encourage population growth among native Hawaiians and advance agriculture and commerce. His first objective was not easy to achieve, as even in his own royal household he and his wife remained childless. But the second could be more easily addressed. Attempts to negotiate a reciprocity treaty with the United States had sputtered in recent years, as the kingdom was being wracked by royal deaths and succession battles. At the request of the sugar planters, Kalākaua decided to try again and began planning a U.S. trip.

The following day he boarded the American warship USS *Benicia*, accompanied by John Dominis, who remained governor of O'ahu under the new king, as well as by the U.S. minister and Maui's governor. For three months, Kalākaua would tour the United States, a trip that some white residents of the islands criticized as a "grandiose move by the King;" to others it seemed to confirm suspicions of Kalākaua's pro-American bias.

San Francisco mayor James Otis, along with a crowd of upwards of six thousand people, waited to welcome the Hawaiian king on the wharf. Kalākaua charmed the city, winning praise as "urbane," "gracious," "amusing," and "extremely handsome."

Shivering their way across the snowy Rocky Mountains by train, the royal party arrived in Washington, D.C., on December 12, 1874. As an exotic, dark-skinned visitor, the king of Hawai'i attracted attention. "Kalakaua is a large, well-built man, standing about 5 feet 11 inches, and weighing about 180 pounds. "The general cast of his features resembles the American negro," the reporter wrote, but added that his skin color was closer to that of a "mulatto," or a mixed race person. "His expression is one of good nature, and does not indicate any particular strength of character. His bearing is easy and his manner and conversation those of an intellectual gentleman." The rings he wore on each of his little fingers caught the journalists attention.

Kalākaua met with President Ulysses S. Grant and the members of his cabinet and was invited to address a joint session of Congress—the first king ever granted such an honor. Unfortunately, the cold climate of America did not agree with him: he caught a severe cold and became too hoarse to speak himself, so instead he instructed his chancellor to read his message. Even so, Washington's lawmakers cheered him afterward and Mrs. Grant offered to provide him with a cough remedy.

The king's trip to the nation's capital was a public relations victory that raised Americans' awareness of his distant island kingdom, and one that Lili'u would later try to repeat. Kalākaua also stopped in New York, shopping on Fifth Avenue, riding a sleigh in Central Park, and eating breakfast with the editor of *Popular Science Monthly*, with whom he had corresponded years earlier about inventions he had tinkered with, such as a submarine torpedo and an improved bottle stopper. He also spoke before a temperance league, making gentle fun of himself. He noted that he had once embraced the ideals of temperance brought to the islands by the missionaries "but humanity is weak, you know, and I do not know how they [the missionaries] consider my case now."

Rumors circulated back in the islands that the king had rung up enormous bills and that he and his brother-in-law John Dominis had cavorted their way across the country. Kalākaua suggested as much himself in a letter he wrote to Lili'u at 3 a.m. on December 29, 1874, in which he explained he was "besieged with invitations & visitors, in fact I am not my own master." He wrote he was sleeping just three or four hours a night, adding that his "hotel bills from San Francisco to Washington and New York have been paid by the City Authorities," with cars and trains furnished in the same way. After having been showered in foreign hospitality, Kalākaua and his party returned to Honolulu in February 1875. At least in the eyes of the islands' white merchant class, he was triumphant for having returned with strong prospects for a reciprocity treaty between Hawai'i and its largest trading partner.

Hawai'i's cultured and dignified monarch was likely somewhat different from what readers of the *Sacramento Union*, then one of the most influential newspapers in the western United States, had expected. In a series of articles for the paper a few years before Kalākaua's first trip to America, Samuel Langhorne Clemens, writing under the pen name Mark Twain, had humorously portrayed the Hawaiian royal family and its courtiers—with their grand titles and fancy dress uniforms—as ruling little more than a "play-house kingdom."

Twain had arrived in the islands for a four-month visit in 1866 on the first steamship to make the trip from San Francisco to Honolulu. Writing a series of letters for the newspaper, he followed with a lengthy lecture tour in the late 1860s and 1870s, stirring up interest in Hawai'i and shaping Americans' views of the islanders. Usually calling it "Our Fellow Savages of the Sandwich Islands," Twain's talk on Hawai'i was his favorite as he became America's foremost lecturer, repeating it to the amusement of his audience almost a hundred times.

Twain, like many Americans, was skeptical of monarchy as a form of government. That, coupled with the writer's famously sharp eye for the preposterous and pedantic, led Twain to scoff at what he saw as the pretensions of Hawaiian royalty in an entertaining mix of truth and prejudice.

"In our country, children play 'keep house,' and in the same high-sounding but miniature way the grown folk here, with the poor little material of slender territory and meager population, play 'empire.' " Adding to his satirical portrait a mention of the practices of eating dogs and rumored orgies, he drew a titillating portrait of a people who, in his words, were ruled by "sceptered savages."

The flame-haired writer with the droopy mustache was still struggling financially at that point in his career. Undoubtedly aware of the pocketbook interests of his newspaper's readers, he used his sharp eye to size up the economic prospects of the islands for his American readers. So in addition to his more colorful dispatches, which included reports on his visit to a volcano and the place of the death of Captain Cook, he added reports that the business readers of the *Sacramento Union* might find useful.

He wrote a letter on the burgeoning sugar industry, entitled "The High Chief of Sugardom." With his well-known propensity to exaggerate, he reported that Hawaiian sugar plantations were producing up to 13,000 pounds of sugar, or 6.5 tons, to the acre on unfertilized soil. The actual number at the time was closer to 1.5 tons to the acre, still slightly more than the 2,500 pounds per acre Twain claimed was produced on fertilized soil in Louisiana. "This country is the king of the sugar world, as far as astonishing productiveness is concerned." After visiting all the principal wonders of the islands, Twain concluded that Hawai'i's sugar industry, "in its importance to America, surpasses them all."

Twain wrote for an American audience that increasingly looked west to the Pacific for commercial opportunities and his glowing reports on the prospects for sugar cultivation supported those in favor of stronger ties between the two nations. After the Civil War, the United States experienced an economic boom, fueled by reconstruction. In Hawai'i, Twain observed that his fellow Americans were also in an expansionary mode: "The 3,000 whites in the islands handle all the money and carry on all the commerce and agriculture—and superintend the religion. Americans are largely in the majority. These whites are sugar-planters, merchants, whale-ship officers, and missionaries."

Aware of the disastrous effects that the arrival of foreigners had had on the native Hawaiian population, Twain suggested that the Hawaiian race was dying out due to the "disease of civilization" and predicted that the islands would eventually pass to the United States as its "lawful heirs." Twain's dispatches helped lay the groundwork for discussions of reciprocity and annexation, whetting the general public's appetite for the prospects that awaited across the Pacific.

When the king's steamer entered Honolulu's port on February 15, 1875, a few days earlier than expected, Sanford Dole and the other citizens charged with organizing his greeting were flustered. Only one of the two arches planned as a surprise to greet him was ready. But the government house across the street was decorated as never before: on top of the tower was a large crown and, in large letters, KALAKAUA spelled out.

The king's tour had advanced the efforts of the emissaries he had sent to Washington ahead of him to negotiate a reciprocity treaty. In early 1875, simple terms allowing Hawaiian and American sugar to enter both countries free of duty wound their way through the U.S. House of Representatives. But by the time a treaty made its way through the Senate, an amendment had been added, guaranteeing that the Hawaiian king would not lease or otherwise dispose of any port, harbor, or territory in his dominions "to any other power" than the U. S.. Thus lay the earliest official roots of America's claim on Pearl Harbor.

News of the Senate's approval of the treaty reached Honolulu on April 8. There was rejoicing on the part of the Honolulu business community, with the *Pacific Commercial Advertiser* printing a special edition to trumpet the development. The treaty seemed to be the answer to at least some of the planters' problems and to settle the question of which foreign power the kingdom would draw closer to.

The treaty, of course, was not without its critics. The San Francisco sugar refiners initially protested it because they worried it would flood the market with higher-quality Hawaiian sugar that required little further refining after milling, as opposed to their own second-grade "coffee sugar." Their objections were overcome when the islands' sugar planters initially withheld their crops, then agreed to sell in return for withdrawing their opposition to the treaty. Sugar planters from Louisiana and other southern states also opposed it, fearing the competition. But their protests remained largely unheeded, particularly when weighed against the military and strategic value of Hawai'i to a young nation looking westward for expansion.

Other opponents attempted to stir up fears that Hawai'i would go to the British if the treaty were not passed. The Monroe Doctrine of 1823, which proclaimed separate spheres of influence for America and Europe and warned European powers not to meddle in the affairs of the western hemisphere, still prevailed, and the sentiments it contained had lately been revived and reinterpreted through the lens of "manifest destiny," a term coined by an American journalist named John L. O'Sullivan in 1845.

O'Sullivan argued that the United States was destined to expand westward across the North American continent. In a magazine article, he praised the annexation of Texas as a "fulfillment of our manifest destiny to overspread the continent" and vigorously urged the country to look next at acquiring California. He expressed the belief that the U.S. was destined to expand westward, an aim that was being accomplished largely through purchases of territory, such as Louisiana from France in 1803, the Oregon territory from Great Britain in 1846, and portions of Texas, California, and New Mexico from Mexico in 1848.

Just as America's fears of being trumped by the British in Texas helped move along Texas's bid to join the union, the reciprocity treaty between the United States and Hawai'i was prodded by fears of British influence over the Hawaiian kingdom.

Even Lili'u seemed to have doubted the wisdom of the treaty, though it is not clear whether she voiced them at the time. Decades later, with the benefit of hindsight, she wrote, "There were a few who protested against the treaty, as an act which would put in peril the independence of our nation. The impressions of the people are sometimes founded upon truth; and events have since proved that such was the case here,—that it was the minority which was right in its judgment of the consequences of the Hawaiian concession of 1875 to the power of the foreigner."

One person who did speak out against it was Joseph Nāwahī, a Hawaiian educator, journalist, and legislator who would later become one of Liliʻu's most trusted advisers. As a representative to the legislature from the island of Hawaiʻi, Nāwahī had delivered a fiery and unusually prescient speech, decrying it a "nation-snatching treaty, one that will take away the rights of the people causing the throne to be deprived of powers that it has always held as fundamental."

Nonetheless, King Kalākaua ratified the treaty soon after receiving word of the U.S. Senate's approval. President Grant soon followed suit. On the afternoon of August 24, 1876, the *City of San Francisco* approached the Honolulu harbor. To celebrate the good news it was carrying aboard, the ship was "decked with bunting from bowsprit to spanker boom."

This good news boosted Kalākaua's standing with the kingdom's sugar planters. But he was far from secure on the throne. A spy had come to him with a warning about a plot under way on the part of Emma's supporters, which the king jotted down on a piece of paper. It read:

> Conspiracy of the Queenites.
> It is decided that a few days before the closing
> Of Parliament, that a number of conspirators
> Will assemble secretly for the purpose of
> Killing the King, and the royal family.

His handwritten notes continued to speculate that all the officials loyal to him would also be in danger, and that the goal of the conspirators was to put Queen Dowager Emma on the throne. At the moment of his greatest diplomatic triumph, Kalākaua had reason to fear for his life.

* * *

As history would have it, the *City of San Francisco* also carried a man whose influence would shadow Hawai'i and Lili'u for years to come: the San Francisco–based sugar baron Claus Spreckels.

By the time the reciprocity treaty passed in the summer of 1876, Spreckels—whose first name was pronounced "claws," as in Santa Claus —was forty-eight years old. He had bootstrapped himself from a lowly immigrant grocery clerk to the leading sugar refiner in San Francisco. Born into the age of the tycoon, when industrialists such as Cornelius Vanderbilt and Andrew Carnegie were building their empires largely on America's east coast, Spreckels was creating his own sugar empire in the west.

Like Vanderbilt and Carnegie, Spreckels began life in humble circumstances. His family owned a small farm in a German village called Lamstedt, which was then in the kingdom of Hanover. Born in 1828 as the eldest of six children to villagers who farmed a small plot of land, Spreckels was forced to leave the village school at fifteen to earn money as a farmhand. Three years later, at an age when most of the boys his age were entering mandatory military service, he purchased a ticket in the steerage compartment of a steamer bound for America, evidently dodging the draft.

He arrived in Charleston, South Carolina; the family legend is that he arrived with one German thaler in his pocket, a single silver coin worth less than a dollar at the time. Big-boned and formidable, Spreckels endured teasing from other clerks. It was not for his heavily accented English but for his ruddy complexion: they called him "Red-face." It is not clear why he left South Carolina. (One family story suggests that he noticed the high price of one of the key ingredients in ice cream— sugar—and concluded from that there was money to be made in becoming a sugar producer himself.) But whatever the reason, he eventually headed north to New York, where he thrived as a grocer and married his childhood sweetheart, Anna Christina Mangels, who had emigrated from Germany to join him in America.

A decade after coming to America, Spreckels moved his family across the country to San Francisco, buying the grocery store that his brother had started in a state still booming from the Gold Rush. The family lived modestly and Spreckels's wife bore him thirteen children, though only four boys and one girl survived to maturity. Like Levi Strauss and other San Francisco merchants who made fortunes selling clothing and other goods to miners during California's Gold Rush era, Spreckels poured his early profits back into the business.

Not long after moving to San Francisco, he'd expanded beyond the grocery and opened a brewery and a saloon, both located south of San Francisco's busy Market Street, near the city's sole sugar manufacturer. Overhearing the talk of the sugar workers, as they nursed their beers after work, Spreckels concluded that since it was letting excess juice, or "liquor," as it was known, run out uncaptured, the owner of the town's sugar monopoly wasn't operating efficiently. Figuring he could run a tighter and more profitable operation, he decided to challenge the existing monopoly.

Spreckels founded a rival sugar business, the Bay Sugar Refinery, in 1863. His timing was perfect to take advantage of surging demand for sugar during the Civil War, as fighting disrupted supplies from the southern states. Two of his partners were his brother and his brother-in-law. That same year, he took his eldest son, John D., who was then just ten years old, nearly three thousand miles to New York to study advanced methods of sugar refining by working in the refinery—making this journey despite the dangers of the war that was raging.

Spreckels was deeply committed to making the refinery more efficient. But his relationships with his business partners were not so smooth. He had wanted to expand the business more aggressively, a move his partners resisted. In a pattern that he would repeat often in his professional life, he withdrew from the business. Whether he left in a huff or was thrown out is unclear. But whatever happened he ended up selling the Bay Sugar Refinery back to his coinvestors, making a large profit for himself.

Extraordinarily, after selling his interest in this company, he again left San Francisco for eight months in 1865 to work as a common laborer in a German beet sugar refinery. It may have been he needed some time away from the United States to regain his equilibrium. Whatever it was that fueled his nearly six-thousand-mile journey, he returned to California from his trip brimming with new ideas.

He soon started a second sugar refinery, sourcing the raw sugar from Hawai'i, the Philippines, China, and Java, and patented a way to dramatically speed up its processing. Once again, his move was well-timed: demand was soaring and the United States had become one of the largest users of sugar in the world on a per capita basis, consuming more than 35 pounds per person annually by 1870, second only to Britain's whopping 48 pounds per person.

Spreckels named his new company the California Sugar Refinery and ran it as he saw fit, without answering to fellow investors. Initially, the refinery spun out up to 12,500 pounds of sugar an hour. Soon, he doubled that torrential pace, making it into the most modern refinery in America, producing mountains of crushed and cubed sugar at his massive factory on Eighth and Brannan streets in San Francisco.

But Spreckels's intense focus on the business took a toll on him. Details are unclear, but it appears that he suffered a nervous breakdown due to overwork. On his doctor's advice, he left San Francisco with his family and headed for the soothing waters of health resorts in Germany. After a long rest he returned to San Francisco, his health restored, in 1871.

By 1876, when Spreckels arrived in Honolulu harbor, he was the most powerful sugar magnate on the west coast, displaying a gift for spotting opportunity and a high tolerance for risk. Already grown portly, he had a precisely trimmed salt-and-pepper beard and wafted a strong perfume of tobacco smoke from the cigars on which he was constantly puffing. He never adopted the relaxed habits of some San Franciscans and wasted no time before getting to work in Hawai'i.

In three short weeks he personally paid visits to the owners and managers of the islands' biggest sugar plantations, offering to buy the crops in their fields for cash. By the time he climbed aboard a steamer to return home he'd bought up over half of the islands' anticipated 14,000-ton sugar crop for the following year, betting that the new treaty would send demand for Hawaiian sugar soaring.

His relentless drive was something that the islanders hadn't encountered much of before. In turn, some plantation owners grumbled about Spreckels's sharp-elbowed ways, suggesting that he'd offered them too little for their crops.

"Very well, gentlemen," Spreckels told them. "Sell to anybody you please."

The unhappy sugar producers sent a representative to New York, hoping to drum up better offers, but he returned empty-handed. According to one account, they ended up "begging" Spreckels to buy their crops, which he did—at the price he'd originally offered them.

Although it was Spreckels's first trip to Hawai'i, he was not seduced by its languid charms. Sticking to business, he had calculated that he would profit by the treaty, which allowed duty-free entry of Hawaiian sugar, rice, and other products into the United States, lowering sugar planters' costs by two cents a pound. In addition to cornering much of the islands' sugar crop for 1877, he had even greater ambitions. In the spirit of *If you can't beat 'em, join 'em*, Spreckels decided to grow sugarcane in Hawai'i and become a plantation owner himself.

He would eventually own or control nearly every aspect of the islands' sugar trade—from vast plantations of swaying cane, to sugar mills, and even to the steamships that carried the crystallized sweetener to San Francisco and the railroads that would carry it up and down the coast, in what would now be called vertical integration. "I went to the islands for self-protection," said Spreckels, many years later, "and soon became the largest sugar raiser there."

Spreckels was Teutonic in his approach both to business and parenting. In particular, he was determined to bring his four sons into the family business. So intent was Spreckels in grooming a successor that he enrolled his eldest son—the same one with whom he'd ignored the possible dangers of crossing the country during the Civil War to study sugar refining in New York—at a polytechnic school in Hanover, Germany.

If John D., who was fourteen when he left San Francisco for Germany, minded, his protests soon melted away. After all, he was up against the will of his father, who didn't tolerate disobedience and "always treated us in something of an authoritarian Prussian manner," his son Rudolph later recalled.

An incident in Germany suggests the patriarch Spreckels was decisive in carrying out his parental duties. Visiting his teenaged son early one morning in Hanover, in the rooms where John D. was boarding as a student, Claus encountered a fair, buxom young woman entering his son's rooms, carrying a tray with a cup of hot chocolate and rolls. She set the tray on John D.'s bedside table and quietly left the room. Claus sternly eyed her.

"Who is she, John?" he asked.

"The landlady's daughter."

"H'm! And *what* is she, my son?"

"She's an actress, father."

Claus didn't say another word about it and John D., perhaps a little relieved, assumed the matter was closed. But by the end of the day his father informed him he'd found more convenient rooms for him elsewhere. He expected him to move there that very evening.

In the face of his father's intractable will, John D. didn't bother arguing. He moved into his new rooms before bedtime.

CHAPTER FIVE

Pele's Wrath, 1875–1881

For the *ali'i*, whose numbers continued to plummet as disease and childlessness persisted, one event brought unalloyed joy. On October 16, 1875, a child was born to Miriam Likelike, sister to Lili'u and David Kalākaua, and her husband, Archibald S. Cleghorn, a Scottish-born merchant whose parents had immigrated to the islands and ran a dry goods business in downtown Honolulu.

The couple had married in 1870 at Washington Place, the Dominis home. The Scotsman was then thirty-five and Likelike just nineteen. Five years later, their daughter was born, the first child of the new Kalākaua dynasty. Overjoyed by the news, the king ordered the firing of guns and tolling of church bells.

To further mark the importance of the birth, her christening took place on Christmas Day, 1875, in St. Andrew's Episcopal church. Using the English Book of Common Prayer, the bishop christened the baby Princess Victoria Ka'iulani Kalaninuiahilapalapa Kawekiu I Lunalilo. She was called Ka'iulani, which meant "the royal sacred one." Wrapped in a cashmere blanket and held by her Hawaiian nurse, she was "the hope of the Hawaiian people, as the only direct heir by birth to the throne."

Just two years after the princess's birth, Kalākaua's younger brother, who he had named as his successor, died of rheumatic fever at the age of twenty-three. Since Ka'iulani was still a toddler, King Kalākaua on April 10, 1877, made his sister Lili'u his heir apparent, giving her the royal name Princess Lili'uokalani. She seems to have disliked the name, which means "Lili'u of the heavens." In letters to family members, she continued to sign her name Lili'u—the first of many disagreements within the House of Kalākaua.

Lili'u spent her first few months as heir apparent circling the island of O'ahu. Traveling mostly by horseback and carriage, she witnessed for herself the destruction of the landscape wrought by the island's enterprising planters, particularly at the home of James Campbell, an Irish immigrant who built his fortune as a partner in a Maui sugar mill.

Born in Ireland in 1826, Campbell had made his way to Hawai'i via New York, seeking better prospects. Landing at Lahaina, Maui, as a twenty-four-year-old, he put his skills as a carpenter and woodworker to work repairing ships. Acquiring an interest in the Pioneer Mill Company in 1860, near the start of the U.S. Civil War, he began investing in the sugar business. The firm grew steadily, acquiring less fortunate sugar companies that foundered in the turbulent years prior to passage of the reciprocity treaty. By the time he sold his interest in the company to a partner, seventeen years later, Campbell had earned the Hawaiian nickname "*Kimo Ona Milliona*" (James the Millionaire).

Using the $500,000 proceeds from the sale, Campbell in 1878 purchased the Honolulu home of Archibald Cleghorn, a year after buying a ranch on the 'Ewa plain on O'ahu's leeward coast for $95,000. He also bought 15,000 acres at Kahuku on O'ahu's northernmost tip. The 'Ewa ranch seemed unlikely to return Campbell much in the way of profits, since it was on O'ahu's arid side. But a year later, when he drilled

Hawai'i's first artesian well and began transforming the dry ranch into a fertile plantation, he silenced any doubters.

By 1878 James Campbell was one of the largest private landowners on O'ahu. In addition to the 15,000 acres he already owned at Kahuku, he had purchased his ranch on the 'Ewa plain, consisting of another 41,000 mostly dry acres near Pearl Harbor, the year before Lili'u's visit. He had also loaned money to Lili'u's husband on several occasions, in an early example of ties between the Hawaiian royals and the expanding sugar trade. As Lili'u and her entourage made her 150-mile circuit around the island, she was honored with outpourings of food, song, and gifts. But none outdid the Campbells, who, Lili'u later wrote, "spared no pains to give us an ovation in every way worthy."

With the introduction of large-scale agriculture to the islands by families such as the Campbells, the natural world that Lili'u had known as a girl was beginning to disappear. Sugarcane was replacing taro patches, fish ponds, and forests. The plaintive whistle of the Hawai'i *mamo*, a shy bird then found only on Hawai'i Island, was heard only rarely by the mid-1880s, as cattle ranching and plantations altered the forest canopies where this nectar-loving finch once thrived. Not only was its habitat disappearing but the mongoose, newly introduced to control rats in the sugar fields, ferociously snatched the *mamo's* eggs.

The *mamo* was highly valued by native Hawaiians. For centuries they had painstakingly laid tiny snares to capture it. They'd then pluck out the mamo's golden feathers, tucked behind the wing among mostly black feathers, and release the birds. It took about 80,000 of these bright yellow feathers to make a single feathered cloak and these mantles were so precious they were worn only by Hawai'i's highest chiefs.

Yet within two decades of Lili'u's circling of O'ahu the exquisite mamo would become extinct.

Despite the *aloha* she felt on her first royal tour, Lili'u's health began to falter. Her physician, a resident of Oakland, California, suggested she take a restorative trip to the United States.

Lili'u's marriage to John Dominis was not a close one; the couple continued to spend time apart, with Lili'u in Waikīkī and John ostensibly residing with his mother at Washington Place. They squabbled over money and both suffered pangs of jealousy. There is little doubt that Dominis found his way into other women's beds.

Perhaps realizing that conceiving a child of her own was unlikely, Lili'u explored the idea of adopting a child according to the Hawaiian custom of *hānai*. Her husband had been appointed governor of Maui as well as O'ahu, and the wife of his personal secretary on the outer island was expecting a child. A mutual friend suggested to Lili'u that she might adopt this infant. Lili'u's husband, once he heard of her offer, opposed it. Her brother David Kalākaua wavered, at first supporting the idea then cooling on it.

The matter remained unresolved as Dominis took Lili'u on her first trip to the United States. In early 1878, when Lili'u was thirty-nine years old, the Dominises boarded the steamer *St. Paul* and spent nine days crossing the Pacific bound for San Francisco. The journey provided a distraction, as Lili'u and John were welcomed to California by some of the state's most prominent families. They visited San Francisco's Olympic Club, ate breakfast at the Cliff House, and promised to send Hawaiian butterfly specimens to a member of the Bohemian Club. Crossing the bay from San Francisco, Lili'u was reunited with her teacher Susan Mills, who had helped found a women's seminary in the Oakland foothills. Continuing their trip, the party traveled to the state capital of Sacramento. There, they were entertained by California governor Romualdo Pacheco, a childhood friend of John Dominis's who had spent some of his school years in Hawai'i and who claimed to have once lassoed a grizzly.

Lili'u returned to the islands refreshed and in better health. She soon learned that the mother of the child she had hoped to adopt had died during childbirth. This made it possible for her to overcome the objections to adoption by her husband and brother. Holding in her arms her newly adopted child must have been a moment filled with gratitude and awe for Liliʻu; one can imagine her breathing in the singular scent of the newborn's head, like the scent of freshly plowed earth. She gave the girl her own Christian name, Lydia, and composed *"Lilikoʻi,"* a name chant incorporating her daughter's middle name, which was also the Hawaiian name for the passion fruit plant.

Despite the addition of a baby to the household, Liliʻu found the time to write down a song that had come to her during her tour of the island the prior year. She and her party had stopped at a ranch on the windward side of Oʻahu. Heading away from the coast up steep cliffs on horseback, Liliʻu had paused to take in the view of the sea and spotted one member of her party giving a lover a farewell embrace. Some accounts speculate that the lover was Liliʻu's own sister Likelike; others say the song memorialized a good-bye between a member of the royal party and a local woman. Whoever they were, the couple inspired Liliʻu's most famous composition, the wistful *"Aloha Oe,"* whose lyrics express the poignancy of separated lovers.

During the spring of 1878, while Liliʻu was enjoying the hospitality of friends in California, a circle of white newcomers to the islands drew more tightly around her brother David Kalākaua, seeking to extract as much as they could from the king and his island kingdom.

Claus Spreckels, for one, had been busy expanding his San Francisco–based sugar empire to Hawaiʻi. Heʻd returned to the islands in May of that year, less than two years after his very first arrival in Hawaiʻi aboard the steamer carrying news of the reciprocity treaty. Almost immediately, he and his engineer set off to conquer the key obstacle to growing cane in Hawaiʻi: bringing water from the mountains down to the dry plains near the coastline. He owned neither land nor water rights when he stepped off the boat from the mainland. But he soon bought a half interest in 16,000 acres on Maui and leased 24,000 adjoining acres of crown lands, representing more than 10 percent of the island's total acreage. These lands would become the basis for his island sugar empire.

To make the land productive he needed to irrigate it. So within weeks of his arrival he presented a petition to King Kalākaua and the ministry seeking water rights on Maui, arguing that "a large district now lying waste [would] be brought to a high state of cultivation." Water rights had always been crucial in Hawai'i and were subject to a complex system of regulations. It is no coincidence that the Hawaiian word for wealth, *waiwai*, is similar to that for water, *wai*.

Kalākaua and his cabinet did not immediately grant Spreckels his request. A week passed. The doughty German-American, used to getting his way, grew impatient and decided to force the issue. He invited the king and several others to meet him in a private room at the Hawaiian Hotel, the grandest hotel in Honolulu, which served such Western delicacies as "Cabinet pudding" and "Windsor soup." Champagne flowed and the crowded room grew warm as the gathering stretched into the early hours. It is not clear exactly what happened, but around two in the morning Kalākaua sent a messenger to awaken his ministers and deliver news: he was firing them.

A week later, on July 8, Kalākaua's new cabinet granted Spreckels his water rights. Some began whispering that the sugar king had bribed the monarch during that late night gathering at the Hawaiian Hotel, which sparked outrage in the legislature as well as in the kingdom's newspaper offices and its foreign diplomats' parlors. Upon learning of what had happened, the kingdom's chief justice of the supreme court called a meeting with Spreckels and accused him of corrupting the king.

Spreckels denied it. The justice persisted, suggesting he had first offered the king "pecuniary considerations" and then pressured him by threatening to withdraw his already sizable investments in the islands, which included the interest in 40,000 acres on Maui. It was evident the chief justice had pieced together the story from the imperious way that Spreckels afterward had addressed him and the king.

Spreckels countered that he was only defending his interests. But the justice remained skeptical and produced proof: reaching forward, he held out the king's promissory note—perhaps waving it under the sugar baron's nose—to prove it was bribery. As the judge later wrote, he told Spreckels "it is the first time money has been used in this country to procure official favors, and now with the King. You have injured our pride & done damage to those who are doing good to you." But there was nothing more to be said, since the king had already taken the money and Spreckels had gained his water rights.

In fact, by the summer of 1878 Kalākaua had borrowed much more from Spreckels than the chief justice or almost anyone else in Hawai'i realized. He'd signed four notes, dated July 8, 1878, "in favor of Claus Spreckels for $10,000 each at 2, 3, 4 & 5 years with int. at 7 per cent per annum," according to the king's cash books for this period. Forty thousand dollars represented many times the king's total annual income and was secured by his income from the crown lands.

Those notes plunged him deeply and desperately in debt to Spreckels, with no obvious way out. And with his indebtedness Kalākaua took a step closer to becoming what his critics had begun to call him: a puppet ruler whose strings were being pulled by U.S. businessmen.

Foreign diplomats posted in Honolulu were rightly appalled by what had happened, perhaps understanding more fully than Kalākaua himself did how this indebtedness could undermine Hawai'i's independence. Britain's long-serving commissioner in Hawai'i James Wodehouse grasped immediately that Spreckels's arrival in the islands had drastically shifted the kingdom's balance of power. The new cabinet looked more favorably upon Spreckels's requests. As if underscoring that point, one of the newly appointed ministers spoke to a group of native Hawaiians on the very same day the water rights were granted to Spreckels. The meeting's theme? *E mahalo I ka ona miliona* ("Let us give thanks to the multimillionaire").

The mounting debts of Kalākaua Rex would irreparably change the kingdom and lay the unstable foundation for Lili'u's future reign as queen. And it was a tall, blue-eyed adventurer named Walter Murray Gibson who spurred on the king's spending. He was the sort of character who thrived in the heady climate of the late nineteenth century, reinventing himself again and again, despite setbacks that would have ended his career or perhaps even his life in a different era. But Gibson, like Spreckels, had a genius for spotting opportunities. And the tropical temptations of the Hawaiian Islands drew him like a fruit fly to an overripe mango.

Gibson arrived in the islands on the Fourth of July 1861, just after the start of the U.S. Civil War. A charming southern gentleman with a murky family history, he seized an opportunity to fill a vacancy as head of the Mormon Church in the islands, which had been leaderless for several years. Gibson revived a plan to establish a "City of Joseph" on the island of Lānaʻi, one of the smallest of the major Hawaiian islands where a converted chief had offered the church 10,000 acres. Using funds donated to the church by native Hawaiian congregants, Gibson bought up thousands of acres, ostensibly for the church. But the land deeds were all in the name of Walter M. Gibson.

Gibson didn't think much of the native Hawaiians who were helping him transform the dry land of Lānaʻi's plains into what he called his "Hawaiian Zion." He asked them to work for free, to turn over much of their wealth to the church, and to pay to advance in its hierarchy. As he wrote in his diary, "But the people are poor; in pocket, in brain, in everything. They are material for a very little kingdom. They should not affect the course of trade nor change much of the earth's balance of power."

Gibson's disregard for the native Hawaiians who were helping him build his fortune was matched by his own greed. In his diary, he sketched the outlines of the land deal he envisioned for himself, one that would be repeated again and again in the islands, usually with native Hawaiians on the losing side. He acquired land for a mere twenty-five cents an acre. Once irrigated, the land would be worth ten times as much and more.

The Hawaiian elders in his congregation, however, soon caught on and wrote a letter to Brigham Young charging that Gibson had perverted Mormon doctrine to serve his own ends. Upon investigation, the church excommunicated him. In later years, Gibson's enemies would dig up his shameful early years in the islands and dub him ironically the "Shepherd Saint of Lanai."

Gibson continued to acquire land on Lānaʻi, thanks in part to a mortgage from Spreckels, until he controlled more than anyone else. He then turned his energy to the island nation's capital, with its seething and unstable political scene, arriving in late 1872. By then fluent in Hawaiian, he bought a Hawaiian-language newspaper and used its pages to espouse the populist theme of "Hawaiʻi for Hawaiians," weighing in on elections and the latest scandals in the legislature. Gibson, who had renounced his U.S. citizenship in order to become a citizen of the Kingdom of Hawaiʻi, eventually became a trusted counselor to Kalākaua, with whom he shared ideas on how to expand the Hawaiian race. Although there are some indications that the king was aware of Gibson's cloudy past, he ignored it, seduced instead by his friend's grand ambitions and linguistic talents.

It didn't take long before the king gave his flattering white adviser Gibson certain concessions, such as additional crown lands on Lānaʻi and a strip of land on Maui that gave him a secure seat in parliament. In turn, Gibson became Kalākaua's most steadfast supporter, helping to push through the legislature a long-standing plan to build a new palace, including $50,000 of state funds. When the legislature came up short of the money Gibson, whose holdings on Lānaʻi were now profitable, provided a loan. Likewise, he championed holding a lavish celebration to commemorate the discovery of Hawaiʻi by Captain Cook a hundred years earlier, even though Cook and his men had brought disease and its attendant misery to the islanders.

Archibald Cleghorn, who was then a member of the house of nobles, warned his brother-in-law about his unfortunate choice of advisers. Kalākaua dashed off a furious letter in reply: "You need not preach to me of History and of the value of truthfulness and so forths. I know enough of history and of human nature to discriminate who are honest and who are not."

The tiff drew the attention of the family doctor, who sympathized with Cleghorn's position, warning him in a letter that the king dare not lose the support of the foreigners who'd helped elect him.

The King has completely forgotten the facts and uncertainties at the time. The day of the election had not the marines been landed and the foreigners stood by the King, again he would have lost the Crown. . . .

Were the natives certain that the foreigners would not support the King, they would make a revolution in 24 hours under any able leader. This is no vain talk—I know the feeling of the natives all over the islands—and I know I am right.

Now beware and this is not the only danger. Some foreigners [have] never lost sight of Annexation, and this is another danger but more remote. It is therefore of the greatest importance that the King should *not* turn the foreigners against him as they are his *only* support and he can put no reliance on any of his native retainers, I do not care who they are.

It was a dire yet insightful analysis of the king's unsteady hold on the throne—though not one that Kalākaua probably would have agreed with, had he seen the letter. But the king and his brother-in-law managed to set aside their differences in the fall of 1880, when the young princess Ka'iulani, just before her fifth birthday, fell gravely ill. Increasingly it seemed that Ka'iulani would be the Hawaiian monarchy's sole hope of surviving into the next generation. Her illness was a matter of deepest concern not just for her relatives but for the nation. The king himself attended to the child, writing to Likelike to tell her he thought she might have died if not for the care she received.

The young princess's father was similarly distraught at his child's illness, writing to his wife, "she [Ka'iulani] talks much of her birth day. I hope she will get strong, and be spared to see many of them. I would rather die myself than that she should."

* * *

Steaming back to the islands from San Francisco in September of 1880, Claus Spreckels landed in Honolulu only to learn about the latest government shake-up, which had elevated an adventurer and backer of dubious schemes named Celso Moreno to Kalākaua's minister of foreign affairs. Moreno's appointment touched off an outcry among the diplomats in Honolulu, who considered him a scoundrel.

The Italian-American immigrant had managed to finagle a commission from the king as his "envoy extraordinary and minister plenipotentiary" and soon headed off to Europe to negotiate with foreign heads of state. By the time Spreckels stepped off the steamer, the king had already dismissed Moreno. Nonetheless, a displeased Spreckels couldn't resist scolding Kalākaua for surrounding "himself with a precious set of fools; that every body knew it except himself and that the whole thing was a laugh stock to all his enemies and the enemies of his country."

Unlike the missionary sons, who were born on the islands and whose pursuit of wealth was deeply woven into their efforts to spread their Protestant faith, Spreckels felt no obligation to try to improve the moral life of his plantation workers. Yet he did invest heavily in the islands and that, arguably, brought benefit in the form of new technology to Hawai'i. Indeed, after securing water rights on Maui and becoming the king's lender, Spreckels began pouring some of the fortune he'd made by refining sugar in San Francisco into the island nation.

One of the first things he did was to secure control of transportation between the islands and the mainland. In the 1870s and early 1880s, sailing ships were still the chief method of carrying goods between Pacific ports. One of the fleetest of these was a 132-foot schooner that the sugar baron named after himself, the *Claus Spreckels*. On its maiden voyage in 1879 the ship made the crossing from San Francisco to the port on Maui serving the Spreckelsville plantation in just nine and a half days—one of the fastest recorded passages.

Spreckels soon began adding to his fleet of merchant sailing ships. He named them after his family and friends: the second he called the *John D. Spreckels*, followed by the *Anna*, named after his wife, the *W. H. Dimond*, named after a Honolulu-born San Francisco–based sugar broker who was a friend, and the *W. G. Irwin*, after Spreckels's business partner in Honolulu. Spreckels's fleet of sailing ships faced some competition from steamers, which had begun making Pacific crossings less than a decade earlier. Spreckels got in on the action by founding the Oceanic Steamship Company, offering regular steamer service between Honolulu and San Francisco.

Just as Spreckels's new vessels seemed to break all speed records, so did the man himself, whose entrepreneurial energy was unflagging. He rose each morning by 6:30 and often worked until 1:30 a.m., thriving on five hours of sleep a night. Barrel-chested and powerfully built, he was not a man who tolerated opposition. Soon after winning Maui water rights, he formed his San Francisco-based Hawaiian Commercial Company and began planting 500 acres of sugarcane on Maui.

Anticipating good harvests, Spreckels commissioned the construction of a new sugar mill on Maui, with the capacity to process 25 tons of cane per day—more than other mills were producing at the time. Instead of oxen and mules, the Spreckels plantation used steam plows and railroads to haul cane. Five years before King Kalākaua illuminated the royal palace in Honolulu with electric lights, Spreckels had installed them in his Spreckelsville mill, which made it possible for his laborers to work around the clock.

Spreckels had invested more than $500,000 (worth more than $11 million in today's dollars) to dig his crucial irrigation ditch, transforming the dusty plains of Maui into luxuriant cane fields by bringing water down to them from the mountains. To firm up his claim on the royal lands he was leasing for his Spreckelsville plantation, he entered into an agreement in 1880 with Princess Ruth Keʻelikōlani, half sister to the late Kamehameha V and cousin to Liliʻu's adoptive sister Bernice Pauahi Bishop. He bought her questionable claim to some half a million acres in crown lands for $10,000, as well as making her a loan of $60,000 at 6 percent interest.

From the start, this deal raised questions. For one thing, the going value of the half million acres—if indeed, Princess Ruth had a valid claim to it—would have been closer to $750,000 rather than the $10,000 that Spreckels paid for it. That suggests either that Princess Ruth herself did not believe she had a valid claim to the land or that she genuinely had no idea of what it might be worth. But the sugar baron pre-emptively rallied legal opinion in his favor among powerful lawyers in Honolulu and San Francisco, who argued that the claim was valid.

Kalākaua's government, headed by his newly appointed prime minister, Walter Murray Gibson, supported Spreckels. It introduced a bill into the legislature that allowed the king to quitclaim *all* of Ruth's lands in return for Spreckels gaining title to 24,000 crucial acres at Wailuku, near Spreckelsville. Since Spreckels had threatened to take all of Ruth's crown lands, this was the government's way of mitigating his claim while avoiding a confrontation with Princess Ruth. In turn, it was an instance of how Spreckels, a seasoned capitalist by then, was able to pull the strings of the kingdom's land-rich but cash-poor *aliʻi*.

The scope of Kalākaua's political ambitions—and his zest for adventure—was revealed on a rainy Saturday in early January 1881. The newly installed telephone at Washington Place rang: the king wished to speak with his sister. Liliʻu made her way to the boathouse, which had increasingly become the late-night clubhouse of Kalākaua, Gibson, Spreckels, and others in the group that critics dubbed "the palace party."

Walking into the long building, dark and musty from the heavy rains that month, she found Kalākaua picking out oars for one of his boats. Almost casually, he told her he planned to circumnavigate the globe, something that no monarch had ever before attempted. Kalākaua went on to explain that while he was gone on his months-long voyage, Liliʻu would assume control of the government, albeit with oversight from a "regency council" whose approval would be required in order for her to exercise authority.

Like her brother-in-law Archibald Cleghorn, Liliʻu did not admire her brother's choice of advisers, particularly those who practiced what the Hawaiians call *hoʻomalimali*, the art of ingratiating themselves into royal favor. Liliʻu told David what she thought of that arrangement "in terms too plain to admit of the least understanding," she later wrote, arguing that she ought to be the sole regent.

Liliʻu got her way. Then forty-two, she shed the diffidence instilled by her missionary schoolteachers and, speaking forcefully, no longer as a compliant student or a shy bride, she began to assert herself as heir apparent, even if it meant challenging the wishes of her brother and his advisers.

The night before the king's departure, groups of Hawaiians gathered at the palace grounds. Under the rule of Kalākaua, they had revived the *hula*, which had been condemned by the missionaries. Dancers, holding gourds filled with pebbles, shook them with one hand while gesturing gracefully with the other. They wore *lei* of fragrant flowers. The chanting and sound of rattling gourds lasted late into the night, alternating with Western music played by the military band.

The next morning, January 20, cannons boomed from Punchbowl Hill to mark the departure of the *City of Sydney*, the steamship that would carry Kalākaua to San Francisco. As the steamer rounded Diamond Head, Liliʻu took charge of the Hawaiian kingdom.

Within a few weeks Liliʻu faced the first crisis of her regency. The plantations demanded laborers willing to immigrate to the islands to work in Hawaiʻi's sugarcane fields, work that was so arduous that few Hawaiians were willing to do it. One of the reasons the king had given for setting off on his adventure was to find such laborers.

Those immigrants who'd already arrived had begun to fundamentally change the Hawaiian kingdom. The sounds in the streets of Honolulu, particularly after dark when the taverns and brothels were at their busiest, became a Babel-like mix of languages. One corner of the town became known as Chinatown, where the smells of frying pork and spicy noodles mixed with the early morning fragrance of rising sweet bread, or *pan dulce*, which the Portuguese brought with them. On Chinese New Year, Honolulu's skies were lit by exploding fireworks.

Yet continuing a pattern that began with Captain Cook, this flood of immigration ended up reducing the population of native Hawaiians even further. During the four-month period around the time the king left on his tour, some 4,400 Chinese workers disembarked at Honolulu from steamers chartered in Canton. Some carried the deadly smallpox virus.

A few scattered cases of smallpox had erupted in December, before Kalākaua had departed, and more in January. But the full force of the disease hit the islands in February and raged for six months. Early on, Lili'u grasped the seriousness of the epidemic, having lived through two serious outbreaks of disease before. The second, in 1853, had devastated the city on the heels of the 1848 measles outbreak that had killed her schoolmate Moses. She acted decisively, summoning her cabinet, which prohibited travel between the islands in an effort to thwart the spread of the disease and ordered a strict quarantine of anyone infected or even suspected of being infected.

Hawaiians, whose numbers had plunged in recent decades relative to the overall population of the islands, proved especially vulnerable. Of the 575 cases treated at the smallpox hospital, only 66 were non-Hawaiians. One government minister wrote, "The disease seems to go through our native population like a fire."

Residents of Honolulu grew desperate. On February 7, 1881, a group from the Kaumakapili church presented Lili'u with petitions asking her to stop taking patients to the present quarantine grounds, "as a large proportion of them do not receive sufficient care and medical attendance." Rather than reflexively siding with her native Hawaiian subjects, Lili'u responded with a letter to the group which placed some of the responsibility for the spread of the disease on them, noting that some had tried to evade the quarantine. This willingness to be unpopular with her subjects revealed a strength of character her brother lacked.

Lili'u also revealed her humbler side during her visit to Honolulu's smallpox quarantine hospital, on the outskirts of the harbor. On March 26, after she and her sister-in-law Kapi'olani brought bouquets of ferns and flowers to the patients, Lili'u delivered a short address in which she admitted her uncertainty: "I feel that this is a dreadful visitation upon us, and more especially is it saddening to myself in this the beginning of my imperfect endeavors to guide the affairs of our Government."

Lili'u declared a day of national prayer. The U.S. minister to the kingdom reported that, during her regency, Lili'u "won praise by the prudence and tact of her course and made friends by the simple dignity of her style and by her accessibility to the people in public receptions and otherwise."

Her brother was more critical of her. Upon hearing about his sister's declaration, Kalākaua wrote her a mocking letter from Cairo.

I see by the papers of your performing your religious duties faithfully. As you are a religious and praying woman. Oh! All the religious people praise you! But what is the use of prayer after 293 lives of our poor people have gone to their everlasting place. Is it to thank Him for killing . . . in my opinion it is only a mockery. The idea of offering prayer when hundreds are dying around you. To save the life of the people is to work and not pray. To find and stop the causes of death of our people and not cry and whine like a child and say to god "that is good oh Lord that thou hath visited us thus."

Kalākaua then abruptly changed the subject to tell Lili'u how he was looking for pearls to purchase in all the foreign countries he was visiting. It is a safe guess that his pious and embattled sister, left to cope with a national crisis at a time when he was shopping for pearls, was deeply irritated by his letter.

As the disease raged, other troubles erupted. That summer, several prominent American newspapers began reporting that the true object of

King Kalākaua's journey was to find the highest bidder for his strategically located island nation. "It is an open secret that Kalakaua, King of
the Hawaiian Islands, is on a voyage around the world for the purpose
of selling his kingdom," proclaimed an editorial in the *New York Times* of
July 13, 1881. Noting the extensive American interests in Hawai'i and the
uncomfortable resulting political situation, the *Times* decreed soberly,
"Although our government cannot afford to promote any policy of annexation, other Governments of the world should be notified that any
attempt on their part to acquire the Sandwich Islands, by purchase or
otherwise, would be regarded by the United States as an unfriendly act."

In a letter the *Times* ran two weeks later, the kingdom's minister to the
United States denied that Hawai'i was for sale. Yet by then the disturb-
ing talk had reached Kalākaua himself, who dismissed the rumors swirling about the motives of his trip around the world, namely that "I was
travelling for the purpose of selling my country and I am travelling to
obtain a loan and all such miserable stuff and nonsense." Instead, he told
his sister in a letter about the delights he had encountered on his journey: "You ought to hear Strauss's Band in Vienna. Oh! Exquisite music.
The best I have ever heard," excluding Hawaiian music from his musings.

In another letter to Lili'u, the king described, somewhat breathlessly,
his brief meeting with England's Queen Victoria at Windsor Castle.
Kalākaua was flattered to have been granted an audience with the British monarch, however short. "I was electrified and Monopolized the
whole of the conversation," he wrote. "Oh! Sister I wish you were here
to see the beauties of Windsor castle and the old relics that this ancient
and noble pile contains." Queen Victoria gave him her box at the Royal
Opera and lent him a carriage. She also made him an Honorary Knight
Grand Cross of the Order of St. Michael and St. George. Perhaps this
was why, after all the places he visited on his trip, England became
Kalākaua's favorite country.

By August the smallpox epidemic had subsided and the government
lifted its travel ban. Traveling as the princess regent with a retinue that

included Princess Ruth and Queen Kapiʻolani, Liliʻu was welcomed by enormous crowds and lavish outpourings of *aloha*, as her subjects clasped her knees and kissed her hands and feet to show their reverence. Liliʻu had decided to revisit Hawaiʻi Island, where she had once seen from a safe distance the fiery glow of the crater of Kīlauea, describing it as "nature's gorgeous fireworks."

That was not the case when Liliʻu returned to Hilo in the late summer of 1881. For six months, Mauna Loa had been erupting, with streams of molten lava inching toward the city and its wooden houses. The churches began holding prayer meetings and Liliʻu was invited to join Hilo's townsfolk in asking God to turn back the lava flow. While she prayed, she also helped organize construction of earthen dams and ditches to divert the flow away from the town. As much as she believed in these practical steps, she told a large church group that "Since the flow has commenced, I have learned that the Sabbath day has not been observed with that strict decorum . . . let me urge upon you all to supplicate heaven, from whence all power and blessings emanate, to avert the danger that threatens us all." When the threat from the lava was turned away by the dams, some believed that their prayers had been answered.

But a wellspring of old belief survived alongside the Christian prayer meetings and the chiefs themselves were divided over where divine power lay. According to one eyewitness, it was not the intercession of Liliʻu and her prayers that had stopped the lava but that of Princess Ruth, weighing four hundred pounds or so and standing six feet tall. After assessing the situation, she took a stack of red silk handkerchiefs and a quart of brandy to the edge of the molten lava. When she drew as close as she could, she threw the handkerchiefs and then the bottle into the advancing flow. The alcohol roared into flames and the enormous chiefess in her booming voice began to pray to Pele.

Early the next morning some of the people who'd witnessed the efforts of Princess Ruth made their way to the lava. To their amazement the flow had stopped right there.

On her return to Honolulu Ruth was greeted by native Hawaiians as a heroine, an *aliʻi* so powerful she could single-handedly halt molten lava. And although Liliʻu—a devout Christian who embraced the West—had helped with the less glamorous work of constructing dams and ditches, her efforts were overshadowed by the dramatic vision of the female descendent of Kamehameha I who had waved her red handkerchiefs and shunned Western ways.

Neither Liliʻu's Christian faith nor her belief in progress helped prevent a frightening accident that forced her to bed in the final weeks of her regency. Returning from a trip to a friend's country estate at Waimānalo on Oʻahu, where thousands of acres of crown lands had been leased to cultivate sugarcane, Liliʻu's driver lost control of the horse-drawn carriage. As it pitched down a steep hill she came tumbling out. Landing on a bit of marshy grass, between two rocks, one thought overtook all others: she was going to die.

In excruciating pain, the injured princess returned to Honolulu on a stretcher. The streets were also unusually subdued following the news of President James Garfield's death at the hands of an assassin; shot in July of 1881 he finally succumbed in September. Some merchants had draped their stores in black crepe in memory of the fallen president. As the wagon carrying Liliʻu rolled through the streets of the capital, she lay prone looking up at the clear night sky lit by a bright moon. Crowds of native Hawaiians lined the way, their silence broken only by smothered sobs. John Dominis walked beside his injured wife.

Liliʻu feared she may have broken her back but her physician determined she was suffering from a severe strain. Even after three weeks of bed rest, however, she still couldn't sit up.

In this condition, Liliʻu helped prepare for her brother's return. After an absence of just over nine months, he entered Honolulu harbor in the early dawn of October 29, 1881. "It is home! It is Hawaiʻi *nei!*" the homesick king and his entourage shouted from the boat. The kingdom had prepared a grand welcome for its prodigal son: arches festooned with flowers and the Royal Hawaiian Band playing "Home Sweet Home." His journey gave him the right to declare himself the first monarch ever to circumnavigate the globe. But during his absence the differences between the royal siblings had multiplied, providing a wedge for their enemies.

PART II
THE HOUSE OF KALĀKAUA

CHAPTER SIX
Merrie Monarch, 1883–1886

By dawn on February 12, 1883, the heavy rains that had muddied Honolulu's streets finally stopped. But because the weather still looked threatening, workmen began attaching a roof of corrugated metal to a temporary amphitheater erected on the palace grounds. A gang of prison laborers spread rush grass along the route to the palace. The king had chosen this day—the ninth anniversary of his accession to the throne—for his royal coronation.

At about 8 a.m. the "morning star" of Venus peeped through the clouds, visible even as the sun shone brightly in the fresh morning air. Two hours later, thousands of islanders, garlanded with flowers, gathered on the palace grounds to witness the crowning. The ceremony was meant to herald the rise of a new ruling dynasty—the House of Kalākaua—and to vanquish any lingering public attachment to the Kamehamehas, as well as demonstrate the kingdom's embrace of modernity. Many of the events would take place at the just completed 'Iolani Palace, boasting modern conveniences such as indoor toilets and telephones, which were still unknown in many parts of the world.

Then at the pinnacle of his powers, Kalākaua had the financial resources and power as king to command a fortnight of balls, parties, and performances to celebrate his reign. But the coronation festivities had the unintended consequence of widening the kingdom's divisions, particularly among those already critical of what they considered Kalākaua's reckless spending. It was the controversial Gibson who had promoted the idea of a coronation and had convinced Hawai'i's legislators to fund a ceremony mixing Polynesian customs with those borrowed from European monarchies.

On that February morning the blow of the conch shell was accompanied by blasts from a trumpet, heralding the arrival of the royal party and Kalākaua's success as a forward-thinking ruler. Emerging from the palace out onto a walkway, the king and queen saw a grandstand holding several thousand people—the native women standing out in the crowd in their brightly colored *holokū*, the modest Mother Hubbard–style dresses first introduced by the missionaries

On the grounds of the palace there were thousands more: Hawaiian fishermen from the outer islands, white planters descended from missionaries, Chinese shopkeepers, and foreigners. The harbor was filled with four men-of-war and twenty-two merchant ships, all flying standards and draped with bunting. They were a reminder of the kingdom's thrall to foreigners and trade.

In turn, the people seated in the amphitheater saw a resplendent royal family that, except for their brown skin and Polynesian features, would not have looked out of place presiding from a European capital. Queen Kapi'olani wore a gown trimmed in ermine, with its crimson train embroidered in gold. On the chest of his white military uniform, the king wore all of the stars, ribbons, and orders he had been awarded during his trips abroad. In a touch that Twain surely would have enjoyed, a red, white, and blue feather plume topped his helmet.

Seated near her brother and accompanied by her husband, whose dark beard framed his long, angular face, Lili'u wore a gold and white silk gown imported from Paris. Its richness contrasted with a delicate wreath of white feathers, pearls, and gold leaves she wore in her dark hair. For the evening festivities, she planned to change into another new gown, this one brilliant crimson and also made in Paris. She later wrote that her two splendid dresses for the coronation were "generally considered to have been the most elegant productions of Parisian art ever seen in Hawai'i."

The youngest member of the royal family also took part in the ceremony. Ka'iulani was then just seven years old, and she wore a light blue silk gown with matching blue lace ribbons in her hair. Flowing down her back, her dark locks framed her delicate face, her skin the color of creamy coffee. Holding a small bouquet of flowers, Ka'iulani was the embodiment of Hawai'i's embrace of the West—a child of mixed race born into a royal family that increasingly patterned itself on the courts of Europe.

There were some notable absences, including Queen Emma, the Bishops, and Princess Ruth, who threw her own three-day celebration around the time of the coronation to celebrate completion of her new mansion, which rivaled the new 'Iolani Palace in elegance and size. Her party included a formal house-warming ceremony, a *lū'au*, and a ball where she danced the quadrille while wearing a rich yellow gown with a ten-foot train.

The timing suggests an active rivalry between the Kamehamehas and the ascendant house of Kalākaua. The *Advertiser*, excerpting a *Daily Bulletin* article, wryly noted, "We regret to say that the Princess is affected with heart disease, and an occasion of great festive excitement would certainly be unfavorable to the health of the distinguished sufferer," an excuse belied by Ruth's own extravagant celebration. But if Ruth noticed the implied criticism in the *Advertiser*, it is unlikely she cared. Unlike the House of Kalākaua, Ruth did not put much store in Western conventions. During a church service at Kawaiaha'o, she once walked to the rear of the church, lay on her back, and called a native Hawaiian boy of about eight years old over to her, commanding him to *lomilomi* her abdomen with his feet. The massage apparently relieved her pain and she ordered the boy to step off. The enormous chiefess then arose and returned to her pew, with no interruption to the church service.

Yet Ruth's apparent competitiveness did not spoil Kalākaua's day. Representatives of the great nations were present to witness the coronation: Japan dispatched a special ambassador, while the Americans, British, and French were represented by resident ministers or commissioners.

Traditionally, Hawai'i's kings had neither worn crowns nor staged Western-style coronations. But Kalākaua had ordered two crowns made for him and his queen in England. Believing he was creating symbols of power that would be handed down for generations to come, he ordered that the crowns be adorned with golden taro leaves, the sacred plant whose roots, when mashed, make the Hawaiian staple food *poi*. Encrusted with jewels, the crowns cost $10,000 (nearly $225,000 in today's dollars). Likewise, Kalākaua ordered a sword modeled after one he had seen in England, made of fine Damascus steel and decorated with the Hawaiian coat of arms inlaid in gold.

"Sire, is your majesty willing to reaffirm your previous oath?" the kingdom's chancellor asked Kalākaua, his formal tone resounding in the soft tropical air.

"I am willing."

The king rose from his throne, raised his right hand, and swore his oath.

The chancellor then declared Kalākaua's accession to the throne. Kapi'olani's sister handed the chancellor the feathered cloak of Hawai'i's ancient kings; he, in turn, placed it on Kalākaua's shoulders and handed him the scepter.

Finally, the chancellor turned to the king and said, "Receive this Crown of pure gold to adorn the high station wherein thou hast been placed." Kalākaua took the crown, placing it on his own head. The chancellor then handed the second crown to the king, who attempted to place it on his wife's head. But because she was already wearing a diadem he had trouble securing it atop her elaborate coiffure.

"The audience watched with intense interest, while hairpins, comb, and veil were being removed," one Western observer wrote. "In vain! The crown would not fit, and in desperation, and apparently in no very good temper, the King made a final effort, and literally crammed the insignia of royalty down on Her Majesty's temples." Recovering their equanimity, the royal couple knelt while the household's Episcopalian chaplain, who was also the rector at St. Andrew's, offered a prayer. The king and queen rose, took their seats, and the ceremony concluded with the royal party returning to the palace, accompanied by the Royal Hawaiian Band playing the "Coronation March."

In their accounts of the event in following days, some of the English-language newspapers took great sport in pointing out that Kalākaua, in Napoleonic fashion, had placed the crown on his own head. The *Hawaiian Gazette*, a *haole* newspaper opposed to the monarchy, on February 14, 1883, ran a long article headlined "The Self-Coronation of King Kalākaua," declaring, "In coronations where the King Crowns himself it is usual for the Monarch to take both hands and in a solemn manner to hold the Crown high in front . . . but by taking hold of the small button or ornament at the top, the effect was rather comical." Emma, the widowed dowager queen, and Princess Ruth were both highly amused by this account.

The festivities continued with a grand coronation ball where Likelike wore a shimmering dress in a shade described as "moonlight-on-the-water." As the guests were swirling to the music, a few drops of rain began pattering gently on the tarpaulin roof over their heads. As the rain became heavier, puddles began forming. Some guests dashed from the tent to the palace. One lady accepted the offer of a seat in a chair, lifted by four gentlemen and carried aloft, above the ground, to avoid muddying her slippers.

The coronation, perhaps more than any other single event in Kalākaua's reign, became a lightning rod for criticism. The cost of the festivities outraged some of the descendants of the missionaries, particularly after they learned that the actual expenditures were more than three times as much as the $10,000 that the legislature had allocated for the events. And while foreign guests repeatedly enjoyed the

Hawaiians' lavish hospitality at these festivities, some still voiced criticism of their hosts. For Honolulu's white merchant class, comprised in large part of Americans who leaned toward republican forms of government versus monarchies, the celebration was symbolic of all they believed was wrong with Hawai'i's king. It seemed to them to demonstrate his unchecked spending, pleasure seeking, and vainglorious displays of pomp at a time when not only the kingdom but Kalākaua himself was already deeply in debt.

For islanders loyal to their monarch, however, the celebrations showed that their king, who had been embraced by the crown heads of Europe and the Far East, would lead their island kingdom into a more prosperous era. At a time when the Vanderbilts were in the final stages of planning what would be the world's most expensive party at their new Fifth Avenue mansion in New York—a costume ball for a thousand people—the kingdom's own celebrations were in the spirit of the age. It seemed a moment to mark Hawai'i's ascendancy, not to count pennies.

Writing in her memoirs some fifteen years later, Lili'u defended her brother's coronation. Hawaiians who had traveled from the countryside and other islands returned to their homes with a "renewed sense of the dignity and honor involved in their nationality," she argued. On a more pragmatic level, she also noted that Honolulu's merchants and traders benefited from the influx of visitors to the capital city, many of whom spent freely. With the benefit of hindsight, Lili'u saw in the criticisms of the lavishness of her brother's coronation the shadows of a conspiracy to rob the House of Kalākaua of its right to rule.

Despite a steadily rising drumbeat of criticism over the king's spending, the new 'Iolani Palace itself was a source of pride and wonder to many in the kingdom. The old, termite-infested palace had been demolished in the mid-1870s; it had become an embarrassment to the king. "The life of my noble wife (ka'u ali'i wahine) and myself is not so pleasant in this place, the houses are filthy and in poor condition, and it is only with great effort to hide the humiliation that we live here," Kalākaua wrote in 1876. "And it would be well that the citizens feel humiliated (*hilahila*) also regarding this thing."

After several years the legislature finally agreed to allocate $50,000 to rebuild it, with construction beginning in earnest during the king's trip around the world in 1881. At just over 34,000 square feet—tiny compared to Versailles or Buckingham Palace—it was the grandest structure in the islands. Built in an architectural style described as "American Florentine," with deep verandas and cast-iron columns painted white, it echoed other grand colonial homes built in the tropics.

The rebuilt palace had every modern convenience. The king's copper-lined bathtub was a full seven feet long and two feet wide, built to accommodate his royal girth. There were an astonishing four bathrooms on the second story, a luxury seen only among the elite or in the finest American hotels in the 1880s. The washbasins were made of Italian marble and, off the dining room, were two water closets, or toilets, for guests, an innovation that few other palaces or residences at the time featured. Two dumbwaiters had been imported from San Francisco, as had crystal door panels, etched with twinned images of dancing maidens. Expenses had ballooned and the palace ended up costing more than six times as much as legislators had appropriated, with close to $350,000, or more than $7 million in today's dollars, spent by 1884.

Fascinated by a display of electric lights he had seen in Paris, Kalākaua, upon reaching New York, had made a point of going to the Fifth Avenue mansion that served as the headquarters of the Edison Electric Light Company. There he met with the inventor Thomas Edison who told him how steam power had been transformed into electricity. The king's eyes lit up at the commercial possibilities.

Upon returning to Honolulu, Kalākaua looked for ways to bring Edison's inventions to the islands. One of the first, and most spectacular, demonstrations would take place at a ball in 1886, where he hoped to dazzle his guests with the new "electric arc lights." And he succeeded, in no small measure. "As we stepped into the ballroom we gave a sudden gasp," wrote Isobel Strong, Robert Louis Stevenson's stepdaughter, who had come to the islands with her husband, Joe Strong, the man commissioned by John D. Spreckels to paint landscapes of Hawai'i for his company's headquarters in San Francisco. "None of us had ever seen it before and the effect after years of kerosene lamps and gas was magical."

Within the palace, gas chandeliers were hung at a level where servants could easily light them in the evenings. But by 1887 they would be replaced by electric lights—more than four years before the White House in Washington, D.C., installed them. This wasn't the only way the tiny kingdom moved ahead of the powers to the east. Just two years after Alexander Graham Bell invented the telephone in 1874, Princess Likelike had ordered one from San Francisco as a gift for her brother. The new palace had a phone that allowed the king to talk to the queen in her separate apartment, across the second-floor hall from his, and the chamberlain's office. Later, the palace's phones would be connected to a city-wide phone system. By the time of the coronation, the Hawaiian Bell Telephone Company of Honolulu was extending service not only to the city but to all of O'ahu and the neighbor islands, and a rival telephone company would be established later that year to speed progress.

Two weeks of celebrations followed the coronation. Two days after the crowning, on February 14, the statue of Kamehameha I that Walter Murray Gibson had helped bring to Honolulu was officially unveiled in front of the judicial building, across the street from the palace. That night, Kalākaua hosted an elaborate, multicourse state dinner, which started with a choice of four soups, eight kinds of fish, six entrees, roasts, curry, and then dessert, with each course accompanied by a wide assortment of wines. It was a far cry from the traditional Hawaiian feast, which always included the beloved *poi*, a purplish paste made from pounded taro root, and whole pig, wrapped in leaves and roasted for many hours in an underground oven. But the king had worldly tastes and loved all kinds of food.

The festivities continued with a regatta, horse races at the new Kapi'olani Park, built in the shadow of Diamond Head, and a grand *lū'au* on the palace grounds for some five thousand people. In the afternoon and evening of February 24, native Hawaiians performed an extensive *hula* recital in a tent erected on the palace grounds, with eighty selections listed in the program. With Kalākaua's encouragement, it was the most public display of this subtle and expressive art form in many years, and one that flouted a decades-long ban on this dance that the missionaries abhorred for its "unabashed expressions of sexuality," particularly the performances known as *hula maʻi*, which celebrated the genitals and procreative vigor, often explicitly, with lusty movements and references to key organs.

The coronation performances also introduced a new style of *hula*, called *hula kuʻi*, which combined elements of the ancient art form with Westernized instrumental music and songs. Men and women dancers partook in the dances, which incorporate languid, curving motions of the hands and arms with fluid hip movement, deep knee bends, and graceful turns. Attended by large crowds of natives and foreigners, these dances were one of the few moments during the coronation festivities where native Hawaiian culture was honored.

Yet the *hula* that produced such a surge in Hawaiian pride in the tent on that day in 1883 also provoked a legal action. The *Hawaiian Gazette* reported that the printed program itself had been "characterized by those who profess to understand the Hawaiian language as obscene in the extreme." Obscenity charges were brought against the printing firm, which, ironically, was run by *haole* who had not understood the meaning of the words in the manuscript that the palace had sent it to print, and that the king himself had apparently written in his own hand. Critics of the king denounced his encouragement of the once-forbidden *hula* as "a retrograde step of heathenism and a disgrace to the age."

Even so, the public embrace of the ancient art form by the king was a crucial moment for native Hawaiians, whose traditions had been frowned upon by the missionaries for decades. By performing *mele* and *hula* over the two weeks of the coronation, after decades in which there had been no public ceremonial performances, Kalākaua helped bring his people together and planted the seeds for a rebirth of Hawaiian culture.

* * *

The coronation was the high point of Kalākaua's reign and perhaps the most public demonstration of his rule as the "Merrie Monarch," as the king soon became known. But while his supporters saw him as genial, generous, and committed to reviving ancient Hawaiian traditions, his critics increasingly portrayed him as an extravagant ruler more concerned with self-aggrandizement than with the efficient workings of his government. While his 'round-the-world journey was seen by some as merely an excuse to travel, others saw it was a valid attempt to achieve world prominence for his nation. Rumors of Kalākaua's dalliance with a woman in Vienna had made their way across the sea to Hawai'i. The late-night *hula* performances and card games in the king's boathouse remained a seemingly ever renewing spring of gossip for the townsfolk.

One of the king's sharpest critics was Lorrin A. Thurston. Fluent in Hawaiian thanks to his childhood on rural Maui as a grandson of one of the first missionaries, he had returned to the islands to work for a local attorney after earning a law degree at Columbia University in New York. Like Sanford Dole, whose critiques of the government were a regular feature in the pages of the *Daily Bulletin* and the *Hawaiian Gazette*, Thurston soon took up strident opposition to what he considered Kalākaua's excesses.

In his memoirs, written many years later, Thurston describes his own upbringing as one of puritanical thrift. His father died when he was eight and, when Thurston attended Punahou, he worked to pay his own expenses. He was expelled before graduating, however, for a series of minor infractions. He kicked a bucket of water out from another student's hands and it created a large clatter when it tumbled down the stairs. He also used an ampersand instead of the word "and" in a school composition. Most egregious, he took liberties in quoting Scripture—apparently using the Bible to make an unflattering comment about his female teachers. While describing himself as a bootstrapping American capitalist, he portrayed Kalākaua as a seemingly idle and dissolute king, in a damning summation of the king's character.

> Kalakaua displayed diverse qualities: a personal charm and a kingly demeanor; an unbalanced mentality and a total inability to grasp important subjects intelligently; a fundamental financial dishonesty; personal extravagance, which merged into the control of community finances, to such an extent that community financial collapse loomed; an immoral disposition, or it might be termed "unmoral," a bent to indulge in political intrigue, a reckless disregard of political honor, which made impossible the continuance of honest government; personal cowardice.

Thurston frowned on Kalākaua's boathouse as a symbol of the monarch's hedonistic tendencies, later describing it as a kind of Sodom and Gomorrah set in the shallow shoals near the docks. Constructed of single-thickness boards, rowboats were secured in slips at water level. The floor above held a social hall, where *hula* performances would take place before the king and his guests. "Liquid refreshments were freely on tap," Thurston wrote many years later. "Poker was the favorite relaxation." Upstairs were several rooms where, it was whispered, some of the kingdom's most powerful men privately indulged their fantasies.

It was from his boathouse on the morning of July 31, 1883, five months after the coronation, that Kalākaua first saw a new ship steaming into Honolulu's port. It was the newest addition to the Spreckels fleet, a steamer named the *Mariposa*. Word quickly spread that one of the passengers was Spreckels himself. The rhythm of Honolulu's days had long moved to the ships entering and leaving the harbor, but this was an exceptional arrival because of the boat itself. Townsfolk dropped what they were doing to make their way down to the waterfront and see the first steamer built specifically to carry even more of Hawai'i's sugar and rice to the mainland.

From his private clubhouse on the water, Kalākaua waved to the *Mariposa* as she passed. The town's leading citizens climbed aboard a smaller steamer, followed by members of the Royal Hawaiian Band. John Dominis, in his capacity as O'ahu's governor, was there, as was Archibald Cleghorn. Hoisting themselves up rope ladders and climbing aboard the *Mariposa*, the welcoming party from Honolulu greeted Claus Spreckels and his wife, Anna, who were joined by a senator from California and his wife. The party made its way to the mahogany-paneled saloon where servants uncorked champagne.

There was cause for celebration: the *Mariposa* had made a record-breaking passage of just five days, twenty-one hours between San Francisco and Honolulu. As the *Mariposa* arrived in port, a twelve-gun salute was fired from the shore battery, bringing still more crowds to the dock, which was lined with spectators.

The king sent his carriage to meet Spreckels, who had been authorized by Kalākaua's cabinet the previous year to mint coins for Hawai'i bearing the king's likeness on them. About ten weeks before the *Mariposa* had reached Honolulu, Spreckels had received his commission from the kingdom in what was yet another dubious transaction. The kingdom could have directly entered into a contract with the San Francisco mint to produce about a million dollars' worth of coins, which would have produced a profit of 10 to 15 percent from the difference between the face and bullion value of the coins for Hawai'i's treasury. But instead Spreckels served as the middle man, reaping a profit estimated at around $150,000 for himself and assuming some of the cash-strapped kingdom's government bonds in exchange. Not surprisingly, the scheme drew fire. Dole, for one, anonymously penned a satirical pamphlet called *Vacuum* involving debased silver currency issued by "His Extravagancy Palaver" [Gibson] aided by "Sir Silvergilt" [Spreckels].

Dole and other critics may have described the coinage scheme farcically, but in fact what it meant was that Spreckels would become chief moneylender not only to Kalākaua but to the Hawaiian kingdom itself. He was quietly tightening his grip on Hawai'i's finances.

What's more, Spreckels had positioned himself and his four sons as leaders in the burgeoning trade between the West Coast and Hawai'i. In

San Francisco, he had incorporated a new holding company, the Hawaiian Commercial and Sugar Company. In 1882, it had its initial public offering, with a single share of stock selling for $60, a respectably high price on the San Francisco exchange, especially when compared to depressed utility and banking stocks. Investors, it seems, were tempted by the possibility of heady profits from Spreckels's fast-growing Hawaiian enterprises.

Perhaps that helps explain why he was greeted so effusively on that day in July, as a second band waited for him on shore. Or the enthusiasm may have had more to do with the enormous success of the Royal Hawaiian Band's trip to San Francisco, which Spreckels had sponsored, introducing Lili'u's tender farewell song "Aloha 'Oe" to American audiences on the mainland for the first time. Whatever the reasons, as the burly sugar magnate strode onto the wharf the band began playing a rousing rendition of "Hail to the Chief."

Spreckels's influence over the kingdom began drawing sharper criticism, particularly as Hawaiian politics entered a tumultuous period of cabinet dismissals and deepening government indebtedness. After one such cabinet reshuffle, a California lawyer named Paul Neumann arrived in Hawai'i. Before landing in Honolulu, Neumann had made an unsuccessful run as a Republican candidate for Congress from California, during which the *San Francisco Chronicle* denounced him as a "sugar-coated candidate" and a tool of the Spreckels interests.

In the fall of 1883 Neumann made several visits to the islands and gained admittance to Hawai'i's bar. Almost certainly with Spreckels's help he landed the plum appointment of the kingdom's attorney general in December. Like his bearded sponsor Spreckels, Neumann quickly befriended the king and became an adviser and companion to Kalākaua at the poker table.

The attacks on Kalākaua and his ex–Mormon premier Gibson intensified in 1884, after the legislature's finance committee, led by the newly elected legislator Sanford Dole, released a harshly critical report on the kingdom's precarious financial position. The previous legislature had authorized a $2 million public loan, whose monies were spent on items such as furnishings for the new palace ($47,500), education of Hawaiian *aliʻi* abroad ($30,000), and the coronation ($10,000)—expenses viewed as frippery by the party that Dole headed, which was alarmed at the 200 percent increase in the national debt since 1882. As a U.S. diplomat wrote to Washington, "With all that can justly be said in defense of the Ministers, it is plain they have been guilty of gross extravagance and irregularity in the administration of the affairs of the Kingdom." Lorrin Thurston in addition to working as a lawyer edited the opposition-minded *Daily Bulletin* during the period when this report came out. While most papers focused their criticism on Gibson and the cabinet, Thurston laid the blame instead squarely on the German-American sugar baron. Regarding Spreckels, he wrote: "We recognize him as a man of unusual enterprise, and one who has in various ways encouraged the business and industries of these Islands. . . . But he has manifested a disposition to exercise undue influence in the affairs of the Government; to control the public administration too much for his own benefit."

The *Saturday Press*, another English-language opposition paper, was even more blunt in its criticism: "It is a fact, painful to admit, but nevertheless acceded on all sides that this government, for the last two years, has been run in the interest of Mr. Spreckels; and to-day his dictation of the national policy is still submitted to."

Although the Honolulu newspapers had begun portraying Spreckels as the puppet master controlling Gibson's and Kalākaua's strings, it is unlikely that the sugar magnate paid the criticisms much mind. He was grappling with much greater worries back on the mainland. Just two years after taking it public in 1882, his San Francisco-based Hawaiian Commercial and Sugar Company by 1884 was stumbling badly. Investors had grown alarmed by its heavy debts. Their fears pushed the price of its shares down from more than $60 a share to just twenty-five cents apiece.

To rescue the flailing company, Spreckels personally loaned it a million dollars and the company's board authorized a bond issue. Both helped push the stock back up. But the dramatic swings in the HCSC's share price led to articles in the *San Francisco Chronicle* and elsewhere charging that the Spreckels family was manipulating the stock price for its own gain. The *Chronicle*, in particular, jeeringly referred to the elder Spreckels as "Sir Claus," which it said was "justified from the fact that Mr. Spreckels Sr. has shown the weakness to accept and the vanity to wear the emblem of an 'order of nobility' from the fantastic Kanaka King." (*Kanaka* is the Hawaiian word for human being, man, or person, but it was sometimes used scornfully, as a racial epithet.)

The *Chronicle* published its story referring to "Sir Claus" and made this explosive allegation of stock manipulation on the eve of an HCSC shareholder meeting. That timing so outraged Claus Spreckels's twenty-seven-year-old son that he decided to take matters into his own hands.

As the second of Claus and Anna's four sons, Adolph—generally referred to by his initials, A.B.—was a young bachelor about town who enjoyed yachting with his brother or spending time at the family's ranch in Aptos, California, where the family raised thoroughbreds. Like his father, he had a reputation for hotheadedness. At about 5 p.m. on November 19, 1884, he stormed into the business office of the *Chronicle*, owned by the city's prominent de Young family. He was searching for the newspaper's owner and publisher, Michael de Young.

"De Young!" A.B. called out. The publisher turned and saw the young sugar scion holding a cocked pistol in his hand. Spreckels fired, hitting de Young in his left shoulder. The publisher tried to duck out of range but stumbled as Spreckels fired twice more, one shot striking his left arm near the shoulder and the other lodging in a stack of children's holiday books, which de Young had been carrying as he entered the office from the street and held up in front of his chest to shield himself from the bullets. A clerk in the office heard the shots and opened a nearby desk drawer, pulling from it a pistol, which he then aimed at Spreckels and fired, grazing his arm. Another employee leaped over the railing of his desk and tackled Spreckels, dragging the would-be assassin to the ground.

Rushed to the hospital, de Young was examined by doctors, who pronounced him in critical condition. The bullets had shattered his left clavicle and come very close to hitting a main artery. The shooting, which involved members of two of the city's leading families, produced sensational headlines. De Young survived and A.B. was eventually acquitted after pleading insanity and self-defense. Michael de Young's brother, Charles, the cofounder of the paper, had been fatally shot in the *Chronicle* offices in 1880 on the exact same spot. History had nearly repeated itself.

The *Chronicle* did not end its campaign against the Spreckels family after the shooting. Nor did Claus Spreckels slow down his whirl of business activities in the islands. He oversaw the digging of new irrigation ditches, ran his steamship line, and expanded his plantations. (The store he owned at his plantation in Maui, for instance, rang up sales of $50,000 a month in 1884, thanks to a wide variety of goods—from truffles to ship anchors—that rivaled the sales of the large mercantile firms in Honolulu.) But so entwined were the Spreckels family's business and personal affairs that in the hours before the jury hearing the case against A.B. returned its verdict of "not guilty" in July of 1885, the family ordered the delay of the departure of the steamship *Mariposa* from San Francisco to Honolulu by several hours. Its goal: to make sure the steamer carried the good news of the Spreckels scion's acquittal back to Hawai'i.

CHAPTER SEVEN
To England, 1886–1887

Compared to his increasingly fraught business life in San Francisco, Spreckels's annual trips to Hawai'i offered him a welcome change. He must have felt some relief in leaving the chilly, fog-bound port town where he lived in an ornate stone mansion with gloomy oil paintings and gilt furniture on Van Ness and Sacramento streets. By then, his adopted city had become the biggest port on the West Coast, boasting block after block of elaborate Victorian homes, many built of redwood cut down and hauled to the city from towering forests along California's northern coast.

Passing a week or so aboard one of his steamers, outfitted with such conveniences as saloons, smoking rooms, and "tonsorial departments" where gentlemen would retreat for a haircut and a shave, he crossed the Pacific. Perhaps he brought with him Andrew Carnegie's newly published book *Triumphant Democracy*, pondering what the industrialist's condemnation of monarchies might mean for the rapidly expanding island kingdom.

After Spreckels and his wife spotted the jutting nose of Diamond Head from deck and approached the swaying masts of the Honolulu harbor, Hawaiians greeted them with flower garlands. Spreckels wore the *lei* he received as gifts with as much entitlement as a Roman emperor might wear a wreath of laurel on his head as he left behind the rancor and ill will that the de Young shooting had caused his family.

But 1886 marked the beginning of the end for Spreckels's reign in Hawai'i, as well as the end of the unconditional *aloha* he received from Hawai'i's royal family. According to the stories that circulated for years afterward, Kalākaua broke away from his longtime patron one fall evening at the king's boathouse.

At the time, Spreckels held nearly half of the kingdom's public debt of $1.3 million, making him Hawai'i's chief creditor. He had also loaned money personally to both King Kalākaua and Premier Gibson, the latter through a $35,000 mortgage on his ranch. Spreckels, the sugar king, was then at the height of his influence.

A political party calling itself the Independents, led by Lorrin Thurston and Sanford Dole, began attacking what they called the "palace party" on charges of corruption and poor financial management. Their target was the triumvirate of Kalākaua, Gibson, and Spreckels. The newspapers and some legislators accused Spreckels of controlling the king and his cabinet. Kalākaua, who was understandably disturbed by such reports, began looking for ways to free himself and his kingdom from Spreckels's grip.

One way he hoped to do this was by finding money elsewhere. Gibson had already proposed an additional $2 million in government borrowings—a move that alarmed Spreckels, since further government indebtedness could undermine the security of his existing loans to the kingdom. Warning of the risks, he urged the monarch to be financially prudent, explaining, "I would rather see him going barefoot, as an independent King, than to see him rolling in luxury for a few years and then to find his kingdom slipping from under his feet," without any apparent sense of irony.

Yet while Spreckels was urging fiscal responsibility on the king, he had also, it was rumored, proposed that he assume control of Honolulu's wharves, waterworks, and electricity plant as security for his loans to the kingdom. Pressure was mounting on Kalākaua to find a way to loosen Spreckels's hold and to find relief from the daily floggings he was receiving in the newspapers for his dealings with the man the papers had dubbed "His Royal Saccharinity" and "Herr Von Boss."

The evening at the boathouse, the king, the sugar magnate, and two visiting admirals—one British and one American—sat around a table, playing a thirty-two-card game called euchre. Blue plumes of smoke drifted toward the ceiling from the cigar Spreckels clenched between his teeth.

Hawai'i's monarch and the sugar king finished their first round: Spreckels held five cards in his hand: three kings, an ace, and one low card. Turning to one of the admirals, he boasted, "If this were poker, I would have the winning hand here."

The admiral, in jest, offered to bet against him, revealing his hand of cards, which held three aces.

"My four kings would still win over your aces," said Spreckels.

"Where is the fourth king?" asked Kalākaua.

"*I* am the fourth king," declared Spreckels.

One can only imagine the resolute set of his lips, as if challenging his host to defy him.

Outraged by the arrogance displayed by his guest, the king stormed off in anger. That evening, the Royal Hawaiian Band was performing on the wharf outside Kalākaua's boathouse. As the livid monarch stomped past, it played "God Save the King." But in a final gesture of hubris, the German-American stood up from the table, turned toward the band, and bowed to the bandmaster, as if the song was being performed in his honor. While the story may be apocryphal, the long-lived tale reflected a break that occurred between the king and the sugar baron, one that would reverberate to Washington, D.C., and even to the United Kingdom.

Indeed, on that very night, King Kalākaua decided to turn to England for help, seeking out a loan from a syndicate in London to help pay off the debts he owed to Spreckels and also to pay for public works projects, such as dredging the Honolulu harbor and improving the water and sewage systems.

Hawai'i's legislators passed a Loan Act that fall—authorizing additional debt—and Spreckels scrambled to protect his interests through a proposed amendment to the act. But his amendment was voted down, prompting a mass resignation by the Spreckels-influenced cabinet ministers. The primary reason for the defeat, explained Gibson in a letter he wrote to Hawai'i's minister in Washington, D.C., was Spreckels's "offensive dictatorial manner."

In a huff, Spreckels returned all of the royal decorations Kalākaua had given him, including the insignia for his most recent honor as a "Grand Officer of the Royal Order of Kapi'olani," which the king had bestowed upon him during a ceremony at the palace a few weeks earlier. It resembled Spreckels's furious departure from San Francisco, after parting ways with his partners in the Bay Sugar Refinery. Hot tempered and excitable, Spreckels by then had earned a reputation for exploding with anger when crossed.

The king's chamberlain tried to calm Spreckels down and convince him to keep these symbols of gratitude. But he refused. So when Spreckels boarded a steamer bound for San Francisco soon after, the king did not go down to the docks to bid him farewell, as he had done so many times before. This time, the Royal Hawaiian Band was silent.

As Spreckels's influence in the kingdom waned, Lili'u remained distant from matters of governance. Instead, she filled her days paying social visits, managing her estates and retainers, and raising money for the Lili'uokalani Educational Society, which she had formed to help educate Hawaiian girls and young women. She took part in the Hale Nauā society, founded by Kalākaua in 1886 as a "temple of science" intended to study and revive ancient and modern Hawaiian sciences, art, and literature.

Like Kalākaua's other efforts to promote Hawaiian tradition and culture, the Hale Nauā was criticized roundly by opponents such as

Thurston, who accused the society of "pandering to vice and debasing influences." Closed to whites, the society was imagined to be the scene of orgies. Lili'u described its rituals as being a blend of Masonic customs with the "old and harmless ceremonies of the ancient people of the Hawaiian Islands, which were then known only to the priests of the highest orders." She also defended them against "mean and little minds [which] can readily assign false motives to actions intended for good, and attribute to lofty ideas a base purpose or unholy intention."

Aside from her cultural activities, however, Lili'u did not engage in politics as much as her position as second in line to the throne might suggest. Princess Lili'u would become Hawai'i's monarch if something happened to her brother. But, barring that event, she felt she held very little sway in politics or business. She confided to her diary that, although people petitioned her for royal appointments, "I am sure I have no more to do with offices than the man in the moon."

It was a lonely time for Lili'u. A few months before her brother's coronation, she had learned of the impending birth of her husband's illegitimate child to a half-Hawaiian woman. The family physician, who was a drinking partner of John's and Kalākaua's, was fond of Lili'u and tried to protect her from the pain that her knowledge of her husband's dalliances might cause her. That became impossible when John's child was born to the young woman, who was a member of Lili'u's household staff.

"I can vouch to how she suffered by it," the doctor later said, referring to John's inconsistencies as a husband. "She was exceedingly fond and jealous of him."

The infant boy, named John Dominis Aimoku, was born in January of 1883 and Lili'u ended up accepting the child as a member of her family. None of her diaries from the time of the child's birth survive, and Lili'u continued to be seen in public with her husband, but by then they were living in separate homes. Eventually, she adopted the boy John Aimoku as her second *hānai* child after Lydia. Not long after that, she adopted a third *hānai* son. While this turn of events in the royal family may have been discussed in Honolulu's private clubs, a series of deaths among the *aliʻi* soon overshadowed royal gossip.

Within a year, three of the most powerful women in the kingdom died. The first was Princess Ruth, who died in May 1883 after a long illness that had begun months earlier, even before the coronation. The next was Liliʻu's *hānai* sister Pauahi, who fell ill at the close of 1883. Traveling to San Francisco in early 1884, she consulted with that city's leading doctors. The diagnosis, when it came, was serious: cancer. Pauahi underwent surgery in a specially outfitted room in the annex of the Palace Hotel, and by June she was well enough to return to Hawaiʻi. After a few months of convalescence at her childhood home in Honolulu, she moved to her seaside home at Waikīkī—near the site of the present-day Royal Hawaiian Hotel—to take advantage of the restorative coastal air. Pauahi asked Liliʻu to stay with her.

Pauahi lingered, grateful for the company of her *hānai* sister. In a second codicil to her will, dated October 9, she bequeathed additional land to Liliʻu at nearby Kāhala, just on the other side of Diamond Head. The same day, her pain only partially dulled by constant doses of morphine, she returned to her late cousin Ruth's mansion in Honolulu and died there just after noon on October 16, 1884, during a ceaseless downpour. Word spread quickly of her death. By early afternoon, shopkeepers closed their doors out of respect for the chiefess and soldiers lowered the capital's flags to half-mast.

Once again Liliʻu returned to what had been Princess Ruth's grand mansion and attended the fifteen-day ritual of mourning. Pauahi's bier occupied the same room as Ruth's had just a year and a half earlier. In the funeral cortege, Liliʻu's carriage was just behind the widower Charles Bishop and the dowager Queen Emma. Struggling through the muddy streets, the long procession reflected the enduring importance of the Kamehameha dynasty, even though Pauahi was the last direct descendant of the chief that had united the kingdom. Mourners carried a hundred or more *kāhili*, some highly unusual or old or with special names, such the *malulani* (shade of the heavens), a handsome large *kāhili* of black ostrich feathers.

The Sunday after Pauahi died, the minister at the Fort Street church portrayed her in his eulogy as a paragon of Westernized virtuous womanhood. He also praised her refusal to become Hawai'i's queen, while delivering a not so subtle slap to Kalākaua and Gibson.

We have heard a good deal in the last few years about "Young Hawaii," and its motto, "Hawai'i for the Hawaiians!" I believe that the hope of Hawaii, so far as the native race is concerned, does lie in a "Young Hawaii," but not the blustering, swearing, obscene, saloon-lounging, young men, facile tools of demagogues, who are facing backward toward the old idolatry, with its unspeakable obscenities and vices. The "Young Hawaii," in whom alone are hope for this nation, are the young Hawaiian girls, provided always they are trained to be modest, virtuous, true, capable wives and home-keepers.

Did Lili'u, who would later challenge the meek role expected of her by the missionaries, bridle at these remarks?

As if to prove the saying that bad news comes in threes, Queen Emma, who had grown corpulent and sedentary after the death of her husband, suffered a series of strokes and died soon after, on April 25, 1885. The following day, an Anglican priest performed the service. An estimated two thousand people filed through her home to view her bier, covered with a pall of heavy black velvet.

The traditional mourning rituals had been followed for Princess Ruth and Pauahi Bishop. But Queen Emma had an unorthodox lying in state and burial, which upset Lili'u, who bridled at the disrespect shown to an *ali'i*. Although Emma had helped found Honolulu's Episcopal church, her remains lay in state at Rooke House, which was the traditional Hawaiian practice, until they were removed to Kawaiaha'o, the Congregational church. Lili'u later wrote that "the persons selected by her agent to guard her remains showed no regard for the sacredness of the place. They smoked, feasted, and sang songs while awaiting the last solemn rites to the dead."

Further upsetting the funeral plans, a violent rainstorm lashed Honolulu on the day the funeral was to take place. Rivers of water rushed down the streets leading to the harbor and litter and broken branches soon clogged the gutters. With the flood, the streets of Honolulu became impassable. Emma's funeral was finally held a week later.

Emma's death left the women of the house of Kalākaua as the highest chiefesses in Hawai'i. Since the *mahele* of 1848, when private land ownership was instituted, *ali'i* landholdings were concentrated into the hands of just a few Hawaiian nobles, as relatives succumbed one by one to disease and death. Ruth not only had been granted twelve *'āina* landholdings directly in the *mahele*; she had also inherited lands from her first husband, her father, her uncle, and three half siblings.

Upon her death, Ruth had willed most of her estate to Pauahi; Pauahi, in turn, bequeathed the majority of her lands—a vast holding of more than 350,000 acres—to fund the establishment of the Kamehameha schools for children of Hawaiian ancestry, which still exist today. An editorial from the *Advertiser* remarking on Pauahi's bequest praised it as "a monument more enduring than any bronze of the aloha for her race" and also praised Charles Bishop's generosity, noting the "self-abnegation of her husband whose guiding hand is conspicuously shown in this generous testament."

Similarly, Emma's will directed that much of her remaining wealth be used for charitable purposes, namely, funding operations at Queen's Hospital. These noble deeds helped fund sorely needed institutions, yet they also tied up vast tracts of *ali'i* lands that might otherwise have brought greater financial security to Lili'u and other members of Kalākaua's family if they had inherited them. For Kalākaua, whose debts were mounting, his lack of significant amounts of personal lands or wealth was one of the pressure points compounding his difficulties as a ruler and goes a long way toward explaining why he became so indebted to Spreckels and other *haole*.

Pauahi was generous with Lili'u, willing her a life interest in coastal lands of Kāhala, properties on Kaua'i, and also on Hawai'i Island. But

Liliʻu was distraught to learn from her brother-in-law that he, and not she, would receive her childhood home, Haleakalā, which was eventually sold and converted into a hotel. "The wish of my heart was not gratified, and at the present day strangers stroll through the grounds or lounge on the piazzas of the home once so dear to me," she later wrote.

Pauahi's decision to leave the home to her husband rather than her *hānai* sister hurt Liliʻu. From what she wrote in her diary during that time, it doesn't seem as if her husband offered her much comfort. To the contrary, he irritated her, with his indiscriminate sociability and apparent lack of attention to her needs. In a diary entry of March 1885, she wrote that she was annoyed by his decision to transport the luggage of some recent visitors to the islands instead of picking up the fish she had requested, presumably for a meal that evening. "Angry because John preferred to take those folks' luggage in his wagon than pick up a small package of fish for me," she jotted down, in a moment of wifely pique. "Glad to get him to sleep at last instead of being bored to death by his silly maudlin stories."

Her anger lingered for days and she began to despair. Refurbishment of her home in Pālama dragged on and she wrote, somewhat peevishly, "I am getting despondent—for one reason or another I cannot move into my house. All alone, alone. Each one attending to their own comfort and *pleasure* and quite forgetful of me," she wrote. Even holding her *hānai* son could not lift her spirits. "Sad, so sad—why should I be sad," she wondered, as she gazed into his eyes, thinking to herself, "The dear little thing does not know yet what he has to meet in the world."

Liliʻu's sense of loneliness deepened further as Princess Miriam Likelike, the fun-loving younger sister with whom she had shared so much over the years, grew gravely ill toward the end of 1886. Already, it had been a difficult year for the Cleghorns: Archibald's dry goods business, which he had taken over from his father, had failed that year, forcing him to turn over his assets to fellow Briton Theo H. Davies for liquidation. Davies helped Cleghorn pay off his debts, with a small amount of money left over to help support the family.

Perhaps Likelike's mysterious illness was brought on by this financial calamity. The best doctors in the islands were summoned to her bedside, but they could not discover what was wrong with her. She refused to eat; some said she was being "prayed to death" by *kāhuna*, traditional Hawaiian priests.

Doctors visited the Cleghorns' Waikīkī estate daily, and Archibald hoped to send his ailing wife to San Francisco, where she could be examined by the city's doctors. But Likelike's strength seeped away and she was unable to make the trip. In January, Mauna Loa began to erupt, unleashing fiery streams of lava down the slopes of the volcano. Lili'u's diary entry noted that Likelike "thinks this bursting of the lava flow in Kau is for her—a piece of superstition." Residents of the island also told of a school of red *akule* fish that had been spotted in the waters off the island of Hawai'i, which traditionally foretold the death of an *ali'i*.

In the late afternoon of February 2, 1887, Likelike died at the age of thirty-six. Her death made Cleghorn a widower and left Ka'iulani, then just eleven, motherless. According to a later account by the governess who comforted the distraught Ka'iulani, Likelike on her deathbed told her daughter that she would never marry and would never be queen.

The wailing began well before midnight and the eerie sounds of grieving Hawaiians reached Ka'iulani's bedroom that night. Mourners brought armfuls of gardenias, Princess Likelike's favorite flower. When her body was removed to the palace, servants burned the blossoms. The scent of the charred flowers was said to have lingered over Waikīkī for days.

That same night, Likelike's body was transported in a hearse to the throne room of the palace to lie in state for three weeks. It lay in the open, in a snowy satin gown, her white gloved hands crossed upon her bosom. A crucifix stood at her feet, with candelabra on either side and a large bouquet of white and pale pink roses. Lili'u, along with Kapi'olani and others, sat at the head of the bier. At her funeral, Likelike's body was placed in a polished koa coffin, adorned with sprays of gardenia, and both the bishop of Honolulu and the clergy of St. Andrew's presided. The procession was so long it took over an hour to pass a single point.

With Likelike's death, Lili'u lost her most intimate friend and only true confidante. "I was tenderly attached to my sister, so much so that her decease had an unfavorable effect on my health," Lili'u wrote years later, only hinting through her restrained words at the profound grief she must have felt.

Lili'u's sorrow in the months after her sister's death was so deep that her brother finally stepped in to invite her to accompany Queen Kapi'olani on a journey to England to celebrate Queen Victoria's fifty years of reign. The very next day, perhaps contemplating the potential dangers of the trip, she wrote, "Must surely make my will. Bright moonlight night. Indeed all my thoughts are for going without any feeling of regret for home."

Lili'u, who had never traveled farther east than Sacramento, looked forward to taking part in Britain's Royal Jubilee. More than seven thousand miles separated the Hawaiian Islands and Great Britain, taking more than three weeks of traveling, but the two nations shared a form of government: both were constitutional monarchies, and ever since Kamehameha IV and Emma had ruled, the leaders of the Pacific islands had looked to England as a role model.

The similarity, however, ended there. Even though monarchies across Europe were under attack from democratic factions, Victoria's British empire was the most powerful on earth. In contrast, Hawai'i's fortunes looked increasingly uncertain, as interests on the part of powerful nations such as Germany, France, Britain, and Japan in gaining footholds in the Pacific—specifically, the strategically located Hawaiian Islands— grew stronger each day.

Just as the European colonial powers had agreed just three years earlier to partition wide swaths of the African continent among themselves, a similar sort of gamesmanship was being played out in distant Polynesia. The year before Lili'u left for England, in 1886, Britain and Germany had divided up parts of New Guinea and the Solomon Island chain. Could a colonial power play for Hawai'i's be far behind?

The most bellicose noises were coming from Hawai'i's neighbors to the east. Although it was four decades after the term "manifest destiny" has first been used, Americans by the mid-1880s had broadened the meaning of the phrase beyond annexation of new territory on the North American continent. By then America had begun proclaiming it was their destiny to spread capitalism, Chistianity, and the white race beyond its borders, an argument that coincided with aggressive moves by American businesses, such as John D. Rockefeller's Standard Oil Co., into foreign markets.

From Lili'u's perspective, Great Britain remained the world power and the United States a mere upstart in comparison. She did not look to America's president as an example of how to preside over a country, but to Britain's diminutive Queen Victoria. Perhaps not coincidentally, just as Lili'u was beginning her three week journey to meet the woman whose empire stretched over half the world, her brother David Kalākaua was launching his own attempts at Pacific empire building. He sought to unite the people of Polynesia into an oceanic empire, with Honolulu as capital and himself as king.

The adviser who most actively fanned the flames of Kalākaua's imperial ambitions was Gibson, who argued in editorials published in his *Pacific Commercial Advertiser* for "Hawaiian Primacy in Polynesia," in which the kingdom would take a leading role in the affairs of the region. By then, the great powers had already established footholds in the Pacific: in 1880, Tahiti became a colony of France after years of warring; in 1885, Germany declared the Marshall Islands in Micronesia a protectorate. And Samoa's fierce internal strife was inflamed by conflicting U.S., German, and British interests.

By 1879 the United States, Germany, and England had all signed treaties with warring native factions of Samoa on the conflict-wracked islands, which between 1876 and 1889 would endure a civil war, two rebellions, and seven attempts to establish governments. Representatives from the three Western countries held a summit in Washington, D.C. in June of 1887 to discuss Samoa, with few concrete results. The Hawaiian kingdom sought to make its views heard through diplomatic channels. This was largely ignored, with Britain's foreign secretary, Lord Rosebery, referring to its efforts as "a mere piece of fussy impertinence."

American and British diplomats repeatedly warned Hawai'i against becoming involved in Samoan affairs, but Gibson, who became foreign minister in late 1886, brushed off such counsel. Instead, under his guidance, the king appointed John E. Bush, a part-Hawaiian politician who had served in various posts for Kalākaua since 1880, including minister to Samoa, Tonga, and "the peoples of Polynesia." By December of that year, Bush had boarded a steamer bound for Samoa, with secret orders to try to negotiate a Polynesian federation headed by Hawai'i.

Kalākaua's choice to head this mission was unfortunate. Soon after arriving in Samoa, Bush hosted a dinner for the embattled Samoan king, which stretched through many toasts to dawn. After the Samoan king agreed to enter into an alliance with Hawai'i, Bush then celebrated with another party, made famous by Robert Louis Stevenson's description of it. Although Stevenson himself did not attend, he heard about it on a trip to Samoa when the memory of it was still fresh in the minds of those he met.

> All decency appears to have been forgotten; high chiefs were seen to dance; and roused, doctored with coffee, and sent home. As a first chapter in the history of the Polynesian Confederation, it was hardly cheering, and Laupepa [the Samoan King] remarked to one of the [Hawaiian] embassy, with equal dignity and sense; "If you have come here to teach my people to drink, I wish you had stayed away."

When news reached Germany, Britain, and the United States that Hawai'i had formed an alliance with Samoa, the three great powers were not pleased. Reports began circulating that Bush had plied the Samoans with liquor and hospitality in an effort to win their favor. Germany, in particular, which was supporting a rival Samoan chief, became incensed by the sheer gall of the tiny kingdom of Hawai'i. A message was sent through diplomatic channels that it was "obviously absurd for the King [Kalākaua] to bring himself in conflict with the wishes of the German Government."

To some, this episode resembled a Gilbert and Sullivan operetta. The kingdom commissioned the *Kaimiloa*, formerly a British steamer engaged in hauling copra (the dried white flesh of the coconut from which oil is extracted) and guano (the droppings of seabirds or bats used as fertilizer), and fitted it out with six small brass cannons and two Gatling guns. The ship's commanding officer was a former lieutenant in the British navy who had become the head of Honolulu's Industrial and Reformatory School. About two dozen of the reform school's older boys became seamen, complemented by a group from the King's Guards.

The ship was scheduled to leave for Samoa on March 18, 1887. But two nights beforehand a drunken brawl erupted among the men, resulting in the dismissal of three of the ship's officers. The ship left, as planned, on the eighteenth, but with few officers or recruits with naval experience. Still, the captain of the *Kaimiloa* and his men made it to Samoa, only to learn that Bush had indulged in a lengthy drinking binge. Overall, the venture was a disaster. As one Hawaiian diplomat wrote, "The 'Kaimiloa' finally became a disgrace to her flag. The captain was taken sick and then all discipline was at an end . . ."

Meanwhile, discussions continued among the great powers over how to parcel up the Pacific islands. One suggestion made during a conversation between Britain's prime minister Lord Salisbury and Germany's state secretary of the foreign office Prince Herbert von Bismarck, son of the "Iron Chancellor," was that Germany take Samoa, England take the Tonga Islands, and the United States take Hawai'i. The Germans didn't bother waiting for these discussions to progress. Instead, Bismarck sent four German warships to Samoa and declared war on its king, who promptly surrendered to avoid bloodshed.

Against the backdrop of much more powerful countries scrambling for footholds in the Pacific, Kalākaua's imperial folly undercut his efforts to be seen as a strong, forward-thinking leader. He later asserted that he sent Bush only after receiving "a repeated call from Samoa as well as all the other South Sea Islands—a call of Confederation or solidarity of the Polynesian Race," adding that "Our Mission was simply a Mission of phylanthropy more than any thing, but the arogance of the Germans prevented our good intentions and . . . we had to withdraw the Mission." But whatever his intentions, the disastrous mission to Samoa made him into a laughingstock.

One person who found humor in the episode was a Honolulu-based satirist named A. T. Atkinson. He published a pamphlet titled the *Gynberg Ballads*, with the heavy-drinking Duke intended to represent David Kalākaua. The pamphlet made fun of almost every aspect of Kalākaua's reign, including Hawai'i's mission to Samoa, featuring a boat called the *Conundrum* (i.e., the *Kaimiloa*) with a bottle of brandy for a bowsprit, whiskey for a funnel, and gin for a poop ornament. When eleven hundred or so copies of the *Gynberg Ballads* arrived in Honolulu in May of 1887 aboard the *Mariposa*, the government seized them. Despite the government's attempt to muzzle Atkinson, his satirical pamphlet made its way into circulation and was wildly popular.

Lili'u was thousands of miles to the east when the *Mariposa* unloaded its shipment of the *Gynberg Ballads* in Honolulu. She had left Honolulu on April 12 on the steamer *Australia* headed for San Francisco and boarded a private car provided by the Central Pacific Railroad for a train ride east, over California's imposing Sierra Nevada mountains which were still covered with snow in the late spring. For someone coming from what she called the "land of perpetual summer," Lili'u later wrote with delight about how some members of her party disembarked from the train, gathered the cold, white flakes in their hands, packed them into spheres, and pelted one another with snowballs, enjoying the sheer novelty of the experience.

When the queen, the princess, and John Dominis, who had accompanied the two women, arrived in Washington, D.C., on May 3, 1887, they paid a social visit to President Grover Cleveland's new bride, the beautiful, dark-haired Frances Folsom. A few days later, the Hawaiian party visited Mount Vernon, the former residence of George and Martha Washington. In its guest book, Lili'u wrote in Hawaiian, "*Ilihia i ka ike i keia*," which means, "I am overcome with awe at the sight of this."

Later that night, a marine band conducted by John Philip Sousa welcomed them to a state dinner at the White House in their honor.

The Hawaiian party also met with America's most influential Freemason, Albert Pike, who had created a system for the secret society based on the so-called Scottish rite. Although the organization was for men only, Lili'u and Kapi'olani were presented with scrolls attesting that anywhere they traveled in the world they could count on the assistance of Freemasons.

Lili'u and other members of the entourage then visited a three-ring circus. Despite the lack of seating cushions and the dusty arena, Kapi'olani, in particular, was amused by a boxing match between a clown and a trained elephant, which drew "outright laughter" from the queen. They also saw an exhibition of Indian warriors on horseback, being chased by American soldiers.

Cowboys and Indians were much on the capital's mind at the time. In February, Cleveland had signed the Dawes Act, which gave every Indian family the right to purchase 160 acres of land they had once freely roamed. The parcels would be held in "severalty," or trust, for him by the U.S. government for twenty-five years. Meant to convert tribally owned lands into private property, the law was authored by Massachusetts senator Henry Dawes, who believed in the civilizing power of private property, explaining that to be civilized was to "wear civilized clothes . . . cultivate the ground, live in houses, ride in Studebaker wagons, send children to school, drink whiskey [and] own property." His views were similar to those of the first missionaries to Hawai'i—with the notable exception of whiskey drinking.

The party then made its way to Boston, where it stayed in the Parker House hotel, owned by members of the family that also owned an enormous cattle ranch on the island of Hawai'i. To welcome the visiting royals, the hotel's staff had decorated Kapi'olani's suite with a plaque on which the words "Aloha Oe" were spelled out in small red, yellow, and purple flowers, a generosity noted by one of the Hawaiian staffers in his diary, commenting that flower buds "are very dear at 25 cents a bud." The city of Boston hosted a number of lavish entertainments and more than a hundred members of the Dominis family gathered at a reunion to ogle the exotic Hawaiian princess that John had married.

The party's next stop was Manhattan, where Lili'u visited the mummies at the Metropolitan Museum of Art. Making their way past a raw patch of Central Park, up a flight of wooden steps, and into the redbrick Gothic structure that housed the museum's growing collection of European art and Egyptian artifacts, Lili'u turned away from the mummy, "because it spoke too plainly of death and burial."

After eleven days in New York Lili'u, Kapi'olani, John Dominis, and other members of the Hawaiian party boarded the *City of Rome*, which was then one of the largest steamers in the world, accommodating more than two thousand passengers.

On board the ship, the queen and Lili'u enjoyed *poi*, the staple food of the Hawaiians, and spent Sunday afternoons singing hymns. A school of porpoises played in the steamer's wake and a whale drew close. The crew of the *City of Rome* finally spied land through a thick haze at about 10 a.m. on Wednesday, June 1. When Lili'u and the rest of the party reached shore, they encountered an extraordinary sight: a huge crowd of thousands of people had gathered for as far as the eye could see, hoping to catch a glimpse of royalty from the Sandwich Islands, as Hawai'i was still called in Great Britain. A military escort of about a hundred red-coated British soldiers served as the party's honor guard. Once they stepped onto dry land a band struck up England's national anthem, "God Save the Queen."

CHAPTER EIGHT

Bayonet Constitution, 1887

When Lili'u set foot on British soil for the first time, she landed on an island that was as distant from her own as could be. Even the breath of the horses seemed different: what caught Lili'u's attention was the steam coming from the nostrils of the chuffing steeds pulling her carriage, although the temperature outside was not cold. "I was told that the peculiar atmosphere of the city of Liverpool, damp to saturation, made this phenomenon quite usual," Lili'u later wrote.

Then the most densely populated town in England, Liverpool was home to an enormous pool of impoverished laborers who loaded and unloaded the British empire's daily shiploads of cotton, sugar, and coal. Ringed by slums, the city also teemed with thieves and prostitutes. The sickly smell of rudimentary plumbing wafted from the grim rows of terrace houses, where a dozen families might share a single water tap and an outdoor toilet.

Nonetheless, the Hawaiian party enjoyed a marvelous meal during their stay in Liverpool, a luncheon at the town hall that included turtle, whitebait, dressed crab, and many toasts to the health of King Kalākaua.

That evening, most of the party attended a performance of *Hamlet*, which Lili'u decided to skip, instead spending a quiet evening in her hotel.

The next day, they left the sprawl of Liverpool for the English countryside, passing fields of brilliant yellow mustard blooms and meeting a member of the Colman family, makers of the famed English mustard. When the royal entourage finally reached London, an escort helped guide them through the thick snarl of carriages and pedestrian traffic arriving for the Jubilee. He led them to a suite of rooms at the Alexandra Hotel, on Hyde Park Corner, where princes from Japan, Siam, India, and Persia were also staying.

The normally raucous street sounds of London were subsumed by a symphony of nail pounding, with hundreds of carpenters and laborers toiling to erect grandstands in a fortnight, before tens of thousands of people converged on London for the Jubilee celebrations. Unlike the relatively quiet streets of Honolulu, Britain's capital bustled at all times of day and night, alive with street urchins, pickpockets, and the working poor. The world's largest city was flooded with immigrants from all corners of Europe and the empire, including more than a hundred thousand fleeing famine-devastated Ireland—a number larger than the entire population of the Hawaiian islands.

By the time the Hawaiian party arrived in London, Queen Victoria herself was on her way from Balmoral, Scotland, with a brief stopover at Windsor Castle. Excitement was rising. Victoria had gradually emerged from years of secluded mourning following the death of her consort, Albert, in 1861. By midday on Monday, June 20, 1887, masses of people lining the streets strained to catch a glimpse of their monarch as her carriage headed toward Buckingham Palace.

That same day, Kapi'olani and Lili'u made their way to the palace past guards in their high bearskin hats to a reception room, where an official held a baton across the entrance to the door, lowering it so the Hawaiian royal party could enter. There they were greeted by Lord Salisbury, a tall, slightly stooped man in his late sixties. Lili'u noticed that she and her sister-in-law were a source of curiosity to some of the British courtiers;

she saw several ladies of the royal household peeking into the room where she and her sister-in-law were sitting, proving, as Lili'u observed, that "human nature is about the same in the palace as in the cottage."

A short time later, Kapi'olani and Lili'u were led into another room where Queen Victoria sat on a sofa. Walking about twenty-five feet toward the sovereign, wearing their specially made court dresses fitted with tight corsets that pinched their waists, Lili'u and Kapi'olani approached the short-statured British queen, who rose to kiss Kapi'olani on each check and then turned to Lili'u and kissed her on the forehead.

Kapi'olani, who spoke no English, sat next to Victoria on the sofa. Their conversation was translated by the Hawaiian king's private secretary, Curtis 'Iaukea. Lili'u sat in a nearby chair, as Victoria recalled having met Kalākaua, when he visited England during his around-the-world trip in 1881. When the visit concluded after more small talk, Victoria arose and once again kissed Kapi'olani on both cheeks and Lili'u on her forehead, as if she were kissing a child. The aged yet vital monarch, then sixty-eight, took Lili'u's hand "as though she had just thought of something which she had been in danger of forgetting, and said 'I want to introduce you to my children.'" One by one they came forward to meet the exotic chiefesses from the faraway Pacific nation.

Lili'u and other members of the Hawaiian party found themselves struggling with the hierarchical protocol followed by Queen Victoria's court. In Hawai'i, as heir apparent to the throne, Lili'u's position was considered equal to Kapi'olani's as queen. But in Britain her status was lower than her sister-in-law's. That bothered Lili'u, who behaved somewhat petulantly by threatening to return to Hawai'i if she didn't get her way, according to the courtier 'Iaukea.

The Princess possessed a strong will and determination . . . her desire to have recognition equal to the Queen's caused me many worried hours and much futile effort trying to persuade her that it was not possible in a country where the customs were different. After consulting with her husband, whose calm judgment was wise and sensible, however, she finally gave up her threatened departure for home and matters settled down to a busy routine again. But not for long.

Indeed, because John Dominis was not titled and thus not considered a member of the Hawaiian royal family, he was not seated with his wife or assigned the same carriage. Lili'u soon wrote to her brother, asking him to make both her husband and Archibald Cleghorn princes, to avoid such embarrassment in the future. Although Lili'u and the other members of the Hawaiian royal family admired and patterned themselves on Britain's royal family, they felt very much like outsiders during their Jubilee visit.

When Lili'u finally reached the waiting room for the royal ladies, after her sister-in-law, she discovered everyone was standing. A grand duchess turned to her and asked, "Why does not the queen sit down, so that we may all be seated," referring to Kapi'olani, the highest-ranking royal in the room. Hawai'i's gentle and slightly befuddled queen had not understood that the rest of the ladies would not take their seats until she did. Lili'u signaled Kapi'olani to sit.

Once the reception began, Lili'u was dazzled by the tiaras and necklaces worn by royalty and ambassadors' wives. She had never before seen such a grand display of priceless gems and the experience seems to have heightened her sense of just how far off and relatively impoverished her island kingdom was compared with the capital of the British empire. In the letter she wrote to Archibald Cleghorn from London, she said she was enjoying herself and mentioned that she and John would sit on the balcony of their hotel room, watching the handsome horse-drawn carriages go by. "It is magnificent, but sometimes I get tired of all that show," she wrote.

Yet in a letter she wrote to her coachman in Honolulu, she alerted him to a package she'd arranged to have sent to him. It contained half a dozen coachman's uniforms, the blue one of which she directed him to wear when he met her upon her return. Her purchase suggests she was far from indifferent to adopting European court customs herself.

The culmination of England's glorious show took place on Jubilee Day. By late morning on June 21 the crowds lining the route to Westminster Abbey were dense—an estimated 3 million people came to London that day to celebrate, adding to the already-thronging population of 5.5 million. Some people had secured their spots along the route by spending the night on camp stools, huddling beneath blankets to keep warm. By midmorning the dense crowds, coupled with the warm weather, caused several ladies to faint.

Even the dignitaries invited to attend the service at Westminster Abbey arrived many hours ahead of time, drinking from flasks and nibbling on sandwiches brought wrapped in paper. As the Hawaiian royal party approached, the congregants inside the abbey heard a roar of cheers for the queen of the Sandwich Islands. Then came a blare of trumpets announcing that Queen Victoria had entered her carriage. The lords and ladies hurriedly stashed the newspapers that had helped them pass the time during their long wait and hastily rewrapped the uneaten portions of their sandwiches. The crowd let out a loud and continuous roar, punctuated with cries of "Here she is!," "I have seen her!," and "She is alive!"

Westminster Abbey, where every English king had been crowned since 1066, was packed, with the ladies brightening its gloomiest recesses with their pink, mauve, and saffron gowns. In contrast, the small figure that Lili'u saw as she made her way down the central aisle wore her usual gown of somber black, brightened only by a white hat with a plume of white feathers and a tightly spaced row of diamonds. As Victoria proceeded through an arched door and into the nave, accompanied by a Handel processional thundering from the abbey's great organ, Lili'u and the entire congregation of some nine thousand people rose as one.

Kapi'olani and Lili'u sat near Queen Victoria, in the choir. Kapi'olani wore an extraordinary blue velvet gown, tightly fitted and trimmed with wide bands and panels made from scores of peacock feathers. Toward the end of the service, Queen Victoria rose and, seemingly out of a spontaneous outflow of feeling, kissed and embraced the nearly three dozen members of her immediate family who joined her that day. Did Lili'u ponder Queen Victoria's blessings of having so many children and a secure throne as she watched?

That evening, Buckingham Palace hosted a gathering for visiting royalty; London's midsummer night sky glowed with streaks of phosphorescence and houses lit with colored fairy lights. Even the grand old lady of Threadneedle Street, the Bank of England, lit no fewer than ten thousand gas lights on the night of the Jubilee, some ruby colored and others in the shape of a dozen large stars. At 10 p.m. Britons lit beacon fires on the highest points of the British Isles, including Arthur's Seat, Edinburgh, an extinct volcano whose name is said to have been derived from the King Arthur legend. Asked how she was afterward, Queen Victoria replied, "I am very tired, but very happy."

A week of Jubilee events followed, including a children's fete in Hyde Park and the queen's garden party, which took place amid the lawns, graveled walks, and rose bushes of Buckingham Palace. But as Lili'u enjoyed the last of the celebrations and visited the Tower of London's rack and the dungeon, reports of a more frightening nature to the heir apparent of Hawai'i's throne began reaching her in London. Some newspapers had began publishing terse reports of "excitement and possible revolution" in Hawai'i.

Lili'u got word of the upheaval immediately following Queen Victoria's garden party, once she returned to her hotel. The royal party made haste for Liverpool to catch the steamer *Servia* back to New York, resting just long enough to secure sleeping cabins on the overland train. It then rushed across the country to San Francisco in uncomfortably hot summer weather and boarded the steamer for Honolulu just fifteen days after leaving London.

Most likely it was in San Francisco where Lili'u received two distressing letters, one from her brother and another from her friend Charles Wilson.

Honolulu, July 5/87

Dear Sister,

We are just passing through a tremendous Crises. Happily averted since Tuesday 28 of June of last week. I have appointed my Ministers. Mr. Green as Minister of Finance and Premier. Mr. Thurston as Minister of Interior and Mr. Godfrey Brown Minister [of] Foreign Affairs. Mr. C.A. Ashford Attorney General. Both Thurston and Ashford have made necessary apologize for their former conduct towards me. So we are now in full sympathy and I think we can get along together.

But the fault of the whole matter is that the firms of Brewer & Co., E.O. Hall & Son, J.T. Waterhouse and Co., S.N. Castle & Co., have distributed promiscuously the arms to every body that now I believe they regret it not being able now to quiet matters.

Lili'u must have puzzled over the news that her brother had seemingly accepted a cabinet comprised of some of his fiercest critics, especially Lorrin Thurston. But Wilson's letter, written the same day, was likely to have unsettled her even more.

Honolulu July 5, 1887

My Dear Princess,

Since my last, everything was peaceable, until this morning, a false rumor got afloat that His Majesty was corresponding with Mr. Gibson and inciting the Native population to an uprising against the Whites and also that His Majesty was having ammunition and Arms prepared in and around the Palace premises.

Wilson reported that his inquiries found the rumors to be "false and without any foundation" and wrote that the king and the new cabinet met that morning, with the ministers assuring Kalākaua they would direct that "the Citizens disperse and go quietly to their homes." Wilson ended by assuring Liliʻu that "everything has quieted down."

Liliʻu and Kapiʻolani had plenty of time to ponder the meaning of those letters aboard ship, as they took in the fresh ocean air on deck. They tried to distract themselves by knitting, reading, and singing Hawaiian songs. On July 23, while still at sea, Liliʻu wrote, "A lovely day—nothing but knitting to do—but as fast as my needles fly my thots seem to fly even faster."

Her worries multiplied overnight, and the following day she wrote in her diary, "My heart is sad thoʻ—for affairs at home seem dark. My poor brother!"

In Honolulu, the sun shone brightly on June 21, the day planned for Queen Victoria's Jubilee celebrations. Stores and government offices were closed and residents flew flags in front of their homes to celebrate. At 8 a.m. gunfire erupted from the battery on Punchbowl Hill as churchbells rang. At Kapiʻolani Park, in the shadow of Diamond Head, a series of sporting events got under way, including shotput throws, high jumps, and sack races. The *Advertiser* declared the rush for free food "execrable," reporting that "a crowd of young hoodlums, dark skins as well as fair . . . rushed the booth, crowded round the buffet, seizing in their fists lumps of meat and whatever else came their way." Eventually the police were called in. But the crowd was more orderly that evening. The Royal Hawaiian Band played for a dance attended by several hundred people, while the British minister hosted an elegant reception at his home attended by some *aliʻi*.

Yet a crisis was building in Kalākaua's kingdom. For one thing, Walter Murray Gibson, the statesman upon whom the king had increasingly relied to help him govern, was burdened by a host of physical and personal problems. He was still a tall, handsome man but his shoulders now drooped, his long beard had turned snow white. The gauntness brought on by illness made him look more than ever like an Old Testament prophet. For months, the kingdom's prime minister had been suffering from various chest and stomach ailments. Compounding his troubles, the widower then in his early sixties was named in a lawsuit filed by a woman who claimed he had broken his promise to marry her. In his diary, he described her as "a miserable schemer."

Just as his personal affairs grew more vexing, Gibson's worries over affairs of state multiplied. His anxiety about the *Kaimiloa*—the retrofitted guano steamer heading to Samoa—kept him up at night. Also vexing him were two "gifts"—one for $75,000 and the other for $80,000—that the king had allegedly accepted from two separate Chinese men, each seeking to win a single potentially lucrative opium license that the government planned to grant. The *Hawaiian Gazette* caught wind of the story and published an investigative bombshell about the bribes paid to the king to win the license, based on lengthy affidavits. Public opinion, particularly in the *haole* community, rapidly turned against both Kalākaua and Gibson with what was presented, perhaps unfairly, as the latest example of his corruption.

Reflecting this sentiment, the American minister to Hawai'i forwarded to Washington, D.C. a complete set of the affidavits supporting the story and detailing what became known as the opium scandal. "Of late I have heard it remarked that no change would be satisfactory unless it was one deposing the King, changing the Constitution, and adopting a republican form of government," the minister wrote, adding that he had urged the king's critics to be moderate.

But the *Gazette*, the most outspoken of the papers opposed to the king, hammered away at Kalākaua and Gibson on an almost daily basis, editorializing that "the end must come to the present era of extravagance, corruption, and incompetence."

Such strong views were not confined to newsprint. In Honolulu, a secret organization that would become known as the Hawaiian League had formed earlier in the year with the goal of reforming government and reining in the powers of the king. Sanford Dole hosted the first meeting in his home and the leader who emerged was none other than Dole's friend Lorrin A. Thurston, a lawyer and firebrand editorial writer for the *Bulletin*, who had been elected to the legislature in 1886. Dole and Thurston served on an executive committee of thirteen men—all of them *haole*—that became known as the Committee of Thirteen. With a membership that rapidly grew into the hundreds, the group split into radical and conservative wings. Among the extremists, there was talk of creating a republic and even of assassinating King Kalākaua by shooting him in cold blood.

Despite the distractions of his personal affairs, Gibson was alert to the rising danger posed by the Hawaiian League and its military arm, a volunteer militia known as the Honolulu Rifles. He had already placed an informer inside the two groups and soon began to obtain information about their plans. He quickly grasped the threat they posed. In his diary entry from June 10, he wrote, "The tempest seems to be rushing to a climax . . . Had I been in good health perhaps I might have prevented some of these disasters but my poor body cannot keep up with mind or spirit. I am weary, languid, listless, oh, so weary."

The king's enemies came from the white business class and they organized rapidly. To avoid police surveillance, Kalākaua's opponents held meetings at different locations each evening. As the atmosphere in town grew tense, many members of the Hawaiian League began arming themselves—buying rifles and ammunition at Honolulu hardware stores. On Tuesday, June 28, fresh supplies of arms arrived aboard the steamer *Australia* from San Francisco. Castle & Cooke and other merchants put them on sale the next morning. They were popular: the *Daily Bulletin* reported "for several hours a regular run was kept up on the deadly weapons."

Aware of this surge in arms sales, Kalākaua's government began fortifying the palace and other government buildings to prepare for an attack by *haole* opponents, including barricading the palace gates, just as Charles Wilson's letter had described. Kalākaua's ministers and loyalists could not have missed the notices posted around town of a mass meeting planned by the league in two days, on June 30. When the time came,

Kalākaua himself called out the Rifles—whom he mistakenly thought were still loyal to him—before noon that day to maintain order.

Composed of Honolulu's mercantile leaders, the league held tremendous sway. It ordered all of the town's grog shops closed and set guards to watch for fires and to prevent possible contamination of the water supply. It also posted more than 150 men in uniform, carrying fixed bayonets and fifty rounds of ball cartridge apiece, at the front entrance to the armory of the Honolulu Rifles, a one-story building on the corner of Beretania and Punchbowl streets, just a few blocks from the palace. The militiamen wore uniforms that bore a close resemblance to a standard U.S. Army pattern of dark blue with red facings.

At 2 p.m. Dole called the meeting of perhaps a thousand or more people to order. Although he had resigned from the Hawaiian League after the radicals in the party began pushing to overthrow the monarchy, he still agreed to open the gathering. After Dole spoke, Lorrin Thurston mounted the podium wearing the uniform of the Honolulu Rifles.

In a booming voice that could be heard to the very back of the overflowing hall, he read a set of resolutions that he and other members of the league's Committee of Thirteen had prepared. Casting his dark eyes downward, the young politician with the thinning hair and handlebar mustache read a list of demands to the king. These demands might have been reasonable, from citizens of the Kingdom, but many of the people making them were, in fact, resident aliens who wanted to vote and hold office even though they were not naturalized citizens. Calling for the dismissal of the cabinet and of Walter Gibson, Thurston railed against the payments for the opium license, calling "to remove the stain now resting on the throne."

He then moved on to the heart of the league's demands: the king should not interfere with the election of representatives, "unduly influence" legislation or legislators, or use his official position for private ends. Many have had their businesses almost entirely ruined by the king's "mal-administration," he fumed. Would they ever take Kalākaua at his word again?

"No!" shouted the men in the room.

What they needed was a radical change in the constitution!

Amid cheers, Thurston declared that the Committee of Thirteen would personally present their list of demands to Kalākaua and give him just twenty-four hours to reply. "We want the King to think of the public good, not of personal ends," added another of the king's critics. "We have just seen the Jubilee of Queen Victoria, and if Kalākaua would follow her example, he might reign as long." In other words, they wanted a largely ceremonial figure on the throne, not one who would attempt to actively rule the country. The crowd passed the resolutions read by Thurston with a resounding chorus of "ayes."

Without a pause, members of the Committee of Thirteen took the printed resolutions and marched to the palace, demanding a written response from the king within twenty-four hours. Tensions in rumor-rife Honolulu rose even higher, the next morning, as a fresh delivery of seven cases of firearms arrived on the *Mariposa*. Word spread that the arms were meant for the government, to put down the rebellion. The Honolulu Rifles sprang into action, seizing the cases. Only upon prying the boxes open did they discover they contained guns of a type commonly used by Chinese planters to drive birds from their rice fields.

Order rapidly broke down, as members of the Hawaiian League and the Rifles turned their fury on Walter Murray Gibson. At this point, the Committee was in charge of the city. Confined to house arrest on June 30, he jotted down in his diary entry that day: "Threats of violence . . . Rumors of armed mob, purpose to lynch me. Col Ashford [the head of the Honolulu Rifles] informs me that I will be shot down if I attempt to leave my house. The mob around my house—an anxious night."

The next day, however, was even worse for the statesman once satirized as the Shepherd Saint of Lāna'i. Gibson's son-in-law paid him a visit around ten that morning at his home. The two men sat together talking in Gibson's parlor when Colonel Ashford burst into the room, ordering them to put on their hats and follow him. A detachment of artillerymen from the Rifles prodded the pair past jeering crowds lining the sidewalks to the Pacific Navigation Company's warehouse near the docks, apparently intending to hang them both.

When they entered the vast iron structure, they saw a noose already dangling from one of the roof beams and an area cleared of freight and baggage for the hanging. The high silk hat that Gibson had been wearing was knocked to the ground as the sergeant in charge, tying their hands behind their backs, pushed him and his son-in-law toward the rope. The crowd shouted obscenities at the pair, hungering for an execution. The son of a prominent missionary family made his voice heard above the crowd, shouting, "Hang them! Hang them!"

Just as the militiamen were dropping the noose around Gibson's neck, an infuriated, shouting female, using her folded umbrella as a weapon to poke and prod her way through the crowd, confronted the surprised soldiers and demanded that they halt. It was Talula, Gibson's daughter, who had arrived to try to save her father and husband from the noose.

Described as a "brave girl" in Gibson's diary entry of July 1, Talula had stood up for him against what had rapidly turned into a vigilante mob. James Wodehouse, the lanky British consul to Hawai'i, notable for his drooping mustache and his daily walks with his pair of red dachshunds, also broke through to intervene, claiming that Gibson was of English parentage and that harming him would touch off an international incident. This was enough to halt the hanging. Gibson and his son-in-law were then allowed to return home until July 5.

During the period when Gibson was under house arrest, he tried to pass messages to the king, according to an account by Isobel Strong, who wrote about her experience of having been enlisted as a courier by the embattled ex-premier. She arrived at the gate of Gibson's house and saw two young men, salesmen who had waited on her in downtown shops, dressed in military uniforms.

> I nodded amiably and was about to walk in when, to my amazement, they crossed their rifles before me with a curt "Halt!"
>
> "Don't be silly," I said. "What's the matter with you?"

"You can't go in," was the surprising answer. "Mr. Gibson is under arrest and no one is allowed to see him."

It struck me as ridiculous and with a "Pooh to you!" I dodged under the rifles and walked up the path. As they had no orders to shoot ladies in the back I reached the house safely.

Gibson then gave her a message in Hawaiian to relay to Kalākaua. She went to the palace and found him under watch. Thinking quickly, Strong feigned she was sketching but instead wrote out the message, which she did not understand the meaning of. The king read it, thanked her, and Strong left the palace. A week or so later Kalākaua received her in the palace's empty throne room.

"I am not asking you what the message meant," Strong said. "But I would like to know why the Missionary Party is making so much trouble for your Majesty?"

"It is not me, personally, at all," he explained. "What they want is my country. They are hoping to annex Hawai'i to the United States. It has been a steady fight ever since I came to the throne."

"Take the islands away from you," she exclaimed.

"Not while I live," said the king. He then rewarded her with the Order of the Star of Oceania for her service to the kingdom.

Despite Isobel Strong's success in passing along Gibson's mysterious message to the king, Gibson and his son-in-law were indicted on embezzlement charges and moved to the O'ahu prison, preventing further such communiqués.

The day of the June 30th mass meeting, representatives of the Hawaiian League had told Kalākaua that they would be delivering a new constitution for his signature. The rumor was that if the king refused to sign there would be bloodshed. Tension mounted as hours and then days passed without any word from the king, who remained out of public view. Adding to the apprehension, workmen placed large iron bolts and bars on the palace gates. The *New York Times* reported that in the basement of the palace three hundred armed Hawaiians had formed a volunteer regiment, prepared to defend their king at a moment's notice.

Some people hoped Kalākaua would refuse to sign the constitution, especially since three British warships and one French man-of-war were expected to arrive in Honolulu harbor at any time, potentially serving as a counterforce to the Americans. But on Wednesday, July 6, a group of representatives from the Hawaiian League made their way to the palace. They then read the document to the king, "who listened in a sullen, and somewhat appalling silence," according to an account written by C. W. Ashford, one of the league members present.

The king questioned and argued with the group of *haole*, going back and forth, and then retreated into silence—"for considerable periods appeared to be gazing into space and weighing the probabilities of success in the event of a refusal." Finally, at just after 6 p.m. that day, Kalākaua's "forbidding countenance . . . dissolved into a smile, sweet as seraphs were, as, with apparent alacrity, the King reached for a pen and attached his signature to that instrument whereby he was reduced from the status of an autocrat to that of a constitutional sovereign."

The perspective of the Hawaiian League member who described this moment, however, was very different from that of Kalākaua's supporters, who believed the king had signed the document only under fear of death. Indeed, considering that the new constitution radically reined in Kalākaua's authority, there is little doubt he would have signed it unless he had been under dire threat. Even Lorrin Thurston, chief instigator of the new constitution, noted that, "Unquestionably the document was not in accordance with the law; neither was the Declaration of Independence from Great Britain. Both were revolutionary documents, which had to be forcibly effected and forcibly maintained."

The constitution also reduced the political power of native Hawaiians by imposing property requirements for membership in the house of nobles, and requiring voters to meet those same requirements in order to elect representatives to that body. There was no property qualification for voting or membership in the assembly; now, enfranchisement was no longer a right reserved for subjects of the kingdom but extended to all males of Hawaiian, American, or European descent who were in good standing with their taxes, who took an oath to support the new constitution, and who could read and write Hawaiian, English, or a European language.

However, the new constitution disenfranchised nearly eighteen thousand of the kingdom's subjects of Chinese ancestry. And because it gave the legislature the power to dismiss cabinets, the result was that no single leader, including the king, held power enough to effectively be able to lead the nation. In short, the new constitution produced no less than governance gridlock in the years ahead.

The new constitution outraged many native Hawaiians and, on July 25, about three hundred of them streamed into a Honolulu church for a meeting to discuss the upcoming election. "There is a little goodness in the new Constitution, but much to condemn," said one speaker, J. M. Poepoe, who urged the group to elect representatives who would oppose it. They "want to exercise the same power here as they do in their own country. They are doing it little by little, and it will not be long before Hawai'i becomes an entire republic."

Among those who believed that the king had been forced to sign, the document became known as the "Bayonet Constitution."

The morning of July 26, 1887, dawned clear as the steamer *Australia* made its way across the Pacific. By the time the queen and princess arose for their final day on board the ship, they could see the island of Moloka'i on the port side. After a few miles, they caught sight of O'ahu's tall mountains soaring above the clouds, and then they spotted the jagged promontory of Diamond Head. By 10:30 that morning the steamer had reached Waikīkī. After more than three months away, Kapi'olani and Lili'u had returned safely home.

The large crowd that gathered at the wharf to greet the arriving passengers erupted into cheers when the first of the royal party emerged. But the feeling on that unusually warm Tuesday morning in July was more than just gratitude for the safe delivery of the two chiefesses after their journey nearly halfway around the globe. The mournful expressions on the faces of the native Hawaiians in the crowd alerted Liliʻu that a far more serious chain of events had occurred during her absence than her brother had revealed to her in his letter.

She and Kapiʻolani were met on their arrival by the king's new cabinet, including Lorrin Thurston. Four months earlier, when she and the queen had left for England, Kalākaua's four-member cabinet had included three native Hawaiians. When they returned only white men occupied the cabinet posts, all of whom except Thurston were foreigners born in Britain and North America, and all of whom had been members of the Hawaiian League.

Liliʻu and the queen stepped into the carriage and went directly to ʻIolani Palace. Waiting for them at the entrance, Kalākaua greeted them brightly. But Liliʻu saw that he had suffered during their absence; to at least one member of the royal household, the king's sister seemed to make no attempt to conceal her feelings of disapproval after having learned of his many concessions. Even so, she was not insensitive to the toll of the past few months. "We could see on his countenance traces of the terrible strain through which he had passed, and evidences of the anxiety over the perilous position." Having witnessed for herself the pomp and adoration for Queen Victoria, signaling the British monarch's important symbolic hold over her empire, Liliʻu must have felt deeply apprehensive at the muted homecoming her royal party received, and anxious as well about King Kalākaua's increasingly shaky hold on the throne.

CHAPTER NINE

Be Not Deceived, 1887–1891

To some Westerners, the most beguiling treasure hidden in the Hawaiian Islands was a large estuary about half a day's carriage ride to the northwest of Honolulu. Ancient Hawaiians believed that the shark goddess Ka'ahupahau guarded its treacherous entrance, a narrow channel through coral reefs where saltwater mingled with fresh. But the Pearl River basin had lured a succession of British and American naval officers, carrying their magnetic compasses and surveyor's chains to gauge its suitability as a possible deep water port.

Oyster beds gave the area its English name and through much of the nineteenth century Hawaiians dove for these prizes in the harbor's waters. Sheep grazed on the largest island in the estuary. Gradually, starting in the 1870s, planters began transforming the dry plains to the west of it into sugar plantations. But Western surveyors quickly spotted the larger potential of what Hawaiians called Pu'uloa.

In 1825 the British government sent a surveyor to chart the estuary. After exploring the area on a launch, one of his colleagues concluded that "it would form a most excellent harbor as inside there is plenty of water to float the largest ship and room enough for the entire Navy of England."

Fifteen years later Commodore Charles Wilkes of the U.S. Exploring Expedition arrived on Oʻahu and mapped the entrance to the Pearl River estuary at the request of Kamehameha III. He reported that "the inlet has somewhat the appearance of a lagoon that has been partly filled up by alluvial deposits" and suggested that, if it were deepened, "it would afford the best and most capacious harbor in the Pacific."

The American interest in Puʻuloa only grew. In 1872, a military commission under secret instructions from the U.S. secretary of war examined various ports in the Hawaiian Islands for possible defensive and commercial purposes. A year later, King William Lunalilo became the first Hawaiian monarch to give serious consideration to offering the Pearl River harbor in exchange for the United States allowing Hawaiian sugar to enter the American market on a duty-free basis. The proposal offered America a defensive toehold in the Pacific in return for favorable terms to Hawaiian planters—the vast majority of whom were *haole*— selling their sugar into the American market. Trade and defense were becoming inextricably bound, and in neither case were native Hawaiians reaping the potential benefits.

In his public statements, King Kalākaua had long been opposed to ceding rights to what would become known as Pearl Harbor. Likewise, for years Gibson had argued against giving the estuary to the United States. In 1873 he founded a bilingual newspaper, the *Nuhou*, whose stated purpose was to prevent Hawaiʻi from ceding the basin to a foreign nation. In November of that year, Gibson printed a *mele* expressing Hawaiian opposition to giving away the estuary, without any apparent irony, despite his own grasping history on Lānaʻi. It ended with the warning:

I am a messenger forbidding you
To give away Puuloa,
Be not deceived by the merchants,
They are not only enticing you,

Making fair their faces, they are evil within;
Truly desiring annexation,
Greatly desiring their own good;
They have no thought of good for you,
A presuming set only are they,
A proud and haughty set,
Ever soliciting, at the same time flattering,
Desiring that you should all die,
That the kingdom may become theirs.

In the years following the chant's publication, the king and Gibson successfully fought off efforts by foreign diplomats, mainland politicians, and the islands' own powerful sugar planters to turn over the Pearl River basin to a foreign power. But that became difficult following Gibson's ignominious departure from the islands out the back door of the courthouse and straight onto a Spreckels-owned steamer, which carried him to San Francisco.

With Gibson's exit, the king—now stripped of virtually all of his powers except his ability to veto legislation—stood as the sole bulwark against Hawai'i's cession of Pearl Harbor. The kingdom first signed a reciprocity treaty with the United States in 1876 and had renewed it on a year-to-year basis since 1883. But by 1887 sugar planters in the southern United States had begun to decry what they saw as Hawai'i's unfair advantage in the sugar market. Meanwhile, George F. Edmunds, a U.S. senator from Vermont, journeyed west to California, where the connection to Hawai'i was stronger than in his home state, and returned to the nation's capital "inspired with the idea of acquiring Pearl Harbor." He proposed a Pearl Harbor amendment to the reciprocity treaty in a closed-door session of the Senate.

News of the secret amendment leaked out before Gibson's departure, amid rumors of land speculation in the area. Clearly, if the United States were to gain exclusive rights to the Pearl River basin, widening the entrance channel and dredging the harbor, the surrounding lands could become vastly more valuable to landowners, as more people settled there and businesses sprang up to serve them. So when Gibson and the rest of the cabinet resigned on July 1, 1887, it opened the way for a new set of ministers who supported swapping rights to Pearl Harbor for a sweet commercial treaty with the United States.

America's rivals in the Pacific were not pleased with this prospect. Following the Paulet episode in 1843, Britain and France had issued a joint declaration opposing "the acquisition by the United States of a harbour or preferential Concession in any part of the Hawaiian Kingdom [that] would infallibly lead to the loss of its independence and the extinction of the Hawaiian Nationality. On the above grounds, Her Majesty's Government could not view with indifference the cession of a Harbour to any foreign Power."

Britain and France, in other words, had been willing to keep their hands off the islands for the previous four decades as long as some other contender didn't sweep in ahead of them. Assured that Her Majesty's ships could continue to visit the area, however, the British decided to drop the matter instead of picking a diplomatic fight. Meanwhile, the U.S. Congress swiftly ratified the reciprocity treaty with the Pearl Harbor amendment and Kalākaua's new cabinet urged him to accept it. He did so, apparently reluctantly, and only after insisting on attaching a note explaining that the treaty would not impair Hawaiian sovereignty and jurisdiction.

The editorial writers and the street orators of the kingdom's Hawaiian-language newspapers reacted with dismay, particularly Nāwahī, the respected native Hawaiian journalist, legislator, and Emmaite. He had predicted in 1876 that reciprocity "would be the first step of annexation later on, and the Kingdom, its flag, its independence, and its people will be naught." Nāwahī also objected to cession of the Pearl River area.

Lili'u likewise was distressed by Kalākaua's deal with the Americans for Pearl Harbor. On Monday, September 26, 1887, she wrote, "Today—a day of importance in H. History. King signed a lease of Pearl river to U. States for eight years to get R. Treaty." Seeing the lease as an unequal swap for a treaty that benefited the island kingdom's sugar planters, she concluded darkly, "It should not have been done."

After a slow twenty-four-day passage across the Pacific, Gibson disembarked from the sailing brig *John D. Spreckels* on August 6, 1887, and newspaper reporters sought out the exhausted and hoarse exiled statesman for his comments on the revolution in Hawai'i. "The new Constitution has many admirable features about it," Gibson said, as reported by the *New York Times* the next day. "Still, it is what might be termed a shotgun or rifle Constitution. The King only proclaimed it through fear of his life."

Wearing a long black coat and high silk hat, the old man climbed into a carriage, stopped briefly to meet with Hawai'i's consul general in San Francisco, and made his way to the Italianate-style Occidental Hotel on the corner of Bush and Montgomery streets in San Francisco's downtown financial district. There he collapsed on the bed, summoning just enough energy to ask a chambermaid to light the gas fire in his room.

Gibson wrote and received letters from Honolulu. But because he was convinced he was under surveillance in San Francisco and that his correspondence was being read by spies, he insisted on sending his letters through friends. Meanwhile, Gibson sought to commit his version of events to paper, since he felt the "reformers" who had chased him out of Honolulu had ignored his years of faithful service to the Hawaiian people and his brave, but increasingly unpopular, defense of their interests. Since his excommunication from the Mormon Church, Gibson had joined the Catholic Church, in whose rituals and incense he found solace for what a hymn writer might have called his sin-sick soul.

A fire broke out that fall in the Little Grotto of Lourdes, a small chapel in San Francisco that was part of the same mission where he had stored his manuscript. Gibson panicked and rushed out to witness the flames himself failing to save his writings but catching cold. By early January, he felt well enough to take off his overcoat on his way to have his photograph taken. But he caught a chill and died on January 21, 1888.

According to the newspapers who reported his death, his last word was "Hawai'i."

Priests performed a requiem mass for Gibson at St. Mary's Cathedral in San Francisco. Then his body, embalmed and set in a black, gold-trimmed coffin, was placed aboard the *Zealandia*, which was returning to the islands covered with a Hawaiian flag. In a procession up King Street with a hundred and fifty or so members of Hawaiian societies, the coffin of the kingdom's former prime minister was set in the center of Arion Hall, behind Honolulu's Opera House, for viewing. Peering through a plate of glass the public could glimpse Gibson's face one last time.

The next day, streams of visitors came to view the body as it lay in state. Native Hawaiians outnumbered *haole* and, unlike most funerals of white residents of the islands, native Hawaiians bearing *kāhili*, the feathered staffs of the *ali'i*, flanked Gibson's body.

One visitor was Judge Sanford B. Dole, accompanied by his brother George and Lorrin Thurston. As he was leaving the nearby Ali'iōlani Hale, the government building where trials took place, he turned to his companions and asked, "Well, shall we go and see old Gibson?"

The three men joined the crowd moving past his coffin. Thurston was shocked to see that the embalming fluid had turned the skin very dark, eerily contrasting with Gibson's long white beard and silver locks.

They left the reception room and stepped out onto the street. "What do you think of it?," Dole asked his brother and Thurston,

After a few seconds' pause, George answered, "Well, I think his complexion is approximating the color of his soul."

Lili'u was disturbed by the accounts she heard of Gibson's treatment by the group she and others had began to refer to as "the missionary party." When she heard the story of how a missionary descendant had shouted "Hang them!" "Hang them!" she began to question how he could have forgotten the spirit of religion his parents taught. Unlike the Christians who had first arrived in the islands in the 1820s, devoting themselves to spreading the good word, Lili'u came to believe that many of the sons and grandsons of those same missionaries had failed to absorb the forgiving message of Christ.

Her brother, likewise, identified his enemies as mainly the sons and grandsons of missionaries and he was at a loss as to how to handle them. The Honolulu Rifles—now an overtly military force made up of clerks and stock boys from *haole* shops—were a threat to the monarchy. To Kalākaua's dismay there was no readily apparent way to disband them without starting a fight. As Lili'u noted in her diary that November, "The King, the Court, the City wants to get rid of the Rifles & yet do not dare to. How—laughable." The distance between Lili'u and her brother was growing at a time when their enemies were organizing against them.

Hawai'i's gracious and well-spoken king, who just a few years earlier had been embraced by fellow monarchs around the world, was trapped by his personal financial woes. That fall, the cabinet had tried to persuade Kalākaua to return one of the "gifts" he'd received for the opium license, but in doing so it discovered that the king's debts totaled a quarter of a million dollars (more than $5.5 million today) and that he was unable to make restitution to the Chinese man who had given him this bribe in hopes of winning the license.

To dig his way out of this financial mess, Kalākaua in November of 1887 agreed to assign his private estate and crown land revenues to three trustees, who would manage his finances for him. A three-person commission had administered and managed the crown lands since 1865. For the first time the income previously spent by the king at his own discretion was placed under control of the trustees. Kalākaua's lavish spending had cost him control of his personal finances, even though he'd chosen the trustees himself. An intelligent man who was truly ashamed by the depths to which he had fallen, Kalākaua wrote to Robert Wilcox: "It is true that I have been humbled, that I have been mortified, that I have been crushed . . ."

The king earned some much-needed income in a venture that also helped preserve Hawaiian culture. Not long after Gibson's funeral, a New York firm partly owned by Mark Twain published *The Legends and*

Myths of Hawaii: The Fables and Folk-Lore of a Strange People by His Ha-waiian Majesty Kalākaua, a dense collection of native Hawaiian folklore, which linked the islanders' tales with those of other ancient cultures, such as the story of Hina, the Helen of Hawai'i. More than five hundred pages long, it was the first major book of its kind with a native Hawaiian named as its author. Twain, who had generated so much interest in Hawai'i through his lectures across the American continent, called the book "very curious, & new . . . full of romantic interest."

Yet the king continued to face almost daily ridicule from the white merchant class, including from the pulpit on Sundays. The Hale Nauā met wilting sarcasm from the *haole*-owned press and became the butt of jokes, centered on a partner-swapping game called *'ume,* supposedly played at or after the meetings, in which a ball of twine was rolled toward the object of one's desire. The *Gazette*, for instance, wrote, "The full dress is believed to consist of a ball of twine and a pocket handkerchief."

Understandably, living in Honolulu became oppressive for the king; in addition to being stripped of much power, constantly battling the cabinet, and facing ridicule in public, he was also financially strapped. So that spring he and Kapi'olani retreated to Kona, partly in an effort to reduce their spending. The king wrote to his chamberlain in April of 1888—five months after the three commissioners had been put in charge to pay his debts—that he could eat for far less than in the capital:

> I can get my poi for less that one-half of $70.00 a month. The meat from our ranch we can live on $108.00 a month. . . . I do not see any other alternative than to make further reductions and live entirely in the country here. We won't be obliged to entertain but if we live in Honolulu the expenses can never be kept down.

The king had hoped a loan from a London firm might bail him out. But that effort stalled and so, during a visit with Lili'u at Washington Place late in the fall of 1887, shortly after his fifty-first birthday, he pulled out letters from the company, hoping to convince his sister that he could solve his problems if only she would agree to sign away some of her lands. Liliʻu refused, explaining sheʼd been advised against doing so.

Kalākaua returned, hoping to talk her into affixing her signature to the documents. Once again she refused, holding her ground. That night, she wrote in her diary about her brother, "How sorry I am for him for he appears to be anxious to make up for the past."

Yet her refusal drove the siblings apart even further. A few weeks later, amid rumors of plans by Hawaiian loyalists to raise a company of militiamen, Liliʻu heard through a Hawaiian that the king had said she was a *kipi*—a rebel or a traitor. That split only grew deeper as both Hawaiians and *haole* approached her about taking over the throne if her brother were deposed. An eighteen-year-old white man representing the white merchants came just before Christmas of 1887, when Liliʻu was in her country house. Would she accept the throne if her brother was overthrown? Being approached by such a young messenger offended the princess.

"No," Liliʻu answered indignantly.

A few days later, a man with considerably more influence in Honolulu approached her: William R. Castle, who was a member of the Hawaiian legislature and a principal in what was by then the kingdomʼs leading sugar factor and merchandiser, Castle & Cooke. Arriving at ten that morning, Castle asked Liliʻu if she would take the throne or, if not, "go to the King and influence him to sign bills." Liliʻu replied she "could not sit on a throne where violence was used to my brother." She assumed, it seems, they would once again use their bayonets on him.

Still, Liliʻuʼs doubts about Kalākaua were growing. As the holiday season passed, Hawaiians also began seeking her out. On January 16, 1888, two Hawaiian loyalists paid her a visit in order to strategize with her on how to convince Kalākaua to step down from the throne. Liliʻuʼs suggestion was that they advise him to abdicate for a year, until the dustup over the opium affair settled down. During that time, she would rule until he returned. Evidently, Liliʻu felt she could do a better job governing than her brother.

The two men made their case to the king, as Lili'u waited in the little cottage on the grounds of Washington Place known as Hinano Bower. For years, it had been her refuge from the critical eye of her mother-in-law. But by then Mary Dominis was ailing. Perhaps Lili'u pondered the changes that time had brought to her domestic situation, or maybe she just passed the time hoping that her brother would agree to step down from the throne. But Kalākaua declined. Had he guessed his sister was behind the request?

Tensions between the royal siblings soon bubbled up again. Two days after the loyalists asked Kalākaua to abdicate, Lili'u attended a breakfast at the palace in honor of some visitors from Scotland. Her brother made a passing comment that shocked her—something along the lines of "Supposing I should sell the country, what then?" Lili'u didn't bother to hide her look of displeasure. Kalākaua, who had noticed this, again called her *kipi*, behind her back. When Lili'u learned he'd called her this, she wrote in her diary, "What he said on Wednesday was a threat. I don't care what he does but I fear that Million will burn his fingers." She apparently thought he was corrupt.

One visitor to the islands, Robert Louis Stevenson, the poet and novelist, who arrived in Honolulu in the afternoon of January 24, 1889, aboard a ninety-four-foot chartered yacht named the *Casco*, would become a staunch supporter of the Hawaiian royal family. The famed Scottish author of *Treasure Island* and *The Strange Case of Dr. Jekyll and Mr. Hyde*, was greeted by his stepdaughter Isobel Strong and her husband the artist Joe Strong, who lived what one biographer called "the strange life of the Pacific whites—at once trashy and exalted," as members of the inner circle of court life centered around 'Iolani Palace.

The Honolulu that greeted the frail, sunken-chested writer was a far cry from the cluster of grass houses and the dry plains that the first company of missionaries encountered nearly seven decades earlier. Shining with electric lights and bustling from the comings and goings at the wharf, Stevenson described it as a modern town, "brisk with traffic, and the palace with its guards." He also noted "Mr. Berger's band with their uniforms and outlandish instruments," referring to the Royal Hawaiian Band and its German conductor.

Honolulu was starting to resemble an American town. Mule-drawn streetcars carried holiday makers and mothers with children out to Waikīkī as well as the shopkeepers and stock boys out to the racetrack and pleasure gardens of Kapiʻolani Park, the plain beneath Diamond Head where Cleghorn, Dominis, other members of the royal circle in 1876 had formed a private corporation to develop the area as an exclusive residential retreat. Honolulu had a telephone system before many American cities did so and even boasted its own Opera House, decorated with red velvet, gilt, gas lights, and a drop curtain decorated with a bucolic scene of Italy's Lake Como flanked by purple mountains.

Most of all, the capital of the island kingdom had a vibrant social scene, with endless suppers, card parties, and *lūʻau*. Stevenson, accompanied by his wife and mother, were immediately drawn into the busy court life by the Strongs. One such afternoon took place on February 3, 1889, when King Kalākaua and Liliʻu were the special guests at a *lūʻau* thrown by a local resident and held at the Waikīkī bungalow borrowed by the Stevensons, decorated with such "South Sea curiousities" as war clubs, idols, pearl shells, and stone axes.

The table that day was overflowing with dozens and dozens of bowls of food and crowded with bottles of champagne. The menu included chicken, roast pig, raw fish, seaweed, which Hawaiians called *limu*, roasted kukui nuts, and baked dog—one of the king's favorite dishes. Sitting on woven mats, Kalākaua and Liliʻu presided at the head of a table, with Stevenson on their right and the novelist's mother on their left. During the evening, Fanny Stevenson, Robert's wife, presented the king with a golden pearl from their voyages and Stevenson stood to read a sonnet he had composed to accompany the gift, ending "The ocean jewel to the island king."

Afterward, Liliʻu and Stevenson found time to talk quietly with each other on the bungalow's *lānai*. All the guests were inebriated by the day's end, but the king especially lived up to his reputation as the Merrie Monarch. Writing to his friend and literary agent in Britain two days after the *lū'au*, Stevenson described the king as "a very fine, intelligent fellow, but O, Charles! what a crop for drink! He carries it, too, like a mountain with a sparrow on its shoulders. We calculated five bottles of champagne in three hours and a half (afternoon) and the sovereign quite presentable, although perceptibly more dignified, at the end."

When not entertaining, Stevenson padded around the bungalow in his pajamas, playing his flageolet in bed when he wasn't writing. He also struck up a friendship with Princess Ka'iulani, the daughter of his fellow Scotsman Cleghorn and the late Princess Likelike. The Cleghorn's ten-acre Waikīkī estate was within walking distance of the Stevensons' bungalow. Ka'iulani's father had transformed what once had been a mosquito-plagued marshland into an estate where peacocks strutted through the gardens, their high-pitched screams piercing the quiet days, and the air perfumed by the flowers called by the same name in Hawaiian—*pīkake*, or jasmine. It was named 'Āinahau, "the cooler place," because of the refreshing winds that came down from the mountains.

Cleghorn, a talented horticulturalist, had poured his energy into turning 'Āinahau into a tropical paradise. Visitors would pass *kapu* sticks at the gate, forbidding trespass and signifying divine royalty, then follow a road bordered by towering date palms. Then came mango, teak, and cinnamon trees, hidden glades, lily ponds, and fishponds where tortoises basked in the sun. Flowers bloomed all year round, including fourteen varieties of hibiscus. The huge tree in front of the main house, known as "Ka'iulani's banyan," was believed to be the progenitor of all the banyans in Honolulu.

The Stevensons and the Cleghorns visited back and forth, with the young princess inviting Stevenson to enjoy some "good Scotch *kaukau*," Hawaiian for "food," and the Scotsman, in turn, sitting under the spreading banyan tree at 'Āinahau, regaled her with tales of England, which she was about to visit for the first time, and lent her books.

As the date of her departure approached, Stevenson wrote a farewell poem to the princess in the small red autograph book that she planned to bring with her to boarding school in England.

> Forth from her land to mine she goes,
> The island maid, the island rose,
> Light of heart and bright of face,
> The daughter of a double race.
> Her islands here in Southern sun
> Shall mourn their Kaiulani gone.
> And I, in her dear banyan's shade,
> Look vainly for my little maid.

Ka'iulani and her father departed from Honolulu on May 10, 1889, aboard the SS *Umatilla*, wished farewell by a large crowd on the wharf. As the ship drew out of the harbor, heading to San Francisco, Ka'iulani expected to be gone no more than a year or so.

Her friend Stevenson sensed the changes under way in the kingdom and already felt a sense of loss. He had just returned to Honolulu on the day of their departure from a trip to the rural Kona coast. From his travels to its quieter corners, he'd gained a more critical perspective on the changes being wrought on it by the powerful white foreigners who now controlled its fortunes. To a friend, he wrote,

> I have just been a week away alone on the lee coast of Hawaii . . . a lovely week among God's best—at least God's sweetest—works, Polynesians. It has bettered me greatly. If I could only stay there the time that remains, I could get my work done and be happy; but the care of a large, costly, and no' just preceesely forrit-gaun family keeps me in vile Honolulu, where I am always out of sorts, amidst heat and cold and cesspools and beastly haole. What is a haole? You are one and so, I am sorry to say, am I. After so long a dose of whites, it was a blessing to get among Polynesians again, even for a week.

Hawaiian warriors in their canoe, as depicted by John Webber, the official artist of Captain James Cook's final voyage of discovery.
(State Archives of Hawai'i)

This 1837 drawing by Louis-Jules Masselot depicts the *hale kauila*, the king's reception hall. Kamehameha III and his entourage, on the raised dais, confer with crew members of a French frigate and a British sloop-of-war.
(State Archives of Hawai'i)

In 1820, American missionaries arrived in the islands and began teaching the native population Western mores. Missionary Gerrit Judd, left, accompanied the princes Alexander Liholiho, center, and Lot Kamehameha, right, on a tour of the U.S. and Europe in 1849.
(State Archives of Hawai'i)

Left, an early photo of Lili'u, then called Lydia Paki Kamaka'eha, around 1853—age fifteen. At right, Lili'u's hanai sister, Bernice Pauahi, who was the last direct descendent of Kamehameha the Great and married a haole, Charles Bishop. (State Archives of Hawai'i)

Lili'u as a young married woman, 1863 or 1864. Like her hanai sister, Pauahi, before her, Lili'u chose a haole, or non-Hawaiian, for a husband. (State Archives of Hawai'i)

John Dominis and Lili'u married September 16, 1862. (State Archives of Hawai'i)

David Kalakaua, Lili'u's biological brother. In a contentious election in 1874, he was voted king of the islands. (State Archives of Hawai'i)

Honolulu's waterfront as seen from the harbor, circa 1873. (State Archives of Hawai'i)

When their brother Leleiohoku died in 1877, Kalakaua named Liliʻu as his successor and bestowed upon her the name Liliʻuokalani. (State Archives of Hawaiʻi)

Victoria Kaʻiulani Cleghorn, born in October 1875 and pictured here in 1881 or 1882, around age six. (State Archives of Hawaiʻi)

Claus Spreckels arrived in Hawai'i in 1876 and soon became the islands' "sugar king." (Spreckels family collection)

William Gibson, the "Shepherd Saint of Lanai." (State Archives of Hawai'i)

When Kalakaua circled the globe in 1881, rumors were rife that he intended to sell the islands—prompting the *Wasp* to publish the cartoon at right showing him auctioning off the kingdom to the highest bidder. (Kahn Collection, State Archives of Hawai'i)

A LILIPUT KINGDOM FOR SALE CHEAP.

Kalakaua on the steps of 'Iolani Palace, which was completed in 1882 and featured electric lights four years before the White House in Washington had them. (State Archives of Hawai'i)

Performers sing and dance the hula on the 'Iolani Palace grounds in 1885, in honor of Kalakaua's birthday. In the background is the pavilion where Kalakaua staged an elaborate coronation ceremony in 1883. (State Archives of Hawai'i)

Harvesting sugar cane,
circa 1885.
(State Archives of Hawaiʻi)

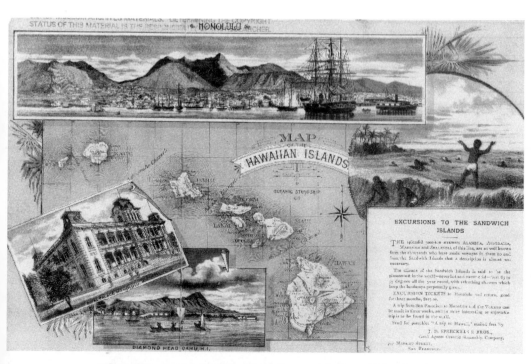

This 1887 map advertised the Spreckels steamship line, which enjoyed
a monopoly with Kalakaua's support. (Bishop Museum)

In 1887, Lili'u accompanied Queen Kap'iolani to England to attend the jubilee celebrations marking the fiftieth year of Queen Victoria's reign. In this formal portrait, Kap'iolani (in the foreground) wears a gown trimmed with peacock, while Lili'u's coiffure is embellished with a diamond butterfly brooch.
(State Archives of Hawai'i)

A painting of the scene of Queen Victoria's jubilee service in Westminster Abbey where Kap'iolani, and Lili'u occupy positions of honor.
(*Queen Victoria's Golden Jubilee Service* by William Ewart Lockhart, The Royal Collection © 2011 Her Majesty Queen Elizabeth II)

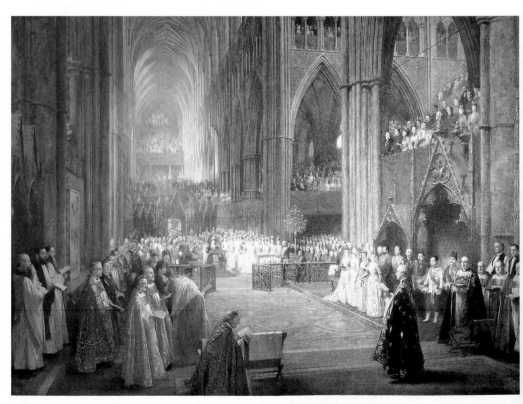

✦ ✦ ✦

Lili'u, like Stevenson, was also growing weary of the "beastly *haole*." In the summer of 1889 she escaped "vile Honolulu" to spend a few weeks on Kaua'i, where the slower pace of life and the reverence for *ali'i* were a relief from the dissonant clamor of the capital's politics. She visited the plantation town of Waimea, where a Russian-built stone fort lay in ruins at the mouth of the silvery Waimea River. Captain Cook had first landed there more than a century earlier and she was eager to find out how a small project of hers there was faring.

Several years earlier, she had arranged to bring three pairs of the rapidly vanishing 'ō'ō bird from Hawai'i Island to Kaua'i, hoping they would form a new colony. A honey feeder similar to the shy momo, the 'ō'ō was a black bird prized for the yellow tuft of feathers beneath its wings, which the Hawaiians plucked out and used in the feather cloaks of their chiefs. One of her hosts had been trying to raise the birds, but Lili'u soon learned that only a single pair were now known to be living there, taking sustenance from the nectar of the mimosa bush that grew near her host's house. "They are true Hawaiians," Lili'u wrote. "Flowers are necessary for their very life."

The year had begun with the death of "Mother Dominis" in April and by the time Lili'u returned from Kaua'i by schooner she felt restored. She made her way home to Washington Place and found her husband in bed, suffering from rheumatism but well cared for by their servants. She then left to visit her home in Pālama, a district on the west side of Honolulu. As she was about to leave, she heard someone on the front steps. Lili'u went to the door and looked through the grating, reluctant to open it to a stranger.

Standing there was Robert W. Wilcox, a tall, slender half-Hawaiian man who was then thirty-four years old. Lili'u had befriended Wilcox, the son of a New England sea captain and an *ali'i* woman, giving him permission to use the Pālama home in her absence.

In 1881 Wilcox had been one of the three young Hawaiian men whom Gibson and Kalākaua had sent abroad for a military education. In 1883,

Wilcox had sent Kalākaua a copy of Machiavelli's *The Prince*. He had returned to Honolulu from Italy at about the same time that Liliʻu had returned from her trip to London. Trained as an engineer, Wilcox fully expected the king to reward him with an important government post. Because Kalākaua had lost many of his powers under the new constitution, no such job was forthcoming.

The plight of Wilcox and his young bride, an Italian contessa, moved Liliʻu. She took the young couple into her home and petitioned her brother on their behalf. Yet the contessa felt only disdain for Liliʻu, whom she believed was intelligent but took her role as heir apparent too seriously. As for her relations with Kalākaua, the contessa believed Liliʻu felt "a queenly scorn" for "her brother whose weakness and lack of capacity she understands, and she actually aspires nonetheless to rob him of the throne and put herself in his place. With this goal in mind, doubtless, did she wish us to be close at hand: my husband who is basically a big boy, does not realize that he is only an instrument of this woman's ambition, and he follows her advice."

By the time Liliʻu saw Wilcox standing on her doorstep on July 29, 1889, looking anxious and haggard, the contessa had left him. For months he had been holding secret meetings at Liliʻu's Pālama house, whose shutters entirely closed off the interior from the view of anyone who might be outside. Several Italians, a German, a Belgian, and another part-Hawaiian attended the early gatherings organized and run by Wilcox; later, some Chinese and native Hawaiians joined in. The group's overall goal was revolution—overthrowing the hated *haole*-controlled government. But the precise details of what Wilcox planned are unclear: it appears he wanted to depose Kalākaua, whom he viewed as having weakly submitted to the Bayonet Constitution, and put Liliʻu on the throne instead. Whatever the case, Liliʻu was aware of his intentions.

Wilcox had begun buying firearms. After gathering in Pālama on the evening of July 29, the band of about eighty men set out a few hours before dawn to march on ʻIolani Palace, lightly armed with thirty-five rifles, a scattering of ricebird guns, and some pistols. Wilcox wore an

Italian military uniform. Inspired perhaps by the Italian revolutionary Giuseppe Garibaldi, he issued red shirts to his men. In his pocket, Wilcox carried a copy of the new constitution he expected Kalākaua to sign.

As daybreak approached, the company reached the palace, which was then surrounded by an eight-foot-high masonry wall. Wilcox's troops positioned themselves on the palace grounds and across the street at the government building, dragging out four small cannons to guard the four gates. By the time they arrived the king had left the palace, tipped off about the attempted coup. Accompanied by his longtime private secretary Curtis ʻIaukea, they rode through the silent streets of Honolulu to the wharf. Kalākaua spent the night at his boathouse so he was not at the palace when Wilcox's men arrived.

Early the next morning, Liliʻu rose from her bed at Washington Place and took a walk in the garden, which bordered the palace grounds. She saw troops running toward the armory, some dressing themselves as they ran. Liliʻu stopped a young man who worked at the customhouse to ask what was going on. He told her that Wilcox and his men had taken control of the palace. Her appearance on the street that morning took on a different meaning to a white observer, who later wrote that "Mrs. Dominis" was "riding around that day covered in leis," as if anticipating that she shortly would triumphantly take her brother's place on the throne.

Later that morning Liliʻu heard shots ringing from the palace, which lasted intermittently all day long, some "whizzing past our house." Led by Robert Waipa Parker, the government had stationed sharpshooters on the roof of the Opera House and other buildings surrounding the palace yard. Wilcox and about thirty of his men surrendered, but others took refuge in a small, delicately latticed bungalow on the northern corner of the palace grounds, which became the focus of intense rifle fire.

That was not all. Two white men on government orders had climbed out onto the roof of the Hawaiian Hotel's stables. They hurled crude bombs made out of small metal spikes attached to sticks of dynamite off the roof of the bungalow, creating a huge boom and explosion. Six of Wilcox's men died that day and a dozen more lay wounded.

What came to be known as the Wilcox Rebellion was an abject failure. Yet when Wilcox was tried before a jury of native Hawaiians he was found not guilty of the charge of conspiracy. There were widespread rumors afterward not only that had Lili'u known of the secret meetings held by Wilcox in her Pālama home, but that she had sympathized with the rebels in their attempt to depose her brother.

The *haole* cabinet suspected that the revolutionaries were backed by at least some members of the House of Kalākaua in their efforts to topple the government. To prevent future insurrections, it swiftly removed all munitions and military equipment from the palace grounds to the police headquarters, lowered the high masonry wall around the palace grounds three feet or so, to less than half its previous height, disbanded the native battalion of Hawaiian Volunteers, and cut the size of the King's Guard.

Lili'u later wrote almost wistfully about Wilcox and his attempted revolution: "His enthusiasm was great, but not supported by good judgment or proper discretion. His efforts failed; and indeed, it is not easy to see how under the circumstances it could have been otherwise." Had she hoped it would succeed?

Wilcox was cheered in the courthouse after his acquittal and became a resistance hero. Taking up the mantle of the late Walter Murray Gibson in championing the cause of native Hawaiians, he ran for a Honolulu seat in the House of Representatives. With fiery language, he decried the white "missionary party" and maintained, "Today our homeland is being run not for the good of the people but to enhance the wealth of the few."

Wilcox won his seat by a three-to-one margin and the elections of that year swept out many reform party candidates, bringing in those who were in favor of restoring rights to native Hawaiians. Within a few months he and other legislators had managed to oust the hated cabinet and replace it with a more moderate group of ministers. Wilcox, positioning himself on the radical end of his party, along with the more moderate Joseph Nāwahī began pushing for a constitutional convention, hoping to complete through legislative methods what Wilcox's rebellion had failed to achieve.

At the same time, others were introducing bills amending the 1887 constitution, including limiting voting privileges to only subjects of the kingdom (versus residents) and reducing the property qualification for voting from $3,000 to $1,000, which would result in more native Hawaiians being able to vote.

But Wilcox grew frustrated over the slow progress toward a constitutional convention and his verbal attacks on the floor of the House became racially tinged and even violent. The English-language press quoted him as saying that legislators who voted against the convention "ought to be torn limb from limb." That same day, speaking on another subject, he said, "If the people are not granted their rights the streets will be sticky with blood." In part because of this kind of rabid rhetoric, the effort to draw up a new constitution stalled and Wilcox's party split into moderate and radical factions.

Such talk was soon overtaken by a far greater worry: the passage in the United States of the McKinley tariff bill, which President Benjamin Harrison signed into law on October 1, 1890. Under this law, the financial advantage that sugar from Hawai'i enjoyed in the U.S. market through the reciprocity treaty was wiped out, as raw sugar from all foreign countries would be admitted into the United States duty free, while sugar produced in the United States would receive a bounty of two cents a pound. The new law was set to go into effect on April 1, 1891, and it would effectively annul the treaty for which the islands' planters had fought so hard, and for which Kalākaua had sacrificed exclusive access to Pearl Harbor.

The threat posed by the McKinley Act to the kingdom's economy was severe, for Hawai'i by then had become dangerously dependent on sugar: production had quadrupled over the previous decade to nearly 260 million pounds by 1890. The plantations now covered so much arable land that they were the main business of the islands; sugar made up the vast majority of the nation's output, representing $12.16 million of Hawai'i's total exports of $13 million in 1890. Either directly through exports or indirectly through businesses supporting the trade, King Sugar ruled the Hawaiian Islands.

And who ruled King Sugar? As of October 1, 1890, there were seventy sugar plantations, mills, and cane growers in Hawai'i. Forty of the largest were incorporated, with the value of their capital stock totaling $28.4 million that year. By comparison, the estate of Bernice Pauahi Bishop the year she died in 1884 was valued by the government at just $800,000, a tiny fraction of the value of the kingdom's sugar trade. And of those large sugar producers, Americans held the majority of the stock—some $22.45 million, or 79 percent. By far the largest producer was the Hawaiian Commercial and Sugar Company, controlled by Claus Spreckels and his sons. The second largest was William G. Irwin, a Briton who was Spreckels's business partner.

The other leading British sugar magnate in the islands was Theo H. Davies, a friend to Archibald Cleghorn and his daughter Ka'iulani. Overall, the British were a distant second in terms of the dollar value of their shares in Hawaiian sugar companies, trailing far behind the Americans. Native Hawaiian ownership of shares in sugar corporations was a scant $266,250, or less than 1 percent, with their shares held mostly in the Waimanalo Sugar Co. Lili'u was one of those shareholders and she carefully watched the price of the stock, buying and selling shares over the years, tracking them in her diary.

It is not clear whether Kalākaua also owned shares in sugar companies. But he was well aware of the importance of sugar to Hawai'i's economy and remained willing to exercise his remaining personal appeal and charisma on its behalf. Now reduced to little more than a figurehead, David Kalākaua had lost much of the gaiety and expansiveness that had charmed so many during his trip around the world. Staffers noticed that weariness had come over him. On November 14, 1890, he managed to preside over the end of the legislative session for that year, but illness prevented him from attending a formal dinner the following week.

Nonetheless, the planters soon approached the monarch about performing a crucial service for them and the kingdom: traveling to the United States to try to regain Hawai'i's favored nation status. The following day, some of those same people attended the celebrations for the king's fifty-fourth birthday, which included fireworks in the evening and the somewhat threatening spectacle of a new all-white organization called the Sons of Hawaii, mounted on some of the city's finest horses and galloping into the palace yard, with each *haole* rider carrying a lit torch. Many of the horsemen were the sons and grandsons of Hawai'i's missionary settlers who seemed intent, Lili'u wrote, on outdoing "those of native birth in their manifestations of loyalty and respect."

Soon after Kalākaua's birthday celebration, Lili'u took to her bed for three weeks, citing a "slight fever" and exhaustion. Her brother visited her at her home, informing her of his plans to visit the United States and appointing her as regent in his absence. Unhappy he was leaving and concerned about her own ability to cope, Lili'u later wrote that she had implored Kalākaua to stay by arguing not only that he was in failing health but also that, if anything should happen to him, she might have difficulty serving as the acting ruler.

Her arguments failed to sway him. On November 25, 1890, he bade farewell to his sister and wife at the palace, made his way to the wharf, and climbed onto a barge that took him to the USS *Charleston*, whose commander had offered to take Kalākaua to San Francisco as his guest. Remaining in the palace, Lili'u and Kapi'olani heard the guns from the warships fire a royal salute. But in Honolulu harbor an ill omen had appeared: schools of the reddish-pink fish that the Hawaiians called the *alalau* appeared—a sign that an *ali'i* would soon die. Hawaiians asked, "*O wai keia?*" "Who is it?"

By midmorning on December 4 the *Charleston* had passed the rocky outcroppings of the Farallon Islands and entered the mouth of the San

Francisco bay. When it reached the pier, Kalākaua was greeted by cheering crowds and a twenty-one-gun salute. Wearing a loose blue suit and a straw hat, he stepped into a carriage drawn by four horses, which made its way to the Palace Hotel on New Montgomery Street. Built in 1875, the Palace was one of the largest and most luxurious hotels in the world, with eight hundred rooms and the kind of engineering marvels that Kalākaua loved: electric bells in all the rooms, air-conditioning, even novel hydraulic elevators, dubbed "rising rooms."

The king hoped that the temperate climate of California would improve his health. But instead of resting upon his arrival Kalākaua embarked on an exhausting round of social engagements, including an especially memorable dinner at the Bohemian Club—where Claus Spreckels was a member—and musicians performed a specially arranged version of "Aloha Oe." As one of the musicians who played that evening recalled, "His Majesty turned to our President, and with beaming countenance said in that soft and gentle way of his, and in a tone as full of deep affection and love, *that piece* was composed by *my Sister* . . . we repeated it, and played it often during the evening—Every one was touched by this charming incident."

He was also feted on another evening by the Spreckels family, and the king hosted a late-night party at his suite in the Palace Hotel attended by a journalist named Ashton Stevens. Many years later, Stevens recalled the champagne-soaked night in which Kalākaua played the role of exotic Polynesian king to a tee. He sat in a high-backed chair. Once the naval officers left at midnight, the king's favorite *hula* dancer appeared, performing what Stevens described as "a chaste and comely measure." After more champagne, the journalist felt emboldened to ask him how it felt to rule a kingdom.

> He graciously answered that it didn't feel so good to be a King as it used to before the Missionaries got to plaguing him with embarrassing reforms for his people. No more Sunday picnics, no more all-night hulas, no more gin. The Missionaries, he said, had taken all the fun out of being a King.

To lift the mood of the evening, Kalākaua then led the group in song with his clear tenor voice, and the merriment and drinking continued until dawn. As Stevens recalled, "My last groggy memory is of kneeling while he bent down and decorated me by pinning a Monopole cork to the shirt bosom he had autographed . . . and bade me arise: 'Sir Knight of the Twinkling Banjo.'"

Kalākaua's warm reception in the United States, particularly after the humiliating drubbings he had taken over the past few years in Honolulu, must have been gratifying to him. Far from the labyrinth of politics in the kingdom's capital, he wrote with relief on January 1, 1891,

A spontaneous ovation. I have never seen the like before . . . Not one moments rest. Travelling day and night. Receptions, Balls, dinners, Dinners, Masonic Initiation. All combined it makes no difference Sun Shine, Rain, Stormy, &c its all the same. Wonder that I am not half dead yet.

Anyhow everything has its effect and I have learnt and have seen a great deal. Nice country. Good People and all that but awfully damned cold. Whi'o!

To escape San Francisco's unusually cold weather that December he headed south aboard a parlor car provided by the Central Pacific Railway. In San Diego, he stayed at one of the Spreckels family's most elegant investments in the growing port city, the Hotel del Coronado. It is not clear whether the ailing king climbed the hotel's red-roofed turret to look down upon the beachcombers or across the Pacific, toward Hawai'i. Yet surely it must have occurred to him that the Spreckels family, although not of royal blood, owned a commercial palace that dwarfed his own in Honolulu.

It was on his return north, during a three-day stopover in Santa Barbara, that the king suffered a mild stroke. Returning to the Palace Hotel, Kalākaua was attended by the head surgeon of the U.S. Pacific Fleet.

The doctor diagnosed him with Bright's disease, a serious kidney ailment now known as nephritis, with symptoms that included edema, or swelling, and presence of albumin in the urine. It is likely the king had been suffering from it for several years without diagnosis or treatment, as well as cirrhosis of the liver. He remained in bed for more than a week but stubbornly insisted on attending an event on the evening of Wednesday, January 14, at the Masonic Temple in San Francisco. Although his doctor and aides attempted to dissuade him by explaining the seriousness of his condition, he replied, "I must go . . . and nothing shall prevent me from going." After having slept most of the day he made it to the temple, spending less than an hour there, then returned to his hotel suite.

Some time over those fraught days, a man representing the Edison Phonograph company came to the king's suite carrying one of Edison's new recording machines. He asked the ailing king, through his chamberlain, "if it would please His Majesty . . . to have the King's voice recorded?" It was hoped that capturing the voice of Kalākaua on a phonograph would help publicize the device invented just a few years earlier by Thomas Edison. The machine sat untouched by the king's bedside for several days. But on Friday, January 16, Kalākaua summoned enough energy to agree. His attendants moved the queer device, with its wax cylinder and sensitive metal etching arm with a steel needle, closer to his bed. They gently raised the king, supporting his back with pillows, and placed the speaking tube near his lips.

The king began to speak slowly in Hawaiian, pausing for breath.

"*Aloha kaua,*" he said with great effort.

"*Aloha kaua.*"

"*Ke hoi nei no paha makou ma keia hope aku I Hawai'i I Honolulu. A ilaila oe e hai aku ai oe I ka lehulehu I kau mea e lohe ai ianei.*"

The king's words were "Greetings to you. Greetings to you. We will very likely hereafter go to Hawai'i, to Honolulu. There you will tell my people what you have heard me say here."

The effort exhausted him and soon he slipped into a coma. The royal party hoped to keep his condition a secret, but by Monday a dozen reporters were waiting in the hotel's corridors and the newspapers began

publishing extra editions on an hourly basis, with huge headlines updating the king's condition. Shortly, hundreds of people flocked to the
Palace Hotel to try to find out what was happening.

An Episcopal clergyman came to Kalākaua's room to deliver a com-
munion service. The king's doctors rigged up tubing that dripped glyc-
erine and brandy into his mouth to try to sustain him. Gathered around
his bedside were eighteen people, including his favorite *hula* dancer,
Kalua, and the man still known as the sugar king of Hawai'i, Claus
Spreckels. At the head of his bed sat his devoted aide-de-camp, his
strong frame bent in sorrow and clasping the left hand of the king.
"Shall we kneel and have the commendatory prayer?" asked an Episcopal priest and then led the group in reciting the Twenty-third Psalm,
"The Lord Is My Shepherd." Froth began forming at the king's lips and
his breathing grew labored. The group sang the hymn "Abide with Me"
and prayed.

"Oh Lord! Oh Jesus Christ," began the clergyman, but his prayer suddenly stopped when the king seemed to stop breathing. For a half minute there was no motion in his chest. Then came a sigh. "cleanse his soul.
Lord Jesus Christ, be with him." Once again, the king's chest stopped
moving. On Tuesday, January 20, 1891, at 2:33 in the afternoon, David
Kalākaua died.

Kalua, a young native girl who served as the king's handmaiden, was
the first to touch him. She had been weeping silently as the end drew
near. She rose from the floor, tears streaming down her face, and placed
her hand upon his chest. When it became evident that it was no longer
moving, she moved her hand to the king's sunken cheek, stroking it gently. Then she turned away from the dead monarch with a sob, sinking
into the arms of the king's aide.

As one of the attending doctors wrote, Kalua and the king's valet Ka-
hikina were the only ones who seemed to reach him in his final hours.
The gentle cadences of his native tongue were "both soothing and comforting in the highest degree," the doctor wrote, and the only language
that "His Majesty could comprehend" at the end was Hawaiian.

*   *   *

The rest of the world learned of Kalākaua's death before Liliʻu did. Thanks to transcontinental and transatlantic cable, young Kaʻiulani in England got the news first on January 21, 1891. When her British guardian, Theo H. Davies, who had received a telegram with the news, told Kaʻiulani, she exclaimed, "Oh! I did not know how much I loved my uncle." She must also have realized that his death put her only one step away from the throne.

Her guardian, who owned vast sugar plantations on Hawaiʻi Island and had invested in the Honolulu Iron Works, understood the responsibilities that this would entail and thus asked Kaʻiulani's father to allow her to stay in England for a while longer: "I honestly hope that there will be no need for Kaiulani to come out before her school course is finished. She is acquiring so much valuable training, and her character is developing so well, that it would be cruel to interrupt it . . . She asked me today if I thought she would have to go out on account of this sad blow. I personally hope not."

Farther west, in San Francisco, an estimated 100,000 people thronged the streets of San Francisco to witness the funeral procession of Hawaiʻi's king on January 22, 1891. But the Hawaiian Islands remained in ignorance. For decades, there had been talk of laying an undersea telegraphic cable in the Pacific Ocean to connect the west coast of America to Asia by way of the Hawaiian Islands. But that project had sputtered off and on, delayed by the difficulties of financing it.

So it was not until seven in the morning on January 29, when the USS *Charleston* rounded Diamond Head, that people on the islands learned their king was dead. The ship flew the American and Hawaiian flags at half-mast and black crepe hung from its spars. By 8:30 Honolulu's telephone system had carried the word to the palace. Liliʻu hurried to the Blue Room. As she entered she saw distressed looks on the faces of the cabinet ministers. By the time the *Charleston* dropped anchor in the naval row she knew Kalākaua was dead.

Early that afternoon, before Kalākaua's body had been moved to the palace, the most powerful men in the land gathered in the palace and summoned her to join them.

"What is the object of this meeting," she asked her husband, who had risen from his sickbed to join her. Dominis told his shaken spouse that they planned to administer to her an oath of office, in which she would promise to uphold the hated so-called Bayonet Constitution of 1887. Liliʻu, writing later, recalled immediately telling Dominis that she did not wish to take the oath just then and would prefer to wait until after her brother's funeral, which would be in about three weeks' time.

Dominis replied that the chief justice and others had decided she must take the oath of office then and there. For whatever reason—her grief over her brother's death or being surrounded by so many powerful white men with only her ailing spouse as her counsel—she agreed. After a prayer, the chief justice and chancellor, assisted by the court's associate justices, administered to her the oath.

> I solemnly swear in the presence of Almighty God to maintain the Constitution of the Kingdom whole and inviolate, and to govern in conformity therewith.
> So help me God
> Liliuokalani

Liliʻu then signed and executed the document before the witnesses. Afterward, the chief justice shook Liliʻu's hand in congratulations and offered her a word of advice. "Should any of the members of your cabinet propose anything to you," he told her, "say yes."

A photograph of Liliʻu taken shortly after she took the oath shows her dressed entirely in black. She wears a stunned expression on her face, as if events had moved just too fast for her to fully absorb. Writing many years later, she recalled feeling as much when she swore to uphold the constitution that had stripped the monarch and the Hawaiian people of so many of its powers.

> I was so overcome by the death of my dear brother, so dazed with the suddenness of the news which had come upon us in a moment, that I hardly realized what was going on about me, nor did I at all appreciate for the moment my situation. Before I had time to collect myself, before my brother's remains were buried, a trap was sprung upon me by those who stood waiting as a wild beast watches for his prey.

When Honolulu's workmen learned of the king's death, they began stripping away the bright decorations and greenery they'd hung for his homecoming and replaced them with dark bunting and black crepe. The shopkeepers draped their storefronts in black and closed their doors to business. The words on the triumphal arch erected by the fire department to welcome the king back were shorn off and replaced with "We mourn our loss."

At five that afternoon, through the drizzling rain, a group of U.S. sailors lifted the coffin containing the embalmed body of the king onto the wharf. Hundreds of British and American sailors marched in columns alongside the hearse as the *Charleston's* band played funeral dirges. The funeral cortege passed firemen standing at attention, each holding a burning torch in honor of the fallen king, as was the family custom. The air was full of coming rain and clouds darkened the sky but a rainbow arched fleetingly over the entire span of the palace just as the funeral cortege reached it.

Inside the yard, hundreds of native Hawaiians had gathered, chanting and wailing for their dead monarch. The king's longtime friend Sam Parker, the part-Hawaiian playboy, was assigned the task of officially informing the king's family of his death. After delivering the news he pulled out a handkerchief to wipe away his own tears. Queen Kapiʻolani at first had trouble grasping Parker's words. She waited on the palace's balcony, directly above the main entrance. Swaying back and forth in anguish, she wept and clasped her hands above her head and even tore at her hair. "When the stricken woman leaned forward in intense agony, one could not but fear that she would inflict bodily injury upon herself from the iron picketed railing," wrote one observer. Others thought she was about to hurl herself upon the cast iron steps below but was stopped just in time by one of her ladies-in-waiting.

Lili'u, too, was overcome with emotion. As she stood on the balcony, she was urged to come inside the palace, away from the cries below, the blare of the band, and the view of onlookers. Military men lifted her brother's coffin from the hearse, carrying it up the steps and into the Throne Room of the palace, placing it on a bier. Lili'u made her way unsteadily down the stairs and viewed the casket, leaning on the arm of John A. Cummins, a part-Hawaiian and close friend who was minister of foreign affairs. The plaintive cries of the mourners penetrated the palace walls.

In the Throne Room, the handmaiden Kalua made her way to Kapi'olani and prostrated herself before her, sobbing and kissing the queen's hand. Kalua then gave her a small purse that contained the key to the late king's jewel box and a locket containing a photograph of the dowager queen. Holding the belongings of her deceased husband threw Kap'iolani into further paroxysms of grief.

"The King went cheerfully and patiently to work for the cause of those who had been and were his enemies," Lili'u later wrote. "He sacrificed himself in the interests of the very people who had done him so much wrong, and given him such constant suffering. With an ever-forgiving heart he forgot his own sorrows, set aside all feelings of animosity, and to the last breath of his life did all that lay in his power for those who had abused and injured him." The late king had thought he'd done it for the good of his country.

Surely he believed that bringing economic prosperity to the islands would help his people, and that's why he supported the sugar planters and the reciprocity treaty that benefited them too. He also presided over a revival of native Hawaiian culture, which proved controversial to *haole* residents of the islands. But by brokering the treaty that gave foreigners not only economic but military concessions, he had helped lay the groundwork for the impossible situation in which Lili'u would soon find herself.

CHAPTER TEN

Enemies in the Household, 1891–1893

The sounds of grief penetrating the palace walls before King Kalākaua's funeral were far different from those Lili'u remembered from her childhood. Each evening, groups of native Hawaiians gathered on the palace grounds and poured out their sorrow in dirges drawn from the Christian hymnal—a far cry from the traditional *uē*, the atonal dirges that Hawaiians considered an art form yet some whites heard as "senseless wailing."

One such dirge began:

Mourn ye sons of Hawaii,
Sad news to you we bring,
No more we'll gaze with loving eye,
Upon your generous King

Each verse ended with the doleful refrain "King Kalākaua's no more," repeated over and over, as twenty or more voices blended together under the electric arc lights of the palace.

The king's funeral reflected the passing of the old ways. Before the Anglican service began, the secret society that Kalākaua had founded to help preserve knowledge of Hawaiian genealogy and traditions—the Hale Nauā, or Temple of Science—performed an ancient funeral ritual. A dozen Hawaiian women approached the late king's body, which was lying in state in the Throne Room at 'Iolani Palace. Carrying lighted candles, each in turn offered a short prayer, saying a few words at the dead king's head, shoulders, elbows, hands, thighs, knees, ankles, and feet. The six torchbearers on each side of the body concluded by chanting prayers in unison.

The Anglican bishop of Honolulu then began a traditional Christian service by reading a passage from the Bible in Hawaiian, and the choirs of both St. Andrew's Cathedral and Kawaiaha'o church performed a chant, into which Lili'u, drawing from knowledge of the Bible rather than Hawaiian traditions, had woven a sobering reflection on the brevity of life, from Psalm 90: "For a thousand years in thy sight are but as yesterday when it is past."

A long funeral procession made its way up the mountains, toward the royal mausoleum. Kalākaua's casket was covered by a yellow cloak made of thousands of tiny feathers from the rare mamo and 'ō'ō birds.

When they arrived, the bishop said a few words, the choir sang another hymn, and then almost everyone left the chamber so that another service—this one Masonic—could take place. Before his death Kalākaua had attained the highest degree among Freemasons and now his Masonic brethren filed into the dark crypt and circled his casket. After the master spoke, each Mason, in turn, paused at the late king's casket and dropped onto it a sprig of green, the freshly cut branches releasing their sharp, clean scent into the crypt's still air.

Soon after the king's death, condolence letters poured into 'Iolani Palace from around the world. The U.S. president Benjamin Harrison expressed his sympathy, as did Pope Leo XIII. Robert Louis Stevenson, living in Samoa, scrawled a letter in his untidy handwriting assuring

Liliʻu of his support and politely suggesting that her brother may have lived a little too extravagantly. "The occasion is a sad one, but I hope, and trust, the event is for the ultimate benefit of Hawaii," he wrote, "where so much is to be hoped from, as much is sure to be effected by a firm, kind, serious and not lavish sovereign."

Liliʻu must have been gratified to receive this pledge of support from Stevenson, who was then nearing the height of his literary fame. She likewise received flattering praise from some of her late brother's sharpest critics, including the Reverend Sereno E. Bishop, the Hawaiian-born son of Protestant missionaries who edited the *Friend*, a journal concerned with Christian morals and sailors' welfare. In the spring of 1891 he wrote about the new queen that "Her gentle and gracious demeanor, her good sense, and her fine culture, have also commanded the high regard of the foreign community."

The regard waned as soon as Liliʻu signaled her intention to be a powerful ruler, in the tradition of Kamehameha I. Just one day after the official mourning period for her brother had ended, Liliʻu met with the cabinet and demanded that the ministers from her brother's reign submit their resignations to her, as was her legal right to demand as the new sovereign. When they resisted she turned to the supreme court, bluntly laying out her reasons in a manner sure to embarrass the cabinet. She stated to Chief Justice Albert F. Judd that its members were unpopular, had failed to act in concert, and had neglected to "correct what I consider corrupt practices hurtful to the standing of a good and wise Government."

The court studied the queen's request for two weeks. One of the changes under the constitution of 1887 was that, for the first time, the monarch's cabinet appointments required legislative approval. Liliʻu took the position that her brother's death necessitated that his cabinet resign and that she, as the new sovereign, had the right to appoint their replacements without approval from the kingdom's fractious parliamentarians.

After a fortnight of deliberation, the chief justice of Hawaiʻi's supreme court supported Liliʻu, allowing her to reappoint ministers of her own choosing. By taking this stand, she made it clear that she did not intend to be a malleable figurehead like her brother, but to restore power to the monarchy and the Hawaiian people lost after the imposition of the Bayonet Constitution.

While the court had considered Liliʻu's claim, government business ground to a halt. For weeks the monarchy was without an heir. The succession question was settled soon after the supreme court rendered its verdict, and by March 18 the news had been cabled to England and delivered to Kaʻiulani that she was named heir to the throne. But in Honolulu the "mischief," as Liliʻu called it, had only begun. She faced opponents not only from the white business class but from among her native people.

Robert Wilcox led the most radical faction alongside John E. Bush, the former leader of Kalākaua's Samoan fiasco. Bush had returned to Honolulu and was running a Hawaiian-language opposition newspaper. Bush had initially supported most of the queen's choices for cabinet members, but both he and Wilcox felt snubbed by Liliʻu, because she hadn't appointed either of them to government posts. Wilcox appealed to her to reconsider her decisions and name him as chamberlain, but she declined.

By April Bush had accused Liliʻu's administration of "downright idiocy." Bush and Wilcox preached ending the monarchy in favor of republicanism, decried the influence of the "sugar barons," and fanned rumors of the queen's supposed love affair with her handsome marshal the half Tahitian, half British Charles B. Wilson.

Liliʻu was infuriated by their criticisms and rumormongering. To her chamberlain, the chief officer in her household, she railed against Bush and his paper.

The chamberlain later wrote that Liliʻu "had a good mind to send some of the household soldiers over and smash his printing materials to pieces. When word of her anger over the newspaper reports began to circulate, it fueled talk among her opponents of the queen's hot temper.

Charles Bishop, who was then living in San Francisco, along with fellow businessmen in Hawaiʻi, were alarmed by the new queen's forceful debut. They wanted her to leave the business of governing to the cabinet, which had been comprised mostly of *haole* during her brother's reign. Bishop expressed this view in a letter he wrote to Lili'u in March of 1891, in which he suggests she'd received poor advice concerning the need to change her cabinet members and explained, somewhat paternalistically, that "the simple fact of a man's being a native does not fit or entitle him to hold a responsible and difficult position."

Bishop then went on to offer her advice on what her role should be: "In the politics and routine of the Government the Ministries have responsibility, annoyances and blame—and usually very little credits—Let them have them, and do not worry yourself about them. You will live longer and happier and be more popular by not trying to do too much."

Painful and condescending as that advice must have been, he was suggesting that Lili'u play a role in Hawai'i similar to the one that Queen Victoria played in Britain—essentially that of a figurehead who left most of the daily business of governing to her prime minister and Parliament. But Lili'u, born into a culture that had long revered its high chiefs as demigods, declined to take this advice.

Even before Bishop suggested she not try "to do too much," Lili'u was described by her late brother's ally Claus Spreckels as a monarch who would not jeopardize the kingdom's status quo. In an interview with the *San Francisco Examiner*, Spreckels described her as "a shrewd, sensible woman . . . who will never go the length of setting up her will against the Constitution, as interpreted by the Supreme Court." Acutely aware of the fact that American businessmen in Hawai'i wanted political stability in the country, he confidently told the reporter that there was "no likelihood of Queen Liliuokalani attempting reactionary measures."

Hoping to steer the debate on Hawai'i's future, where he and his family still controlled much of the commerce through steamships, sugar plantations, and the kingdom's largest bank, Spreckels published his views on the value of Hawai'i to the United States—in an article titled "The Future of the Sandwich Islands"—in a prestigious American journal.

Arguing that the strategic location of the archipelago made it vital to the United States, Spreckels wrote presciently that "The power which holds Pearl Harbor, close to Honolulu, and is in direct communication with it by cable, will be mistress of the sea in the north Pacific."

Lest anyone confuse him with an annexationist, Spreckels went on to reason that the kingdom, despite its strategic importance to America, should remain independent.

> The possession of Pearl Harbor as a naval station has been guaranteed to the United States government by treaty for a number of years. Why not improve the harbor and make this condition of occupation perpetual by treaty conferring perpetual reciprocal advantages upon Hawaii? . . . This should not, and, indeed, need not involve any attack upon the independence of the Islands. No one could be more opposed to their annexation to the United States than I am.

Spreckels was reflecting a shift in thinking triggered a year earlier by the publication of Alfred T. Mahan's book *The Influence of Sea Power Upon History*. In it Mahan, a U.S. naval officer and historian, argued that the strength of the British empire rested in large part on its command of the seas. This was a novel idea for Americans, who had focused on expanding western lands across the North American continent. From the nation's founding, Americans had hewed to the anti-imperial idealism expressed by Thomas Jefferson: "If there is one principle more deeply rooted in the mind of every American, it is that we should have nothing to do with conquest."

But Mahan and Spreckels believed that the basic element of power was trade, a belief that was already being energetically pursued by other nations. By 1893 Britain would formalize its relationship with the Gilbert Islands and with the Solomon Islands, Germany controlled Samoa and had annexed the Marshall Islands, and France had annexed Tahiti and expanded its hold over other Polynesian islands as well. Domination of the seas seemed to go hand in hand with expansion of economic interests. With the United States grappling with a powerful economic downturn, some American politicians and journalists had begun calling for Pacific expansion.

Mahan's view quickly won converts, including a young Theodore Roosevelt, whom he had met a few years earlier at the Naval War College. Influential American legislators such as Henry Cabot Lodge and administration officials, including the current U.S. secretary of state James G. Blaine, began advocating for a buildup of naval power and the acquisition of Hawai'i. Indeed, Blaine, in a burst of the expansionist bravado then gripping Washington, wrote to President Harrison in August of 1891 that "there are only three places of value enough to be taken that are not Continental. One is Hawai'i and the others are Cuba and Porto Rico."

None of Lili'u's letters or diary entries from this period suggest she had read Mahan's book or recognized the powerful impact it was having in military and diplomatic circles in Washington and the European capitals. Indeed, after reading it, the German kaiser thought it was so important that he had it translated and placed in all German naval libraries. Lili'u had other matters on her mind than trade relations and naval power. While Americans in Washington and elsewhere began to train their sights more intently on Hawai'i, Lili'u was reeling from yet another personal blow.

Late in the spring of 1891, in the midst of a drought and the beginnings of an economic downturn, Lili'u began the traditional royal tour of the islands, stopping at Moloka'i to visit the leprosy settlement. The plight of the afflicted was expressed in the last known chant of a native Hawaiian named Ka'ehu. Rounded up at gunpoint and shipped away to die on Moloka'i, Ka'ehu had composed a heartbreaking *oli* that asked: "*E aha ana o Hawaii, I nei mai o ka lepela?*" "What will become of Hawaii? What will leprosy do to your land?" After that somber visit, Lili'u moved on to Kaua'i to attend a series of parties hosted by leading white families, including a mutton lunch and a reviving sea bath in the waters off the tiny island of Ni'ihau, near Kaua'i.

When she returned from her trip, she joined her husband at Washington Place, where he was bedridden. Dominis, who was then fifty-nine, had contracted pneumonia. To watch over him more closely, Lili'u arranged to move him to a room on the ground floor of his family home, since climbing the stairs to his first-floor bedchamber had become too difficult for him.

On the warm afternoon of August 27, 1891, Lili'u sat in a room adjoining her husband's sick chamber, attended by three ladies-in-waiting. They spent the time quietly, planning the queen's upcoming birthday celebration on September 2, when she would turn fifty-three. The plan was that the day would start off with a traditional ho'okupu, or ceremonial offerings to the kingdom's monarch by her subjects, followed by a reception at the palace for dignitaries and the general public, a state dinner, and a lū'au. The prior day, Dominis's condition had seemed to improve, and no one saw a reason to call off or curtail the festivities.

Suddenly, the family physician, Dr. Trousseau, stepped into the room where Lili'u sat with her ladies-in-waiting bearing urgent news: "Madam, I believe your husband is dying; your presence is required," he told her.

Lili'u rose and made her way to the foot of Dominis's bedside, watching him as he slept. He and Lili'u had known each other since they were children and had by that time been married for nearly three decades. Together, they had attended the weddings and funerals of most of the remaining chiefs and chiefesses of Hawai'i, witnessing the end of the ruling line of Kamehameha and the tumultuous rise of the House of Kalākaua. Dominis himself had been the contemporary and friend of five reigning sovereigns of Hawai'i, serving each of them. Although she and her husband had had their difficulties, he remained her closest adviser on matters of state.

Lili'u stood in his room for a few minutes when she noticed "a slight quivering motion" pass over his frame, as she wrote years later. She rushed to his bedside and saw him make "a peculiar motion of his hand," which she had seen him and other Masons make when they were praying. She wondered whether this was the moment he died—as his hand fluttered in a final gesture of the fraternal order that was so important to him—when his spirit took flight "to enter that larger and grander brotherhood beyond the things which are seen?"

For four hours her husband's body lay in his deathbed, as the queen and her advisers consulted on the funeral. At 9:15 p.m. a hearse drawn by horses arrived to move the body to 'Iolani Palace, where family friend Sam Parker, marshall of the kingdom Charles Wilson, and other men lifted it and carried it into the Throne Room. Putting ceremony and public duty before her private grief, Lili'u made sure that the arrangements were all in place that evening.

Once her work was done, Lili'u requested that everyone else leave the room that evening so she could be alone. There, standing by her husband's corpse, she finally let her tears flow.

Amid unseasonably hot weather in the fall of 1891 Lili'u mourned. With her husband's death, Lili'u had lost an adviser who had deep experience in spanning the gap between Hawaiians and *haole*. Her letters to Princess Ka'iulani suggest her sorrow at her husband's passing. Lili'u wrote to her niece at Harrowden Hall, her English boarding school, that "You and Papa is all that is left to me."

With her husband, sister, and brother dead, and with her sister-in-law Kapi'olani incapacitated by a stroke, Lili'u had very few confidants, for either matters of state or affairs of the heart. She told one visitor about a week after her husband's funeral that it had become so lonesome for her living in 'Iolani Palace that she had moved back to Washington Place.

Lili'u was so despondent during this time that she avoided public appearances. Rumors began to circulate that she, too, was ill and nearing death. To counter these, she wrote to her niece assuring her of her good health. She also congratulated her on her sixteenth birthday, although admitting "it was always a sad day to me on account of Mrs. Bishop's death," referring to the anniversary of Pauahi's death and explaining that she'd spent the morning in the royal mausoleum to sit beside the remains of many of her dear friends and relatives. She also told Ka'iulani that her father Cleghorn would play a more important role as her adviser, now that Dominis was gone.

> When your dear Uncle [Dominis] was alive he used to advise me in great many things pertaining to ruling a Nation as he has had some experience under the former Kings and under your dear Uncle Kalākaua's reign so when I became Queen he often gave me advice which were valuable to me, but now that he is gone, I will have to look to Your father who is left to me.

Perhaps it was the desire to cling to the last vestiges of her family that caused her to squabble over relics Kalākaua had kept in the palace. The curator of the Bishop Museum, which Lili'u's brother-in-law Charles Bishop had established two years earlier to honor his deceased wife, Pauahi, sought to claim the late king's collection, including the large drum of Kamehameha I and other important artifacts from the Hale Nauā society. Lili'u forbade the removal of her brother's property from the palace and, for a while, the dispute seemed to be heading to court. It instead remained unresolved.

She faced far graver problems: opponents on all sides and a steep downturn in the kingdom's sugar-dependent economy. As one of Cleghorn's friends reported in September of 1891, Lili'u assumed the throne at a time when any ruler, even Kamehameha the Great, would have struggled with such powerful enemies as Lorrin Thurston, Robert Wilcox, and John E. Bush. Thurston, in particular, became alarmed by the populist appeal of Wilcox and Bush. He was convinced that Hawai'i could not remain independent in the face of an economic depression. Even a friend of Archibald Cleghorn's, who was sympathetic to the queen and the royal family, foresaw trouble.

The poor Queen has not had an easy task before her. Her reign, so far, has I think been intelligent and blameless; and the adherence to her constitutional oath is to be regarded as sincere. Her brother came to the Throne with a possible future of untold prosperity before him . . . The Queen comes with commercial depression, with every incentive to activity on the part of annexationists, and with her people only too ready to listen to Bush's threats and Wilcox's promises (both of these "statesmn" being her brother's creations), and moreover with the loss of her husband, whose advise has I believe always been patriotic. I think there are many prayers that God will guide her.

Lili'u continued to seek higher guidance and New Year's Day of 1892 found her at the newly rebuilt wooden church in Waialua, the district on the north shore of O'ahu near her country home. She couldn't help but think of her late husband, writing in her diary, "My poor John—Everything around reminds me of him."

As 1892 began, the quiet of the holiday season quickly gave way to the press of royal engagements. Early that year, Lili'u met with a visitor she knew could influence world opinion regarding her small island kingdom: Sir Edwin Arnold, editor of the London *Daily Telegraph*. Bearing herself with dignity and wearing a widow's gown of black silk crepe, Lili'u rose to meet the influential English newspaperman and author when he visited her at the palace. She extended her hand to him "with all the simplicity of a lady welcoming friends," wearing no ornaments except a diamond ring. He noticed her coffee-colored skin and her luxuriantly thick hair. Impressed, Sir Edwin described Lili'u as "every inch a queen."

But Sir Edwin's kind view of Hawai'i's eighth monarch was not shared by everyone. Vicious descriptions of her as "a black, pagan queen who wanted nothing short of absolute monarchy" had begun, mysteriously, to appear in the *San Francisco Examiner*, the paper owned by William Randolph Hearst and already printing the inflammatory headlines that would make it infamous for the era's so-called yellow journalism.

Some influential men closer to home apparently shared the *Examiner*'s view of Lili'u as a power-hungry absolutist. In early 1892 Thurston, who won election as a representative from Maui in the upper house of the legislature, met a fellow attorney on Merchant Street, in front of his office, and stopped for a chat. The two men immediately began speculating about what might happen if she continued on the independent course she was taking.

"Thurston, if Liliuokalani attempts to subvert the constitution of 1887, what do you intend to do about it?" his colleague asked.

Thurston replied that he would oppose her.

Soon after, he gathered about a dozen like-minded men at his law office, where they decided to form a group called the Annexation Club. Some of them had probably also been members of the secret Committee of Thirteen that brought about the Bayonet Constitution five years earlier. Contrary to what the name suggested, the aim was not to hasten the annexation of the islands to the United States, Thurston later disingenuously claimed, but to be prepared if Lili'u were to make a move against the constitution or "revert to absolutism."

Although Thurston practiced law, he was deeply enmeshed in the kingdom's sugar trade and other business ventures. He had $9,200 invested in sugar, $75,800 in the Halea-kala Ranch Company, and $500 in the O'ahu Railway and Land Company, founded by Benjamin Dillingham to serve the sugar plantations of the Campbells and others. His law partner W. O. Smith, who shared many of his views, was a large shareholder in sugar stocks. Like the other members of the Annexation Club, Thurston was motivated by a belief that Hawai'i's tumultuous politics hurt business. Conversely, he reasoned that annexation would lead to stability and prosperity.

In late March 1892, Thurston headed to Chicago in his role as an honorary commissioner for the upcoming world's fair known as the World's Columbian Exposition. Thurston's mission was to help arrange the details of the Hawaiian exhibit on volcanoes, a panoramic painting that would reproduce in miniature a volcanic eruption, charging awestruck fairgoers fifty cents admission. Displaying an entrepreneurial flair, he had a private concession at the Hawaiian booth as well. By then, the kingdom had begun to grasp the potential of tourism, which would bring more ships and passengers to the islands.

These geologic wonders had captured Thurston's imagination since his youth. Expelled from Punahou for taking liberties in quoting the Bible and other minor acts of disruption and defiance, he nonetheless made his way to New York, where he studied law for two years at Columbia University. Upon his return to the islands, Thurston became one of the owners of the Volcano House Hotel, perched on the rim of Kīlauea, on Hawai'i Island. In early 1892, however, Thurston had a private agenda, funded by the Annexation Club. Tacking on a visit to Washington, D.C., he met with legislators and Secretary of State James G. Blaine to gauge their interest in American annexation of the islands.

Solidly built and pugnacious, Thurston was gratified by his reception, particularly from Blaine, Secretary of the Navy Benjamin F. Tracy (a supporter of Mahan's and a firm believer in bolstering naval forces,) and, indirectly, from President Harrison himself. As Thurston later wrote, a secretary to the president told him, "The President does not think he should see you, but he authorizes me to say to you that if conditions in Hawai'i compel you people to act as you have indicated, and you come to Washington with an annexation proposition, you will find an exceedingly sympathetic administration here." Thurston, who was undoubtedly looking for support, took that as a go-ahead to stage a revolution.

The annexationists weren't Lili'u's only problem as the kingdom prepared for elections in early 1892. Despite the Bayonet Constitution of 1887, voters of Hawaiian ancestry still represented a strong majority of the electorate. Some, including native opposition leaders Bush and Wilcox, had adopted Gibson's old slogan "Hawai'i for the Hawaiians."

But when the elections took place in February of 1892 voters rejected the populist views of Bush and Wilcox. Their party suffered many losses, gaining only thirteen seats, while the parties supporting the queen and the government won thirty-five. With those seats spread over four parties, and a total of twenty-three *haole* and twenty-five Hawaiians elected, the result was no clear majority for any party, leading to legislative stalemate. While *haole* businessmen controlled most of the commerce in the kingdom, they increasingly felt frustrated by their lack of control over its governance.

Nor did the victory calm the waters for Lili'u, as she'd hoped it would. For the first time in her short reign she faced the possibility of civil unrest from voters unhappy with the opposition party's routing. On the day of the election, Sam Parker, her minister of foreign affairs, a commissioner of the crown lands, and one of her most trusted advisers, awoke Lili'u from an afternoon nap to tell her he'd prepared for a riot, in case the opposition party tried to violently unseat the queen from the throne.

As it turned out, there were no disturbances that day or in the weeks following the election. The gloomy mood was lifted shortly afterward by a children's fancy dress party featuring a Fairy Cupid, Lord Nelson, a Gypsy Fortune-Teller, and even a Prince Charming. The accounts of the party so delighted Lili'u that she invited the children the very next afternoon to visit the palace. Accompanied by their mamas, the costumed sprites marched around the ballroom, as the queen inspected them from the upper end of the Throne Room, surrounded by her ladies-in-waiting.

But this charming interlude passed too quickly. With the balance of power in the kingdom so unstable, the government was in a state of near deadlock: no party possessed enough power to assert its political will. Lili'u became frustrated, perhaps longing for other, lighthearted diversions. Not long after the elections, she retreated to her low-roofed cottage set among the Waikīkī palms to escape the tumult of Honolulu.

Despite the sounds of the lapping waves and the breeze through the palm fronds she slept fitfully. In her diary, she wrote, "Dream that a dead man wanted to strangle me—so when I went to bathe in the sea a strange fear came over me that a Shark might take hold of me, so hastened out of the water after a few dips."

* * *

In the following weeks and months, the threats against Liliʻu—real and perceived—became more detailed. There were rumors of a conspiracy being hatched by Wilcox and Bush to topple Liliʻu from the throne and replace the monarchy with a republican form of government. The rhetoric against Liliʻu boiled over, with the ever-shifting Wilcox, who was perhaps still angry after the failed 1889 insurrection. His allegiances seemed to change day by day and aimed his misogynist vitriol squarely at Liliʻu. "I do not wish to be governed by dolls," he fumed in a speech. "I believe no woman ought to reign. They have no brains."

The prospects of annexation, rioting, and an attempted coup, as it turned out, were not Liliʻu's only worries. The kingdom's financial condition was rapidly deteriorating. The McKinley tariff act, which had swept away the trade advantages of Hawaiʻi's sugar planters, had sunk the kingdom into a depression, and government receipts sank dramatically. In 1889, the year before the tariff act passed, close to 95 percent of the nation's total export revenues came from sugar bound for the United States. By 1892 sugar exports were still the single largest export crop. But their dollar value had dropped 23 percent from the previous year, and 44 percent from 1889—a terrifyingly swift plunge for planters and government alike.

Faced with a downturn that was likely to worsen, the legislature slashed government spending with a bill that cut the pay of government officials and employees, including the queen and her cabinet ministers. Liliʻu also began the year with an economizing gesture, scaling back the one-year anniversary celebration in January of her accession to the throne. The move, ironically, drew criticism from some newspapers that the ceremony lacked the "elegance" of her brother's disapproved-of entertainments. No matter what choices she made, she couldn't make the right ones in the eyes of her critics. In her diary, Liliʻu described the event, marred as it was by rain showers and bickering over seating arrangements, as "a disagreeable day."

The kingdom's financial woes also strained relations within the royal family. After Lili'u reduced the allowance of the dowager queen Kapi'olani, reasoning that she could live comfortably off the proceeds from her lands, the relationship between the once close sisters-in-law grew more distant. Likewise, Cleghorn began worrying about how he would continue to pay for his daughter's education in England and her return passage to Hawai'i. That spring, he petitioned the legislature for funds for the heir apparent. His lack of success prompted him to write to his daughter, "It is a shame to cut down on your allowance, and I am quite put out with the ministers for doing so, any way I will try and get an amount for your return."

Yet in June of 1892 Lili'u wrote to Ka'iulani outlining her plans for a European grand tour for her niece before she returned home. Her father would travel to England to meet Ka'iulani in April of 1893 and from there they would head to the continent, where the princess would be presented to the crowned heads of Europe. Returning to England, she would be presented to Queen Victoria, book passage across the Atlantic, and travel to Washington, D.C., where she would meet the president, and after taking in the sights of Boston and Chicago she would return to Honolulu in time for her birthday.

It is not clear how Lili'u intended to fund her niece's travels, though one of Cleghorn's letters to his daughter suggests the queen enjoyed an annual income of $48,000 per year, or more than a million dollars today, in revenue from her lands and other investments. What is clear is that Ka'iulani and her father had become deeply important to Lili'u as her closest remaining family members. In an unusual moment of candor for a woman who often kept her feelings tightly cloaked, Lili'u suggested to her niece that she was feeling lonely.

My health is very good, my dear child and I would like all my friends to know it, for some of our papers make it out that I am sickly and getting old. Of course I am getting old, we all are, but as long as we are well and I feel well and know that I am capable of attending to my duties, it is nothing to me what they say. I am looking forward to the time when I may have you back which will lessen the feeling of loneliness which at present weighs upon me."

Compounding those feelings, she must surely have been experiencing growing unease about her own finances, as well as those of the state, as economic conditions deteriorated. Toward the end of the year, as some residents began pulling money out of the bank, the government barely averted a bank run, partly by borrowing $95,000 from the Honolulu-based bank owned by the Spreckels family. Liliʻu, like her brother, became even more dependent on a foreign businessman whose primary allegiance was to himself.

This crisis in confidence forced Liliʻu and the government to take other desperate measures to raise funds. One was a bill to grant a franchise to a lottery company, a scheme encouraged by a woman named Fräulein Gertrude Wolf, who had been teaching Liliʻu German and also serving as her "medium." The fräulein read cards to receive messages about the supposed noble ancestry of the queen's late husband and wormed her way into the queen's confidences at a time when Liliʻu had few people in whom she could confide.

As Liliʻu noted in her diary, in the early hours of July 8, 1892, after a ball at ʻIolani Palace, the fräulein met with the queen and read her cards, foretelling that at ten that morning a gentleman would call on her at the palace with a "bundle of papers where it would bring lots of money across the waters. She says I must have the House (legislature) accept it—it would bring 1,000,000." Later that day, Liliʻu wrote, "Sure enough—the man came up with a bundle of papers—and spoke of lottery—how strange she should have told me."

A few weeks later Liliʻu elaborated that the fräulein told her the lottery bill would result in $10,000 or $15,000 for herself annually as "pocket money." It may have been that Fräulein Wolf was on the payroll of the lottery promoters, who were the same group behind the Louisiana state lottery. Faced with opposition from the *Advertiser* (which called the lottery scheme "scandalous") the lottery promoters published promotional material arguing: "The country is on the verge of bankruptcy; is there anything in sight that will extricate the Government from the muddle? The lottery people have the means."

Whether or not she was paid by the promoters, Fräulein Wolf fed promises to Lili'u that seemed to support the lottery bill. It may be that Hawai'i's queen was the victim of a confidence game. Or, at the very least, she was a poor judge of character in her dealings with her German soothsayer. Toward the end of the year, while this debate lingered, the government's financial strain was eased a different way: through a $100,000 loan from W. G. Irwin, Claus Spreckels's Honolulu business partner.

The lottery bill wound its way through the increasingly fractious legislature and eventually passed. Legislators also introduced three similarly controversial opium bills, aimed at licensing a trade whose growth had coincided with the importation of sugar plantation workers from China. During the tortured debate over immigration policies, Parliament passed one of these bills. Shadowing the legislative dustups were repeated cabinet shuffles and the undertow of the annexation question, which fueled discontent over Lili'u's governance.

The American envoy to Hawai'i John L. Stevens observed the kingdom's politics with growing alarm. Born in Maine, he had been a Universalist pastor, newspaperman, state Republican party leader, and minister to Paraguay, Uruguay, Norway, and Sweden. Almost as soon as he'd stepped off the steamer in Honolulu for the first time in 1889, the diplomat allied himself with Lorrin Thurston and other members of the kingdom's white business class, pushing for closer ties between the islands and the United States. Perhaps most important, he had a booster in his country's new, expansionist-minded secretary of state, John W. Foster.

Stevens did not bother to hide his disdain for monarchy, quickly managing to insult Lili'u as well as alarm Britain's long-serving minister to the islands James Wodehouse. On the same day as Kalākaua's funeral, Stevens reminded the queen of the limits of her authority under the

1887 constitution. Then, during speeches he delivered on Memorial Day and the July Fourth celebration of American independence, he undiplomatically railed against emperors and kings, referring to the "monarchcursed and enslaved nations of Europe."

Expressing his opinions further afield, Stevens penned an unsigned article in the *Kennebec Journal*, arguing that the time had come to "decide whether the Hawaiian Islands will have unity, liberty, and autonomy with the United States, or become a colonial possession of a European power."

Lili'u was well versed in that line of reasoning. Rumors, fanned perhaps by Stevens, circulated that the British businessman Theo H. Davies hoped to marry off his eldest son, Clive, to Ka'iulani as a way to lay the groundwork for Britain's annexation of the islands. Even before that talk had bubbled up, Cleghorn had arranged for Davies to give the new queen a tutorial on geopolitics—including a map of the world with all of Great Britain's imperial possessions colored in red. Lili'u, however, made it plain she was not eager to fall into Britain's embrace, no matter how powerful its empire was. She wanted her nation to remain independent.

Wodehouse warned Lili'u that Stevens had pledged to support her enemies "under certain circumstances." Even more alarming, the Briton told her that the U.S. minister might come up with a pretext for requesting aid from a U.S. warship.

Not long afterward, an anonymous letter dated December 17, 1892, suggested in even stronger terms that a conspiracy was afoot. Lili'u later described the author of the letter as "a gentleman in whose word I have great confidence as a man who had the best interest of Hawai'i at heart." The writer advised her that there was danger ahead and she should keep "strictest watch" on her cabinet members, warning that "the enemy is in the household."

PART III
MANIFEST DESTINY

CHAPTER ELEVEN
Pious Adventurers, 1893

Just before noon on Saturday, January 14, 1893, Liliʻu strode out of the palace into bright sunlight, determined to right a wrong. Soon after she'd taken the throne in 1891, petitions had begun pouring in to her from native Hawaiians, asking her to replace the hated constitution forced upon Kalākaua. By her count she had received formal appeals with more than sixty-five hundred signatures, representing more than two-thirds of the kingdom's registered voters. Pressure was mounting on her to act. At last, she saw her moment.

Liliʻu had dressed with special care that morning, choosing a lavender silk gown, the color of the delicate crown flower, traditionally threaded by Hawaiians into flower garlands known as *lei*. Before setting out, she asked Archibald Cleghorn whether he liked her dress. Assured by her brother-in-law she looked regal, the queen stepped into the open carriage and settled herself onto the seat.

Even though it was January, when Honolulu is often pelted by rain, the temperature was in the mid-70s and skies were clear. The coronet of diamonds she wore that day complemented the flecks of silver in her dark hair. As soldiers fired a royal salute from the Punchbowl Battery, she climbed into her open carriage and rode the short distance from 'Iolani Palace to the legislative building, Ali'iōlani Hale, to preside over the formal closing of the legislature.

The brief ceremony ended a long and unusually bitter session, marked by four cabinet reshufflings and fierce debate over the contentious lottery and opium bills, which Lili'u had just signed into law that morning. Two days earlier, prompted in part by the cabinet's opposition to the queen on the lottery bill, the legislature had passed a want of confidence motion and voted the ministers out of office. That gave Lili'u the chance to appoint ministers she thought would support her move to change the constitution. But almost as soon as she entered the sparsely filled assembly chamber she sensed something was wrong.

She made her way toward the platform, where a royal feather cloak had transformed a high-backed chair into a throne for the occasion. Sitting down, she looked out into the large hall, some thirty feet wide by sixty feet long, and saw that it was not nearly as crowded as it had been at the start of the session more than seven months earlier. She saw few women; and very few *haole*.

The Hawaiian-language newspaper *Hawai'i Holumua* reported sarcastically a few days later, "The haole Members of the House did not attend for they were sulky and afflicted with dizziness." Most of Lili'u's most prominent political opponents, including Thurston, were absent. Congratulating the nobles and representatives on having completed their "arduous duties," she declared the legislative session closed. "Nobles and Representatives: I ask the Almighty to continue to pour down blessings and riches upon all of you and our Nation, as in the past," she told the half-empty chamber. "I hereby proclaim this Legislature to be prorogued."

Yet the day's real business lay ahead. The previous fall, she had begun working with Joseph Nāwahī and other native legislators to draw up a constitution that would reverse many of the key changes brought about by the 1887 constitution and restore executive powers to the monarch. In her proposed constitution, not only would the monarch have the power to replace the cabinet at any time but could do so without legislative oversight. It also would give her the right to appoint members to the house of nobles without the constraints of elections or cabinet approval. In short, it would have given her much more power.

Furthermore, the proposed constitution would change voter eligibility, giving only Hawaiian subjects, both island-born and naturalized, the right to vote. By doing so, it would undermine the enfranchisement of *haole*, who under the constitution of 1887 could cast ballots without becoming Hawaiian subjects as long as they met residency requirements. It also boosted the voting powers of Asian immigrants, a fast-growing group that had been excluded entirely from voting by the constitution of 1887.

Lili'u's efforts to work with Parliament, however, had failed. During the session that just ended, Lili'u had tried to convince legislators to pass a bill calling for a new constitution. If she'd succeeded, she might have put an end to the scuffles that had so disrupted the past year's session. But in late December legislators defeated a bill calling for a new constitution 24 to 17. The vote, for the most part, ran along racial lines, with Hawaiians in favor and *haole* opposed.

Because she was blocked, on that January day she decided to enact her proposed constitution in a different way: by royal fiat. By pushing it through with the help of her new, handpicked cabinet ministers, she hoped to empower native Hawaiians to retake control of the political and economic direction of their tiny island nation. But it was a threatening document to many *haole*; not only would they lose their vote unless they became Hawaiian subjects, they'd also suddenly be vastly outnumbered by newly enfranchised native Hawaiian, Asian, and Portuguese residents. Stripping the *haole* of their political power threatened their livelihoods. Certainly Lili'u must have known they were likely to strike back.

Lili'u's ride from the government building to the palace was short. Following her carriage were about forty members of a Hawaiian political society called the *Hui Kālaiʻāina*, wearing black broadcloth suits and carrying banners, marching two by two. Their leader carried a large flat package in front of his chest, suspended by ribbons from his shoulders: a copy of the new constitution. Liliʻu had arranged with the society to bring the document to the palace and formally ask her to proclaim it, witnessed by the members of legislature and foreign diplomats."

The liveried driver, wearing a tricornered hat and buckled shoes, halted the carriage and Liliʻu stepped out. Slowly, she climbed the iron steps to the front entrance of the palace, limping slightly from her childhood fall from a swing. She passed household troops, which stood rigidly at attention.

She crossed a wide veranda and passed through two massive double doors with etched maidens surrounded by delicate ferns. Entering the palace, she glanced at the parade of portraits of the past kings and queens of Hawaiʻi, including the fierce king Kamehameha I, who had united the islands eight decades earlier.

The queen did not head upstairs to her private chamber but instead turned left, into a reception area known as the Blue Room. Charles Wilson, the tall, powerfully built, half-Tahitian who had stepped into the role as Liliʻu's protector following her husband's death, stood by the door. Liliʻu turned to him and asked if everything was ready. Wilson told her yes.

"You will have to be brave today," the queen told him, anticipating unrest or even riots.

She strode into the room, which took its name from the heavy blue satin draperies trimmed with velvet, and took a seat at a table. That morning, Liliʻu had informed the ministers of her plans to proclaim a new constitution, giving them several hours to consider her request. Thirty minutes passed before the ministers finally arrived. The queen saw their distress. Unbeknownst to her, one of the ministers that morning had shown his copy of the proposed new constitution to Thurston and several other *haole* lawyers for review. They strongly advised him not to sign it and also to refuse to quit his cabinet post, since doing so could allow the queen to replace him with a more pliant minister.

So confident had the queen been of her ministers' support that she'd invited members of the supreme court and the legislature as well as other dignitaries to attend a ceremony in the palace's Throne Room, just across the hall from where she and the ministers were now conferring. None knew precisely why they had been summoned. By the time the ministers finally arrived, her guests had waited there for nearly an hour. Members of the Hui Kālaiʻāina were drawn up in regular lines, and their president held the speech he planned to deliver open in his hand.

"I was requested by my people to promulgate a new constitution. I want you gentlemen to sign it or to consent to it," Liliʻu ordered the tardy ministers. Adding that her guests were in a nearby room, she warned, "We must not keep them waiting."

The four cabinet members, all of whom she had been convinced would support a new constitution, advised her against taking such a step because of the danger of an uprising. Parker became their spokesman. "Your Majesty," he began, "we have not read the constitution, but before we read it you must know it is a revolutionary act. It can not be done." At that moment Liliʻu's hopes collapsed.

Looking up from her chair, she gathered her strength, "Read it, see what it is."

The ministers refused, suggesting instead that she give up on her plan.

Liliʻu's initial dismay turned to fury. She brought her clenched fist down upon the table.

"Gentlemen, I do not wish to hear any more advice. I intend to promulgate this constitution and to do it now."

Maintaining that she would never have taken such a step if they had not encouraged her, she later wrote that she felt they had led her out to the edge of a precipice and were now leaving her to take the leap alone.

"Why not give the people the constitution and I will bear the brunt of all the blame afterwards?" she argued in frustration, fully aware that many of the most powerful people in the kingdom were now waiting, some undoubtedly impatiently, for her and the cabinet members to arrive.

"We have not read the constitution," said one of the ministers.

"How dare you say that to me, when you have carried it in your pocket for a month?" she asked, not bothering to hide her fury at the bald-faced lie. She demanded they resign, but since they'd been advised not to by Thurston and others, they refused.

Accounts differ on what happened next, but one *haole* historian from that time wrote that Lili'u threatened to go out to the steps of the palace, where large groups of Hawaiians had gathered and the household troops were lined up, to announce that it was the ministers who had blocked her efforts to give the nation a new constitution. Recalling the riots of 1874 that followed Kalākaua's election and fearing a similar eruption of violence, three of the four ministers apparently fled the palace, scurrying to Ali'iōlani Hale to tell Thurston and others what had happened.

That left Sam Parker, the heir to the Parker Ranch on Hawai'i Island and a family friend who was closest to Lili'u, alone with the queen in the Blue Room. Parker was a *hapa-haole* whose American grandfather had arrived in the islands and married a Hawaiian chiefess. His father had done the same, making him three-quarters native Hawaiian. Parker was a longtime friend to the House of Kalākaua, dating back to his days as a Honolulu dandy. An adventurous man-about-town, he wore all-white riding outfits and mounted on a prancing white horse.

Like Lili'u's late brother, Parker was hardly moderate in his habits; his spending regularly exceeded his income. Upon the advice of Claus Spreckels, in 1878 he had decided to carve out a sugar plantation on ocean bluffs owned by the Parker Ranch, which by that time he had inherited along with his brother, and build a mill. He went deeply into debt to carry out the plan, naming the venture the Paauhau Sugar Plantation Company.

From its very first harvest, Parker's plantation proved a failure, due to a delay in the nearby sugar mill that Spreckels had promised to build if Parker grew the cane. That led some to speculate that the German-American sugar baron had intended all along to drive Parker into debt to him. The Parkers were eventually forced to mortgage their ranch to

William G. Irwin and Company, Spreckels's close associates. As Parker later said, "The whole thing was a roller coaster ride conceived in chaos and executed in panic."

But on this day, more than a decade after beginning his sugar venture with Spreckels, Parker counseled moderation, hoping to help Lili'u keep the throne by convincing her to back down from her plan to introduce a new constitution.

Before long, the three ministers returned to the palace, their resolve hardening. They'd been swayed by Thurston, who argued that the queen had violated her oath of office and launched a "revolution" against the government and that they, the ministers, should "declare the throne vacant by reason of her treasonable attitude." The American envoy Stevens and the British minister Wodehouse, whom they met with as well, also urged them to stand firm.

The new cabinet balked at Lili'u's attempt to push a new constitution through by fiat. They saw her stepping outside the bounds of the current constitution, which provided a means for making changes to it through the legislature. But Lili'u may well have reasoned that there was precedent for her actions, since that was exactly how Kamehameha V had proclaimed his new constitution in 1864, declaring it the law of the land without anyone's approval. It became the nation's longest-standing constitution, lasting for twenty-three years until the Bayonet Constitution of 1887. Lili'u seemed to have relied too heavily on this precedent dating to the Kamehameha dynasty. Clearly, she misread her ministers' willingness to support an absolute decree.

Eventually, the ministers, led by Parker, managed to convince Lili'u to delay the new constitution for a few weeks.

The queen and her cabinet then crossed the hall and headed toward the throne room. By that time guests such as supreme court's chief justice A. F. Judd and others had been waiting there for close to four hours. Deeply upset and humiliated by her cabinet's refusal, Lili'u stepped up to the dais and explained to her guests that she had intended that day to promulgate a new constitution, since the one from 1887 was imperfect and full of defects. Turning to the chief justice, she asked, "Is it not so, Mr. Judd?"

The chief justice, she later wrote, answered "in the affirmative, in the presence of all the members assembled." Judd, until very recently, had been a staunch supporter of the queen. Born in Hawai'i, Albert Francis Judd was a son of Gerrit Judd, the former medical missionary who'd served as a minister in the government of Kamehameha III. Like his father, he'd loyally served the monarchy until learning of the queen's efforts to introduce a new constitution. At that point, Lili'u later learned, Judd apparently planted a spy in her household who kept him informed of her plans. As it turned out, the native Hawaiian man whom Lili'u had hired to copy the proposed constitution because of his neat penmanship had been slipping drafts of the constitution to Judd all along.

Turning her attention away from Judd and back to the other dignitaries gathered in the Throne Room, Lili'u explained that she had yielded to the wishes of her ministers because they had promised that she could introduce a new constitution in the future. Return to your homes and keep the peace, she told the gathering, addressing the members of the Hui Kālai'āina in their stovepipe hats. The queen remained calm, believing she had cloaked her true feelings from the assembled dignitaries. But the chief justice described Lili'u's demeanor somewhat differently. "She was under great emotion," Judd wrote. "I never saw her in such a state of agitation."

A crowd of mostly native Hawaiian subjects had gathered outside, on the palace grounds. The chairman of the Hui Kālai'āina left the Throne Room and informed the group that the queen was "quite ready to give a new constitution, but her Cabinet [was] opposed to it. Her Cabinet refused it, so that she could not do otherwise."

The queen stepped out onto the palace's second-floor veranda, which overlooked the grounds toward Ali'iōlani Hale and, beyond that, to the wharves. By then the sun was starting to set. Speaking in Hawaiian, she told the people who had gathered to "go in good hope" and wait for her to act on the new constitution at another time.

The Hawaiian-language newspaper *Ka Leo O Ka Lahui*, owned by opposition editor John E. Bush, reported that the queen had "wanted to fulfill the desires of her Native people, but because of the obstacles which were encountered . . . she was unable to do so." The queen, it also reported, had asked them "to preserve peace in the realm."

Some of her supporters were less than moderate in their expressions of disappointment. One Hawaiian representative climbed up the front steps of the palace and unleashed his frustration in a speech to the crowds gathered there. The cabinet had betrayed them, he railed, and instead of going home peaceably they should go into the palace and kill and bury them. Others rushed over, hoping to stop the intemperate flood of words. After putting up some resistance, the speaker threw up his hands and said he was *pau*—the Hawaiian word for being done with a job. Afterward, the Hui Kālai'āina in their formal black frock coats filed out, looking dejected.

The queen's enemies soon used her words against her. She may have thought that by withdrawing the constitution that day she had averted a crisis. Little did she know it was only the beginning of a much more profound conflict, which would pit her against both her handpicked ministers and a determined and resourceful group of missionary descendants, whom Lili'u would come to despise as "pious adventurers."

The *Pacific Commercial Advertiser* was by then owned by Henry Castle, his brother W. R. Castle, and Henry Whitney, who'd founded the paper back in 1856. Closely allied with Thurston and his followers, it published an English-language version of the queen's speech on Monday, January 16. As translated by Chief Justice Judd, the queen said she had only postponed the introduction of a new constitution for "a few days"— a subtle but potentially inflammatory difference, since it suggested she would soon try again.

The paper also fanned the flames by reporting a comment allegedly made by one of the officers of the queen's Household Guards. According to the paper, he'd boasted that Lili'u's troops "had enough arms and ammunition to kill every haole in the country." Whether or not any such statement was uttered by one of the queen's officers (there is room for doubt that it ever was since the officer that the *Advertiser* quoted was unnamed) it created fear.

Almost as soon as the queen finished her remarks in the Throne Room on Saturday afternoon, Thurston and his followers began to mobilize. Two of the cabinet ministers hurried to the downtown law office of a judge named W. O. Smith to relate what had happened at the palace. They accurately relayed to the group that the queen had not dropped the idea of introducing a new constitution but had merely postponed it. Determined to prevent her from pushing it through at a later date, the thirteen men gathered in the law office that afternoon, all white men and some from missionary families, forming what they called a Committee of Safety. Headed by an American who had recently arrived in the islands and had worked as an attorney for the California Southern Railroad, Thurston and his Annexation Club guided events.

Justice of the Hawaiian supreme court Sanford Dole missed the excitement, though he was alarmed by the turn of events. Two days earlier he had written to his brother George, "The legislature will prorogue on Saturday. Yesterday they helped the lottery bill by a vote of 23 to 21. Today they are going to make another attempt to vote the Cabinet out. The Queen is at the bottom of it. She is showing a greed of power and a disposition to interfere in politics equal to Kalakaua in his (calmest) moments."

Dole went on to tell his brother, who had worked as a supervisor on a sugar plantation and was fully versed in island politics, that one of their mutual friends was happy about the lottery bill passing "because he thinks it will demoralize things here and so hasten annexation."

That Saturday, Sanford Dole had decided to skip the ceremony marking the end of the parliamentary session and take a group of school boys on a sailing trip. Heading back from the wharf, he saw a crowd of men spilling out of Smith's law offices. He soon learned of the queen's attempt to "tamper with the constitution," as he later described it, and her "vehement" address on the balcony "to carry out her scheme within a few days."

One of the men at the gathering was the sugar investor and business-man Charles M. Cooke, one of the sons of Liliʻu's teachers at the Royal School. What, he demanded, was meant by the decision to form the Committee of Safety. "Does it mean no more queen?" he asked. Assured that that was exactly what it meant, Cooke threw his support behind the group of merchants and lawyers, many of whom had strong ties to the sugar industry.

That evening, a "Masquerade on Skates" party was scheduled to be held at the armory—admission twenty-five cents and no skaters allowed with-out masks. The armory, nicknamed the "Skating Rink," was the place in the tropical kingdom's capital where one of the newly popular sports from America, roller skating had unexpectedly taken hold. It was also the de facto headquarters of the Honolulu Rifles, which by then had become the military arm of Thurston's annexationist movement.

Sunday, January 15, passed quietly for Liliʻu. Her Sabbath was spent, in part, in the presence of native pastors, whom she had invited to the palace to pray with her. Her day also included a visit from Sam Parker, who told her that her political opponents were meeting at the govern-ment building.

But Liliʻu's cabinet members did not enjoy a day of rest. Like a tropical Paul Revere, Thurston arrived on horseback on Sunday at 6:30 a.m. to rouse two of them from their beds to report progress in preparing for a provisional government. The queen's ministers spent much of the day ask-ing for advice from some of her most loyal white supporters. Eventually, they decided that if they could convince the queen to sign a document in which she publicly retreated from her goal of promulgating a new consti-tution, they might dampen the flames of the rapidly escalating conflict.

Meanwhile, Thurston and the other committee members became, if anything, even more confident that the American envoy Stevens would support them in their efforts to overthrow the queen. Rumors ricocheted through the kingdom's already rumor-prone capital. In his diary entry for that Sunday, Chief Justice Judd noted that he had gone to the post office and to church, where he'd heard a rumor that the queen would be forced to abdicate, hastening Hawai'i's annexation to the United States.

The queen's marshal, Charles Wilson, grew alarmed. He had assigned spies to tail the committee members and keep an eye on the shops in Honolulu that sold firearms. He also warned Thurston and his backers to back off. "I know what you fellows are up to," he told them, "and I want you to quit and go home."

"We are not going home, Charlie," Thurston replied coolly. "Things have advanced too far." Although Wilson offered to personally make sure the queen didn't make any further moves to force a new constitution like those on Saturday, that wasn't enough for Thurston, who told him firmly, "We will not take any further chances, but are going to wind affairs up now."

Calling the cabinet to meet with him at the police station, Wilson asked them to authorize a warrant so he could arrest the committee members for treason. But one of the ministers talked him out of it, arguing that it was important to avoid conflict. Those "damned cowards," as Wilson later recalled, refused to assist him.

The workweek on Monday began with signs of trouble ahead. Broadsides appeared overnight calling citizens to two different mass meetings that day, both set to begin at 2 p.m.: one was in support of the queen at Palace Square and the other was called by the Committee of Safety at the armory.

The ministers tried to calm matters by issuing the queen's conciliatory statement that they had asked for on Sunday. Within an hour, it was printed and posted throughout Honolulu.

Her Majesty's Ministers desire to express their appreciation for the quiet and order which has prevailed in this community since the events of Saturday, and are authorized to say that the position taken by Her Majesty in regard to the promulgation of a new Constitution was taken under stress of Her native subjects.

Authority is given for the assurance that, any changes desired in the fundamental law of the land will be sought only by methods provided in the Constitution itself.

Such assurances arrived too late: Thurston and the members of the Committee of Safety (all *haole*) seized the opportunity given to them by the rupture between the queen and her cabinet.

By two o'clock most of the merchants in Honolulu had closed their shops and given their clerks and office workers the afternoon off to attend the meeting at the Skating Rink. The marshal banned saloons from selling liquor. Most of the city's white men—more than a thousand—streamed into the building on Beretania Street, near Punchbowl Street and just a few blocks from the palace.

The head of the Committee of Safety, who was part-owner of a steamship company, stood up to focus the attention of the crowd and call the meeting to order. "We meet here today as men, not of any party, faction or creed, but as men who are bound to see good government," he began, looking out over the packed hall, where clerks and bankers jostled for space side by side. Some committee members, along with the American Stevens, were convinced that Lili'u was surrounded by corrupt advisers and that she had succumbed to pressure to sign revenue-raising lottery and opium bills in return for support in promulgating a new constitution. "Good government"—the opposite of the autocratic rule of the queen, as they saw it—was essential to protect their stakes in the kingdom, totaling many millions of dollars worth of business and properties owned by the white merchant class in Hawai'i by that time.

The steamship owner's relatively mild remarks were just a warm-up for Lorrin Thurston. Perhaps because of sleeplessness and an earlier attack of grippe that had weakened him, the lawyer's rhetoric was even more volcanic than usual. He began by ridiculing the queen's apparent climb-down and then launched into a full-scale attack on her motives, with all the passion he could summon, calling her attempt to push through a new constitution a "revolutionary" act.

"I say, gentlemen, that now is the time to act!"

Cheers rose from the crowd.

"The Queen says she won't do it again."

Someone in the crowd yelled "Humbug!"

"Fellow citizens," Thurston continued, "have you any memories? Hasn't she once before promised—sworn solemnly before Almighty God—to maintain this constitution? What is her word worth?"

"Nothing! Nothing!," shouted voices from the crowd.

Thurston then urged the men gathered that day to rise up and protect their liberties.

The queen, he thundered, "wants us to sleep on a slumbering volcano which will some morning spew out blood and destroy us all." His call for a resolution to denounce the action of the queen and her supporters met with thunderous applause.

Others then rose to the podium to speak, including the Maui sugar planter H. P. Baldwin, who suggested moderation. But the crowd shouted Baldwin down. As the meeting ended and the men returned to their homes, the kingdom teetered on the edge of a crisis. Rumors began circulating that angry Hawaiians planned to burn down homes owned by *haole*. By 4 p.m. there was scarcely anyone on the streets. The city was eerily quiet.

The American minister Stevens, who had just returned home after spending a few days aboard the USS *Boston* with his daughter, sprang into action. The *Boston* had been stationed in the Honolulu harbor for two years. Its orders from the U.S. government were to protect the life and property of American residents, of whom there were about two thousand in the island kingdom's total population of around ninety thousand. It had just returned from a cruise of Hawai'i Island, where it stopped at the rainy town of Hilo on the island's windward side intending to do some target practice. Finding it too windy, the *Boston* headed instead to Lahaina on Maui.

Late that morning, as the tide began to turn, the ship moored about a half mile from the landing docks at Naval Row. As soon as he could, Stevens hurried ashore to find out about the latest developments from the Committee of Safety. One of the people he met with was J. B. Atherton, one of the richest and most influential sugar barons on the islands, who urged him to use his influence to convince the commander of the *Boston* to land troops.

By 3 p.m. Stevens, his silver hair slicked back, climbed back on board the *Boston* carrying the note he had dashed off, addressed to the ship's commander. Dated January 16, 1893, it read:

SIR: In view of the existing critical circumstances in Honolulu, including an inadequate legal force, I request you to land marines and sailors from the ship under your command for the protection of the United States legation and United States consulate, and to secure the safety of American life and property.

Very truly yours, JOHN L. STEVENS, Envoy Extraordinary and Minister Plenipotentiary of the United States.

Before Stevens arrived, however, the *Boston*'s walrus-mustachioed captain had anticipated such a request and reviewed his standing orders from the U.S. Navy and the secretary of state. He ordered his lieutenant to prepare his ship's battalion for landing. When the officer asked the captain to define the parameters of the mission, he replied, "My desire is that you remain neutral; you are to protect the lives and property of American citizens." He gave no indication that his troops should go beyond that order.

It didn't take long for the three companies of sailors, the artillerymen, and the marines to pack their knapsacks and hitch on their cartridge belts. Shortly before 5 p.m. 154 men and 10 officers climbed into four landing boats for the short trip to the docks.

They lined up, guns strapped across their chests and each man armed with eighty rounds of ammunition. Some of the troops pushed a Gatling gun, a deadly, rapid-fire weapon invented at the start of the U.S. Civil War that could fire four hundred or more rounds of ammunition per minute. They paraded their fearsome machine gun along Queen Street, toward the palace, as dusk approached.

For many years, troops from the *Boston* had practiced drills in the parade grounds on the outskirts of town. American troops had also landed twice during periods of unrest—the 1874 riots following Kalākaua's election and the 1889 Wilcox Rebellion. But the unusual sight of heavily armed troops kicking up dust as they marched through the streets of downtown Honolulu on a Saturday, when there was no obvious unrest taking place, puzzled and alarmed some onlookers.

One soldier separated from the group to stand guard at the U.S. consul general's office. Forty more broke off to guard Stevens's residence. The remaining marched along the unpaved roads, turning onto King Street, which led to 'Iolani Palace and the government building Ali'iōlani Hale, carrying the American flag.

Lili'u sat alone in the Blue Room as shadows deepened across the palace grounds. Earlier that day, as many as a thousand of her supporters had gathered at Palace Square for a rally at the same time as the one at the armory. Their leaders, including Joseph Nāwahī and Robert Wilcox, had urged them to remain calm and "not provoke the haole to violent measures." With cries of *Ae!* they adopted a resolution of support for the queen, prompting Sam Parker to uncork a bottle of champagne, in celebration of what he thought was a peaceful resolution.

Now, at dusk, the lawns and gardens outside the palace were quiet and the barometer began to drop. Parker had left. Servants had cleared away the champagne glasses and some of the queen's supporters lingered on the palace grounds. Suddenly, Dr. Trousseau and a former government minister broke her solitude to tell her that troops were approaching. "Tell the people to be quiet," Lili'u commanded. She wondered why an American battalion would be marching toward the palace when there were no signs of disturbance.

She made her way out onto the veranda to take a look. By then word had come that the commander of the *Boston* had ordered the landing of the troops to ensure the safety of Americans and protect their interests. If that were the case, she thought, then why would they be lining up on King Street, directly in front of the palace, rather than heading to the homes and businesses of Americans? The drummer kept up a low, continuous beating. Trumpets sounded. Troops marched past, giving the queen a royal salute.

To Lili'u, it looked as if the American soldiers and marines were pointing their guns at her as they passed before heading to the grounds of Atherton's estate, which was about six hundred yards down King Street from the palace. There, the blue-jacketed troops rested under trees until nearly 10 p.m., drinking lemonade, eating bananas, and occasionally swatting away buzzing mosquitos, which had first arrived in the islands in the 1820s, along with the missionaries and whaling ships. A few raindrops started to fall, pattering softly on the ground. The soldiers moved indoors to Arion Hall, just behind the Opera House and directly opposite the palace. As the troops drifted off to sleep and Lili'u lay in bed wondering what the next day would bring, strains of music could be heard floating in from the grounds of the Hawaiian Hotel, behind the palace. Henry Berger's band was performing a moonlight concert there of Verdi, Wagner, and the late king's composition "Hawai'i Ponoi" for a group of tourists.

Shortly after the troops landed, Archibald Cleghorn, who was then governor of O'ahu, and Sam Parker rushed to protest the arrival of the marines to Stevens, who lay weak and exhausted on a sofa in his private office. Speaking with difficulty, the American minster insisted that they make their request in writing. He had also been visited that day by representatives from Britain, France, and Portugal—all asking the same question. Why were U.S. Marines camped in downtown Honolulu? Stevens's formal response to the palace, delivered Tuesday, was infuriatingly vague, perhaps intentionally so.

The queen sent a note to Stevens assuring him that the "present constitution" would be upheld. Pleading illness, Stevens refused to see anyone except Sam Parker and one of his fellow ministers. Stress-induced illness seemed to be making the rounds. Thurston also took to his bed early Monday night. Other members of the Committee of Safety, blithely assuming the success of their overthrow, had gathered to decide who among them should serve in a provisional government. They wanted Sanford Dole, the associate justice of Hawai'i's supreme court, to serve as president. Widely respected for his moderate views and his deep knowledge of the country, they knew Dole would legitimize their efforts if he'd accept the job.

He was at home, sitting in his parlor with his wife, Anna, when one of the comittee members knocked on his door. The emissary quickly relayed his message: the committee wanted Dole to head up a new government.

"No," Dole answered, asking why Thurston wouldn't take the job.

He explained that Thurston had become ill from toiling day and night on the annexation scheme. Perhaps unsaid was that Thurston was seen as a fiery radical, which might hurt their cause in Washington.

Dole agreed to meet with the committee members at their de facto headquarters in the downtown law office, in a room dominated by tall bookshelves, bound volumes, and a heavy safe on rollers. He was, at least initially, reluctant to go along with their plans. He argued that though Lili'u should be deposed, the Princess Ka'iulani should be named her successor, ruling under a regency until she was old enough to assume the throne on her own. The others dismissed his idea, arguing that the monarchy had to go. Dole went home to sleep on the decision of whether to accept the presidency. He later wrote that he had "passed a very unpleasant night."

By Tuesday morning Dole had changed his mind. He made his way before breakfast to consult with several friends, including Lorrin Thurston, at their homes. They helped him decide to accept the presidency, knowing that Stevens supported their cause. He also visited Stevens that day, who told him with little apparent evidence of conscience, "I think you have a great opportunity." He then wrote out his resignation as a judge, a post that Kalākaua had appointed him to in 1887.

Thurston became convinced the monarchy was about to collapse. The committee was winning support, including from a German military group known as Drei Hundert ("the three hundred"). Thurston was unable to rise from his sickbed on Tuesday, January 17, but nonetheless he dictated to his law clerk a draft of the proclamation to be used in deposing Liliʻu, overthrowing the monarchy, and establishing a new government made up of his allies until the United States annexed Hawaiʻi. By two-thirty that afternoon all the members of the Committee of Safety had signed Thurston's proclamation. They passed the four or five burly Hawaiian policemen who were posted across the street from the law office where they met and headed as a group down Merchant Street, toward Aliʻiōlani Hale.

As Thurston worked in bed, the Honolulu Rifles spent the morning gathering firearms and ammunition. Just as the committee members left their headquarters, a few blocks away, the Rifles' ordnance officer, an employee of Castle & Cooke, was driving a wagon loaded with ammunition toward the armory. An unarmed Hawaiian policeman grabbed the reins of the team of clomping horses pulling the wagon, trying to stop the wagon. A streetcar rattled along the tracks running up King Street, momentarily delaying the wagon, and another policeman attempted to climb into it. A tussle broke out and the ordnance officer shot the policeman in the shoulder.

At the sound of gunfire, people began running toward Fort and King streets. The distraction drew away the burly Hawaiian policeman who had been watching the committee's headquarters from across the street and permitted its unarmed members, about twenty of them including Dole, to reach the government building with no one stopping them. The gunfire also drew away the crowd of about a hundred Hawaiians who had gathered on the steps of the Opera House, poised for a confrontation at the government building. The distraction left the kingdom's seat of government almost deserted except for a few clerks, who fled their offices.

The chairman of the committee climbed to the top step of the building. His hands shook as he read the proclamation that Thurston had drafted to a half dozen or so spectators. It painted a portrait of a kingdom wracked by corruption and favoring "adventurers and persons of no character or standing in the community" during Kalākaua's reign. As well as detailing the perceived outrages perpetrated by Lili'u, the rambling statement also accused the recent legislature of "corruption, bribery and other illegitimate influences." It continued:

Her Majesty proceeded on the last day of the session to arbitrarily arrogate to herself the right to promulgate a new constitution, which proposed among other things to disenfranchise over one-fourth of the voters and owners of nine-tenths of the private property of the Kingdom . . .

Five uprising or conspiracies against the Government have occurred within five years and seven months. It is firmly believed that the culminating revolutionary attempt of last Saturday will, unless radical measures are taken, wreck our already damaged credit abroad and precipitate to final ruin our already overstrained financial condition.

The chairman then abolished the Hawaiian monarchical system of government and declared a provisional government established in its place, "until terms of union with the United States of America have been negotiated and agreed upon." Reading the statement took just ten minutes. By the time he finished reading this shaky pretext for overthrow, more and more armed supporters of the committee had gathered. Still confined to his sickbed, Thurston himself missed the moment of revolution.

Shortly after 3 p.m. Dole sent a note to Stevens. From his sickbed, the U.S. minister recognized the new government. Some time that afternoon, a photographer captured the image of Dole in his new role as president of the provisional government. Wearing an all-white suit and a straw boater tilted forward, Dole at six-foot-two towered above the captain of the USS *Boston* and the other *haole* who stood on the street curb that day, watching the American troops parade down King Street, within sight of the palace yard. Judged by his jaunty attire he might have been enjoying a Fourth of July day parade.

CHAPTER TWELVE

Crime of the Century, 1893

The House of Kalākaua rose amid violence and conflict. But its fall, on Tuesday, January 17, 1893, was surprisingly swift and almost bloodless. Liliʻu had remained indoors all afternoon. Soon after the proclamation one of her former ministers crossed the street from the government building to the palace carrying the bad news: Aliʻiōlani Hale occupied and a new government with Sanford Dole as its president which had won recognition from the American minister. He told the queen it was his painful duty to inform her that she must abdicate. Liliʻu replied hotly she had no intention of doing so.

Her options were narrowing. All four of her cabinet ministers made their way to the palace. Although Marshal Wilson had asked the cabinet for permission to surround the insurrectionists at the government building and "shoot them down, as they were only a handful," the ministers refused. Wilson, in turn, refused to surrender the station house until he was ordered to do so by the queen. Wilson certainly had a sizable enough force to regain control of the government building: 272 guards of the household, 500 or so royalist volunteers, and 30,000 rounds of ammunition, compared with the 164 American troops and officers armed with just over 13,000 rounds of ammunition and the provisional government's own troops, numbering fewer than 50 men. The ministers, it seems, were reluctant to get into a fight with the United States and may have had an exaggerated idea of the force at the Committee of Safety's command.

When the ministers met with Lili'u in the Blue Room, they advised her to surrender to avoid bloodshed. Perhaps thinking back to the Paulet episode of 1843, resolved by the British government restoring the Hawaiian king to power after five months of British rule, Lili'u agreed. She was counting on Washington to rule in her favor. Agreeing to yield, she issued a carefully worded protest, delivered to Dole at dusk.

I, Liliuokalani, by the Grace of God and under the Constitution of the Kingdom, Queen, do hereby solemnly protest against any and all acts done against myself and the constitutional government of the Hawaiian Kingdom by certain persons claiming to have established a provisional government of and for this Kingdom.

That I yield to the superior force of the United States of America, whose minister plenipotentiary, His Excellence John L. Stevens, has caused United States troops to be landed at Honolulu and declared that he would support the said provisional government.

Now, to avoid any collision of armed forces and perhaps the loss of life, I do under this protest, and impelled by said force, yield my authority until such time as the Government of the United States shall, upon the facts being presented to it, undo the action of its representatives and reinstate me in the authority which I claim as the constitutional sovereign of the Hawaiian Islands.

Dole signed the back of this protest, indicating he'd received it. He may have been so stunned by her surrender that he did not absorb the full implications of her note: she had refused to acknowledge the provisional government's authority, yielding instead to the United States as the ultimate arbiter of the matter. She'd characterized Stevens as having orchestrated her overthrow. And she had refused to abdicate.

The wording of her protest, drafted by her lawyer, would later be the subject of lengthy U.S. congressional testimony and debate. With a few strokes of a pen, Lili'u and her allies had transformed what might have been a minor coup in a remote kingdom into an international incident, one that became a test of America's first major imperial push. For months and even years afterward, scandalous headlines and lengthy investigations would dog the U.S.-supported takeover of the Hawaiian kingdom.

That evening, as the troops shared hardtack, corned beef, and a huge urn of coffee from a nearby saloon, they worked in the occupied government building until after nine o'clock. Perhaps concerned that the glow of the lights from the government building could be seen from the palace, they worked at the back of the building.

Dole declared martial law and suspended the right of the writ of habeas corpus. Working under electric lights, first installed in the building a few years earlier, it is likely he could hear the sounds of American troops singing to pass the time that evening: they sang the abolitionist ballad the "Battle Hymn of the Republic."

Mine eyes have seen the glory of the coming of the Lord
He is trampling out the vintage where the grapes of wrath are stored

That night, the queen retired to her private chamber on the second floor of the palace and wrote down the day's events. She noted that the Hawaiian flag would not change, nor would the royal standard. Relieved that no lives had been lost, and perhaps failing to grasp how the world had changed since the British restored her predecessor to the throne back in 1843, she wrote, "Things turned out better than I expected."

The next morning, the queen woke to the soft tones of *mele hoāla*, one of the songs that her chanter would sing to stir her from her sleep. After breakfast, she looked forward to the bouquet of red lehua blossoms and other flowers brought to her every day. But her sense of relief quickly vanished.

Soldiers surged through the corridors of the palace. The smells of bread and roasting meat rose from the basement, as overnight the former royal residence became a barracks. Lili'u may have heard the thump of rifle butts on concrete floors or the sound of their hobnailed books pacing across the polished wood floors.

Hastily she gathered her belongings. Unshaven soldiers now lounged in the former throne room, beneath the crystal chandeliers. Clerks hurried in and out of the dining room, which was littered with boxes and papers. To escape the chaos, the deposed queen and her household retainers hurriedly decamped to Washington Place.

Perhaps to calm herself, Lili'u visited the mausoleum that afternoon and went swimming off of Waikīkī. Upon returning home, she received a note from the provisional government ordering her to permanently haul down the Hawaiian royal standard that had long flown over Washington Place. After consulting with her attorney, she reluctantly agreed. Aside from writing appeals to the U.S. president, Queen Victoria, the emperor of Germany, and the president of the French republic, Lili'u wrote in her diary that she sought to "remain perfectly passive till we heard from our Commissioners to Washington."

Sanford Dole, for his part, was less jubilant about the turn of events than one might have imagined. In a letter to his brother George just two days after the overthrow, he wrote, "How I have regretted this whole affair. Had I my way about the matter I would have used far more tactful ways than the treatment that we have thus rendered. I have reiterated time and again my desire that we hold the power of the throne in a trust and we hold the regency in the name of the young Princess Kaiulani, Mr. Cleghorn's daughter, who is away in England, until she reaches her majority and is able to govern her own affairs. I am sorry to say this plan has not met with approval."

Yet Dole's actions as head of the new government displayed little of this remorse. As commander in chief of the newly established National

Guard of Hawai'i, he ordered the disbanding of the Royal Household Guards, leaving the queen with only a small squad of sixteen men and one officer to protect her at Washington Place. Meanwhile, American troops also sandbagged the government building in case of a counterattack from royalist forces. The new government banished even small symbols of monarchy: Lili'u's remaining guards were required to remove the gold crown royal insignia from the front of their caps. It even stripped the "By Authority" column in the newspapers—which for decades had contained official communications from the palace—of its coat of arms.

Dole did not allow the feelings he confessed to his brother to enter into his decisions about how to present the news of the coup to the outside world. Recognizing the need for speed, the new government specially chartered a steamer to bring its version of events to America. When officials of the deposed government learned of this they too, requested to send commissioners on the same boat to the mainland. But the provisional government denied that request. Its representatives, led by Lorrin Thurston, would arrive in Washington, D.C., a fortnight ahead of the queen's, allowing them to present their side of the story first to lawmakers and the president.

As the new government's emissaries began their race across the Pacific, Dole's government quickly repealed the lottery and opium bills. The provisional government's troops moved into the royal barracks on the palace grounds. With the risk that some of the soldiers might start taking treasures from the palace home to adorn their own mantels, the administrator of Kalākaua's estate wrote Dole a letter dated two days after Lili'u had vacated the palace demanding that he return the king's property still at 'Iolani Palace, referring to an itemized list of the late king's belongings submitted seven months earlier. Lili'u earlier had resisted this request, preferring to keep priceless Hawaiian artifacts with her in the palace instead of turning them over to the Bishop Museum.

Under martial law, the capital remained calm. Mounted troops patrolled the streets and, much to the relief of some of the neighbors of a Chinese theater, the gong it rang each night was quieted. Women soon felt safe enough to leave their homes unattended, classes resumed at the

Punahou school, and saloons reopened. American troops remained stationed downtown, moving into one of the places that remained closest to Liliʻuʻs heart: her beloved childhood home, Haleakalā, which had become a hotel. The troops nicknamed it "Camp Boston."

But the presence of nearby troops didn't ease Dole's anxiety. After hearing rumors of threats against him, he was afraid to sleep at home. So at night he moved into a small room adjoining the former royal apartments on the second floor of the palace, where a bed had been moved. Tacitly acknowledging its inability to preserve the peace on its own, the provisional government petitioned Stevens for American protection. It also requested a ceremony that, to the Hawaiians who witnessed it, would painfully display their country's occupation by a foreign military force.

At 8:30 a.m. on February 1, the captain of the *Boston* and a battalion of troops arrived at the government building, joined by three volunteer companies. At nine the American warship fired a booming salute and U.S. Marines hoisted the American flag over the tower of Aliʻiōlani Hale. Stevens declared the former Kingdom of Hawaiʻi a U.S. protectorate.

Some rejoiced; one *haole* historian, for instance, wrote at the time that he hoped the "glorious sight" of the "ensign of Freedom floating over the tower of the Government Building" would "send up" government bonds and plantation stocks—suggesting that the conspirators were driven by financial concerns above all else. Privately, that same historian wrote to his son recounting Liliʻu's overthrow, blaming it on what he considered her crazed decision to appoint "four drunken gamblers" as her cabinet ministers. "*Quos deus vult perdere, prius dementat* [the Latin for "Those whom a god wishes to destroy he first drives mad"]. How true this is of Liliuokalani!"

Liliʻu, for her part, felt a furious desire for revenge upon seeing the American flag fluttering over Aliʻiōlani Hale. "Drove by the Palace and would not look at the American flag over the Government building," she wrote. "Time may wear off the feeling of injury by and by—but my dear flag—the Hawaiian flag—that a strange flag should wave over it. May heaven look down on these Missionaries and punish them for their deeds."

* * *

One of the people most pained by the swift fall of the monarchy was Archibald Cleghorn. A few days after the overthrow, the Scotsman wrote a long, heartfelt letter to his daughter Kaʻiulani, who by then had left her boarding school. The princess was living in the English seaside town of Brighton, where she was being privately tutored in physics, literature, and history as well as dancing, painting, and deportment. Aside from missing Fairy, her white pony back in Waikīkī, Kaʻiulani's life was relatively carefree, and her letters to her aunt over the previous year had bubbled over with details of the dainty summer dresses she was having made and her success at raising £400 for charity.

Cleghorn wrote to tell her how he had waited with the other dignitaries in the Blue Room for three and a half hours on Saturday, January 14, as Liliʻu prepared to introduce a new constitution. Furious with what he considered the trouble the queen had started, he fired off nineteen anguished pages to his daughter.

> I have never given the Queen anything but good advice. If she had followed my advice, she would have been firm on the throne, and Hawaiian Independence safe, but she has turned out a very stubborn woman and was not satisfied to Reign, but wanted to Rule. If she had followed in the example set by [Queen] Victoria, She would have been represented by all good people, and by my dear daughter—[the] Govt may think that it is best you should not come to the Throne. you may be happier in private life and be an example to your people . . .
>
> If the Queen had abdicated the night of the 16th or early in the 17th in your *favor*, the Throne I think could have been *saved*, but she did not think they would do as they did. She still followed the advice of poor Ministers, wretched men, and we have all to suffer.

He ended his letter with these words: "I am ashamed to write any one. My poor country."

*   *   *

Kaʻiulani learned of the problems weeks before her father's letter arrived. Her guardian in England, Theo H. Davies, received three telegrams on January 30. The first read "Queen Deposed." The second: "Monarchy Abrogated." The third: "Break news to Princess."

After a few days Davies asked the seventeen-year-old princess to accompany him to Washington, D.C., where he hoped she could help sway public opinion toward the cause of restoring the Hawaiian monarchy. She agreed, reasoning it was better to try and fail than to answer criticism from the Hawaiian people if she never tried at all. Her instincts were good, since at almost exactly the same time, the U.S. minister Stevens wrote to the American secretary of state John W. Foster, "The Hawaiian pear is now fully ripe and this is the golden hour for the United States to pluck it."

On February 18, Kaʻiulani issued a statement to the London newspapers, declaring, "I am coming to Washington to plead for my throne, my nation and my flag. Will not the great American people hear me?" A few days later she boarded the *Teutonic*, accompanied by her guardian, his wife, and a companion, and arrived in New York harbor on March 1. Even before reaching the pier, a cutter pulled up alongside the liner carrying two of Liliʻu's former ministers, who were there to welcome her. As the liner approached the pier, Kaʻiulani could see a crowd of reporters and curiosity seekers, who in turn were eager to catch a glimpse of the crown princess of Hawaiʻi.

What the gentlemen of the press saw was a slender young woman with creamy skin and soft brown eyes. Fashioning her hair in a high, twisted knot and wearing a simple gray traveling gown, her composure was striking enough for a *New York Times* reporter to write, "She talks in a very simple, dignified way and seems possessed of decidedly more common sense than most young women of seventeen or eighteen." Wearing glasses that did not conceal "her decidedly good eyes," the newsman sized her up as a "Yankee school-marm type." But Kaʻiulani's arrival that day was overshadowed by stories of Tammany Hall politicians heading to Washington for President Cleveland's inauguration.

Despite the blustery, overcast weather and her inexperience with public speaking, Ka'iulani stood on the pier, clutching an appeal written for her by Davies, her ruddy-faced British guardian.

> Seventy years ago Christian America sent over Christian men and women to give religion and civilization to Hawaii. Today, three of the sons of those missionaries are at your capitol asking you to undo their fathers' work. Who sent them? Who gave them the authority to break the Constitution which they swore to uphold?
>
> Today, I, a poor, weak girl with not one of my people near me and all these Hawaiian statesman against me, have strength to stand up for the rights of my people. Even now I can hear their wail in my heart and it gives me strength and courage and I am not strong—strong in the faith of God, strong in the knowledge that I am right, strong in the strength of seventy million people who in this free land will hear my cry and will refuse to let their flag cover dishonor to mine!

It was a moving appeal, sure to touch the hearts of even the most hardened journalists. But beneath the sentimental plea lay the implied promise that the fetching and pliable Ka'iulani could replace Lili'u on the throne, thus setting up a potential rivalry between niece and aunt. With an accent and graceful bearing reflecting her English boarding school, Ka'iulani won admirers as she traveled from New York to Boston and then on to Washington, trailed by thirteen trunks and eight bags, all stamped with the initials VK.

The favorable stories about her in the American press came at a time when public officials and editorial writers, initially favorable to annexation in the weeks after the overthrow, by March of 1893 had begun questioning the actions of Thurston, Dole, and the provisional government. The *New York Herald* concluded that the revolution was "of, by, and for sugar," while the St. Louis *Chronicle* reported that "The revolution was not a movement of the people but . . . by those who were not permitted by the queen to plunder the land." The *New York Times* ran a lengthy story on the affair, headlining it "A Shameful Conspiracy in Which the United States Was Made to Play a Part." The story's subtitle was even more inflammatory, decrying it as "The Political Crime of the Century."

Much of the coverage had an ugly racial tinge. Shortly after news of the overthrow reached America, the lead editorial in the Fresno (California) *Expositor* read, "The Hawaiians have 'revoluted' and dethroned the fat squaw they have hitherto chosen to call a queen." But four days later the same paper reversed itself and wrote, "The more closely it is examined the more the so-called Hawaiian 'revolution' looks like a deliberate scheme on the part of a band of schemers to deliberately create a crisis in order to precipitate annexation to the United States." By the time of Ka'iulani's arrival in Washington, the American papers, which had first referred to Thurston and his supporters as revolutionaries, were now calling them "adventurers" who had stolen a kingdom at the behest of the sugar barons.

Grover Cleveland also had growing doubts about the overthrow. One of his first moves as the new Democratic president after taking office on March 4 was to hastily withdraw the Hawaiian annexation treaty, which his successor the Republican Harrison had hoped to push through before leaving office. He appointed a special commissioner to investigate the matter: James H. Blount of Georgia, who had been head of the House Committee on Foreign Affairs.

Ka'iulani had arrived in Washington at just the right moment, as public opinion was already shifting. Her delicate beauty and elegant manners quickly swept away any lingering image, planted by the pro-annexation propagandists, of the heir apparent as a "barbarian princess." She was invited to the White House and arrived in the late afternoon of March 13 wearing a sophisticated long-sleeved gown with a tightly fitted bodice, topped off with an enormous Gainsborough-style hat trimmed with ostrich plumes to be received by the portly president and his much younger first lady. The teenager was a sensation.

Yet little did Ka'iulani realize when she boarded a steamer on March 20 to return to England that her embattled aunt had started to see her as a threat to her own hoped-for restoration to the throne.

Back in Honolulu, Lili'u spent the long weeks before Commissioner Blount arrived worrying about money, fending off unwanted visitors, parrying attacks on her public image, and calming her supporters. To pay for her representatives to travel to Washington, she mortgaged her three homes—her modest cottage and surrounding lands at Waikīkī, her home at Pālama, and Washington Place—to the Bishop bank, raising $10,000. She cashed in the postal savings accounts of her two wards and wrote to Claus Spreckels regarding her shares in the Hawaiian Agricultural Co., which she hoped to sell.

A ceaseless downpour dampened Lili'u's spirits, as did the screeds issuing forth from the pulpits of some of the island kingdom's churches. "It is a gloomy day and it rains, rains, rains," wrote Lili'u in her diary entry for Sunday, February 5. "Do not feel like going to Church—perhaps never more. I never saw a more unchristian like set as these Missionaries and so uncharitable as to abuse me in the manner they do from the pulpit. Is it godly—No—It makes me feel as if I would not like to do any thing more for Churches."

She took little comfort from practitioners of native religion either. About a week later, Lili'u had received some unwelcome visitors at Washington Place: three Hawaiian women dressed in white with yellow handkerchiefs tied around their necks and red bands on their hats. They were *kāhuna*, practitioners of the old Hawaiian religion, apparently offering themselves as sacrifices to appease the gods so that the queen would be restored. All too aware of how these visitors might give her enemies more ammunition against her, Lili'u wrote in her diary, "I wish they would not come here."

Rumors circulated almost daily that Lili'u might be the target of an assassination plot. At the end of February the provisional government withdrew the guards from Washington Place. Lili'u heeded cautions not to go out onto the streets of downtown Honolulu and spent more time at her home in Waikīkī, where she supervised weeding the garden and employed now unemployed royalist troops to cut fence railing from the date trees. As she prepared new furnishings for her bedroom there and awaited the arrival of mosquito netting to keep away the ever present pests that bred in Waikīkī's swamps, a sense of loneliness overcame over her. To pass the time, she wrote out a list of all the songs she'd composed, tallying a hundred in all.

One bright moment came in mid-March. Almost as soon as it had seized power, Dole's government began requiring all former government employees to swear a loyalty oath. Among those who refused were the musicians of Berger's Royal Hawaiian Band, declaring they'd rather "eat stones" than swear their allegiance to the provisional government, by then known as the P.G. As a result, all but sixteen members of the band were sacked. Berger ended up hiring Portuguese musicians and recruiting through the San Francisco musicians' union to fill out the band's ranks.

Early that morning, however, to support Hawai'i's beleaguered queen, the unemployed former band members gathered outside Washington Place to serenade Lili'u. Listening to them play, she admired their patriotism. Tears filled the eyes of some of the people heading to work that morning who heard the strains of music in the deposed queen's garden, among its tamarind and monkeypod trees.

Several letters that Lili'u received from friends and supporters reported on Ka'iulani's trip. In one, the queen's correspondent warned her that "Ka'iulani's appearance upon the scene will embarrass us very much more especially as she does not appear to care for anyone but herself, and wants the Throne at once."

Those worries were soon overtaken by the arrival of the Honorable James Blount and his wife aboard the *Rush*, which entered Honolulu harbor on March 29. Lili'u sent her chamberlain to the steamer at eleven that morning to offer the commissioner a ride in her carriage. Speaking in a soft Georgia drawl, Blount politely declined. Likewise, he turned down the offer of transport and a furnished home from representatives of the provisional government, to avoid the appearance of accepting any favors from either side. Anticipating his arrival, the town was decked with American flags.

On the morning of Saturday, April 1, three days after Blount's arrival, the American flag flying over Ali'iōlani Hale came down. On Blount's orders, soldiers hauled down the Stars and Stripes from the government building and the U.S. troops returned to the *Boston*. Lili'u, through Joseph Nāwahī, had asked her subjects to restrain themselves from cheering. Standing silently, native Hawaiian men held their hats in their hands as soldiers lowered the standard. Tears streamed down their cheeks. Afterward, the queen slept most of the day, writing in her diary, "I am more tired from thinking than from actual work."

That same night, Lili'u heard from her chamberlain that some of the departing troops had looted the palace. Several hundred spent the evening in the palace basement, stripping decorations from the walls and stealing one of the crowns she had hidden. An Irish-American recruit found Kalākaua's crown and pried off the jewels, which he then used as payment in a game of dice. He managed to avoid gambling them all away and kept one of the biggest diamonds, which he sent to his sister on the mainland, not realizing its value.

The pro-government *Advertiser* ran a splashy story soon after the theft, headlined "PLUNDERED!" The newspaper declared it "almost a certainty" that the crown, which had been kept in a locked trunk in what had been the chamberlain's office in the palace basement, had been stolen before the overthrow—not during the Dole government's watch. But that turned out to be wishful thinking when Ryan, one of the new government's recruits, was caught red-handed with some of the jewels he'd stolen. He was arrested, found guilty, sentenced to three years in jail, and ordered to pay a $200 fine.

The snowy-haired Blount, a taciturn man, kept his orders from Washington a secret, earning himself the nickname "Reticent Blount." Others called him "Paramount Blount," since his authority was thought to be supreme in matters relating to the American presence in the islands. Working from a cottage on the grounds of the Hawaiian Hotel, he diligently gathered testimony, letters, affidavits, and documents from both sides over the next five months—although not, puzzlingly, from Dole or many members of the Committee of Safety. It may be that they declined to cooperate, having concluded, based on the royalist company he was keeping, he was biased in favor of the queen.

Blount's meeting with Lili'u took place shortly after he arrived and she submitted a written statement to him laying out her version of events. Well before Blount was finished, Minister Stevens was dismissed from his post and recalled to the United States.

Lili'u, who'd long felt insulted by the minister's disrespect, had showed little pity when soon after the overthrow one of Stevens's three daughters drowned off of Hawai'i Island. She had been gathering signatures on a pro-annexation petition. Lili'u's diary entry of May 24, 1893, on the day Stevens left, echoed the remorselessness of her warrior ancestors: "May he be made to suffer as much as the many pangs he has caused amongst my people. He took back with him the remains of his daughter. Her death I consider a judgment from heaven."

Steaming into the Honolulu harbor Claus Spreckels disembarked from the *Australia* on the rainy morning of April 18. The sugar king of Hawai'i himself wanted to size up the situation in Honolulu. He had been attending to his business in California at the time of the overthrow, preoccupied by a war against a band of eastern sugar producers, known as the Sugar Trust. Once it wound to a conclusion, largely in his favor, he turned his attention back to the islands.

Hosting Thurston and his fellow provisional government commissioners when they stopped in San Francisco in late January on their way to Washington, he briefly seemed to favor a closer relationship between the kingdom and the United States. Spreckels reasoned that annexation would mean more freight and passengers for his steamship line and less expensive sugar from the islands for his California sugar refineries. Like many West Coast businessmen, he figured it would boost Pacific trade.

But Spreckels rapidly switched his position when he realized his interests would be better served by supporting the queen, particularly since annexation could mean an end to the kingdom's planter-friendly labor laws. The islands' inexpensive labor and laissez-faire regulations, he reasoned, would end under the exclusion laws of the United States. And they were far more valuable to Spreckels than any benefits gained from annexation. "We could get along—the majority of the plantations—without any [tariff] subsidy if we had labor, but without labor we could not get along at all."

Joined by his wife, daughter, and son Rudolph, Spreckels and his family settled into the graceful, white-pillared home they owned in the Punahou neighborhood of Honolulu. Within days, he sat down separately with Blount, Dole, and Lili'u to find out for himself what had happened. As the owner of the kingdom's largest sugar plantation, its principal steamship line, and a leading bank, the German-American remained a silent but significant economic force in the kingdom. Some of the American reporters who'd journeyed to Hawai'i to cover Blount's investigation sought out his opinions.

One of the most prominent of these reporters was Charles Nordhoff, who wrote for the *New York Herald*. When Nordhoff asked Spreckels if stability would be possible in Hawai'i without annexation, he replied, "I can't see why we should not have stable independent government. I am sure that stable, orderly, and economical government is possible here, and as I am the largest taxpayer on the islands, and have more property at stake and pay more taxes than the whole Provisional Government, you will admit that my interests make me conservative. I need a stable and economical government more than any man on the islands."

So Spreckels, with his powerful build and large head, bullheadedly refused to admit defeat. He devised a plan to topple the provisional government using a weapon readily available to him. He called in the

$95,000 loan made to the government under the monarchy, for which the new government had assumed responsibility, from his bank. His hope was that Sanford Dole's government would default thus triggering a destabilizing crisis of confidence. Lili'u first heard of the plan from Sam Parker and later from Spreckels himself that it would be "the means of putting me back on the throne."

But the P.G. wasn't to be outmaneuvered so easily. It responded by sending representatives out onto the streets of downtown Honolulu to raise funds to meet the demand. Within just two hours it'd collected the $95,000 from local merchants. That meant Spreckels's gambit had backfired, souring his relations with the P.G. and making the sugar king a target for scorn in the P.G.-friendly newspapers.

"Since the days of Shakespeare, the calling in of gold has been a typical method of taking revenge on the unsuspicious debtor," one outraged commentary in the *Gazette* fumed. The same paper later said, with rhetorical flourish, that Hawai'i "had refused to be reduced to bankruptcy at the nod of the chief Hawaiian boodler and politician."

Even more incendiary was an article aimed at Spreckels published in the pro-P.G. *Star* entitled "Herr Rothschild von Katzenjammer." Set in imperial Germany and painting Katzenjammer (Spreckels) as a large landholder who had been living abroad, the story contained an implied threat. "It was easy therefore to prove that he was a conspirator against the peace and dignity of the Provisional Government of Germany. The sentence of the court was that his estates and credits should be confiscated and his person banished from the country." So outraged was Spreckels by the story that he filed a libel suit against the newspaper.

The anger directed at the sugar king wasn't confined to newsprint. On the morning of June 22, just as he was preparing to step into his carriage outside his home, Spreckels spied a bloodred sign nailed to the gatepost of his large, two-storied home. Above a crudely drawn skull and crossbones, it read "Gold and Silver will not stop lead!!!"

Spreckels was outraged by this anonymous threat. A masculine man cast in the mold of his contemporary Thedore Roosevelt, he was not however particularly contemplative. His strengths lay in his enormous capacity for work and his intuitive grasp of opportunities. But whatever his shortcomings as a thinker, who might have seen that this threat was as thin as the parchment it was scrawled on, he demanded from Blount protection for himself and his family.

True to form, he got it. Soon a Hawaiian policeman was assigned to guard his home. Liliʻu, for her part, was familiar with what Spreckels and his family were experiencing: she continued to hear rumors of plots against her, including one in which the P.G. planned to send sixteen men with masks and guns to carry her off and deport her and another in which explosives were planted in her unopened letters. She also believed her mail was being intercepted and that the P.G. had planted spies to watch her every move. During his visits with the queen at Washington Place, Spreckels had tried to reassure her by stating his belief that the provisional government would not dare harm her and urging her to let him know if she ever needed money.

A few weeks after discovering the threatening sign, Spreckels and his wife paid Liliʻu one last visit before leaving for San Francisco. Spreckels expressed the deposed queen's own most fervent wish: that the monarchy be restored with her at its head and a new constitution promulgated. Promising to travel to Washington to press her case, Spreckels then could not resist asking for Liliʻu's cooperation in return, particularly when it came to her choice of what ministers to appoint to the cabinet and laws governing the sugar industry.

Having seen where horse trading with Spreckels had landed her late brother, Liliʻu balked at making him any promises.

The next morning, Spreckels left his home and climbed on board the *Australia* as the old Royal Hawaiian Band, granted permission by the provisional government to do so, serenaded him and the other passengers from the wharf. He stood on the deck of the steamer, his blue eyes crinkled from the wide smile on his face and his cheeks ruddy from the champagne he'd enjoyed after boarding. A dozen or more *lei* circled his neck and festooned his straw boater.

One can only imagine the overwhelming fragrance of tropical flowers that Spreckels experienced at that moment, intensified by the tropical heat as well as the smoke from his ever present cigar. He was surrounded by Hawaiian women, perhaps members of the women's branch of the Hui Hawai'i Aloha 'Āina, a mostly native league formed immediately after the overthrow to support the queen, clothed in white and wearing flower garlands. Did he feel a sense of *aloha*? Or did he feel merely relief at having escaped Honolulu and what some called the Murder Society—that band of missionary descendants intent on taking over the kingdom?

If he did, his relief was short-lived upon his return to San Francisco. In late 1893 an incendiary family fight broke out, and it ended up costing Spreckels control of the Hawaiian Commercial and Sugar Company. His two younger sons, aggrieved by their father's complex financial engineering in the midst of the company's financial troubles, filed a $2.5 million suit against him and their two older brothers. In essence, they alleged that they had been cheated out of their rightful shares of the company by the other family members. Their claims seem to have been valid, since Claus and the two older siblings were ousted after an out-of-court settlement that gave the younger sons control of the company. Like Lili'u, Spreckels, too, suffered a rift in his family and the loss of his Hawaiian kingdom.

Lili'u's sense of foreboding deepened toward the end of the year, as heavy rains hammered the earth. Blount had left Honolulu not long after Spreckels, forwarding his findings to the U.S. secretary of state, who submitted his report to President Cleveland in October. Its conclusions were unambiguously in Lili'u's favor: she had been illegally overthrown with the help of Minister Stevens and aided by the presence of U.S. Marines.

That a deep wrong has been done the Queen and the native race by American officials pervades the native mind and that of the Queen, as well as a hope for redress from the United States, there can be no doubt.

In this connection it is important to note the inability of the Hawaiian people to cope with any great powers, and their recognition of it by never offering resistance to their encroachments.

The suddenness of the landing of the United States troops, the reading of the proclamation of the Provisional Government almost in their presence, and the quick recognition by Mr. Stevens, easily prepared her for the suggestion that the President of the United States had no knowledge of these occurrences and must know of and approve or disapprove of what had occurred at a future time . . .

The undoubted sentiment of the people is for the Queen, against the Provisional Government and against annexation. A majority of the whites, especially Americans, are for annexation.

To try to rectify that wrong, the secretary sent Albert S. Willis, a new minister, to the islands in mid-October with instructions to express to the queen "sincere regret" for the "reprehensible conduct" of Stevens and to rely on the justice of the American government to undo the "flagrant wrong." The president, in turn, expected Lili'u to assume all the debts of the provisional government and to grant full amnesty to those who'd overthrown her.

But Lili'u remained an *ali'i* above all else. Despite the values of obedience and humility impressed upon her by her missionary teachers, she balked at the thought of meekly submitting to these demands. It was not until a week after Willis's arrival in Honolulu, where he installed himself in what was known as Snow Cottage—the same residence that his predecessor "Paramount" Blount had recently vacated on the grounds of the Hawaiian Hotel—that he finally summoned Lili'u to call on him at the American legation, a breach of protocol that was an early hint of the grave misunderstanding ahead. Lili'u overcame her offended feelings of being asked to travel through the streets of Honolulu when she believed it was Willis, a former congressman from Kentucky, who should have come to her. She made her way to the legation at 11:30 on the morning of November 13, accompanied by her chamberlain. By insisting that she travel to see him, Willis may have been making it clear, right from the start, that the balance of power lay with him.

Ushered into the parlor, Lili'u met the short-statured, balding minister unaccompanied by her chamberlain, who had withdrawn to another room. Willis began by sending greetings from Cleveland, telling her that the president wished to express his regret that, through the unauthorized intervention of the United States, she had been obliged to surrender her sovereignty. It was his hope that, with her consent and cooperation, the wrong done to her and to her people might be redressed.

Lili'u, who was seated on a sofa, bowed her head slightly to acknowledge his words. So far, her audience with Willis seemed to be going well.

"The president not only tenders you his sympathy but wishes to help you," the minister continued. "Before fully making known to you his purposes, I desire to know whether you are willing to answer certain questions which it is my duty to ask?"

"I am willing," Lili'u replied.

"Should you be restored to the throne, would you grant full amnesty as to life and property to all those persons who have been or who are now in the provisional government, or who have been instrumental in the overthrow of your government?"

Lili'u hesitated. Willis asked her to speak from her heart, assuring her they were alone. Yet she knew that Mrs. Willis was in the next room and later wrote that she suspected someone was listening to their conversation, perhaps from behind a Japanese screen or some curtains. Cautiously, she replied that she would have to consult with her cabinet before granting the P.G.s their lives or amnesty.

There is no need to consult them, Willis countered. What is your decision?

At that moment, she spoke candidly and perhaps out of anger. She would later suffer from the terrible consequences of her words.

"Our laws read that those who are guilty of treason shall suffer the

239

penalty of death, and their property confiscated to the government," Lili'u told him. "If any amnesty was to be made, it was that they should leave the country forever—for if they were permitted to remain, they would commit the same offense over again, seeing that they had once caused a revolution in 1887 and this was a second offense, and the next I fear would be more serious than this for our country and our people."

Willis heard the queen's response differently. As he later reported to Washington and in a memorandum that Lili'u later signed, her words were: "My decision would be, as the law directs, that such persons should be beheaded and their property confiscated to the government."

Taken by surprise, Willis asked her to repeat what she had said: "It is your feeling that these people should be beheaded and their property confiscated?"

"It is," the queen replied.

"Do you fully understand the meaning of every word which I have said to you, and of every word which you have said to me, and, if so, do you still have the same opinion?"

"I have understood and mean all I have said, but I might leave the decision of this to my ministers," Lili'u said, beginning to backpedal as the realization of how she'd responded sank in. Nonetheless, likely fueled by months of simmering outrage at the bold, unapologetic theft of her country, she did not retract her explosive threat to behead her enemies at that moment—when doing so might have changed everything.

"If that is your decision, I will write to President Cleveland and inform him of this," Willis said, adding that he was likely to hear back from Washington with further instructions in three to four weeks.

Three days later, Willis sent a telegram to Secretary of State Walter Gresham about his interview, hinting that the restoration would not proceed according to plan: "Views of first party so extreme as to require further instructions." In a testy response demanding further details, the secretary of state replied, "The brevity and uncertainty of your telegrams are embarrassing."

Lorrin A. Thurston, son of missionaries, and chief instigator of the 1887 "Bayonet Constitution." (State Archives of Hawai'i)

Robert Wilcox, who plotted an attempted coup that sought to restore Kalakaua's right to rule. (State Archives of Hawai'i)

At an 1889 lu'au, guest of honor Robert Louis Stevenson (at the head of the table, at left) sits next to Lili'u (seated second from left, in light skirt); to the right of her is Kalakaua (third from left, with bow tie). (State Archives of Hawai'i)

A bereaved Liliʻu assumed the throne on
January 29, 1891. (State Archives of Hawaiʻi)

Kalakaua lying in state, February 1891. (State Archives of Hawaiʻi)

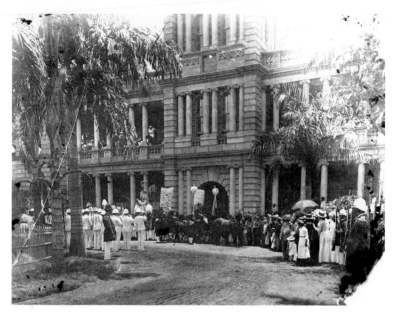

Lili'u arrives at the legislature to close the session on January 14, 1893. Later that day she would announce her intent to promulgate a new constitution restoring executive powers to the monarchy. (State Archives of Hawai'i)

The thirteen members of the "Committee of Safety" reacted quickly to news that Lili'u wanted to enact a new constitution and organized a coup that toppled the Hawaiian government.
(State Archives of Hawai'i)

Lorrin Thurston, right, and Sanford B. Dole, at Dole's legal offices in Honolulu. Dole would go on to assume presidency of the Provisional Government. (State Archives of Hawai'i)

Troops from the USS *Boston* landed on January 16, 1893, backed by the U.S. envoy, John L. Stevens. (State Archives of Hawai'i)

This December 1893 cartoon from the *Judge* depicts a barefoot Lili'u clutching papers that read "scandalous government" and "gross immorality." (Bishop Museum)

Claus Spreckels (second from left, festooned with lei) tried to help the queen. He traveled to the islands in 1893 and called in his debts, hoping to bankrupt the Provisional Government and restore her to the throne. The attempt failed, and Spreckels returned home after claiming to have received death threats. (State Archives of Hawai'i)

Lili'u's niece, Ka'iulani.
(State Archives of Hawai'i)

On January 16, 1895, the republic accused Lili'u of participating in a failed rebellion that attempted to restore her to the throne. She was arrested and imprisoned in 'Iolani Palace. Above, the only photo of her arrest shows Lili'u, in a long gown at right, mounting the stairs to the palace under government escort. (State Archives of Hawai'i)

In this newspaper illustration from the *San Francisco Examiner,* Lili'u, in a black gown, is defended by attorney Paul Neumann, standing in foreground, against charges of knowing about a plot to overthrow the government. (State Archives of Hawai'i)

In her nearly eight months of imprisonment in ʻIolani Palace, Liliʻu and her attendant stitched a quilt, whose images and words chronicled the key events in her life. (The Friends of ʻIolani Palace)

In 1896, Liliʻu traveled to the United States to plead for restoration of Hawaiʻi's sovereign independence. This picture was taken after her departure, perhaps in 1899 or 1900. (State Archives of Hawaiʻi)

The Hawaiian flag is lowered and replaced with the Stars and Stripes on Annexation Day, August 2, 1898. (State Archives of Hawaiʻi)

Lili'u at Washington Place in the 1890s. (State Archives of Hawai'i)

Lili'u's statue outside the Hawai'i
state legislature. (Author photo)

After a dispatch from Willis finally arrived to clarify matters, Gresham sent another telegram, specifying, "Should the Queen ask whether, if she accedes to conditions, active steps will be taken by the United States to effect her restoration, or to maintain her authority thereafter, you will say that the President can not use force without the authority of Congress." The irony of this—considering it was the presence of U.S. troops that led to her overthrow—was apparently lost on the secretary.

On December 14, a U.S. cutter named the *Carver* appeared unexpectedly at dawn, rounding the coast at Diamond Head. It was carrying the secretary of state's second set of instructions to Minister Willis from Washington, which the captain of a pilot boat retrieved and rushed to the American legation in Honolulu. A few hours later, the *Star* newspaper published an extra edition on the streets, reporting President Cleveland's message: "Our only honorable course was to undo the wrong that had been done by those representing us, and to restore as far as practicable the status existing at the time of our forcible intervention."

Acting on these orders, Willis invited Lili'u to his cottage for a second time, suggesting she bring with her an adviser. She chose the *haole* Joseph O. Carter, who had served in her privy council and acted as her business agent. He had stood by her, against some of his own family members and even after losing his job at C. Brewer & Co. This time, they met at nine in the morning and a stenographer joined them in the parlor to transcribe the conversation.

Before Willis launched into their second interview, he read to Lili'u from a memorandum purporting to be notes on their interview on November 13. After he was done, with Carter as a witness, she placed her elegantly rounded signature on it, using her full royal name Lili'uokalani Rex. She may not have read the document herself but, for whatever reason, she apparently did not dispute the explosive word that the document contained and that her enemies would later use to seal her downfall: her statement that her enemies should be "beheaded."

After she'd signed the paper, Willis again asked her in the presence of the stenographer "whether the views expressed at that time, as read to you now, have been in any respect modified since that conversation?"

"They have not," answered the queen, more confident in answering the homely American minister than she was a month earlier, perhaps since the newspapers were reporting she would soon be restored to the throne.

"You still adhere to your judgment, as then expressed, that all of those persons should be punished according to the law under the constitution of 1887, which is that they should be punished with capital punishment and their property confiscated?"

Having had a full month to reconsider her last interview with Willis, Lili'u softened her position. "I feel that if any change should be made that they must not be permitted to remain in the country, and that their property should be confiscated. That is my view."

Her adviser Carter pushed her to clarify what she meant: "You do rescind so much of that interview as pronounced upon them the death penalty?"

"I do in that respect."

Carter urged her to be more specific. "You feel that their remaining in the country would be a constant source of trouble to you and your people?"

"I do," she said, maintaining that because she felt they would remain "dangerous for the community and the people," they and their children should be banished from the islands, but not put to death, as she had previously said. Finally—after much urging—she retracted her apparently vindictive urge to behead her enemies.

The interview ended and, by December 18, Lili'u had set aside her own feelings "of personal hatred or revenge" and capitulated to the American demands. She agreed to offer unconditional amnesty to everyone who participated directly or indirectly in the revolution of January 17, agreed to uphold the hated Bayonet Constitution of 1887, and agreed to assume all the financial obligations of the provisional government.

But she had retracted her inflammatory threat too late. On December 19 Willis officially notified the P.G. that Cleveland had decided against signing the annexation treaty and that the president now expected the P.G. to agree to stand down, just as the queen had agreed to the stipulations about amnesty. Reports from Thurston in Washington assured Dole and his advisory council that U.S. troops would not be called in to enforce Willis's request.

Two days before Christmas, Dole himself personally delivered a message back to Willis at Snow Cottage. He arrived at midnight on the grounds of the Hawaiian Hotel, long a hotbed of royalist sentiment. The hour may have been so late because he'd consulted first with Thurston, who'd just returned to Honolulu from Washington. In the bluntest possible terms, Dole told Willis that the American government should mind its own business, stating forcefully, "We do not recognize the right of the President of the United States to interfere in our domestic affairs."

The sheer gall of Dole's answer must have infuriated Lili'u and darkened even further her already dim view of the descendants of the Christians who'd arrived in the islands seven decades earlier with a mission to save souls, not to steal a country. Writing in her diary on December 31, she noted that at the same time the sons and grandsons of the original missionaries to the islands were singing praise to God in the Central Congregational Church, just opposite her front gate large groups of armed guards, whom she described as spies, were congregating on street corners.

Lili'u retired to her bedchamber that evening after receiving assurances that the American and British ministers were doing what they could to defuse the rising tension. Perhaps she thought back to the Paulet episode half a century earlier, taking comfort in its happy outcome. But while that takeover was the result of a rogue British commander and rapidly reversed with the stroke of a pen, the P.G. and its supporters not only controlled the kingdom's banks, plantations, and businesses, but also proved fearsome opponents in shaping public opinion in the United States.

Lili'u still hoped to be restored to the throne by President Cleveland and the U.S. Congress, but she was aware that her enemies were literally digging into their position: piling sandbags and assigning overnight volunteer guards around the government's headquarters at 'Iolani Palace while also issuing rifles and ammunition to the Citizen Guard. At midnight, Lili'u awoke with a start to church bells pealing in the new year and popping firecrackers. Confused by the sounds that had interrupted her sleep, she mistook the fireworks for exploding bombs.

CHAPTER THIRTEEN
Secrets of the Flower Beds, 1894–1895

Before 6 a.m. on January 17, 1894, some of Honolulu's children were bounding out of their beds, pulling on street clothes, and scampering outdoors. Even though it was still dark, they hurried downtown to Fort Street, where a costume parade of "Antiques and Horribles" was scheduled to begin—the first of many events organized that day to mark the first anniversary of Lili'u's overthrow.

By 6:30 a.m. the members of the provisional government and their supporters walking in the parade had slipped on their masks and costumes, transforming themselves into comical and outrageous creatures for the amusement of the bystanders. One was a send-up of Blount, the minister first sent by Cleveland to investigate the overthrow. Carrying a rat trap, the character held a sign that said "Blount's instruments."

The day continued with a military parade, troops saluting the fluttering American flag, and the band playing the "Star-Spangled Banner." That was followed by an afternoon reception at the former palace—now the executive building—where Sanford Dole and his wife, Anna, greeted guests in what had been the throne room. Mrs. Dole was attended by the equivalent of at least twenty-eight ladies-in-waiting. Her husband, who had sought to relieve the stress of the past months by racing his sailboat, fishing for shark, and traveling to other islands to study birds, appeared relaxed.

The Doles' reception included some speakers who compared their cause—evidently with straight faces—to that of the citizens toppling Louis XVI during the French revolution and to the Greek triumph over the Persians at Thermopylae in 480 B.C. Chairing the event was J. B. Atherton, the sugar magnate who'd offered his grounds near the palace to billet the troops the first night of the occupation. He declared, "Annexation is manifest destiny, and we are bound to have it!"

The next speaker described how embattled the P.G. had become following Willis's request that it restore Lili'u to the throne. Wearing full morning dress for the occasion, he sketched a picture of a young government surrounded by adversaries: Lili'u, her royalist supporters, the Spreckels family in San Francisco, and a rising numbers of Portuguese, Chinese, and Japanese immigrants to the islands, who'd first come to work in the sugar fields but since had turned to commerce.

After the speeches ended and the last visitor signed the guest book, Dole and his wife prepared for the long evening ahead. As the skies of Honolulu darkened, the streets and alleyways and squares exploded with the sounds of celebration, from guns, firecrackers, and skyrockets to tin horns and every other kind of instrument or noisemaker the P.G.s and their families could dig out of their cupboards or garden sheds. Sulfurous smoke filled the air and the spectators who gathered that night near the palace were greeted by an ocean of delicately swaying green and red paper lanterns, suspended from the branches of trees.

Yet the day was not entirely successful. President Dole's reception had been marred by the absence of royalists and almost the entire foreign diplomatic corps—including the U.S. minister Willis. That night, the illuminations, too, had rocketed out of control. Although the incident was only barely mentioned in the *Advertiser*'s report the next day, it was a mishap that could have ended tragically. The organizers' plan was to launch fireworks from the roof of 'Iolani Palace, so spectators in Palace

Square and on the grounds that evening could better see them. But to their dismay the entire cache of fireworks accidentally caught fire and roared into one big blaze.

Lili'u stayed away from the festivities, though it would have been impossible for her not to have heard the fireworks or explosions from her home at Washington Place. In her diary, she wrote, "One year ago I signed away under protest my right to the throne." And with apparent satisfaction she noted the diplomatic corps' chilly response to the invitations they'd received to attend the P.G.'s anniversary celebrations. "They all declined," she noted, "which made Mr. Dole feel very bad."

The *Advertiser* thundered its disapproval of the diplomatic snubs the next day. "A great deal of indignation is felt at the discourtesy, to use no stronger word, shown by the diplomatic corps towards the Provisional Government yesterday," it said, placing particular blame on Minister Willis. The paper's editors were also incensed that American warships did not fire a salute to the new government. "Is this Government at peace with the United States or not? Does the United States recognize its sovereignty or not? Who shall say? Does Mr. Willis himself know?" it asked, continuing, "Whichever way he [Willis] turns he finds himself confronted with the bristling horns of a dilemma. Everywhere bloody prospects of impalement, and no way of escape."

Lili'u's supporters, meanwhile, prepared for an anniversary of their own: the one-year mark of the Royal Hawaiian Band members resigning after refusing to sign a loyalty oath to the new government, vowing to *Ai pohaku*—eat stones—rather than submit to the will of the P.G. On February 1 they joined together in singing a newly composed patriotic song titled "Kaulana na pua o Hawaii," or "Famous Are the Flowers," which became known as the "Stone-Eating Song." Its lyrics saluted the native Hawaiian band members who refused to bow to the "evil-hearted messenger" of the P.G., with its "greedy document of extortion." The song was as electrifying for Hawaiians as the revolutionary anthem "Marseillaise" was for the French.

Lili'u did not attend this gathering of loyalists. Although she claimed to be "entirely removed from politics and living in complete retirement," she welcomed a daily stream of supporters, who brought her rumors, petitions, protests, and suggestions for who should be her new cabinet ministers when she regained power. In effect, she remained head of a shadow government.

To foreign visitors, she assumed a pose of peaceful forbearance, as she waited for the U.S. Congress to restore her to the throne. The garden that her mother-in-law had first planted half a century ago was crowned with its magnificent tamarind tree, whose branches spread out across the lawns and whose delicately scented yellow blossoms closed tightly at night and opened again at dawn. The grounds were her tropical retreat from hostile Honolulu.

Lili'u rarely ventured now outside the grounds of Washington Place for fear of being kidnapped or shot at in her carriage. She knew that spies lurked on street corners and a network of informers had been paid to collect information on royalists. Still, Hawaiians continued organizing in opposition to Dole's government. The primary groups were the *hui*, political associations formed by both men and women that grew to thousands of people. The first was the Hui Kālai'āina, which had grown out of opposition to the 1887 constitution and in 1894 had chosen Joseph Nāwahī as its leader. The second, also led by Nāwahī, was called Hui Aloha 'Āina—"the group that loves the land," which came to be known as the Hawaiian Patriotic League. It was made up of both women and men.

Lili'u's supporters expressed their opposition in two dozen Hawaiian-language newspapers and a handful of English-language ones, publishing fiery editorials against Dole and in favor of Hawaiian independence. Lili'u helped fund one of them, *Hawai'i Holomua* ("Hawai'i Progress"), until she came under pressure from the P.G. to stop. Joseph Nāwahī and his wife, Emma, who was a leader of the women's branch of the Hawaiian Patriotic League, would later found *Ke Aloha 'Āina* ("The Hawaiian Patriot"), another leading opposition newspaper. But unlike the *Advertiser,* which attracted much more advertising and benefited from new presses and speedier linotype machines, the opposition papers struggled by with type set laboriously by hand.

Even so, the P.G. was so threatened by the papers that it began arresting editors for libel and curbing freedom of speech, which had been guaranteed by each of Hawai'i's constitutions since 1851. It also forbade native Hawaiians to carry firearms or gather in large groups.

To circumvent these rules, Lili'u's supporters began composing songs with double meanings and speaking to each other at funerals and church meetings in allegories. That's how plans were made for a gathering that took place in October of 1894 in the Pauoa Valley, ostensibly to celebrate the first planting of a piece of land that Lili'u had donated as a public park. The deposed queen and some members of her household traveled to the park the night before the ceremony. To the sounds of the Nu'uanu stream and a small waterfall that cascaded through the property, the group planted a design using small shrubs near the entrance that spelled out *Uluhaimalama*, which means "as the plants grow up out of the dark earth into the light, so shall light come to the nation." It metaphorically suggested a growing resistance movement.

By taking the risk of venturing out after dark to help plant this subversive message in the soil, Lili'u let her people know that she continued to hope for restoration. The next morning, government troops lined the roadways to the park. Although the queen did not attend, the ceremony became an occasion for an outpouring of royalist feelings. Once again, they sang the stone-eating song, with its defiantly hopeful refrain:

We will back Liliu-lani	*Mahope makou o Lili'u-lani*
Who has won the rights of the land	*A loa'a e ka pono a ka 'aina.*
(She will be crowned again)	*(A kau hou 'ia e ke kalaunu)*

Such *aloha* hardly soothed the painful sting of what seemed to be a vigorous propaganda campaign being waged against Lili'u in the American press. Soon after her overthrow, scurrilous reports about her began appearing in newspapers: in the spring of 1893 the *San Francisco Chronicle* had reported that she was a heathen who sacrificed black pigs to Pele, relied on a sorceress for advice, and "delight[ed]" in orgies, as did her late brother Kalākaua. Although there were also sympathetic stories about her, vicious press reports dogged her through the year. When details of Lili'u's interview with Minister Willis emerged, even the august *New York Times* published his first-person account with the sensational subheading that "The Queen Wanted to Behead the Men Who Deposed Her."

The most stinging attacks on her came from the political cartoons published in American satirical magazines, which portrayed her as a comical dark-skinned savage. A cartoon from the December 2, 1893, issue of *Judge* showed her as an Indian squaw clutching a paper in one hand reading "Gross Immorality" and a paper in the other reading "Scandalous Government," as she sat on a throne held up by the bayonets of white soldiers and sailors. Another, published in the same magazine in February 1894, portrayed her as a Negro "fancy lady," dressed provocatively in feathers and high heels. The caption read:

Lili to Grover.
You listened to my DOLE-ful tale
You tried your best—'twas no avail.
It's through no fault of yours or mine
That I can't be your VALENTINE.

It is not clear whether Lili'u, who had been educated by Christian missionaries and remained deeply devout throughout her life, ever saw these caricatures of herself. Her diary entries suggest she saw at least some of the American news stories about her, such as the report of her beheading her opponents.

Closer to home, Lili'u heard rumors that the provisional government planned to try to buy her off. "They talk of offering me $20,000 & Kaiulani 10,000 a year," she wrote in her diary in mid-June 1894. "Not a cent will I accept and sacrifice the rights of my people." Even more insulting than the idea that she would accept money in exchange for her rights to the throne, she found herself responding to those who questioned her right to the throne based on her genealogy.

Was she a queen? A savage? A heathen? Someone who could be bought off for a mere $20,000?

On January 20, 1894, Lorrin Thurston returned to Washington, D.C., as the P.G.'s minister. He soon found a champion in John Tyler Morgan, an ardent annexationist and chairman of the Senate Foreign Relations Committee. Morgan "couldn't have taken more interest in Hawai'i if it had been part of his own state," Thurston wrote enthusiastically. "At all times, day or night, the Hawaiian legation had access to him, either at his senatorial office or at his residence."

The Hawai'i question became the subject of bitter partisan wrangling in Congress, with ugly racist overtones. Morgan, a former brigadier general in the Confederate army and one of the most outspoken proponents of racial segregation, had little interest in the perspective of native Hawaiians. As Thurston recalled the snowy-haired senator from Alabama saying early on, "Thurston, I have a suggestion for you. If you will take one thousand Confederate soldiers to Hawai'i and give to each one of them a small piece of land on which to make a farm, and a rifle, you can do what you please out there." Thurston thanked him for the suggestion, but declined, explaining, "We don't do things that way in Hawaii."

Nonetheless, Morgan helped Thurston's cause by launching his own crusade to determine "whether any, and if so, what irregularities have occurred" in the Cleveland administration's handling of the "Hawai'i affair." With the authority to hold public hearings under oath and cross-examine witnesses, Morgan seemed intent on embarrassing President Cleveland as much as possible by reexamining not only the takeover in Hawai'i but also whether Cleveland overstepped his executive authority in commissioning Blount and requesting that the P.G.s stand down.

The highly partisan hearings, which took place from December 1893 through February 1894, resulted in the 1,176-page Morgan report, which largely contradicted Blount's findings. Just as the equally hefty Blount report built a case that the United States should help restore the queen, the Morgan report asserted that "Hawai'i is an American state" over which the United States already exercised "moral suzerainty"—a position as overlord that had to be defended against Lili'u's attempt to "grasp absolute power and destroy the constitution and the rights of the white people." Morgan likened the takeover to the Reconstruction of the American South. As Lili'u's supporters would later point out, Morgan neglected to call many native Hawaiian or royalist witnesses to the stand in his hearing, just as Blount had failed to interview many of the key members of the provisional government.

President Cleveland, meanwhile, had to decide whether to enforce Willis's request. That would have meant ordering U.S. troops to go to war against the sons of American missionaries. When it suited them, men such as Thurston and Dole were quick to call on American resources, though neither could claim to be American citizens: both had been born in Hawai'i and were subjects of the kingdom. But they now led the Hawaiian provisional government, and did so without the backing of the U.S. Congress. Given that Cleveland was already under investigation by Morgan's commission over Hawaiian affairs and taking criticism from the press, he decided that proceeding unilaterally was not a wise course of action.

Since Morgan's and Blount's contradictory reports essentially canceled each other out, the Hawai'i affair was debated on and off until the end of the second session of the Fifty-third Congress on August 28, 1894. Although the House had censured Stevens, the former minister to the islands, Congress did not take the next step of authorizing intervention against Sanford Dole's government. Thus Cleveland's efforts to restore Lili'u to the throne were effectively stymied.

At the same time, a fundamental shift was occurring in how America saw itself in relation to the rest of the world. On July 12, 1893, a professor at the University of Wisconsin named Frederick Jackson Turner delivered a paper at an American Historical Association meeting titled "The Significance of the Frontier in American History." Turner drew attention to the little-noticed fact that three years earlier, in 1890, the U.S. Bureau of the Census had declared that the American frontier was closed, since it had become so "broken into by isolated bodies of settlement." Turner, who would later write a Pulitzer Prize–winning book on the same subject, argued that the "safety valve" western expansion had provided was now gone. The implications were that the country would now begin looking beyond its continental borders for new markets, including the Pacific.

For Thurston and others who supported closer ties between the United States and Hawai'i, this burst of expansionist sentiment couldn't have come at a better time. The provisional government, sensing Cleveland's dilemma and realizing that annexation might take longer than they'd hoped, enacted a constitution that made it even more difficult for impoverished or poorly educated Hawaiians, Portuguese, or Chinese to serve in the legislature or to vote for senators. In effect, it further disenfranchised much of the population. As Minister Willis, the successor to Blount, quipped, "It is certainly a novelty in governmental history—a country without a citizenship."

For Americans living in Honolulu, July 4 was celebrated as America's Independence Day. For the rest of the capital's residents, the fourth of July that year, which fell on a Wednesday, was a normal workday. But at 8 a.m. that morning, troops fired a twenty-one-gun-salute in honor of the newly formed Republic of Hawai'i, which chose America's Independence Day as its own as well.

Sanford Dole, his silver beard grown even longer, stood on the front steps of the palace-turned-executive building, surrounded by a large crowd of black-suited *haole*, and took the oath of office as president. Hawaiians, for the most part, stayed away. Although Nāwahī had urged members of the patriotic leagues to maintain the peace, the anger that many Hawaiians felt began to well up. Sensing this, Dole continued sleeping in different places each night and ordered troops to sandbag his residence in case of attack. He and the other leaders of the new republic feared for their safety and suspected that a plot was under way to topple the government.

Those suspicions were justified. By August the three commissioners Lili'u had sent to Washington to find out from the U.S. President himself whether he would help restore her to the throne, one of whom was Sam Parker, received a crushing answer. Cleveland wrote:

> The recognition and the attitude of the Congress concerning Hawaiian affairs of course leads to an absolute denial of the least present or future aid or encouragement on my part to an effort to restore any government heretofore existing in the Hawaiian Islands.

But in their informal communications with Cleveland's secretary of state, they came away with the impression that the United States would not meddle if there were a popular uprising against the new government either. The American warship USS *Philadelphia* did indeed withdraw from Hawaiian waters. Some saw that as implicit support of their aims. Whether that was true or not, by the fall royalists began secretly gathering weapons, traveling to San Francisco to purchase and arrange transport of guns and ammunition to the islands.

How much Lili'u knew of the plans is not clear: the diary entries she was making during this time only obliquely hint at a plan to restore her to the throne—noting in December, for instance, just that she had "heard good news for our side." Waiting for developments, she struggled with financial worries, deciding whether she should sell off property or stocks to pay the interest on her debts.

Her problem was a pressing one. After the overthrow, the new government had assumed ownership of the crown lands—nearly a million acres—which had produced about $50,000 a year in income for Lili'u through long-term leases. Commoners who had leased the lands now paid their rents to the *haole* government. And Dole, for one, believed that large tracts of former crown lands should be broken up and sold to homesteaders. She later wrote she never received from the provisional government or the Republic of Hawai'i a cent of income from those seized lands, although from the time of Kamehameha V they had been the property of the throne and its successor office acting as a steward for the land and not the private property of the monarch, which could be sold off, as Dole's government would argue.

Her financial worries, along with a rising sense of despair over her prospects for regaining the throne, contributed to Lili'u's poor health during the fall of 1894. She explained it as a consequence of all she had suffered since assuming the throne—the death of her husband, her overthrow, and a tortuous year of waiting for restoration. "For two years I had borne the long agony of suspense, a terrible strain, which at last made great inroads on my strength," she wrote.

Her doctor diagnosed her with severe "nervous prostration," a weakness of the nervous system first identified in 1869 and also known as neurasthenia. It was a condition believed to be especially prevalent among women and attributed to "overwork, worry, hereditary predisposition . . . and fright."

Aside from prescribing a rest cure, some doctors, including Lili'u's, prescribed electricity to treat it. The application of about forty-five minutes of gentle electrical stimulation was meant to be not painful but soothing, leading the patient to experience "contractions" followed by a "delicious slumber," according to a medical treatise on remedies for the disorder published around that time. Indeed, at the 1893 world's fair in Chicago (the same one where Thurston helped organize Hawai'i's volcano display), an exhibit could be found in its Electrical Building of these increasingly popular pleasure-producing devices.

Whatever kind of relief it might have provided, the electricity treatment seemed to have helped. Lili'u ventured out to take a carriage ride with friends on the day after Christmas of 1894. It was the first time she'd left Washington Place for a long trip since September 1893 and the drive refreshed her. A few days later, she signed eleven commissions, lining up the men who would play important roles in her new government when she was, at last, restored to the throne.

At 11 p.m. on January 2, 1895, the steamer *Waimanalo* made its way from Honolulu up the coastline off Diamond Head. As arranged, a small boat signaled with a lantern and pulled up alongside. Using the password "missionary," crews began transferring Winchester rifles packed in white pine boxes onto the steamer. The two captains agreed on a final rendezvous to land arms on shore at 1 a.m. on January 4.

That dark night, lit only by the moon breaking through the clouds, two whaleboats rowed up to the steamer. It was high tide and the two heavily loaded boats managed to make it over the reef and onto the headlands of Kūpikipiki'ō, a lava point off Diamond Head now known as Black Point: the men buried one cache of arms in a small, dry gulch and the other in the sands some distance away. In total, they hid about three hundred rifles near the beach, exposing them to sand and corrosive saltwater.

The next morning, word went out among Lili'u's supporters that the time had come. Their leader was Samuel Nowlein, former head of the Royal Guard, who still watched over Lili'u's safety at Washington Place. At the last moment, Robert Wilcox had also decided to join the uprising. Their recruits ranged in age from men in their early fifties to fourteen- and fifteen-year-old boys and included carpenters, blacksmiths, tram drivers, and stevedores as well as members of some of the islands' richest families. Some of the revolutionaries were impoverished Hawaiians who walked the seven miles to the rendezvous point to save the twenty-five-cent tram fare and others were *haole* businessmen. An American, Major William T. Seward, purchased the arms in San Francisco for the royalists, he said from Rudolph Spreckels. Wealthy sugar planters such as Seward's close friend John Cummins and the British-born William Rickard also helped buy guns.

The plan was for the Hawaiians to gather and distribute their weapons at Diamond Head and join the downtown forces, which were to include a large number of foreigners. But the government had planted spies among the royalists. At four o'clock on the afternoon of Sunday, January 6, a twenty-three-year-old Hawaiian who later received a "gift" of $300 for his services made his way to the house of one of the policemen to inform him that rifles would be distributed at the beachside bungalow of a local *hapa-haole* builder named Henry Bertelmann, which faced west toward Waikīkī. The message was: "Overthrow to take place tonight—2000 men . . . Will start in from Diamond Head between one & 2 a.m."

By dusk the marshal had posted policemen around Bertelmann's grounds, where some eighty rebels had gathered, far fewer than the thousands expected. It didn't take long before shots rang out; men shouted, women screamed, and children began to cry as bullets struck the back slat door of the bungalow. Because all of Honolulu was alerted that a revolt was under way the skirmish was a disaster. Sam Nowlein led one group of about ninety men, who sheltered behind boulders, while Robert Wilcox led another up the slopes of Diamond Head. Meanwhile, the government soldiers mobilized, pushing some of the rebels into the verdant Mānoa Valley. After a week of hardship they were forced to surrender.

In Honolulu, Dole's government declared martial law, permitting only those with passes to ride the tram and walk down the street. Enflamed by stories of "bloodthirsty rebels," more than a thousand men were armed and billeted in the armory, as well as the Central Union and Kawaiahaʻo churches. Policemen led groups of ragged Hawaiian rebels, often in chained groups, to the grim, coral-block prison known as the Reef, near the red-light district along Honolulu's waterfront. By Wednesday the government had imprisoned forty fighters captured in the field and another thirty civilians suspected of having collaborated with them, including prominent Hawaiian-language newspaper editors and a dozen or more Britons with royalist leanings. In total, 355 were arrested.

Exuberant republicans who gathered afterward at the Central Union church called for Liliʻu's immediate arrest. On Tuesday, the government dispatched Henry Baldwin on a nighttime mission by boat to gather information about possible rebel activity in other parts of the island. "Everything quiet," the planter reported two days later. "Sugar mills grinding without interruption."

When the skirmish at Bertelmann's cottage took place, Lili'u was at home, protected by her normal guard of sixteen men and officers. She heard the news through a phone call from Diamond Head to Washington Place. Ten days passed as she waited anxiously for further information. Her supporters had shielded her from the details of the defeat, but she knew it had been disastrous, with many casualties and several deaths, including Charles L. Carter, a nephew of her adviser Joseph O. Carter.

On January 16, two men approached Washington Place at about 10 a.m. After knocking, they told Lili'u's ladies-in-waiting they wished to speak with Mrs. Dominis. Representing the government, one of the men was Captain Robert Waipa Parker, cousin of the dashing former minister Samuel Parker and the man who led the government troops to put down the Wilcox rebellion. Lili'u, who had been in her bedroom, approached them wearing a simple morning dress. The men informed her they had a warrant for her arrest. They instructed her to accompany them, with a companion if she wished.

"All right; I will go," she told them.

Captain Parker was distraught. Tears streamed down his face as he told Lili'u he never thought he would be the one to arrest her. "Were they crocodile tears?" Lili'u wondered.

Retrieving her handbag and changing into a black gown, as if in mourning again, Lili'u left her home and climbed into the marshal's carriage. A second carriage followed, carrying a lady-in-waiting. Lili'u rolled past the crowd that had gathered near the gates of Washington Place. Expecting to be taken to the police station for a brief visit, she hadn't packed any luggage. Lili'u was surprised when the carriage instead pulled up to the palace steps. She saw soldiers resting on the green grass of the palace yard near tents, their arms stacked nearby.

Since leaving the palace almost exactly two years earlier, at the time of the overthrow, Lili'u had not gone back. Now, as she climbed the back steps and entered the central hall, she saw that it had been stripped of all of its decorations and most of its furniture. Following an officer who had been assigned to escort her, she climbed silently up the broad carpeted staircase, made of the island's dense *koa* wood. In the hallway on the second floor, she glanced at a stately, life-size oil portrait of herself hanging from the wall, her dark hair lustrous and her bosom decorated with the star and bright blue sash of the Order of Kalākaua.

Lifting a linen handkerchief she was carrying to her eyes, Lili'u brushed away tears. In the two years since her dethronement her hair had turned gray. She turned her gaze back to the officer, who led her to a back bedroom suite at the southeast corner of the second floor. It was sparsely furnished, with a single bed in one corner, a sofa, a small square table, a single common chair, and a cupboard, with an adjoining bathroom. The colonel withdrew.

Lili'u looked at her companion and said, "I am a prisoner."

The officer returned in about an hour and spoke to her kindly, asking if there was anything she required. Lili'u requested that her meals be prepared and sent to her from home, as well as her clothes, sheets, and pillows. She also asked for a pencil and some paper; the colonel replied that she could write whatever she wanted but asked that she present it to him so he could see it was carried out. He left again and the large, bare room—thirty by thirty-five feet—seemed lonely. As the sun set she read from a small Book of Common Prayer that she had brought with her, illuminated by electric lights.

That evening, as government troops were rifling through Washington Place and digging up her flower beds on a tip that weapons were buried there, Lili'u reached for a pencil and looked for somewhere to keep a diary that would not be read by the colonel or her other captors. She chose a page from the Bible. On the top of the first page of the Book of Psalms, she wrote, "Iolani Palace. Jan 16th 1895. Am imprisoned in this room (the South east corner) by the Government of the Hawaiian

Republic. For the attempt of the Hawaiian people to regain what had been wrested from them by the children of the missionaries who first brought the Word of God to my people."

She later wrote that the first night of her imprisonment was the longest night she had ever passed. She could hear the rattling of arms from the soldiers below her room. There was also a sentry in the hall and an officer on duty. She found it difficult to fall asleep as they paced back and forth outside her door. "The sound of their never-ceasing footsteps as they tramped on their beat fell incessantly on my ears," she wrote. "I could not but be reminded every instant that I was a prisoner."

Meanwhile, the seemingly innocuous fragment of concrete that sat on the desk of her private study at Washington Place, as well as the well-tilled earth beneath its flower beds, would yield secrets that her enemies would soon use against her.

CHAPTER FOURTEEN
Kingdom Come, 1895–1896

During Liliʻu's first restless night back at the palace, Captain Parker and two Hawaiian policemen quietly entered the back of her garden at Washington Place, carrying shovels and lanterns. In the shadows of the last quarter of the moon they dug into the dirt. Four feet down they struck metal. Just as one of the captured rebels had told them, they found a rusty but usable cache of weapons hidden in the cellar and buried in the flower beds: thirty-four rifles, eleven large pistols, more than a thousand rounds of ammunition, five swords, and twenty-one homemade bombs. Four of the bombs were metal, sixteen were cement, and one was made from the shell of a coconut.

The next morning, citizen guards patrolled the grounds of Liliʻu's home. Chief Justice Judd, who had made his first inspection of Liliʻu's papers on Dole's orders about two hours after she was arrested, returned for a closer look. Among the papers seized were her diaries for 1893 and 1894, personal letters from Kaʻiulani, signed petitions asking for a new constitution, and a note in her handwriting titled "Course to pursue on receiving news of restoration." He also confiscated the odd concrete fragment sitting on her desk.

Judd swept up her personal and official documents filling two large grain sacks with the papers and notebooks he gathered from the drawers and pigeonholes of her desk. He also emptied the contents of the safe in her study.

As Judd was examining papers, Lili'u faced her first full day of house arrest. It was January 17, the second anniversary of her overthrow, which the republic marked with a twenty-one-gun salute at noon. Almost certainly she could hear the sound of the sharp crack of the gunfire coming from the Punchbowl Battery. About an hour later, Lili'u said good-bye to the lady-in-waiting with whom she had spent the first night of her imprisonment. She pressed a ten-dollar gold piece into her hand, knowing that the woman's husband was imprisoned and that the family would need the money.

Charles Wilson's wife, the former Eveline "Kitty" Townsend, offered to stay with the queen instead. Mrs. Wilson had been one of Lili'u's protéges and, in recent years, had become her "particular personal friend." Lili'u was also permitted visits by her physician every morning at 9:30. The first morning of her imprisonment, the doctor arrived with his "electric battery" and taught Mrs. Wilson how to use the device. He also brought medicines, which Lili'u was to take three times a day.

Banned from reading newspapers, Lili'u relied on visitors for information. But since all of her visitors had to be approved, she received very few. The Anglican priest from St. Andrew's had not been allowed in to see her at the palace and it is unlikely that Lili'u wanted a visit from the minister of Kawaiaha'o church, since he had turned against her in his Sunday sermons from the pulpit. The foreign office insisted on written requests for any items from Lili'u and guards even searched the bundles of soiled clothes that Lili'u and Kitty sent out for laundering.

Meanwhile, Dole's government arrested her household retainers, numbering about forty people on all her estates, and threw them into jail. Unbeknownst to Lili'u at the time, her long-serving coachman was among them. As Lili'u later described his imprisonment, he was "stripped of all his clothing, placed in a dark cell without light, food, air or water, and was kept there for hours in hopes that the discomfort of his position would induce him to disclose something of my affairs." He refused and suffered further imprisonment for about six weeks, Lili'u wrote, even though no charge was ever brought against him.

Gazing out the windows of her second-floor bedroom prison, Lili'u may have noticed some young women on the streets of Honolulu wearing unusual striped dresses in a silent protest against the arrests. They'd sewn gowns from fabric of dark blue and white stripes, similar to the ones worn by the royalist prisoners at the Reef, as their sons and husbands languished in jail. As the Hawaiian-language newspaper *Ka Makaainana* reported, "The wailing and crying of wives and children for their fathers was heartbreaking."

Lili'u remained incommunicado for four days, receiving neither news nor visitors, until the attorney Paul Neumann, whose ties to the Spreckels family went back many years, was permitted to speak with her. He asked her a troubling question: if all of the rebels must pay for their participation with their lives, was she prepared to do the same?

Yes, Lili'u answered.

Neumann then told her that the government had decided to execute her and six others for treason and he would provide details soon.

Fear gripped her and Lili'u's physical symptoms mirrored her inner turmoil. "I was very weak and threatened with paralysis," she wrote. A day or two passed without further information and Lili'u's anxiety mounted. She had suffered a bout of neurasthenia at the time of the rebellion and the subsequent events had compounded her ailments. Her pulse was irregular and her doctor brought her medicine to calm her nerves. Neumann did not reappear but, according to Lili'u's later recollection, Charles Wilson handed her a document to review on January 22. It was an abdication letter.

Lili'u felt anguish at the thought of those who'd already needlessly died trying to restore her to the throne. As hereditary chief, her first responsibility was to her people. Liliʻu had successfully avoided blood-shed three years earlier by deciding not to confront U.S. troops as they marched through the streets of Honolulu. She made the same decision again, although this time it would cost her the kingdom.

Just after ten-thirty on the morning on January 24, as she remained confined to house arrest at the former ʻIolani Palace, Liliʻu abdicated, signing a document stating that she had done so freely "after free and full consultation with my personal friends, and with my legal advisors." It also stated she was acting in the interests of those "misguided Hawai-ians" who attempted to overthrow the present government and she for-mally renounced all claims, rights, and emoluments to the "late throne." Her signature was witnessed by six of her closest allies, including Sam Parker and Charles Wilson, as well as a notary.

Her shaky signature suggests her abdication was excruciating for her. Although the document stated sheʻd signed voluntarily, she later wrote that she did so under extreme duress—believing that to do other-wise would have led to the murders of six of her imprisoned support-ers. She also felt the name she was told to use in signing the document, Liliʻuokalani Dominis, was intended to humiliate her. As she later explained her decision,

> For myself, I would have chosen death rather than to have signed it; but it was represented to me that by my signing this paper all the persons who had been arrested, all my people now in trouble by reason of their love and loyalty towards me, would be immediately released. Think of my position,—sick, a lone woman in prison, scarcely knowing who was my friend, or who listened to my words only to betray me, without legal advice or friendly counsel, and the stream of blood ready to flow unless it was stayed by my pen.

Doleʻs men had stripped ʻIolani Palaceʻs once-gracious Throne Room of any traces of gilt or royal trappings. It was now turned to a different purpose: the trial of the deposed queen before a military tribunal and a public display of the new government's power. As spare as a New England church and as orderly as a banking house, the room was converted to a courtroom where Lili'u would face charges of "misprision" of treason, an archaic legal term meaning she had failed to report her knowledge of treasonous activities.

As Lili'u was confined to the bedroom suite upstairs, the trial began below on January 17. Robert Wilcox strode into the chamber looking defiant in a light gray suit and white tie, at the head of a group of thirteen fellow prisoners, some wearing boutonnieres of carnations and ferns. Soldiers were posted inside the courtroom and the seven members of the military tribunal sat in roughly the same place as the thrones once stood. Two of the leaders of the rebellion, Sam Nowlein and Henry Bertelmann, had already pled guilty, agreeing to turn state's evidence against the others. Paul Neumann served as the defendants' attorney, and after three days of testimony he called for leniency toward those who had been "misled into rebellion."

He spoke eloquently on their behalf, weaving in references to the Bible in an effort perhaps to shame the missionary descendants in the courtroom. He argued that "The planning of a new government—call it 'Kingdom Come' or what you will—is not treason."

Some lighthearted moments broke up the the long days of incriminating testimony. One morning, during the testimony of a native Hawaiian who'd waited to unload arms from the *Waimanalo*, a large chunk of plaster fell from the ceiling, barely missing the president of the military commission. "I guess we'll take a short recess," the president told the court, his uniform covered with white dust. The Hawaiians interpreted it as a sign of the power of the old ways: "The *kahuna* are working for us!"

The question was not whether the defendants had attempted rebellion but whether they should be punished by being put to death. By January 24, the day of Lili'u's abdication, the commission had sentenced six of the leaders—including Nowlein and Wilcox—to be hanged. Others received lesser sentences of imprisonment and fines. But Sanford Dole, who would make the final decision as the republic's commander in chief, pored through the trial transcripts late into the night. "The question of fixing the punishment is a serious one," he wrote to his brother George.

Surely, Dole would have weighed the diplomatic risks of executing the queen against what such a severe punishment would have gained for the young and still unstable republic. He heard arguments from both sides. The mother of Charles Carter, who was killed by the rebels, wrote a scathing letter to President Dole before the trial began, urging him to show no mercy.

"This country must be purified," she wrote. "Do not waste time & expense upon the Rebels but take their lives at once, and banish the woman who with her presence and influence keeps up the spirit of Revolt. God will give you strength, wisdom to nobly destroy every one."

Others advised Dole toward moderation, including a missionary who reasoned incisively that Lili'u would become a martyr if she were executed or banished from the kingdom: "The execution of the ex-queen . . . would be a political blunder, and one which I fear would damage the prestige and promise of our little republic."

Neither Lili'u's abdication nor her signed oath swearing her allegiance to the Republic of Hawai'i produced the immediate pardon of the prisoners, as Lili'u, perhaps naively, had hoped it would. But Dole eventually did decide to commute all death sentences.

Far more troublesome for the young republic was the trial of "Mrs. Dominis," as the pro-government *Advertiser* and *Star* disparagingly referred to the deposed queen in their pages. Late in the morning of February 5, Lili'u descended the staircase from her prison bedchamber to appear before the military tribunal, entering the former throne room with great dignity. She wore an all-black gown, brightened only by violets and the fronds of maidenhead ferns that trimmed her fan.

When asked her plea to the charge of misprision of treason, she answered calmly, "I decline to plead." The court entered a plea of not guilty on her behalf.

The government's lawyers presented testimony from Sam Nowlein and others that suggested—but did not prove decisively—that Lili'u had understood a rebellion was being planned. In great detail, one of her household guards described digging up homemade bombs that had been buried in the ex-queen's flower beds and testified that his orders from Nowlein had been to "hold Washington Place against all comers." He also recounted a conversation in which he told Lili'u on the evening of January 3 that the movement would begin that night. According to the guard, Lili'u had told him she'd hoped it would be a success.

More damaging was the evidence of her own diaries, particularly the entry from December 28, in which she noted signing eleven commissions. Her secretary testified that he had prepared the commissions, which she then immediately signed, appointing Robert Wilcox secretary of foreign affairs and Sam Nowlein minister of the interior. Her secretary also testified that he'd drawn up a new constitution for her not long before drafting the commissions, as well as a proclamation of martial law—documents that the witness said had been destroyed after the first of the counterrevolutionaries were arrested. He added that one of Lili'u's retainers had taken the log of guests who'd visited Washington Place and burned it in the backyard.

The prosecutor cross-examined Lili'u about these conversations with her guard. Sitting heavily in a chair flanked on either side by guards, grown stout after the strain of the recent years, she denied she had any knowledge of what was taking place. Answering only in Hawaiian, she maintained that the arms found at Washington Place were merely the collection of antique muskets and swords that had belonged to her late husband. She protested what she considered an unlawful proceeding. Judd, who testified against her that same day, wrote in his diary that evening, "L. looks pale & angry."

On her behalf, her lawyer delivered a long written statement in which Lili'uokalani described the series of events since her overthrow. "A minority of the foreign population made my action the pretext for overthrowing the monarchy," it read, then went on to claim that Lili'u had no knowledge of the plans to overthrow the republic. Had she known, the statement claimed, she would have dissuaded the leaders from carrying them out.

The statement was read in court in Hawaiian. An interpreter for the tribunal translated it into English and typed it out on parchment paper. After studying the translation overnight, government representatives struck out long passages, including the reference to the coup orchestrated by "a minority of the foreign population."

Yet her autobiography, written two years later, suggests she did indeed know of the plans for a counterrevolution, at least in broad strokes. "I have no right to disclose any secrets given to me in trust," she wrote, adding, "I told them that if the mass of the native people chose to rise, and try to throw off the yoke, I would say nothing against it, but I could not approve of mere rioting."

Her trial ended with the prosecuting attorney making a vicious and sarcastic attack on the deposed queen, mocking her insistence upon knowing nothing of the plot, comparing it to a child's treats "hidden in a Christmas stocking" to be opened on Christmas morning. He gave a scornful nod to her sex, dismissing her decision to waive any rights to immunity or consideration for herself as meaningless, since "she is a woman, and much that is in her statement may be well passed by." He argued that by all the rules of evidence Lili'u must be found guilty.

After her three-day trial, Lili'u waited another three weeks to hear the tribunal's judgment. On the afternoon of February 27, Charles Wilson and others climbed the stairs to her second floor suite with news. The military commission had found the fifty-six-year-old deposed queen guilty, handing down the maximum sentence of a $5,000 fine and five years' imprisonment at hard labor. Judd exulted in his diary that it had been a "beautiful day" and that he'd received "70 callers at home!," many of whom certainly offered him their congratulations.

The California poet Joaquin Miller, who'd worked as a cook in Gold Rush camps, a pony express rider, and a newspaperman, sat a few rows behind Lili'u during the trial. He was a peculiar-looking figure: wearing old-fashioned top boots, his long hair flowed on either side of his head and framed a shiny bald dome. Sent by a mainland newspaper that had expected him to side with the provisional government, the author of "Songs of the Sierras" instead became outraged by what he saw and heard of the treatment of Hawaiian prisoners.

"There are hundreds of good men down there kept in the vilest prisons," he told a *New York Times* reporter, explaining that he had himself fled the island nation for fear of being imprisoned for his outspoken views. Miller continued that if the captives weren't released and the crown lands returned to the queen, he'd personally go to Japan to "state the case and promise political rights to the oppressed 20,000 contract slaves of Japan down there to get an iron-clad (commitment for intervention)." Comparing Dole's government to France under Robespierre (both with a committee of public safety) the poet fumed that "There has been nothing near so monstrous as the Reign of Terror."

With views like these reaching New York and Washington, Dole was cornered. He realized that public opinion would not look favorably on the republic if he stood by as the proud queen with her careworn face were forced to perform five years of hard labor. So he commuted her sentence.

Dole surely also felt private sorrow at the passing of the monarchy, which had ruled the islands ever since he was born. Perhaps that's why some aspects of the old ways were adopted by the men of the new republic. On April 23, 1895, a group of about seventy of Dole's old friends, some from his days at Punahou and Williams College, surprised Sanford and his wife as they sat in the parlor of their Honolulu home. The friends ascended the front steps and made their way across the wide veranda, "each carrying a hookupu for his chief," including a chicken, a few eggs tied in a cloth, mangoes, figs tied in *ti* leaves, and two small squealing pigs.

It was Dole's birthday, and because he had resisted calls to celebrate it as a public holiday his friends decided to surprise him. As they approached him, some called out *Alo-ha, Maikai*, ("You are looking well") and also, to tease him, *Elemakule no oe* ("You are getting to be an old fellow"). Thurston, who was in on the prank, performed a long, quavering Hawaiian chant. Two others carried in tall stalks of sugarcane, bent into arches that capped the gifts.

Dole had been born in the islands and nursed by a Hawaiian woman. He was a lifelong subject of the kingdom until its overthrow and, like Thurston, was unusual among his fellow whites in that he could read, write, and speak fluent Hawaiian. Surely with such history, the gift bearing must have been poignant for him. As one biographer wrote, "All was in great good fun of course, yet with seriousness too and overtone of homesickness for the old Hawai'i which had already passed beyond recall."

During that time and for nearly eight months in total, Lili'u remained a prisoner in the former palace's upstairs bedroom suite. She passed the time quietly as the business of governing the new republic took place all around her.

From Washington Place, potted ferns and a cage of canaries were brought to her. Almost every day, she and Mrs. Wilson stitched, embroidered, and appliquéd the pieces for an extraordinary crazy quilt. Using plush velvets, satins, and silks, the two women pieced together fabric blocks and embroidered messages into them, including what seems to be a fervent political statement in the center block. Eloquent in its simplicity, it read: "Imprisoned at Iolani Palace . . . We began this quilt there."

The project became a way to bring order to the improbable story of Lili'u's life. In nine blocks made from what most likely was fabric from her wardrobe and that of her retainers, the two women imposed a structure on a riot of different shapes, colors, and materials. They poured their love for the lost kingdom of Hawai'i into its panels, stitching the Kalākaua coat of arms and a series of crossed pairs of Hawaiian flags.

Lili'u wrote to Ka'iulani during her imprisonment and mentioned her sewing as one of the ways she passed the time: "After breakfast and for the rest of the day we are occupied in sewing fancy work or darning stockings or mending some rent in garments or in reading and composing music. And so the day goes by quickly enough." She wrote that letter at the end of July, 1895, perhaps before completing the center panel containing her life story and the death of Hawai'i's monarchy. Beneath a crown and a wreath of *maile*—a garland made of a native vine—is Lili'u's name, followed by the dates she was born and ascended the throne. On red silk she embroidered:

Dethroned
January 17th, 1893
Uprising
January 6th, 1895

Then, on a blue panel, she stitched:

H.M. Queen
Lili'uokalani
Abdicated on the
24th of Jan. 1895

When she wasn't stitching, Lili'u used the lead pencils and paper provided to by her guards to compose music. She set to work transposing "Aloha Oe" and also composed a song for Ka'iulani, recognizing that they would both need strength to forgive the enemies who had wrested the throne from them. Later known as "Lili'uokalani's Prayer" or "The Queen's Prayer," the song's Hawaiian title is "Ke Aloha O Ka Haku" or "The Lord's Mercy."

She wrote the song in Hawaiian a few weeks after Dole had commuted her sentence. Its second and third verses suggest her faith in God hadn't weakened, despite her ordeal.

I live in sorrow	*Ko'u noho mihi 'ana*
Imprisoned	*A pa'ahao 'ia*
You are my light	*'O 'oe ku'u lama*
Your glory, my support	*Kou nani ko'u ko'o*
Behold not with malevolence	*Mai nānā 'ino'ino*
The sins of man	*Nā hewa o kānaka*

But forgive	*Akā e huikala*
And cleanse	*A maʻemaʻe nō*

Liliʻu's guards did not allow her to see the newspapers, so some of her friends began sending her bouquets of freshly cut flowers from her garden at Uluhaimalama—the same garden she had traveled to under cover of darkness the previous fall, planting the name as encouragement to her supporters—the flowers were often wrapped in the day's news. Liliʻu took comfort in the information she could glean from slightly sodden pages.

It was difficult for Liliʻu to communicate with her people as guards searched all the gifts and items coming in or going out of her rooms. Even so, four *mele* were apparently smuggled out of the queen's prison room (or perhaps memorized by one of her supporters) and brought to the newspaper *Ka Makaainana*, where they were published in weekly installments, according to the historian Noenoe Silva. The *mele* speak in the first person about the deposed queen's experiences, and include details—such as the view of Diamond Head from her prison bedroom—that would have been difficult for someone other than her to know. Whether or not she wrote them, they express a fiery anger not found in the English-language press or in the songs celebrating forgiveness that Liliʻu chose to include in her memoirs.

Just as Liliʻu was able to let her people know through the *mele* that her heart was still with them, other prisoners also sent *mele* out from their jail cells to be printed in the Hawaiian-language newspapers. As Silva noted, "The mele acted like conversations between people who were physically unable to talk to each other because they were imprisoned in different locations and separated on different islands . . . The queen's message in the various mele was consistent: she had not abandoned them, and she was fighting the provisional government in every way she could, including through spiritual appeals." The songs, like Liliʻu's, frequently included the coded word "flowers," referring to native Hawaiians loyal to the monarchy.

She passed her fifty-seventh birthday under guard at the palace. On September 4, the heaviest rainstorm of the year drenched Honolulu and loud claps of thunder shook the night sky. Dole and his advisers had decided to grant her a conditional pardon.

The next morning, Lili'u returned to Washington Place. As if to welcome her after her eight-month absence, the soaked garden was prolific with blooms: the orchids, the violets, the chrysanthemums, the geraniums had all come into flower; red bananas hung heavily from their stems and the red berries of the coffee tree brightened its dark leaves. At the same time, she was greeted by friends and members of her household, most of whom also had been released from prison. Although she was restricted to the grounds of Washington Place, it seemed like an Eden after so many months of imprisonment in the palace, listening to the sound of guards pacing outside her door.

CHAPTER FIFTEEN

Born Under an Unlucky Star, 1896–1898

By New Year's Day of 1896 all the prisoners but one had been released from jail. Of the 183 prisoners from the uprising who had come before the court, most were charged with some form of treason but none were executed. Dole's decision to try civilians in a military court in a situation where there was no ongoing fighting would later be judged a travesty by judicial experts and historians, but the United States had not stopped it. Dole did this knowing that no jury in a civilian courtroom in Honolulu would ever convict her. Meanwhile, the government passed a law requiring English to be the sole medium of instruction in all schools, effectively banning Hawaiian.

Lili'u, meanwhile, remained at Washington Place under house arrest. In the spring she wrote a candid and defiant letter, dated March 19, 1896, to Ka'iulani about her ordeal.

"My dear Kaiulani—you have read in the papers everything that has been done to me, and naturally you think that I have suffered. I must convince you to the contrary," she wrote on stationery with a royal crest.

Our family is above such things. I would not let them have the satisfaction to know that I suffered or cried for all the humiliation ... Did I suffer? Yes—for my people, for yours and mine and while they suffered and were imprisoned with myself for the sake of their country and ours. I suffered with them and yet I felt proud of it. When I signed away my rights as an Alii and to the throne and other promises made in that paper—it only concerned myself for I had no rights to sign away my peoples' rights or anybody else's rights except my own—and I do not regret it, for the lives of seven people depended on my signature and I gave it freely for their sakes.

Lili'u then went on to offer advice to her young niece, whom she realized was old enough to understand the burden as well as the privilege of being an *ali'i*.

You must learn to control your feelings, that was what saved my life. I would have worked myself up to that pitch of excitement as to have been injurious to my health and to be calm and cool at all times is the easiest way—be self possessed and it will be sure to react on the opposite party—but the true secret is to know your own worth. If you were to mould your character in everything that is upright it would be your signpost through life & carry you through many dangers that often assail us through life. It will comfort people to respect you and that is a great deal. They may not like you, still they have to respect you.

But Lili'u was wrong in one thing: although she wrote to her niece that "Providence was good to one and to all those who have been imprisoned" she did not fully realize the toll it had taken on one of her most loyal supporters: Joseph Nāwahī. In the weeks before the uprising, he and the newspaper editor John E. Bush had been arrested on charges of sedition—inciting rebellion against Dole's government. Nāwahī had languished in the miserable conditions of the Reef for nearly three months over the rainy season of late 1894 through early 1895. In the jail's cramped and filthy cells he contracted tuberculosis.

He succumbed to the disease on September 14, 1896, at the age of fifty-four, leaving behind his wife, Emma, who was also his partner on the newspaper. Lili'u, like many Hawaiians, considered his death a great blow. The members of the Hawaiian patriotic societies he headed turned out in great numbers for his funeral and his last words, written down at his deathbed by Emma, were later printed in their newspaper, *Aloha 'Āina*: "Give my love to my queen and the nation that I have loved," he told her just after 10 a.m., lying in a bed in a clinic on the edge of San Francisco where he'd hoped to recover. Asking his wife to forgive him for bringing her to a foreign land, he blamed himself for working when his body was weak. But most of all he wanted Emma to carry on his mission. "Speak for me on my behalf. Continue to be steadfast in your love of the land."

When his casket returned to Hawai'i aboard the *Australia*, the news of his death swept through the islands. His funeral was one of the largest ever seen by most; by one count, more than sixteen hundred turned out to mourn and the members of the patriotic associations wore black arm- and hatbands for a month. In death, Nāwahī became a martyred resistance hero to discouraged Hawaiians.

Not long after the funeral, Lili'u was separating and transplanting potted ferns at her cottage in Waikīkī when an aide to Sanford Dole approached her. "It gives me, Madam, very great pleasure to hand you this paper," he said. It was a full pardon, signed by President Dole on October 23, restoring her civil rights. Lili'u set down her trowel, took the paper, and, after reading it, replied, "It gives me a very great pleasure, indeed, to receive this."

By the end of the year, after making a brief courtesy call on the Doles at their home, she boarded a steamer bound for San Francisco, ostensibly to visit her husband's relatives in Boston and her niece in England but in fact to continue her campaign for restoration of the monarchy. In San Francisco, Claus Spreckels and his family welcomed her, as did her brother-in-law Charles Bishop, who nominally remained a loyalist but left Hawai'i for the last time in 1894. Riding an eastbound train, she gazed out the window onto the vast western landscape and couldn't help but wonder, with such vast expanses of arable land, why Americans seemed intent on taking over Hawai'i.

Lili'u sent a telegram to her brother-in-law Archibald Cleghorn, asking him and Ka'iulani to join her in Boston. But upon receiving her request, Cleghorn demurred, possibly still angry over her role in the events leading up to the overthrow. He had traveled to England early in 1895 and was tending to Ka'iulani, who was ill and rapidly losing weight. Writing from the Langham Hotel, he explained that he could not join her on her trip, warning that their enemies would find a way to use the trip against them by asserting a conspiracy. "We cannot therefore be too cautious, not to give any ground for suspecting us of any secret work."

His answer angered Lili'u and compounded her suspicions. After Ka'iulani's trip from England to the United States shortly after the overthrow, Lili'u had heard rumors that her niece sought the throne for herself. Lili'u interpreted Cleghorn's refusal as evidence that Ka'iulani and her father were unwilling to support her and perhaps even plotting their own ascendancy. The former queen believed, without any convincing evidence, they were campaigning to convince the American journalist Julius A. Palmer to take up their case.

Lili'u's mistrust and disappointment were relieved by a happy reunion with family and friends. On Christmas night, Lili'u's train pulled into Boston, where Palmer took her to what was then the grandest hotel in the city—the Parker House—where a group of relatives were waiting for her, including her husband's cousin, Sara Lee, who had so passionately taken up the cause of Hawaiian independence on her behalf. After a few days Lili'u moved to more modest accommodations in the Boston suburb of Brookline, where she marveled at the icicles forming on the trees and the snow whirling around her cottage.

About a month after her arrival, Lili'u left Boston with Palmer, whom she had retained as her unpaid private secretary. Since reaching America, she'd received letters and petitions from the Hawaiian patriotic leagues asking her to seek restoration. Without substantial funds beyond those she'd raised by mortgaging properties to James Campbell, she sought to do that in two ways: writing her story, with Palmer's help, and waging a quiet campaign of her own of private teas and receptions. Her goal was to demonstrate her civility to the wives of the politicians and government officials who might decide Hawai'i's fate. She hoped to show them that she was far from being what some American newspapers called her: a barbarian queen.

Reaching the nation's capital in late January, she received an invitation to call on President Cleveland. The newspapers had grown increasingly disrespectful toward the deposed monarch, referring to her as "Queen Lil" and "her erstwhile Majesty." Some openly speculated about why she had come to Washington. Lili'u kept quiet about her purpose but certainly wished for more than just a courtesy visit. Although the setting was elegant—Cleveland and Lili'u met in the White House's "little red Reception Room," under a thirty-six-light chandelier and amid furniture featuring carved shapes of dolphins, sphinxes, and a lion's head—it was disappointing nonetheless.

"Fifteen minutes of pleasant conversation during which time I gave him a handsome present decorated prettily with a red ribbon. Our conversation was common place, about the crooked streets of Boston—and cold weather in Washington—and how long I was going to stay." She answered she wasn't sure and that she hoped to call on Mrs. Cleveland. "I then rose and left him—*Mahalo no!*," she wrote, meaning that she'd offered the president her great thanks.

A few days later, Lili'u received a note inviting her to attend a private reception hosted by Mrs. Cleveland. As cordial as these visits were, though, the Cleveland administration was on its way out of office, soon to be replaced by that of the Republican William McKinley. From her suite of rooms in Washington's tallest building, the luxurious 156-foot-tall Cairo Hotel on Q Street, she left to attend a series of parties leading up to the inauguration, as well as the ceremony itself, enjoying a simple lunch of ham sandwiches, apple pie, and coffee. Exhausted, she decided to skip the inaugural balls, but she spent the months afterward working with Palmer on her autobiography—dictating it to him in the morning, as he typed up her words in the afternoon.

Her efforts to change Americans' minds about her people led her to compile and translate into English the lyrics of more than a hundred Hawaiian songs. She wrote to her publisher, "I want to get this work out in good shape, so that my enemies may see that I am more intellectual than they want to give me credit for." Aside from that, there was little she could do to advance her people's cause but wait and see.

Meanwhile, she carried on a heartfelt correspondence in Hawaiian with Emma Nāwahī, who continued to publish a newspaper and was one of the leaders of the Hawaiian women's patriotic league. By the spring of 1897, as the leagues in Hawai'i were gathering signatures for anti-annexation petitions, Emma Nāwahī became convinced that the letters she had received from Lili'u had been opened and scrutinized for hidden messages by their enemies. To avoid prying eyes, she suggested sending them through friends in the future. Nāwahī sent the queen news from Honolulu. Lili'u, who was always sensitive to the natural world around her, sent a rare botanical specimen to the islands for her friend. As Nāwahī wrote back, "I saw your greeting and everything and this extremely beautiful flower which I've only heard its name, a tulip. This is the first time I've seen one. Its rainbow petals layered and its delicate body made dainty and neat by the devoted soft hands of Her Majesty. I kiss it unceasingly and dampen it with my falling tears."

Soon Lili'u's quiet contemplation of the capital's springtime blossoms and her mornings spent working with Palmer in front of the gas fire in her parlor suite at the Cairo came to a halt. She received word that President McKinley, on June 16, 1897, had sent an annexation treaty to the Senate. She immediately filed an official protest, focusing not only on its denial of civic rights to Hawaiians but also on the confiscation of 1.8 million acres of crown, public, and government lands.

The treaty languished in the Senate through the annual summer recess. In September, Lili'u received a letter from William Lee, Sara's husband, warning her that her manuscript would need substantial editing. He called some of her remarks "injudicious as they stood" and added that they "would surely have to be modified before a reputable Publishing House could print them." The Lees, who were acting as Lili'u's agents, feared that she could face libel charges if the book was published in the form she'd submitted it.

In the manuscript, Lili'u had unleashed her fury at one person in particular: Lorrin A. Thurston. Lili'u recalled the bravery of his missionary grandmother Lucy Goodale Thurston, who underwent surgery for breast cancer without anaesthesia, and wrote that her enemy "comes rightfully by his determination and inflexibility." But she went on to describe him as a barely educated "rascal" who had waged an unrelenting propaganda campaign against her. She dubbed him the "evil genius" of the missionary party and "absolutely without scruple." Her editors cut many pages from the original manuscript, including her lengthy tirade against Thurston.

As autumn descended on the capital, Lili'u was confident that her book, due out in early 1898, would persuade politicians of the righteousness of her cause. The publication of *Hawaii's Story* did indeed draw further attention to her plight. The *New York Times* review, which appeared on January 22, 1898, described Dole's government as having "extorted her abdication." Although the *Philadelphia Inquirer* ended its generally favorable review by raising the question of how much of the book was written by Lili'u—a charge that Thurston would make against it—it concluded that "its cleverness must be admitted," and "it does cast a serious shadow upon the morality of the missionary party." Even the *Watchman*, a church newspaper, grudgingly conceded that the book was the work of "a character remarkable for probity, discretion, and self-control; and her life, as set forth by herself, is evidence that the work of American missionaries, whose memory is now unsavory to her, was not in vain."

The *Chicago Tribune*, however, asserted in its review that the ex-queen's own injudicious words had played a role in her downfall. Its headline read, "Volume Is Dignified and Tactful, Doing Credit to Her

Literary Judgment, but Practically Admitting All the Chief Charges Upon Which She Was Dethroned—Weak Attempt to Deny Her Intentions of Beheading the Leading Revolutionists."

Such a review was surely deflating. A long-awaited visit the previous fall, however, in October of 1897, from Ka'iulani buoyed Lili'u's spirits. The graying ex-queen hadn't seen her young niece for eight years and misunderstandings had sprung up between them. But now Ka'iulani, nearly twenty-two and with a slender grace that captivated the reporters who met her, was heading home to the islands. She stopped briefly in the capital to pay her respects to her aunt. They shared a grief for the fallen Hawaiian monarchy, with Ka'iulani writing to friend, "I must have been born under an unlucky star as I seem to have my life planned out for me in such a way that I cannot alter it." Lili'u may well have felt the same.

Ka'iulani returned to the islands aboard the SS *Australia*, catching her first sight of her home on November 9, 1897. Honolulu had spread out in the years she had been gone, the streets wider, electric lights installed in many more households, and the markets filled with the exotic foods and rich smells of Chinese cooking. Straight from the wharf, she rode in a carriage up to the royal mausoleum to visit her mother's remains. Then she returned to the new house at 'Āinahau that her father had completed in time for her homecoming. In the days and weeks that followed she traded her tightly fitted European gowns for more comfortable, loose-fitting *holokū*, fed the estate's peacocks, and rode her white pony Fairy, which was still alive after so many years.

She wrote to her aunt, sharing her impressions of how Hawaiians seemed to have changed following the events of the past few years. "It made me feel so sad to see so many of the Hawaiian people looking so poor," she wrote. "In the old days, I am sure there were not so many people almost destitute."

Lili'u remained circumspect toward her niece. Concerned that Ka'iulani might be approached by members of Dole's government to take her place on the throne, Lili'u asked her to prove her loyalty by refusing to become a figurehead monarch for the Republic.

It has been made known to me that it is the intention of the members of the Republican Government of Hawai'i to ask *you* to take the throne of Hawai'i *in case* they failed in their scheme of Annexation . . . You will have a few followers who will love you but it will only be the 2,600 who now is supporting Dole's government and still have over 80,000 opposing you. It is through their mismanagement that their Government has not been a success. It is for this reason that knowing their instability they want to annex Hawai'i to America—and the reason why their Govt has not been a success is, the people *is not with them* and they are fully aware of the fact. So as a last trial they wish you to take it.

The prospect of Ka'iulani taking the throne upon her return to Honolulu in November 1897 soon became moot. On February 15, 1898, a U.S. warship sent into Havana harbor to protect American interests in Cubans' revolt against their Spanish overlords exploded violently. Two hundred and sixty-seven American sailors aboard the USS *Maine* were killed—sending a shock wave through the United States and inspiring the rally cry "Remember the *Maine!*"

Talk of war with Spain immediately dominated proceedings in the U.S. Congress. Thurston, who was then the republic's annexation commissioner in Washington, suggested the idea of drawing up a map as visual aid to convince the legislators of Hawai'i's strategic importance. His argument was that Hawai'i was the only place where a ton of fuel or a loaf of bread could be had between America's Pacific Coast and Asia. A nation controlling Hawai'i would virtually control naval operations in the Pacific because there was no battleship, in existence or planned, that could cross the ocean without refueling and obtaining supplies, to say nothing of making repairs. His case became even more compelling when President McKinley asked for and the Congress agreed to war against Spain on April 25.

Suddenly, the Pacific Ocean became a theater of war. The black coal that was piled up along Honolulu's esplanade, normally reserved for the merchant and passenger steamers refueling at the Hawaiian port, instantly became enormously valuable to the American war effort. The U.S. Navy bought up all the coal available in the islands and dispatched transport ships to make Honolulu "the most important coaling station in the entire Pacific Ocean," as the pro-annexation *Advertiser* enthusiastically reported.

Yet, a treaty for annexation requiring 75% of the votes for approval had stalled in Congress. In part, that was because native Hawaiians who opposed it had organized petition drives in the islands, gathering more than twenty thousand signatures against the treaty. So proponents of annexation instead drafted a resolution requiring just 50% of the votes to pass.

Meanwhile, residents of Honolulu prepared to welcome the first convoy of Manila-bound troops, which were heading to battle the Spanish naval vessels there. A women's committee prepared the food: a ton of potato salad, more than two thousand pounds of roast beef, eight hundred pineapples, and two thousand pies. The excitement was mostly among the white merchant class, but some *ali'i* also embraced the new reality of their islands' importance to the war effort. Ka'iulani and Archibald Cleghorn opened 'Āinahau to American visitors. Robert Wilcox's chiefess wife hosted a *lū'au* and even the royalist stronghold the Hawaiian Hotel threw open its doors. "Camp McKinley" was established on the verdant grounds of Kapi'olani Park, the late Kalākaua's holiday playground.

But troops ransacked local gardens for food, infected the citizenry with a wave of measles, and caused innumerable drunken disturbances. By fall the garrison had worn out its welcome; in response to Mrs. Dole's call for food donations to the troops for Thanksgiving, the *Independent* noted the irony. "We have been smothered, abused, conquered and finally annexed, and yet the Hawaiians are asked to put up money, turkeys, chickens, ducks, etc. etc. for the benefit of the men who, to us at least, represent only a people that took away our country, our independence and our flag." Within weeks of the all-American holiday the troops were gone.

In the end, it was not the wishes of the islands' powerful sugar industry but the Spanish-American War that provided the final push for annexation of Hawai'i. To some, it was simply the fulfillment of American destiny. Others saw Hawai'i's annexation as the first significant example of American imperialism. The United States snapped up a vulnerable Polynesian nation at a time when the nation's businessmen, diplomats, and military thinkers were pushing beyond American borders. No wonder, then, that in the midst of war fever a joint resolution on annexation passed Congress with a simple majority. President McKinley signed it on July 7, 1898.

For all the hand-wringing over empire that had occurred over the past five years, the reaction from Europe was surprisingly muted. After deciding not to ally with Spain against the United States in the war, the European powers were unlikely to fan the flames by protesting the demise of the Hawaiian kingdom. Britain, the most persistent suitor of the Hawaiian Islands over the years, had clashed verbally with the United States in 1895 over affairs in Venezuela, and its envoys to Hawai'i had logged countless hours defending British subjects and denizens who had participated in the failed attempt to restore Lili'u to the throne.

After briefly considering a joint protest with Germany, Britain stood aside. Eager to smooth relations, Britain hoped to collaborate with its former colony on diplomacy toward China. When asked to state its official stance on annexation, the British Foreign Office issued an even-handed statement: "H. M. Government recognize the annexation of these islands as having taken place, although no official communication formally recording the fact has passed between H. M. Government and the government of the United States." Republican France, meanwhile, was focused instead on the scramble for Africa and Indochina, having already secured Tahiti as a foothold in the Pacific.

Japan, the country that the pro-annexation supporters had suggested would swoop in to snatch up Hawai'i if America didn't do so first, issued a strongly worded protest, focusing on protecting the rights of Japanese citizens in Hawai'i. The Japanese government even dispatched a cruiser to the islands in July 1897. Theodore Roosevelt, who was then assistant secretary of the Navy, responded swiftly. He began preparing to strike back. As it turned out, that was unnecessary. At the urging of the United States the Republic of Hawai'i paid Japan $75,000 to settle the dispute.

Native Hawaiians, meanwhile, donned black armbands in protest. In the weeks following the news that the islands had been annexed, hundreds began showing their opposition to the United States, wearing hatbands created by the Women's Patriotic League that read *Ku'u Hae Aloha* (I Love My Flag). The annexation petitions they'd sent to Washington, containing tens of thousands of signatures and representing the vast majority of native Hawaiians, were ignored.

Their plight was not forgotten by McKinley's predecessor Grover Cleveland, though. Living in retirement in Princeton, New Jersey, he spoke eloquently for those who'd opposed annexation of the distant island nation. "Hawai'i is ours . . . as I contemplate the means used to complete the outrage, I am ashamed of the whole affair."

Lili'u returned to Hawai'i just after midnight on August 2, 1898. A crowd of hundreds waited that night to welcome her home. When the deposed queen appeared, leaning on the arm of Prince David Kawananakoa, who was Kapi'olani's nephew, she made her way down the gangplank slowly, with dignity. Dressed entirely in black, the crownless queen's face looked sad and worn, lit only by the moon that shone at intervals through the cloud banks. Despite the large crowd, Lili'u's arrival was met with silence. To break the spell, she said, "Aloha," pausing for a moment for response. When none came right away, Lili'u said it again in a low voice: "Aloha."

"Instantly, a storm of alohas broke from the crowd and they pressed to the gangplank as though they would touch her," wrote Mabel Craft, who witnessed the moment as a reporter for the *San Francisco Chronicle*. Craft followed the crowd heading to Washington Place. Some of the older Hawaiians began to wail. The drive to the home was lit with *kukui* nut torches and its white pillars and doorway wrapped with greenery. The fragrance of jasmine and spider lilies filled the air. Lili'u, exhausted from her long journey, settled into a chair at her own table. Servants brought her a meal of raw fish, *poi*, and fruit. Some of her retainers dropped to the floor and advanced on their knees to greet her in the old Hawaiian court manner. Liliʻu called each of them by name, as they wept and kissed her hands.

For those who couldn't be there to welcome back the crownless queen, *Ke Aloha ʻĀina*, one of the Hawaiian-language newspapers, reported: "We went to see the aliʻi, *Moi wahine* [Queen] Liliuokalani, and we did see her in person, and it was as if She were still on her throne, and her conversation was as if She were [still] ruling for the pono of Her people whom She loves. Her stature as a sacred *aliʻi* continues, and this can never be changed or taken from Her, until the last days of her life." To her supporters Liliʻu remained queen.

Ten days later, the republic marked Hawaiʻi's annexation to the United States in a tense, sparsely attended ceremony that began at noon. Under threatening skies, troops carried first the Hawaiian flag, then the American flag, to the former palace where Dole and members of his government waited. Very few Hawaiians attended; one was the Hawaiian wife of a *haole* cabinet officer and she wept quietly throughout the ceremony. When the time came, a gentle rain began to fall.

A minister led a prayer. Then Dole rose to speak, offering the sovereignty and public property of the Hawaiian Islands to the American minister, who nervously fingered a large blue envelope containing the resolution. The band performed the first strains of "Hawaiʻi Ponoi," the song by Kalākaua urging "Hawaii's true sons, look to your chiefs," but the anthem could not be completed. As Craft reported, "The natives threw away their instruments and fled around the corner out of sight and hearing . . . Some wept audibly and were not ashamed."

A moment later, a soldier lowered the Hawaiian flag down the halyards. Two others caught and folded it. To one observer, it looked "like the fluttering of a wounded bird." Then an admiral gave the order and the buglers played, followed by the "Star-Spangled Banner." The thirty-six-foot American flag rose up the flagpole, hanging lifeless for a moment until it "caught the breath of a passing breeze and flung itself in wide magnificence."

Liliʻu, Kaʻiulani, and other royalist Hawaiians gathered behind the closed doors of Washington Place. Although the deposed queen and other members of the royal family had received invitations from Dole's government to attend the ceremony, they sent their regrets, ignoring what some later described as an intentionally crude insult. Liliʻu's invitation, for one, was addressed to Mrs. J. O. Dominis.

That afternoon they posed for a photograph, Liliʻu seated with a bouquet of flowers in her lap, the others—all native Hawaiians except Liliʻu's close friend Mary Carter—clustered around her. The interior of the parlor was dim, perhaps because they'd drawn the shades, as if in mourning. In that instant, the photographer caught the expression of defeat and inexpressible sorrow on their faces.

EPILOGUE

The Kingdom of Hawai'i vanished more than a century ago but traces of it still exist. The geological oddity known as the Punchbowl is now the site of the vast National Memorial Cemetery of the Pacific. Perched over downtown Honolulu with a view of the harbor, the caldera of the extinct volcano is striped with rows of granite stones marking the graves of tens of thousands of U.S. military personnel killed in the Pacific since the Second World War.

From the cemetery looking northwest a visitor can see the deep inlet of Pearl Harbor, which was created in the early twentieth century by massive dredging of coral reefs. The U.S. naval base at Pearl Harbor is headquarters to the commander of the Pacific Fleet, the world's largest fleet command, responsible for patrolling a hundred million square miles of ocean. Just as Pearl Harbor has become the Pentagon of the Pacific, Hawai'i, which became America's fiftieth state on August 21, 1959, has become the nation's Gibraltar, a crucial military stronghold between the United States and Asia.

The economy of the islands is still influenced by companies founded by missionary families, though many of their enterprises are now subsidiaries of multinational corporations. After annexation, Sanford Dole became the first governor of the territory of Hawai'i, and then a federal district judge. Although he never had children of his own, the Dole name lives on thanks to his cousin's son James, who arrived in Hawai'i in 1898 and began cultivating pineapples.

The Dole Food Company eventually became part of Castle & Cooke, and now both are privately owned by Los Angeles–based billionaire David H. Murdock. Dole still sells pineapples, most of which are grown in the Philippines. Castle & Cooke develops hotels, golf courses, and residential real estate. In mid-2012, Castle & Cooke agreed to sell its 98% stake in the island of Lāna'i to the reclusive software billionaire Larry Ellison for an estimated $500 million. The fate of the island where William Murray Gibson once shepherded his Mormon flock, then became the world's largest pineapple plantation, and now is focused on luxury tourism, remains uncertain.

Thurston directed his gift for oratory into print, buying the *Pacific Commercial Advertiser* in January of 1899 for a reported $5,000. In addition to serving as chief executive, he continued to contribute spirited commentary, including diatribes against plantation laborers' attempts to unionize in the early 1900s. When Thurston died in 1931, his younger son, Lorrin P. Thurston, took over as publisher. He was ousted in early 1961 by Thurston Twigg-Smith, Lorrin Thurston's grandson. In 1993 Twigg-Smith sold the *Advertiser* to Gannett for a quarter of a billion dollars. An opponent of modern sovereignty efforts in Hawai'i, Twigg-Smith published an anti-monarchy book, *Hawaiian Sovereignty: Do the Facts Matter?* in 1998, 105 years after his grandfather led the overthrow.

As the monarchy collapsed, Claus Spreckels's dreams of creating a lasting business dynasty collapsed as well. Four years after the lawsuit between the Spreckels family members in which Claus lost control of the Hawaiian Commercial and Sugar Company to his two youngest sons, the Castle family, in league with Spreckels's competitor Alexander & Baldwin, staged a hostile takeover, buying up the company's stock and ousting Gus and Rudolph Spreckels from the board of directors. The Spreckels family's reign as the sugar royalty of Hawai'i came to an abrupt end in 1898, the same year Hawai'i was annexed to the United States.

Spreckels left a lingering corporate legacy in California and Hawai'i, though his name has largely disappeared. After losing the family lawsuit, Spreckels and his two older sons, John and Adolph, focused on their steamship line and their California beet sugar operation. Over the years, they exerted strong control over the Golden State by owning railroads, a power company, and a San Francisco newspaper, San Diego's *Union* and *Tribune* newspapers, and the Coronado Beach Company. Adolph became president of the Spreckels Sugar Company after Claus's death in 1908; Amstar, the predecessor to Domino Foods, Inc., makers of Domino brand sugar, bought the family's interest in 1963 and the company is now owned by the Southern Minnesota Beet Sugar Cooperative.

Sugar from what was once Spreckels's plantation on Maui is now sold by C&H Sugar, a company best known for its bubble-gum pink boxes and its advertising jingle "C&H, pure cane sugar, that's the one!" Adolph's wife, Alma de Bretteville Spreckels, became a San Francisco philanthropist who helped found the Palace of the Legion of Honor art museum. A statue of her stands in the city's Union Square and the couple's mansion in Pacific Heights, built in 1913 and nicknamed the "Sugar Palace," is now home to novelist Danielle Steel.

Hawaiian sugar production peaked in 1933, when more than a quarter million acres were planted to cane. But as the islands' cane workers pushed for unionization and humane working conditions, new sugar plantations sprang up in other parts of the world, and eventually Hawai'i's plantations could no longer compete. Castle & Cooke, Alexander & Baldwin, Amfac, C. Brewer & Co., and Theo H. Davies & Co.—the sugar firms once known as the Big 5—divested their Hawaiian sugar operations and turned to retail development and tourism instead. Matson, owner of the former Oceanic Steamship Co., is now itself owned by Alexander & Baldwin and remains the largest cruise-ship operator between the West Coast and Hawai'i.

The Hawaiian Commercial and Sugar plantation on Maui, once owned by Spreckels, is still owned by Alexander & Baldwin and is the last remaining sugar producer in the state. The sugar produced at the plantation is shipped to California's C&H refinery and is marketed under the C&H brand. In 2010 the Hawaiian Commercial and Sugar Company was in talks with the military to use its Maui plantation to produce experimental biofuel for use in fighter jets.

The water rights Kalākaua so controversially awarded Spreckels in 1878 are once again the subject of debate, with native Hawaiians seeking to restore natural stream flows to support small-scale taro farming and indigenous wildlife. In May 2010 the state water commission ordered the plantation to restore flows to six streams. The shy Hawaiian o'o was last seen in 1934, the Hawaiian mamo in 1898.

Lili'u's birthplace at the base of Punchbowl Hill is unmarked. It lies *mauka*, or on the mountain side, of Queen's Hospital, under what is now Lusitania Street. The area around her birthplace is a neighborhood of low-rise apartment buildings and modest homes. The bus stops are crowded in the mornings with people heading to work downtown.

The Chiefs' Children's School, whose building long ago disappeared, sat behind what is now the Hawai'i State Library, which lends more than 7 million books and other materials in both English and Hawaiian per year. Its successor, the Royal School, still operates. Across the street is the mighty Kawaiaha'o church, where some choristers still stand barefoot during Sunday services, reflecting a Hawaiian informality that never gave way to starched missionary ways, and continue to sing hymns in Hawaiian.

Nearby Thomas Square, the first public park on O'ahu, is a popular place for the homeless, some of them native Hawaiians, who seek shade under its spreading banyan trees. Across the street the city's elite lunch at the Honolulu Academy of Arts, which was founded by Anna Rice Cooke, the daughter of missionaries and daughter-in-law of Lili'u's Royal School teachers.

The quiet seaside estate at Waikīkī, where Lili'u would relax in her cottage and transplant ferns, has been gone for decades. Lili'uokalani Avenue runs through the property she once owned, including fourteen hundred feet of beachfront. Along the waterfront is Kalākaua Avenue, Waikīkī's main tourist thoroughfare, lit up at night with tiki torches and neon in a colorful pageantry that the "Merrie Monarch" himself probably would have enjoyed. A McDonald's occupies the corner of Lili'uokalani and Kalākaua avenues: the smells of diesel bus fumes and sunscreen mingle with fries and burgers.

At the site of Lili'u's other Waikīkī cottage, farther inland, sits the present Lili'uokalani Gardens apartment complex. 'Āinahau, the lushly planted Waikīkī estate of her niece Ka'iulani, has been paved over, but peacock screams can still be heard from the nearby Honolulu zoo. A plaque marks 'Āinahau's location in a courtyard surrounded by high-rises. Well-wishers have left peacock feathers in tribute to the princess who once lived there.

Washington Place, where the queen lived until her death in 1917, has been home to a dozen of Hawai'i's governors and, since 2003, has offered public tours. The garden that Mary Dominis first planted more than a century ago still flourishes to the delight of the beneficiaries of the Lili'uokalani Trust, some of whom have been invited there in recent years to celebrate Lili'u's birthday. Inside are many of the things that surrounded Lili'u in her later years—the dark Chinese furniture brought to Honolulu by Captain Dominis, a koa piano presented to Lili'u during her reign, *kāhili* passed down to her over the years, and the walnut canopy bed in a ground-floor bedroom from where she could hear the laughter and cries of children playing in the yard of St. Andrew's church seen from her window. Outside, the original, magnificent tamarind tree survives, with its sour-sweet-tasting seeds.

A few of her relics are also preserved behind glass at the Bishop Museum, including the Parisian ball gown she wore to her brother's coronation in 1883. Finely beaded with puffed sleeves and a high neck, it still sparkles as it did while she was dancing the quadrille alongside her sister Likelike. The other artifacts she once owned include a diamond bracelet and a delicate tobacco pipe.

Once the grandest building in Honolulu, 'Iolani Palace now looks like an elaborate toy alongside the high-rise office buildings of downtown Honolulu. Tourist guides suggest visiting it on a rainy day, describing it as the only royal palace on American soil. No longer an executive building, it has become a museum, preserving royal objects and the second-floor bedroom where Lili'u embroidered the words "I am imprisoned" on a quilt and listened to the footsteps of guards pacing outside her door.

Docents wearing floral *mu'umu'u* and aloha attire lead visitors on tours of the palace called 'Iolani, or "bird of heaven." One of the highlights is the dining room where guests such as Robert Louis Stevenson were said to have drunk Château Lafite from crystal goblets imported from Bohemia. The Palace volunteers are frequently asked where Jack Lord's office is, referring to the actor who starred in the 1970s television police drama *Hawai'i 5-0*, which was filmed in part at the palace.

On most Fridays at noon, the Royal Hawaiian Band plays on the palace grounds near where Kalākaua's coronation ceremony took place. One of the longest-playing municipal bands in the United States, it performs "Mele Ai Pohaku," the "Stone-Eating Song," and usually ends its weekly program with "Aloha Oe," a familiar favorite, which prompts any audience to stand up to listen and sing along. The members of the Royal Hawaiian Band still wear the formal whites of the Hawaiian kingdom as they play to retirees, tourists, and state office workers picnicking during their lunch hour.

A statue of Queen Lili'uokalani faces Hawai'i's modern legislature building, with its back to the palace. Like all Hawaiians, she became a U.S. citizen when Hawai'i became a U.S. territory in 1900. On the centennial anniversary of the overthrow of the Hawaiian kingdom, in 1993, supporters heaped her statue with floral tributes, with *lei* of shells and feathers, and small Hawaiian flags. People still regularly drape flower garlands around the statue's neck or leave flowers in her extended hand to honor the deposed queen's memory.

Lili'u's most powerful legacy may be her music. The *mele* of Lili'u and her royal siblings are performed at the annual Merrie Monarch Festival on Hawai'i Island, where giant portraits of Kapi'iolani and Kalākaua preside over the stage. Individuals and groups, dressed in brilliant costumes crowned with flowers and greenery, vie for prizes in traditional and modern hula. "Aloha Oe," Lili'u's most famous refrain, is known the world over and is heard in the soundtrack of everything from Elvis Presley's "Blue Hawaii" to the Disney movie *Lilo and Stitch*.

Lili'u's financial legacy is harder to trace. Despite the lasting popularity of her songs, Lili'u struggled with money for much of her life and her letters and diaries in her later years are sad testaments to her lost land and fortune. She repeatedly sought compensation for the crown lands; her struggle culminated in a lawsuit, *Lili'uokalani v. the United States* which came to trial in 1909, when she was in her seventies. The territorial government paid her a modest $12,000 annual pension in the final six years of her life. Still, the bitter legal wrangling she endured in her last years with lawyers and members of her own family made it difficult for her to trust anyone.

Ka'iulani's death in 1899 compounded Lili'u's grief. The deposed queen left the bulk of her estate, which totaled about $200,000 or about $5 million today, to a trust which triggered her second cousin Prince Jonah Kuhio Kalaniana'ole to file a lawsuit alleging she was mentally incompetent when she made her will. The Queen Lili'uokalani Trust prevailed and exists today, managing 6,400 acres of lands that Lili'u had inherited from her mother. Its mission is to help orphaned and destitute children, particularly those with Hawaiian blood. Its headquarters is about three miles from Lili'u's birthplace. The trust, along with the Kamehameha Schools founded by Lili'u's sister Bernice Pauahi Bishop, are among the largest landowners in the state, holding more than 370,000 acres.

Queen Lili'uokalani's most lasting gift may be the memory of her efforts to restore the rights of her people. In 1993, on the hundredth anniversary of the overthrow, President Clinton issued a formal apology to native Hawaiians. In early 2010, with President Obama's support, the House passed legislation that has been circulating for more than a decade. The Akaka bill would give native Hawaiians political authority similar to the sovereignty granted to American Indian tribes. If the bill passes, the new Hawaiian government would begin discussing its furure, including negotiating for land making up one-quarter of Hawai'i's mass and worth billions of dollars.

While the Honolulu that Liliʻu knew has mostly disappeared, the questions she asked are yet being debated in the U.S. Congress, the courts, and among scholars. Who owns the crown lands? When will native Hawaiians regain sovereignty? How will Liliʻu be remembered? More than a hundred years ago Liliʻu asked, "Has this mission of mine accomplished anything?"

Her struggle continues to this day. Liliʻu's motto ʻonipaʻa—"steadfast"—has been adopted by Hawaiians as a rallying cry and she has become a potent symbol. Despite the hot anger that led her to declare a desire to behead her usurpers shortly after the overthrow, her ability to forgive her enemies late in life inspired the Hawaiʻi Forgiveness Project and an annual festival with slack-key guitar and prayers. In recent years, it has been held on Honolulu's Dole Street, an unintentional irony.

Hawaiʻi was lost to both Liliʻu and her unlikely ally Claus Spreckels. But the ongoing work of scholars, musicians, activists, and educators has kept Liliʻu's memory alive. And because of their efforts, in one form or another, the Kingdom of Hawaiʻi is remembered.

A NOTE ON LANGUAGE AND SOURCES

The last queen of Hawai'i used many names during her lifetime. Her missionary teachers called her Lydia. As a young bride she was known as Lydia Dominis. As princess and queen she became Lili'uokalani. In letters to her intimate friends and family, she called herself Lili'u, the name she was given at birth. I've chosen to call her Lili'u because it's the name she most frequently called herself.

Telling the story of a woman whose mother tongue was Hawaiian was challenging for me, a non-Hawaiian speaker. But I was fortunate in that Lili'u wrote the vast majority of her diary entries and her letters in English, as did most of the members of her immediate family. She learned to write in English before she learned to write in Hawaiian as a student at the Royal School. And as heir apparent and then queen, fully grasping that English was the language of the nineteenth century's ruling classes, she strove to speak it well, despite struggling early on with spelling and grammar. Westerners who met her were continually surprised by Lili'u's fluency in the language of Shakespeare and Emily Dickinson.

English, alongside Hawaiian, became the predominant language used for most government documents by the 1870s, which made my efforts to understand the kingdom's affairs easier. But as the political situation in Hawai'i grew grave for Lili'u in the mid- to late 1890s she switched to writing in Hawaiian to some close friends because she believed her letters were being intercepted and read by her English-speaking enemies. Most of these letters have been translated into English. During that same period, she began coding some of her diary entries, using a preexisting code that equated numbers with letters of the Hawaiian alphabet. In 1971 a volunteer at Honolulu's Bishop Museum decoded the entries into Hawaiian. Some years later, the decoded Hawaiian words were translated into English at the Hawai'i State Archives.

Because Hawaiian is a complex language that often contains multiple meanings for the same word, translation can be difficult and may not always reflect subtleties. There is also a tradition among native speakers of using metaphor, or *kaona*, which is often translated as "hidden meaning." An example of this is contained in the letters written in Hawaiian from Emma Nāwahī to Lili'u when she was in Washington hoping to stave off annexation. Those letters are rich in metaphorical language, which, from the distance of more than a century, makes it now impossible to more than guess at what she really meant: even the English translations are cryptic.

I've relied on the translations of Lili'u's writings that are preserved alongside the original manuscripts in the Hawai'i State Archives and elsewhere, as well as transcripts of her diary entries from the state archives and the Bishop Museum archives. Usually, but not always, these translations were made at the behest of the archive staff and are often many decades old. For translating individual Hawaiian words, I have used the Hawaiian dictionary of Mary Kawena Pukui and Samuel H. Elbert, as well as Ulukau, the Hawaiian Electronic Library. This wonderful resource is an extension of the many-pronged efforts by educators and native speakers of Hawaiian to revitalize the language and save it from extinction. The revitalization of Hawaiian, now in its third decade, is ongoing.

Lili'u's native language is far more nuanced than many nonspeakers realize. Because the written language was given only twelve letters in its alphabet by missionaries, many Hawaiian words may initially seem very similar in spelling and pronunciation. What distinguishes the sound and meaning of many of the words are a glottal stop, or ʻokina, separating vowels (the symbol ʻ), and the kahakō or macron (the symbol ¯ over a vowel) indicating that the sound of that vowel is drawn out. The word pau, spelled without any diacritical mark, for instance, means finished, ended, or all done. But when spelled paʻu, with an ʻokina, it describes soot, smudge, or ink powder; when spelled paʻū it means moldy or moist.

During the queen's lifetime, the kahakō was not used and the ʻokina used only intermittently. Indeed, Hawaiian was not a written language until the arrival of Christian missionaries in 1820, eighteen years before Liliʻu was born. When the missionaries translated the Bible, one of the first texts in written Hawaiian—they did not include diacritical markings and that set the standard for written Hawaiian for the next 150 years.

Starting in the 1970s, consistent diacriticals were introduced into written Hawaiian to reflect the subtlety of the language and help modern speakers understand and pronounce it more easily. I have not inserted diacritical markings into the nineteenth-century diaries, letters, and documents that I cite, following their original form, but I do use them for Hawaiian proper names, as a way to help readers navigate through the subtle differences in the pronunciation of so many vowel-filled Hawaiian names.

Additionally, I have used a word that nineteenth-century Hawaiians themselves often used in referring to white people: haole. In its modern usage, this term is sometimes used derisively, but its original meaning merely indicated that a person—or even a plant, an animal, or a language —was foreign. In referring to the people native to the Hawaiian Islands, whom some Hawaiian activists and scholars now call kanaka maoli (kanaka means "people" and maoli refers to a native), I simply use "native Hawaiians," which is what Liliʻu herself called her people. Respecting the Hawaiian usage of the word, the term haole is not pluralized with an s, as it would be in English. Thus, throughout the book I refer to groups of haole—not haoles—and flower garlands as lei.

As much as possible, I've tried to tell Liliʻu's life story using transcripts of her diary entries, her letters, and other primary source documents. I am enormously fortunate to have been granted early access to a collection donated in late 2009 to the Hawaiʻi State Archives by David W. Forbes, the state's leading bibliographer. Mr. Forbes spent four years collecting and transcribing letters and other significant documents of the members of the kingdom's last royal family, some of which have never before been published. The Forbes Collection runs to some 1,852 pages.

I've also relied on Liliʻu's English-language autobiography, *Hawaii's Story by Hawaii's Queen*, which she published in 1898 as a weapon in her campaign to stave off annexation. It is the only autobiography ever written by a Hawaiian monarch. By comparing earlier drafts of the manuscript against the published book, I discovered large sections that her editor had cut out because she or Liliʻu's publisher considered them too inflammatory.

It should be noted that there has been some dispute over how much of the book was written by Liliʻu herself and how much should be attributed to her collaborator, an American journalist named Julius A. Palmer. Mr. Forbes describes *Hawaii's Story* as a "told to" book, one in which Liliʻu dictated her story to Palmer, who then typed it and added linguistic refinements. Based on my examination of her letters and diaries, I believe the book largely reflects her perspective, though some of the flowery and more dramatic language in it was certainly Palmer's.

Another primary source was *The Queen's Songbook*, the result of a monumental twenty-five-year project by the Hui Hānai Council. It provided me with insight into Liliʻu's life and creative process for which I am deeply grateful. The president of the Hui Hānai at the time of publication was Agnes C. Conrad, Hawaiʻi's state archivist from 1959 to 1982.

As for secondary sources on the queen's life, there are surprisingly few. Helena G. Allen's *The Betrayal of Liliuokalani*, first published in 1982, is a highly sympathetic though not entirely credible account of the queen's life, which depends in part on taped interviews and other source material that I was unable to either locate or substantiate. The other biographies on Lili'u are shelved in the young adult or children's sections of the library. Albertine Loomis's *For Whom Are the Stars?* is an excellent and well-researched account of the overthrow, despite lacking endnotes.

For an overall view of Hawaiian history, I've relied on Ralph S. Kuykendall's three-volume *The Hawaiian Kingdom*, with a particular focus on volume III, covering the years of the Kalākaua dynasty. Kuykendall spent forty years producing his life's work, beginning in the late 1920s and traveling to Washington, D.C., London, and elsewhere to gather documents for it. In comparing his work to the primary documents I examined, I found him consistently admirable in terms of his fact gathering and generally evenhanded in his treatment of the complex, racially charged series of events leading to the overthrow.

Kuykendall, who passed away in 1963 before finishing the final chapter of his third volume, is now targeted by some modern historians of Hawai'i for not including more of the native Hawaiian perspective in his work. This is a valid criticism. Kuykendall did much of his work before the renaissance of Hawaiian language and culture began in the 1970s and '80s, and he did not have the benefit of many of the English translations of Hawaiian newspapers and chants that are available today. While I've retraced many of his steps and examined the same documents he cited from the Hawai'i State Archives, the Hawaiian Historical Society, Hawaiian Mission Children's Society, and Bishop Museum Archives, I also relied on crucial materials that were not available when he wrote his study, for example, the recently unsealed Judd Collection at the Bishop Museum.

To balance out the mainly *haole* accounts of Lili'u's world, I've sought to include the native Hawaiian perspective as much as possible. I've sought out translations of Hawaiian-language newspapers from the nineteenth century, as well as incorporated the perspective of traditional Hawaiian historians, such as David Malo and John Papa 'I'i. I've also turned to some excellent works of more recent scholarship on this period of history, including Noenoe K. Silva's *Aloha Betrayed*, Jon Kamakawiwo'ole Osorio's *Dismembering Lāhui*, Davianna Pōmaika'i

McGregor's *NāKua'āina: Living Hawaiian Culture,* Tom Coffman's *Nation Within,* John Van Dyke's *Who Owns the Crown Lands of Hawai'i?,* (see this book's bibliography.) and Neil Thomas Proto's *The Rights of My People.*

Because Hawaiian history was passed down entirely through chants and stories until the first few decades of the nineteenth century, there are far more accounts available of the island kingdom written by foreigner travelers and missionaries in English than there are by native Hawaiians. As researchers and historians continue to translate Hawaiian-language newspapers and other source materials, however, the already-rich portrait of Lili'u and other Hawaiians who lived through the overthrow will gain even more texture and depth.

ACKNOWLEDGMENTS

On my first research trip to Hawai'i, I visited the University of Hawai'i's Mānoa campus, set in a lush valley above downtown Honolulu. There, I heard a tale about the *kōlea*, a migratory bird from the mainland that traveled great distances across the sea every year until it reached the islands. Once there, it plucked the most luscious berries and choicest fruits, gorging on all it found. After it had grown fat, the bird took off again for the mainland. The moral of this true tale, based on the migratory patterns of the Pacific golden plover, seemed to be that the bird, like so many other visitors, took from Hawai'i without giving back.

That story lingered in the back of my mind as I studied Hawai'i's history of loss and exploitation. Was I like the *kōlea*, feasting on the state's delicacies and, after fattening up my research files, flying back home? Could I find a way to give instead of merely take? By the end of my research I felt overwhelming gratitude toward the many scholars, librarians, and archivists in Hawai'i who went out of their way on so many occasions to help this book germinate. So in addition to thanking them collectively and individually for their help my hope is that this book will inspire readers to learn more about the important work they're doing to preserve and understand Hawaiian culture.

I am deeply grateful to the staff at the Hawai'i State Archives, beginning with the archives administrator Susan E. Shaner, who early on in her three-decade-long career at the archives identified and indexed photographic images of the monarchy and helped proofread Lili'u's diaries. Her wonderful colleagues endured countless requests from me with patience and humor: Jerry Fulkerson, Nicole Ishihara, and Victoria Nihi. I'd like to give a special thanks to Luella Kurkjian, head of the archive's historical records branch, who safeguards many of the most precious documents that are locked away in a safe.

Early on, Susan pulled me into her office with the words, "You've got to meet David!" Sitting at her conference table was a courtly, somewhat curmudgeonly man with silver hair, wearing a blue button-down oxford shirt and khakis. I soon realized he was David W. Forbes, author of the four-volume *Hawaiian National Bibliography* and the man who'd acquired and organized the massive Kahn Collection for the state archives. David has an encyclopedic knowledge of archives and his generosity in sharing so much of what he knows still astonishes me. Thank you, David.

At the University of Hawai'i, Professor Jon Osorio offered suggestions on the chapters of this book about the Bayonet Constitution, as well as providing me with a copy of an English-language biography of Joseph Nāwahī. Likewise, Davianna McGregor, a professor and founding member of Ethnic Studies at the University of Hawai'i at Mānoa, read and commented on early chapters of the book.

Also at the University of Hawai'i, the remarkable Puakea Nogelmeier fielded questions on language; Craig Howes, director of the Center for Biographical Research at the University of Hawai'i and an English professor, provided introductions and wise counsel. Law professor Jon M. Van Dyke author of *Who Owns the Crown Lands of Hawai'i?*, and the late Judge Samuel P. King and Professor Randall Roth, co-authors of *Broken Trust*, were helpful and encouraging.

At the Bishop Museum Archives, library and archives collection manager De Soto Brown gave crucial help in my understanding of Lili'u's often cryptic diary entries as well as offering to read the manuscript. As a great-great-grandson of the Hawaiian historian John Papa 'I'i, who wrote *Fragments of Hawaiian History*, it is no surprise that De Soto has devoted himself to preserving history. Also at the Bishop, many thanks to Charles Myers, B. J. Short and Tia Reber.

A thank you, as well, to Toni Han Palermo, program specialist at the King Kamehameha V Judiciary History Center; Barbara Dunn, director and librarian of the Hawaiian Historical Society; Carol White, head librarian of the Hawaiian Mission Children's Society Library; Kippen de Alba Chu, executive director of 'Iolani Palace; Stuart Ching, 'Iolani's former curator; and Zita Cup Choy, the palace's docent educator, who read and commented on the manuscript and is a treasure trove of knowledge about the House of Kalākaua. Others in the islands who taught me the meaning of aloha are Colette Higgins, the department chair of Arts & Humanities at Kapi'olani Community College and Jamie Conway, director and founder of the Distinctive Women in Hawaiian History conference.

One of the most pleasant few hours I spent in the islands was with Claire Hiwahiwa Steele, sitting outside and enjoying lunch together at the Mission Houses Museum café. Claire, a graduate student in Hawaiian studies and a native Hawaiian herself, not only offered to read and comment on my manuscript but invited me to join her in singing Lili'u's own songs with the choir of the Kawaiaha'o church. What an unforgettable experience.

Others who helped me understand Lili'u more deeply included Corinne Fujimoto Chun, curator of Washington Place, the gracious, white-columned home in downtown Honolulu where Queen Lili'uokalani spent the last years of her life. Corinne offered me a private tour of Washington Place and suggested I study *The Queen's Songbook*, a massive decade-long project. That, in turn, led me to the marvelous Amy Ku'uleialoha Stillman, a Harvard-educated associate professor of music and American culture at the University of Michigan. Amy reviewed the sections of the book on the queen's music. Helping me appreciate island plant life was Carol Russell, a docent at the Ho'omaluhia Botanical Garden, and introducing me to island *kau kau* were Inger Tully, Molly Mayher, Cliff Colvin, and Waltraut and Art Mori.

Back on the mainland, several branches of the family descended from Claus and Anna Spreckels shared with me photographs, newspaper clippings, and family stories of their great-grandfather. A big thanks to Alex and Bob Phillips, their daughter Alix Phillips Becker, Lyn and Terry Wilson, and most of all Adolph Rosekrans, with whom I had the marvelous experience of having lunch under the stained-glass dome of San Francisco's Palace Hotel, where the last king of Hawai'i spent his final days. Thanks to Catherine Pyke for arranging this memorable meal.

Also in San Francisco were the helpful staff of the California Historical Society and, in Berkeley, the wizards at the Bancroft Library. In Santa Cruz, the late author James D. Houston, who loved Hawai'i, offered me some good advice shortly before he died. The distinguished historian Walter LaFeber also provided guidance. I couldn't have done this work without the support of North 24th Writers, a group of women nonfiction authors and journalists who have been together for more than a decade. With good humor and patience, they read too many early chapters of this book to recall. Warm thanks to Allison Hoover Bartlett, Leslie Crawford, Frances Dinkelspiel, Katherine Ellison, Sharon Epel, Susan Freinkel, Katherine Neilan, Lisa Wallgren Okuhn, and Jill Storey.

Another source of unwavering support from the very beginning of this project was Catherine Thorpe, a novelist and a researcher extraordinaire. My brilliant friend Sarah Mott gave me invaluable feedback. Constance Hale, who grew up in Hawai'i and has a wicked way with style and syntax, helped shape early versions of this manuscript. Colleagues at the *Wall Street Journal* continue to teach me how to tell a good story: Eben Shapiro, Steve Yoder, Pui-Wing Tam, Carrie Dolan, Suein Hwang, Rob Guth, Jim Carlton, Sharon Massey, and Don Clark. My friend and former *Journal* colleague Scott Miller led me to helpful historians. Liz Epstein, a book group maven and literature whiz, shared suggestions on an early draft. Thanks also for their friendship and support, Jason Roberts and Katy Butler.

Michael Carlisle, a dear friend and my literary agent, believed in this project from the very beginning, as did his colleagues Ethan Bassoff and Lauren Smythe. Michael opened many doors and offered wise counsel. The most important of these doors was that of Grove/Atlantic, where my wonderful editor Joan Bingham works. The time and care that Joan has devoted to shaping this book makes me believe that I found my fairy godmother in the publishing world. I'm also deeply grateful to Grove/ Atlantic's managing editor, Michael Hornburg, associate publisher Judy Hottensen, publisher Morgan Entrekin, and the publicity team of Deb Seager and Jodie Hockensmith.

Thanks are also in order to Paula and William Merwin for a magical visit to their palm paradise on the north shore of Maui.

Finally, my family has been my cheerleading squad throughout this project. Not only did my late mother, Roberta Grant Flynn, and my sister, Jennifer Israel Flynn, agree to join me on a weeklong history tour of O'ahu, but they both made invaluable suggestions on early drafts of the manuscript. My brother, Greg, offered his encouragement. And my husband, Charles Siler, somehow managed to keep a straight face while I was describing how I needed to take just one more research trip to the islands.

Thank you, Charlie, for everything, and especially for our *kupaianaha* sons, Cody and Andrew. This book is dedicated with love to the three of you and to my beautiful mother Berta.

BIBLIOGRAPHY

PRIMARY SOURCE MATERIALS

Chief among the primary source materials were the correspondence and documents contained in the David W. Forbes Collection at the State Archives of Hawai'i. The collection includes:

- Lili'uokalani Letters, Parts I–IV
- Kalākaua Letters, Parts I–III
- Cleghorn Letters, Parts I–II

Further photo and document files in the State Archives of Hawai'i provided additional information, in particular:

- Queen Lili'uokalani Manuscript Collection
- Archibald Scott Cleghorn Manuscript Collection
- Dole Manuscript Collection

Together, the state archives and the Bishop Museum Archives hold a number of Lili'uokalani's personal diaries:

- Diary of Lili'uokalani, 1878. MS MC LILIU Bishop Museum
- Diary of Lili'uokalani, 1885. MS MC LILIU Bishop Museum
- Diary of Lili'uokalani, 1886. MS MC LILIU Bishop Museum
- Diary of Lili'uokalani, 1887. State Archives of Hawai'i

+ Diary of Lili'uokalani, 1888. State Archives of Hawai'i
+ Diary of Lili'uokalani, 1892. MS MC LILIU Bishop Museum
+ Diary of Lili'uokalani, 1893. State Archives of Hawai'i
+ Diary of Lili'uokalani, 1894. State Archives of Hawai'i
+ Diary of Lili'uokalani, 1898. MS MC LILIU Bishop Museum

The Bishop Museum Archives additionally holds a number of useful documents, in particular:

+ The General Letters file box contains miscellaneous correspondence by members of the royal family
+ Judd, Albert Francis. "Diary of Albert Francis Judd, 1890–1895." Honolulu, Bishop Museum Archive

The Alexander & Baldwin Collection at the Hawaiian Mission Children's Society provided primary source material on missionary families.

NEWSPAPER ACCOUNTS

The author consulted nineteenth-century accounts in the following Hawaiian newspapers:

+ *The Evening Bulletin*, Honolulu. Founded in 1882.
+ *The Pacific Commercial Advertiser*, Honolulu. Founded in 1856.
+ *The Polynesian*, Honolulu; 1840–41 and 1844–64.

In addition, the newspapers' modern descendants have sporadically published special sections focusing on history in the islands:

+ "Hawai'i Looking Back," published in 1999 on the occasion of the millennium by the *Star-Bulletin*. http://archives.starbulletin.com/specials/millennium/index.html
+ "150 Years of Hawai'i's History," published to commemorate the *Honolulu Advertiser's* 150th anniversary, in 2006. http://the.honoluluadvertiser.com/150

Mainland coverage of Hawaiian affairs during the nineteenth century included:

+ *The Boston Globe*, for coverage of Lili'uokalani's visits following the 1893 overthrow.

- *The New York Times*, dating from Kalākaua's first visit to the United States, in 1874.
- *The San Francisco Chronicle*, from 1863 onward.

Finally, articles from the *Times* of London provided invaluable details about Queen Victoria's Jubilee in June 1887.

OTHER RESOURCES: A PARTIAL LIST

Abbott, Elizabeth. *Sugar: A Bittersweet History*. New York: Overlook Press, 2010.

Adams, Henry Austin. *The Man, John D. Spreckels*. San Diego: Press of Frye & Smith, 1924.

Adler, Jacob. *Claus Spreckels: The Sugar King in Hawaii*. Honolulu: University of Hawai'i Press, 1966.

―――, ed. *The Journal of Prince Alexander Liholiho: The Voyages Made to the United States, England and France in 1849–1850*. Honolulu: University of Hawai'i Press for the Hawaiian Historical Society, 1967.

―――, and Robert M. Kamins. "The Political Debut of Walter Murray Gibson." *Hawaiian Journal of History* 18 (1984): 96–115.

Alexander, William De Witt. *A Brief History of the Hawaiian People*. New York: American Book Company, 1891.

―――. *History of Later Years of the Hawaiian Monarchy, and the Revolution of 1893*. Honolulu: Hawaiian Gazette Company, 1896.

Ali, Mehmed. "Ho'ohui'aina Pala Ka Mai'a: Remembering Annexation One Hundred Years Ago." *Hawaiian Journal of History* 32 (1998): 141–54.

"Ali'i Diplomatic Missions and Other Business Travel to Washington D.C.: Research Phase I." Washington, D.C.: Office of Hawaiian Affairs, 2007. http://www.oha.org/pdf/Alii_Diplomatic_Missions_2007.pdf.

"Ali'i Diplomatic Missions and Other Business Travel to Washington D.C.: Research Phase II." Washington, D.C.: Office of Hawaiian Affairs, 2009.

Allen, Helena. *The Betrayal of Liliuokalani: Last Queen of Hawai'i 1838–1917*. Honolulu: Mutual Publishing, 1982.

―――. *Kalakaua: Renaissance King*. Honolulu: Mutual Publishing, 1994.

―――. *Sanford Ballard Dole: Hawaii's Only President*. Glendale: Arthur H. Clarke, 1988.

An Act to Provide for the Allotment of Lands in Severalty to Indians on the Various Reservations, 1887 (General Allotment Act or Dawes Act), Statutes at Large 24, 388-91, NADP Document A1887. As found on National Archive "Our Documents" Web site http://www.ourdocuments.gov/doc.php?flash=false&doc=50&page=transcript.

Anderson, Rufus. *The Hawaiian Islands: Their Progress and Condition Under Missionary Labors.* Boston: Gould and Lincoln, 1864.

Andrade, Ernest. "Great Britain and the Hawaiian Revolution and Republic, 1893–1898." *Hawaiian Journal of History* 24 (1990): 91–116.

———. *Unconquerable Rebel: Robert W. Wilcox and Hawaiian Politics, 1880–1903.* Niwot: University Press of Colorado, 1996.

Armstrong, William Nevins. *Around the World with a King.* New York: Frederick A. Stokes, 1904.

Bailey, Paul. *Hawaii's Royal Prime Minister: The Life and Times of Walter Murray Gibson.* New York: Hastings House, 1980.

Barrère, Dorothy B., Mary Kawena Pukui, and Marion Kelly. *Hula: Historical Perspectives.* Honolulu: Bishop Museum Press, 1980.

Baur, John E. "When Royalty Came to California." *California History* 67, no. 4 (December 1988): 244–65.

Bingham, Hiram. *A Residence of Twenty-one Years in the Sandwich Islands.* New York: Sherman Converse, 1847.

Biographical Research Center. *Mai Poina: Visitor's Guide 2010.* Honolulu: Kamehameha Schools, 2010.

Bird, Isabella. *Six Months in the Sandwich Islands: Among Hawaii's Palm Groves, Coral Reefs, and Volcanoes.* Honolulu: Mutual Publishing, 2007.

Bishop, Bernice Pauahi. "Ke Ali'i Bernice Pauahi Paki Bishop: Will and Codicils," 1883. State Archives of Hawaii. http://www.ksbe.edu/pauahi/will.php.

———, and Mary Hanna Krout. *The Memoirs of Hon. Bernice Pauahi Bishop.* New York: Knickerbocker Press, 1908.

Brennan, Joseph. *The Parker Ranch of Hawaii: The Saga of a Ranch and a Dynasty.* New York: John Day, 1974.

Briggs, Lloyd Vernon. *Experiences of a Medical Student in Honolulu: and on the Island of Oahu, 1881.* David D. Nickerson, 1926.

Brown, Henry A. *Revised Analysis of the Sugar Question: Embracing Foreign and Domestic Cane and Beet Sugar Production—Imports of Sugar—Consumption—Classification—Cost . . . Tariffs . . . Etc.* Saxonville, Mass., 1879.

Cady, John F. "The Beginnings of French Imperialism in the Pacific Orient." *Journal of Modern History* 14, no. 1 (March 1942): 71–87.

Campbell, I. C. *A History of the Pacific Islands*. Berkeley: University of California Press, 1989.

Carleton Green. "Trollope in Hawaii." *Trollopian* 3, no. 4 (March 1949): 297–303.

Carnegie, Andrew. *Triumphant Democracy*. New York: Cosimo Classics, 2005.

Carter, George R., and Mary H. Hopkins. *A Record of the Descendants of Dr. Gerrit P. Judd of Hawaii, March 8, 1829, to April 16, 1922*. Honolulu: Hawaiian Historical Society, 1922.

Castle, William Richards. *Life of Samuel Northrup Castle: Written by his Grandson*. Honolulu: The Samuel N. and Mary Castle Foundation, in cooperation with the Hawaiian Historical Society, 1960.

Chapin, Helen Geracimos. *Shaping History: The Role of Newspapers in Hawaii*. Honolulu: University of Hawai'i Press, 1996.

Chaplin, George. *Presstime in Paradise: The Life and Times of The Honolulu Advertiser, 1856–1995*. Honolulu: University of Hawai'i Press, 1998.

Coffman, Tom. *Nation Within: The Story of America's Annexation of the Nation of Hawaii*. Honolulu: Epicenter, 2003.

Coleman, Kit. *To London for the Jubilee*. Toronto: George N. Morang, 1897.

"Commander, U.S. Pacific Fleet, Official Military Web site," http://www.cpf.navy.mil/.

Cook, James, John Cawte Beaglehole, Philip Edwards, and Hakluyt Society. *The Journals of Captain Cook*. New York: Penguin, 1999.

Cooke, Amos Starr, Juliette Montague Cooke, and Mary Atherton Richards. *The Hawaiian Chiefs' Children's School*. Honolulu: Honolulu Star-Bulletin, 1937.

Cordray, William Woodrow. "Claus Spreckels of California," thesis dissertation. Los Angeles: University of Southern California, 1955.

Craft, Mabel Clare. *Hawai'i Nei*. San Francisco: William Doxey at the Sign of the Lark, 1899.

Cushing, Robert L. "The Beginnings of Sugar Production in Hawai'i." *Hawaiian Journal of History* 19 (1985): 17–34.

Dabagh, Jean, ed. "A King Is Elected: One Hundred Years Ago." *Hawaiian Journal of History* 8 (1974): 76–89.

Damon, Ethel M. *Sanford Ballard Dole and His Hawaii: With an Analysis of Justice Dole's Legal Opinions*, first edition. Palo Alto, Calif.: Pacific Books for the Hawaiian Historical Society, 1957.

Da Pidgin Coup. "Pidgin and Education: A Position Paper." Honolulu: University of Hawaii, November 1999.

Davies, Theo H. *Letters Upon the Political Crisis in Hawaii: January and February, 1894.* Honolulu: Bulletin Publishing Company, 1894.

Daws, Gavan. *Holy Man: Father Damien of Molokai.* Honolulu: University of Hawai'i Press, 1973.

———. *Honolulu: The First Century.* Honolulu: Mutual Publishing, 2006.

———. *Shoal of Time: A History of the Hawaiian Islands.* Honolulu: University of Hawai'i Press, 1968.

———, and Bennett Hymer. *Honolulu Stories: Voices of the Town Through the Years: Two Centuries of Writing.* Honolulu: Mutual Publishing, 2008.

Day, Arthur Grove, and Carl Stroven. *Hawaiian Reader.* Honolulu: Mutual Publishing, 1994.

Devine, Michael J. "John W. Foster and the Struggle for the Annexation of Hawaii." *Pacific Historical Review* 46, no. 1 (February 1977): 29–50.

"Discovery: The Hawaiian Odyssey." Produced by East West Communications. Honolulu: Bishop Museum Press, 1993.

Dole, Sanford. *Memoirs of the Hawaiian Revolution,* edited by Andrew Farrell, 3 vols. Honolulu: Book Company Publishing, 2008.

Dolin, Eric Jay. *Leviathan: The History of Whaling in America.* New York: W. W. Norton, 2007.

Dorrance, William H. *Sugar Islands: The 165-Year Story of Sugar in Hawaii.* Honolulu: Mutual Publishing, 2000.

Duggard, Martin. *Farther Than Any Man: The Rise and Fall of Captain James Cook.* New York: Pocket, 2001.

Dukas, Neil Bernard. *A Military History of Sovereign Hawai'i.* Honolulu: Mutual Publishing, 2004.

Elbert, Samuel H., and Noelani Māhoe. *Nā Mele o Hawai'i Nei.* Honolulu: University of Hawai'i Press, 1970.

Evenhuis, N. L. *Barefoot on Lava: The Journals and Correspondence of Naturalist R.C.L. Perkins in Hawai'i, 1892–1901.* Honolulu: Bishop Museum Press, 2007.

Field, Isobel. *This Life I've Loved.* New York: Longmans, Green, 1937.

Fischer, Steven Roger. A History of the Pacific Islands. New York: Palgrave, 2002.

Fishkin, Shelley Fisher. *A Historical Guide to Mark Twain.* New York: Oxford University Press, 2002.

Forbes, David W, ed. *Hawaiian National Bibliography, 1780–1900*, vol. 4. Honolulu: University of Hawai'i Press, 2003.

Forwood, Sir William B. *Recollections of a Busy Life: Being the Reminiscences of a Liverpool Merchant, 1840–1910*. Liverpool: Henry Young & Sons, 1910.

Frost & Frost, AIA. *Ali'iolani Hale: A Century of Growth and Change, 1872–1977*. Honolulu: Department of Accounting and General Services, State of Hawaii, 1979.

Gardiner, Herbert G. "The Early Lodges in Hawai'i and Some Prominent Brethren of That Bygone Era," n.d. http://www.calodges.org/ncrl/PROM-MAS.htm.

Garrett, John. *To Live Among the Stars: Christian Origins in Oceania*. Suva, Fiji: Institute of Pacific Studies, 1982.

Gibson, Walter Murray. *The Diaries of Walter Murray Gibson, 1886, 1887*, ed. Jacob Adler and Gwynn Barrett. Honolulu: University of Hawai'i Press, 1973.

Grant, M. Forsyth. *Scenes in Hawaii; or, Life in the Sandwich Islands*. Toronto: Hart and Company, 1888.

Gray, Francine du Plessix. *Hawaii: The Sugar-Coated Fortress*. New York: Random House, 1972.

Hackler, Rhoda E. A. "'Earnest Persuasion but Not Peremptory Demand': United States Government Policy Toward the Kingdom of Hawai'i, 1820–1863." *Hawaiian Journal of History* 42 (2008): 49–67.

———, and Michael D. Horikawa. *'Iolani Palace*. Honolulu: Friends of 'Iolani Palace, 1995.

———, Loretta G. H. Woodard, and Friends of 'Iolani Palace. *The Queen's Quilt*. Honolulu: The Friends of 'Iolani Palace, n.d.

Hale Nauā. "Constitution and By-Laws of the Hale Naua or Temple of Science." San Francisco: Bancroft Company, 1890. Bancroft Library, University of California.

Hammond, William Alexander. *Cerebral Hyperaemia, the Result of Mental Strain or Emotional Disturbance*. Brentano's, 1895.

Harman, Claire. Myself and the Other Fellow: *A Life of Robert Louis Stevenson*. New York: HarperCollins, 2005.

"Hawaiian Dictionaries," n.d. http://wehewehe.org/.

Hayashi, Leslie Ann, and Kathleen Wong Bishop. *Aloha Oe: The Song Heard Around the World*. Honolulu: Mutual Publishing, 2004.

Herring, George C. *From Colony to Superpower: U.S. Foreign Relations Since 1776*. New York: Oxford University Press, 2008.

Hibbert, Christopher. *Queen Victoria: A Personal History.* New York: Basic Books, 2000.

Hochschild, Adam. *Bury the Chains: Prophets and Rebels in the Fight to Free an Empire's Slaves.* New York: Houghton Mifflin Harcourt, 2005.

Hoover, Will. "Curtis I'aukea." *Honolulu Advertiser,* July 2, 2006, special section: Celebrating 150 Years. http://the.honoluluadvertiser.com/150/sesq1iaukea.

———. "Samuel Mills Damon." *Honolulu Advertiser,* July 2, 2006, special section: Celebrating 150 Years. http://the.honoluluadvertiser.com/150/sesq1damon.

Horwitz, Tony. *Blue Latitudes: Boldly Going Where Captain Cook Has Gone Before.* New York: Henry Holt, 2002.

Hoyt, Edwin Palmer. *Davies: The Inside Story of a British-American Family in the Pacific and its Business Enterprises.* Honolulu: Topgallant Publishing, 1983.

'Iaukea, Curtis Pi'ehu, and Lorna Kahilipuaokalani Iaukea Watson. *By Royal Command.* Honolulu: Hui Hanai, 1988.

Iaukea, Sydney Lehua. "E Pa'a 'Oukou: Holding and Remembering Hawaiian Understandings of Place and Politics," thesis dissertation. Honolulu: University of Hawaii, 2008.

'I'i, John. *Fragments of Hawaiian History.* Honolulu: Bishop Museum Press, 1959.

Irwin, Bernice Pi'ilani Cook. *I Knew Queen Liliuokalani.* Honolulu: First People's Productions, 1960.

James Campbell, Esq. Kapolei, Hawaii: Estate of James Campbell, 2003.

Jarves, James Jackson. *History of the Hawaiian islands.* Honolulu: Henry M. Whitney, 1872.

Judd, Albert Francis. "Diary of Albert Francis Judd, 1890–1895." Honolulu, n.d. Bishop Museum Archive.

Judd, Charles Hastings. "Interview with Charles Hastings Judd, 1882, 'Affairs in Hawaii: San Francisco, 1882,'" December 17, 1882. Hubert Howe Bancroft Collection, Bancroft Library, University of California.

Judd, Laura Fish. *Honolulu: Sketches of Life.* New York: Anson D. F. Randolph, 1880.

Kalākaua. *The Myths and Legends of Hawaii.* New York: C. L. Webster, 1888.

Kamakau, Samuel Manaiakalani. *Ruling Chiefs of Hawaii.* Honolulu: Kamehameha Schools Press, 1961.

Kamehameha IV. "The Teaching Explained," preface. *In Book of Common Prayer.* Honolulu, 1863. http://justus.anglican.org/resources/bcp/Hawaii_BCP_preface.htm.

Kanahele, George S. Emma: *Hawaii's Remarkable Queen.* Honolulu: Queen Emma Foundation, 1999.

———. *Pauahi: The Kamehameha Legacy,* first edition. Honolulu: Kamehameha Schools Press, 1986.

Karpiel, Frank J. "A Multinational Fraternity: Freemasonry in Hawaii, 1843–1905." *Hawaiian Journal of History* 34 (2000).

Kashay, Jennifer Fish. "Agents of Imperialism: Missionaries and Merchants in Early-Nineteenth-Century Hawaii." *New England Quarterly* 80, no. 2 (June 1, 2007): 280–98.

Kealoha, G. Poki. "G. Poki Kealoha to Kalakaua, 4/3/1860," letter, April 3, 1860. David W. Forbes Collection, Kalakaua Letters Part 1. State Archives of Hawaiʻi.

Kelley, Darlene E. "Historical Collections of the Hawaiian Islands: Keepers of the Culture—A study in Time of the Hawaiian Islands," n.d. http://www.rootsweb.ancestry.com/%7Ehikalawa/koc/koc.htm.

———. "Queen Liliʻuokalani and Her Hanai (Adopted) Children," n.d. http://files.usgwarchives.net/hi/statewide/newspapers/queenlil7nnw.txt.

———. "Queen Liliuokalani and Her Music." Parts 1–4, 2007. http://files.usgwarchives.org/hi/keepers/qlili01.txt.

Kenton Clymer. "Review: [untitled]." *American Historical Review* 104, no. 2 (April 1999): 585.

Korn, Alfons L. *The Victorian Visitors: An Account of the Hawaiian Kingdom, 1861–1866.* Honolulu: University of Hawaiʻi Press, 1958.

Kovacevic, Ante. "On the Descent of John Owen Dominis, Prince Consort of Queen Liliuokalani." *Hawaiian Journal of History* 10 (1976): 1–24.

Krauss, Bob. *Grove Farm Plantation: The Biography of a Hawaiian Sugar Plantation.* Palo Alto, Calif.: Pacific Books, 1976.

Kuykendall, Ralph S. *The Hawaiian Kingdom: Vol. I, 1778–1854.* Honolulu: University of Hawaiʻi Press, 1938.

———. *The Hawaiian Kingdom: Vol. II, 1854–1874.* Honolulu: University of Hawaiʻi Press, 1953.

———. *The Hawaiian Kingdom: Vol. III, 1874–1893.* Honolulu: University of Hawaiʻi Press, 1967.

La Croix, Sumner J., and Christopher Grandy. "The Political Instability of Reciprocal Trade and the Overthrow of the Hawaiian Kingdom." *Journal of Economic History* 57, no. 1 (March 1997): 161–89.

Lafeber, Walter. *The New Empire: An Interpretation of American Expansion, 1860–1898,* 35th ed. Ithaca, N.Y.: Cornell University Press, 1998.

Lili'uokalani. *Hawaii's Story by Hawaii's Queen*. Boston: Lothrop, Lee and Shepherd, 1898.

———. *The Kumulipo*. Honolulu: Pueo Press, 1978.

———, Dorothy K. Gillett, and Barbara Barnard Smith. *The Queen's Songbook*. Honolulu: Hui Hanai, 1999.

Lind, Andrew William. *An Island Community: Ecological Succession in Hawaii*. Chicago: University of Chicago Press, 1968.

Linnea, Sharon. *Princess Ka'iulani: Hope of a Nation, Heart of a People*. Cambridge, UK, and Grand Rapids, Mich.: Erdmans Books for Young Readers, 1999.

Liittschwager, David, and Susan Middleton. *Remains of a Rainbow: Rare Plants and Animals of Hawai'i*. Washington, D.C.: National Geographic, 2001.

"Living on Active Volcanoes—The Island of Hawai'i, Fact Sheet 074-97." U.S. Geological Survey, 2004. http://pubs.usgs.gov/fs/fs074-97/.

Loomis, Albertine. *For Whom Are the Stars?* Honolulu: University of Hawai'i Press, 1977.

———. "Summer of 1898." *Hawaiian Journal of History* 13 (1979): 93–98.

Maclean, Alistair. *Captain Cook*. Garden City, N.Y.: Doubleday, 1972.

Mahan, Alfred Thayer. *The Influence of Sea Power Upon History, 1660–1783*. New York: Little, Brown, 1918.

Maines, Rachel P. *The Technology of Orgasm: "Hysteria," the Vibrator, and Women's Sexual Satisfaction*. Baltimore, Md.: Johns Hopkins University Press, 2001.

Malo, David, and Nathaniel Bright Emerson. *Hawaiian Antiquities (Moolelo Hawaii)*. Honolulu: Hawaiian Gazette Company, 1903.

Marsh, Rebecca. "Shortcomings in American Adoption Policies: And a Hawaiian Alternative." *Hohonu: A Journal of Academic Writing* 2, no. 2 (2004). http://www.uhh.hawaii.edu/academics/hohonu/writing.php?id=28.

May, Ernest R. *Imperial Democracy: The Emergence of America as a Great Power*. New York: Harper and Row, 1973.

McBride, Christopher Mark. *The Colonizer Abroad: American Writers on Foreign Soil, 1846–1912*. New York: Routledge, 2004.

McGregor, Davianna. *Nā Kua'āina: Living Hawaiian Culture*. Honolulu: University of Hawai'i Press, 2007.

McGuire, James W. L. "A Short Description of Queen Kapiolani's Voyage to England to Attend the Jubilee Celebration of Queen Victoria of England in the Year 1887," 1887. State Archives of Hawai'i.

Mellen, Kathleen Dickenson. *An Island Kingdom Passes: Hawai'i Becomes American*. New York: Hastings House, 1958.

Melville, Herman. *Typee; or, a narrative of a four months' residence among the natives of a valley of the Marquesas Islands; or, a peep at Polynesian life.* London: John Murray, 1847.

Menzies, Archibald. *Hawai'i Nei 128 Years Ago.* Honolulu, 1920.

Merry, Sally Engle. *Colonizing Hawai'i: The Cultural Power of Law.* Princeton, N.J.: Princeton University Press, 2000.

Merwin, W. S. *The Folding Cliffs: A Narrative of 19th Century Hawaii.* New York: Alfred A. Knopf, 1998.

Mohr, James C. *Plague and Fire: Battling Black Death and the 1900 Burning of Honolulu's Chinatown.* New York: Oxford University Press, 2005.

Morgan, Theodore. *Hawaii: A Century of Economic Change, 1778–1876.* Cambridge, Mass.: Harvard University Press, 1948.

Moses Handy, ed. *The Official Directory of the World's Columbian Exposition, May 1st to October 30th, 1893.* Chicago: W. B. Conkey, 1893.

Muir, Ramsay. *A History of Liverpool.* London: Williams and Norgate for the University Press of Liverpool, 1907.

Nordyce, Eleanor, and Martha Noyes. "'Kaulana Na Pua': A Voice for Sovereignty." *Hawaiian Journal of History* 27 (1993): 27–42.

O'Brien, Victor H. "Claus Spreckels: The Sugar King." *Ainslee's Magazine,* February 1901.

"Official Castle & Cooke Web site." *Castle & Cooke, History,* n.d. http://www.castlecooke.net/about/history.aspx.

"Official Washington Place Web site." *Historic "Washington Place"—Office of the Governor,* n.d. http://hawaii.gov/gov/washington_place/.

Okihiro, Gary Y. *Cane Fires: The Anti-Japanese Movement in Hawaii, 1865–1945.* Philadelphia: Temple University Press, 1992.

———. *Island World: A History of Hawai'i and the United States.* Berkeley: University of California Press, 2008.

Osorio, Jonathan Kay Kamakawiwo'ole. *Dismembering Lāhui: A History of the Hawaiian Nation to 1887.* Honolulu: University of Hawai'i Press, 2002.

"Our History—International Cotton Association." *International Cotton Association,* n.d. http://www.ica-ltd.org/about-us/our-history.

Palmer, Julius Auboineau. *Memories of Hawai'i and Hawaiian Correspondence.* Boston: Lee and Shepard, 1894.

Pearce, Frank Savary. *A Practical Treatise on Nervous Diseases for the Medical Student and General Practitioner.* New York: D. Appleton, 1904.

Photo of Abner Paki. Photograph, undated. PP98-17. State Archives of Hawai'i..

Photo of Lili'uokalani in front of Washington Place, 1894. Photo Collection. State Archives of Hawai'i.

Porter, David. *Journal of a Cruise Made to the Pacific Ocean.* New York: Wiley and Halsted, 1822.

Pratt, Julius W. *Expansionists of 1898: The Acquisition of Hawai'i and the Spanish Islands.* Chicago: Quadrangle, 1964.

Preble, George Henry. *A Chronological History of the Origin and Development of Steam Navigation.* Philadelphia: L. R. Hamersly, 1895.

Proto, Neil Thomas. *The Rights of My People: Liliuokalani's Enduring Battle with the United States 1893–1917.* New York: Algora, 2009.

Pukui, Mary Kawena, and Samuel H. Elbert. "Hawaiian Dictionary at Ulukau: The Hawaiian Electronic Library." *Ulukau: The Hawaiian Electronic Library,* n.d. http://ulukau.org/elib/cgi-bin/library?c=ped&l=en.

———. *New Pocket Hawaiian Dictionary.* Honolulu: University of Hawai'i Press, 1992.

———, and Esther T. Mookini. "Place Names of Hawai'i at Ulukau: The Hawaiian Electronic Library." *Ulukau: The Hawaiian Electronic Library,* n.d. http://ulukau.org/elib/cgi-bin/library?c=pepn&l=en.

Pukui, Mary Kawena, and Alfons L. Korn. *The Echo of Our Song: Chants & Poems of the Hawaiians.* Honolulu: University of Hawai'i Press, 1979.

"Punahou School: History," n.d. http://www.punahou.edu/page.cfm?p=1788.

Reports of Committee on Foreign Relations 1789–1901, Volume 6 (The Morgan Report). U.S. Senate, 1894. http://morganreport.org/.

Rickman, John. *Journal of Captain Cook's Last Voyage to the Pacific Ocean, On Discovery; Performed in the Years 1776, 1777, 1778, 1779.* London: E. Newberry, 1781.

Ridley, Jasper. *The Freemasons: A History of the World's Most Powerful Secret Society.* New York: Arcade, 2002.

Sadie, Julie Anne, and Rhian Samuel. *The Norton/Grove Dictionary of Women Composers.* New York: W. W. Norton, 1994.

Samwell, David. "A Narrative of the Death of Captain James Cook (1779)." *Hawaiian Historical Society Reprint no. 2.* Honolulu: Hawaiian Historical Society, 1917.

Sauvin, Georges. *A Tree in Bud: The Hawaiian Kingdom, 1889–1893.* Honolulu: University of Hawai'i Press, 1987.

Scharlach, Bernice. *Big Alma: San Francisco's Alma Spreckels.* San Francisco: Scottwall Associates, 1990.

Schmitt, Robert C. *Demographic Statistics of Hawaii, 1778–1965.* Honolulu: University of Hawai'i Press, 1968.

———. "Some Transportation and Communication Firsts in Hawai'i." *Hawaiian Journal of History* 12 (1979): 99–119.

Schweizer, Niklaus R. *His Hawaiian Excellency: The Overthrow of the Hawaiian Monarchy and the Annexation of Hawai'i.* New York: Peter Lang, 1987.

Sheldon, J.G.M. "The Biography of Joseph K. Nawahi." Translated by M. Puakea Nogelmeier. Honolulu, 1908. Hawaiian Historical Society.

Silva, Noenoe K. *Aloha Betrayed: Native Hawaiian Resistance to American Colonialism.* Durham, N.C.: Duke University Press, 2004.

———. "He Kanawai E Ho'opau I Na Hula Kuolo Hawai'i: The Political Economy of Banning the Hula." *Hawaiian Journal of History* 34 (2000): 29–48.

Simpson, Alexander. *The Sandwich Islands: Progress of Events Since Their Discovery by Captain Cook. Their Occupation by Lord George Paulet. Their Value and Importance.* London: Smith, Elder, 1843.

Sobrero Wilcox, Gina. *An Italian Baroness in Hawai'i: The Travel Diary of Gina Sobrero, Bride of Robert Wilcox, 1887.* Trans. Edgar Knowlton. Honolulu: Hawaiian Historical Society, 1991.

Spaulding, Thomas Marshall. *The Crown Lands of Hawaii.* University of Hawai'i Occasional Papers. Honolulu: University of Hawaii, 1923.

Spreckels, Claus. "The Future of the Sandwich Islands." *North American Review,* March 1891.

Stannard, David. *Before the Horror: The Population of Hawai'i on the Eve of Western Contact.* Honolulu: Social Sciences Research Institute, University of Hawaii, 1989.

Stevenson, Robert Louis. *A Footnote to History: Eight Years of Trouble in Samoa.* New York: Charles Scribner's Sons, 1895.

———. *Travels in Hawaii.* Honolulu: University of Hawai'i Press, 1991.

———. *The Works of Robert Louis Stevenson.* Garden City, N.Y.: Charles Scribner's Sons, 1922.

———, and Mehew Ernest. *Selected Letters of Robert Louis Stevenson.* New Haven, Conn.: Yale University Press, 2001.

Stillman, Amy Ku'uleialoha. "Aloha Aina: New Perspectives on 'Kaulana Na Pua.'" *Hawaiian Journal of History* 33 (1999): 83–99.

———. "History Reinterpreted in Song: The Case of the Hawaiian Counterrevolution." *Hawaiian Journal of History* 23 (1989): 1–30.

Strachey, Lytton. *Queen Victoria*. New York: Harcourt, Brace, Company, 1921.

Takaki, Ronald. *Raising Cane: The World of Plantation Hawaii*. New York: Chelsea House, 1994.

Taylor, Albert Pierce. *Under Hawaiian Skies*. Honolulu: Advertiser Publishing Company, 1922.

"The Golden Era. Honolulu, H.I., Sept. 1, 1892. Volume I, Number I," n.d. State Archives of Hawai'i.

The Shepherd Saint of Lanai. Honolulu: Thos. G. Thrum, 1887.

The Transactions of the Royal Hawaiian Agricultural Society, 1850, Vol. 1, No. 1. Honolulu: Henry M. Whitney, Government Press, 1850.

Thomas, Nicholas. *Cook: The Extraordinary Voyages of Captain James Cook*. New York: Walker & Company, 2003.

Thrum, Thomas G. *Hawaiian Almanac and Annual for 1891*. Honolulu: Black & Auld, Printers, 1890.

———. *Hawaiian Almanac and Annual for 1893*. Honolulu: Black & Auld, Printers, 1892.

———. *Hawaiian Almanac and Annual for 1894*. Honolulu: Black & Auld, Printers, 1893.

———. *Hawaiian Almanac and Annual for 1896*. Honolulu: Black & Auld, Printers, 1895.

Thurston, Lorrin A. *Memoirs of the Hawaiian Revolution*. Edited by Andrew Farrell. Vol. 2. 3 vols. Honolulu: Book Company Publishing, 2008.

———. *Memoirs of the Hawaiian Revolution*. Edited by Andrew Farrell. Vol. 3. 3 vols. Honolulu: Book Company Publishing, 2008.

Thurston, Lucy Goodale. *Life and Times of Mrs. Lucy G. Thurston, Wife of Rev Asa Thurston, Pioneer Missionary to the Sandwich Islands, Gathered from Letters and Journals Extending Over a Period of More Than Fifty Years . . .* Ann Arbor, Mich.: S.C. Andrews, 1882.

Tompkins, Calvin. *Merchants and Masterpieces: The Story of the Metropolitan Museum of Art*. New York: E.P. Dutton & Co., 1970.

"Transcript of the Proceedings of the Military Commission," 1895. Archives of Hawaii.

Trial of a Queen: 1895 Military Tribunal. Honolulu: Judiciary History Center, 1996.

Turner, Frederick Jackson. *The Frontier in American History*. New York: H. Holt and Company, 1921.

Twain, Mark. *Mark Twain in Hawaii*. Honolulu: Mutual Publishing, 1994.

———. *The Complete Essays of Mark Twain: Now Collected for the First Time*. Garden City, N.Y.: Doubleday, 1963.

———. *Mark Twain's Letters from Hawaii*. Edited by A. Grove Day. Honolulu: University of Hawai'i Press, 1975.

Twigg-Smith, Thurston. *Hawaiian Sovereignty: Do the Facts Matter?* Honolulu: Goodale Publishing, 1998.

"The US Navy and Hawaii: Pearl Harbor Origins and History," n.d. http://www.history.navy.mil/docs/wwii/pearl/hawaii-2.htm.

U.S. House of Representatives. *House Executive Documents. 53rd Congress, 3rd Session. No. 47. Affairs in Hawaii.* (The Blount Report). Washington: U.S. House of Representatives., 1895. http://libweb.hawaii.edu/digicoll/annexation/blount.html.

Van Dyke, Jon M. *Who Owns the Crown Lands of Hawaii?* Honolulu: University of Hawai'i Press, 2008.

Vandercook, Charles. *King Cane: The Story of Sugar in Hawaii*. New York: Harper and Brothers, 1939.

Various contributors. *Onipa'a: Five Days in the History of the Hawaiian Nation*. Honolulu: Office of Hawaiian Affairs, 1994.

Waldron, Elsie. *Honolulu 100 Years Ago*. Honolulu: Fisher Printing Co., 1967.

Warinner, Emily. *A Royal Journey to London*. Honolulu: Topgallant Publishing Co., 1975.

Webb, Nancy. *Kaiulani: Crown Princess of Hawaii*. Honolulu: Mutual Publishing, 1998.

Weigle, Richard D. "Sugar and the Hawaiian Revolution." *Pacific Historical Review* 16, no. 1 (February 1947): 41–58.

Wellmon, Bernard Brian. *The Parker Ranch: A History*. Fort Worth: Texas Christian University, 1969.

Weyeneth, Robert. *Kapi'olani Park: A History*. Honolulu: Native Books, 2002.

Whitney, Henry Martyn. *The Hawaiian Guide Book, for Travelers*. Honolulu: Henry M. Whitney, 1875.

———. *The Tourist's Guide through the Hawaiian Islands, Descriptive of Their Scenes and Scenery*. Honolulu: Hawaiian Gazette Company, 1895.

Williams, Riánna M. *Deaths and Funerals of Major Hawaiian Ali'i*. R. M. Williams, 2000.

————. "John Adams Cummins: Prince of Entertainers." *Hawaiian Journal of History* 30 (1996): 153–68.

Young, Lucien. *The Real Hawaii: Its History and Present Condition: Including the True Story of the Revolution.* New York: Doubleday and McClure, 1899.

Zambucka, Kristin. *Kalakaua.* Honolulu: Mana Publishing, 1983.

ENDNOTES

Introduction

xvii   *the Hawaiian chant:* Martha Warren Beckwith, *The Kumulipo: A Hawaiian Creation Chant*, (Honolulu: University of Hawai'i Press, 1951), 44, 58.

xviii   *changing color of the air: Discovery: The Hawaiian Odyssey*, (Honolulu: Bishop Museum Press, 1993), 27.

xviii   *as early as 200 A.D.:* Estimates vary as to when the first humans landed versus colonized the Hawaiian islands. For a discussion based on carbon dating of archeological materials, see The Polynesian Settlement of the Hawaiian Archipelago: Integrating Models and Methods in Archaeological Interpretation, Michael W. Graves and David J. Addison, *World Archaeology*, Vol. 26, No. 3, Colonization of Islands (Feb., 1995), pp. 380–399.

xviii   *including tiny shoots of sugar cane:* There are no written accounts of these voyages, but the first western visitors to the islands reported that the Hawaiians were growing sugar cane. Archibald Menzies and William Frederick Wilson, *Hawai'i nei 128 years ago* (s.n., 1920), 34, 75.

xix   *humans were thrown into the volcano's depths:* Archibald Menzies and William Frederick Wilson, *Hawai'i nei 128 years ago* (s.n., 1920), 162–163.

xix *carved wooden statues:* John 'I'i, *Fragments of Hawaiian History* (Honolulu: Bishop Museum Press, 1959), 33–37.

xx *master of song: Discovery: The Hawaiian Odyssey,* (Honolulu: Bishop Museum Press, 1993), 35.

xx *a distinct race:* William Ellis, *Journal of William Ellis: A Narrative of an 1823 Tour Through Hawai'i,* (Honolulu: Mutual Publishing, 2004), 21.

xx *risked instant death:* John 'I'i, *Fragments of Hawaiian History* (Honolulu: Bishop Museum Press, 1959), 28.

xx *the Hawaiian creation chant:* Martha Warren Beckwith, *The Kumulipo: A Hawaiian Creation Chant,* (Honolulu: University of Hawai'i Press, 1951), 44, 58.

xx *Fear falls upon me:* Ibid. 92.

xxi *Their favorite pastime was surfing:* Kamakau, *Ruling chiefs of Hawaii,* 106.

xxi *men, women and children would paddle out:* Ben Finney and James D. Houston, *Surfing: A History of the Ancient Hawaiian Sport,* (Rohnert Park, Calif.: Pomegranate Artbooks, 1996), 27.

xxi 24 Ibid.

xxi *heights of several hundred feet or more:* Kamakau, *Ruling chiefs of Hawaii,* 82.

xxii *their dark hair streaming:* Archibald Menzies and William Frederick Wilson, *Hawai'i Nei 128 Years Ago* (Honolulu: 1920), 180.

xxii *"This is indeed Lono":* Kamakau, *Ruling chiefs of Hawaii,* 93.

xxii *fields flush with yams and taro:* Menzies and Wilson, *Hawai'i Nei 128 Years Ago,* 124, 128.

xxii *a plant brought to the islands:* Robert L. Cushing, "The Beginnings of Sugar Production in Hawai'i," *Hawaiian Journal of History* vol. 19 (1985). See also Menzies and Wilson, *Hawai'i Nei 128 Years Ago,* 34.

xxii *Cook was venerated:* David Malo, *Hawaiian antiquities (Moolelo Hawai'i)* (Honolulu: Hawaiian Gazette Company, 1903), p. 190.

xxiii *"death-dealing thing":* Kamakau, *Ruling chiefs of Hawaii,* 94.

xxiii *the chief kept questioning him:* David Samwell et al., *The death of Captain James Cook* (Paradise of the Pacific Press, 1791), 8.

xxiii *offering themselves up:* John 'I'i, *Fragments of Hawaiian History* (Honolulu: Bishop Museum Press, 1959), 87. The historian 'I'i is referring to a later period, but accounts of Cook's visits by his officers describe Hawaiian women engaging in barter for sexual favors, as well.

xxiv *Wrapped in a feather cloak:* The fight in which Cook died, the ensuing slaughter, and the delivery of the body parts were documented in the journals of several members of Cook's expedition. Native Hawaiian historian David Malo, p. 134, describes how in traditional Hawaiian society, bodies were routinely salted, and the bereaved would frequently exhume the bodies of their loved ones in secret to keep a leg bone or hands/feet.

Preface

xxvi *the population of native Hawaiians was estimated at:* Davianna McGregor, *Nā Kuaʻāina: living Hawaiian culture* (University of Hawaiʻi Press, 2007), 30. McGregor notes that 400,000 was the estimate from Cook's voyage, but cites David E. Stannard, *Before the horror: the population of Hawaiʻi on the eve of Western contact* (Social Science Research Institute, University of Hawaiʻi, 1989). Kuykendall, *The Hawaiian Kingdom: Vol. I, 1778–1854* (Honolulu: University of Hawaiʻi Press, 1938), 336, notes that by 1823 the population was 142,050 and estimates this represents fifty percent of the population at contact.

xxvi *weapons drawn and ready to fire:* Liliʻuokalani, *Hawaii's Story by Hawaii's Queen* (North Clarendon, Vt.: Charles E. Tuttle, 1971), 386, appendix B. "I was told that it was for the safety of American citizens and the protection of their interests. Then why had they (the troops) not gone to the residences, instead of drawing a line in front of the Palace gates, with guns pointed at us, and when I was living with my people in the Palace?"

xxix *a royal salute:* Lucien Young, *The Real Hawaii: Its History and Present Condition: Including the True Story of the Revolution* (New York: Doubleday & McClure, 1899), 187.

xxix *claimed for America:* Jon M. Van Dyke, *Who Owns the Crown Lands of Hawaiʻi?* (Honolulu: University of Hawaiʻi Press, 2008), 170, citing the 1993 "Apology Resolution," supra note 16, whereas para. 8.

xxx *four to one:* There are varying reports on how many troops the queen had at her command. Biographer Helena Allen says she had only a handful of household troops, while historian Ralph S. Kuykendall put the Hawaiian army at 272, commanded by Capt. Nowlein. *Onipaʻa*, published by the Office of Hawaiian Affairs in 1993, says the "Queen's government" had 600 troops, plus 30,000 rounds of ammunition, eight cannons, and two Gatling guns, although it's unclear if the 600 people were part of the official army or household troops or included the police force commanded by Marshal Charles B.Wilson.

xxx *small pox, syphilis, and measles:* Ralph S. Kuykendall, *The Hawaiian Kingdom: Vol. I, 1778–1854* (Honolulu: University of Hawai'i Press, 1938), 336; other discussions of population on 364, 386–87.

Chapter 1: Born in Paradise

4 *". . . schools, and churches.":* Lucy Goodale Thurston, *Life and Times of Mrs. Lucy G. Thurston, Wife of Rev Asa Thurston, Pioneer Missionary to the Sandwich Islands, Gathered from Letters and Journals Extending Over a Period of More Than Fifty Years* . . . (Ann Arbor, Mich.: S.C. Andrews, 1882), 15.

4 *"Can these be human beings?":* Hiram Bingham, *A Residence of Twenty-One Years in the Sandwich Islands* . . . (New York: Sherman Converse, 1847), 81.

4 *The guests, astonished at this act* . . . : Ralph S. Kuykendall, *The Hawaiian Kingdom: Vol. I, 1778–1854,* vol. 1 (Honolulu: University of Hawai'i Press, 1938), 68, citing an account given by Ka'ahumana to Rev. A. Bishop in 1826.

4 *After the meal was over, he ordered the heiau* . . ." Ralph S. Kuykendall, *The Hawaiian Kingdom: Vol. I, 1778–1854,* 68, citing an account given by Kamehameha the Great's widow Ka'ahumanu to Rev. A. Bishop in 1826.

5 *such passionate evangelists as Titus Coan:* On a single day in 1838, Coan baptized more than seventeen hundred converts. Within a few years, Coan's flock had swelled to more than six thousand members. Gavan Daws, *Shoal of Time: A History of the Hawaiian Islands* (Honolulu: University of Hawai'i Press, 1968), 100–102.

6 *they deducted its cost:* Lorrin Thurston *Memoirs of the Hawaiian Revolution,* vol. 3 (Honolulu: Book Company Publishing, 2008), 5.

6 *"every interest but Christ's":* Bingham, 126.

6 *a geological oddity:* Isabella Bird, *Six Months in the Sandwich Islands: Among Hawaii's Palm Groves, Coral Reefs, and Volcanoes* (Honolulu: Mutual Publishing, 2007), 13.

6 *reminded them of punchbowls:* Frederick Grantham, *Discover Downtown Honolulu* (Royal Designs, 1998), 7.

6   *made from tree bark*: Liliuokalani, *Hawaii's Story by Hawaii's Queen* (North Clarendon, Vermont: Charles E. Tuttle, 1971), 4.

7   *"That is the sign of our Ali'i!"*: Helena Allen, The *Betrayal of Liliuokalani: Last Queen of Hawai'i 1838–1917* (Honolulu: Mutual Publishing, 1982), 36.

7   *the chiefess named her*: Allen, *Betrayal*, 36–37.

7   *light complexion and reddish hair*: Bernice Bishop and Mary Hannah Krout, *The Memoirs of Hon. Bernice Pauahi Bishop* (New York: The Knickerbocker Press, 1908), 10, and George H. Kanahele, *Pauahi: The Kamehameha Legacy*, 1st ed. (Honolulu: Kamehameha Schools Press, 1986), 10.

7–8 *a photographer captured an image*: Photo of Abner Paki, Photograph, Undated, PP98-17, Hawai'i State Archive.

8   *". . . any strangers who noticed me"*: Liliuokalani, *Hawaii's Story by Hawai'i's Queen*, 4.

8   *until the court moved permanently*: Kuykendall, *The Hawaiian Kingdom: Vol. I, 1778–1854*, 1:228.

9   *a mild limp all her life*: Bernice Piilani Cook Irwin, *I knew Queen Liliuokalani* (First People's Productions, 1960), 66. Also Helena G. Allen, *The Betrayal of Liliuokalani, Last Queen of Hawaii, 1838–1917*, 1982, 42–44.

9   *Amos Starr Cooke and his wife*: The Cookes, who were Americans, were not related to the British explorer Captain James Cook.

9   *a lamp burning in the courtyard*: "Family School for Children of the Chiefs," *The Polynesian* (Honolulu, July 4, 1840).

9   *one cent a pound*: Noel J. Kent, *Hawai'i, Islands Under the Influence* (Honolulu: University of Hawai'i Press, 1993), 18.

9   *"Forest Trees of the Sea"*: Mary Kawena Pukui and Alfons L. Korn, *The Echo of our song: chants & poems of the Hawaiians* (Honolulu: University of Hawai'i Press, 1979), 217.

10 *even Russian ducats*: According to a table of coinage in use in the kingdom printed by the *Polynesian* in 1848.

10 *a special red-light district*: Eric Jay Dolin, *Leviathan: The History of Whaling in America* (New York: W.W. Norton & Company, 2007), 279–280.

10 *happily surprised*: Dolin, 180, quoting Briton Cooper Busch's history of 19th century whaling.

10 *"mischievous sleeping"*: Sally Engle Merry, *Colonizing Hawai'i* (Princeton

University Press, 2000), 248. In the Pukui/Elbert dictionary, the literal translation is "illegal mating."

10   *stitching modest calico dresses:* Lucy Thurston, *Life and Times of Mrs. Lucy G. Thurston, Wife of Rev Asa Thurston, Pioneer Missionary to the Sandwich Islands, Gathered from Letters and Journals Extending Over a Period of More Than Fifty Years . . .* , 32.

11   *tracts on marriage and intemperance:* Hiram Bingham, *A Residence of twenty-one years in the Sandwich islands* (New York: Sherman Converse, 1847), 615.

11   *fight amongst themselves:* John 'I'i, *Fragments of Hawaiian History* (Honolulu: Bishop Museum Press, 1959), 164. John 'I'i, and his wife became *kahu,* or attendants, at the Royal School. 'I'i later became the kingdom's superintendant of schools.

11   *next generation of rulers:* The purpose of the Chiefs' Children's School may not have been entirely benign, at least from the perspective of some westerners. The *Polynesian,* for instance, wrote in 1840: "The necessity of a family school for these children [i.e., ali'i children] is apparent from the extreme improbability of their being taught to any good purpose unless they are in a measure isolated—cut off from a free intercourse with their former associates. A moment's reflection will show the importance of saving them, if possible, not only from the contagious example of children their own age, but of older though ignorant and superstitious persons, who will flatter their vanity, corrupt their morals, and thus blight the hope of their future usefulness."

12   *"we were growing children:"* Liliuokalani, *Hawaii's Story by Hawaii's Queen,* 5.

12   *hauling away the dead:* John 'I'i, *Fragments of Hawaiian History* (Honolulu: Bishop Museum Press, 1959), 174.

12   *slapped him in the face:* Cooke's journals, as quoted in George S. Kanahele, *Emma: Hawai'i's Remarkable Queen* (Honolulu: The Queen Emma Foundation, 1999), 29.

12   *a rebellious student:* Helena Allen, *Kalakaua: Renaissance King* (Honolulu: Mutual Publishing, 1994), 8.

12   *murdering his wife:* *Pacific Commercial Advertiser,* October 11, 1894 citing an article in the *Polynesian,* Oct. 3, 1840.

12   *witnessed the execution:* Amos Starr Cooke, Juliette Montague Cooke,

and Mary Atherton Richards, *The Hawaiian Chiefs' Children's School* (Honolulu: Honolulu Star-Bulletin, 1937), 86.

12 *saved a piece of the hangman's rope:* Allen, *Kalakaua: Renaissance King*, 8. The story of Kalākaua saving a piece of the rope from his grandfather's hanging may well be apocryphal.

13 *established a supreme court:* Kuykendall, *The Hawaiian Kingdom: Vol. I, 1778–1854,* 159–169.

13 *France expressed a verbal assurance:* Kuykendall, *The Hawaiian Kingdom: Vol. I, 1778–1854,* 194–199.

13 *he had moved his court to Lahaina:* Allen, *Betrayal,* 32.

13 *"a junta . . .":* Herman Melville, *Typee; or, a narrative of a four months' residence among the natives of a valley of the Marquesas Islands; or, a peep at Polynesian Life* (London: John Murray, 1847), 282.

14 *a British possession:* Alexander Simpson, *The Sandwich Islands: Progress of Events Since Their Discovery by Captain Cook. Their Occupation by Lord George Paulet. Their Value and Importance* (London: Smith, Elder and Co., 1843), 51.

14 *the force of the Carysfort's guns:* Kuykendall, *The Hawaiian Kingdom: Vol. I, 1778–1854,* 213–214.

14 *perhaps by Catholic France:* Amos Starr Cooke, Juliette Montague Cooke, and Mary Atherton Richards, *The Hawaiian Chiefs' Children's School* (Honolulu: Honolulu Star-Bulletin, 1937), 165.

14 *to personally press his case:* Kuykendall, *The Hawaiian Kingdom: Vol. I, 1778–1854,* 214–215.

14 *"hoping still for independence":* Kuykendall, *The Hawaiian Kingdom: Vol. I, 1778–1854,* 216.

14 *"men of Britain":* Kuykendall, *The Hawaiian Kingdom: Vol. I, 1778–1854,* 1:206.

15 *"Hear ye!":* Kuykendall *The Hawaiian Kingdom: Vol. I, 1778–1854,* 216.

15 *"That same year, in 1843 . . ."* History of *The Economist* from http://www.economistgroup.com/what_we_do/our_history.html

15 *"they were no longer Chiefs":* Cooke, Cooke and Richards, 169.

15 *"whenever we met (them) on the street":* Cooke, Cooke and Richards, 169, in a footnote citing Elizabeth Kinau Wilder's published reminiscences.

16 *". . . the ships of the whitemen":* Kuykendall, *The Hawaiian Kingdom: Vol. I, 1778–1854,* 1:153, quoting a letter Malo to Kinau, 8/13/1837, AH.

16 *the first boat they could commandeer*: Kuykendall, *The Hawaiian Kingdom: Vol. I, 1778–1854*, 217—the ship left March 11 with Alexander Simpson as emissary for the Paulet government.

16 *spirited back to Honolulu*: Kuykendall, *The Hawaiian Kingdom: Vol. I, 1778–1854*, 217.

17 *he left Valparaiso*: On July 26, 1843—Kuykendall, *The Hawaiian Kingdom: Vol. I, 1778–1854*, 219–220.

17 *Admiral Thomas and the king*: Bingham, 603.

17 *the soldiers hoisted the Hawaiian flag*: William De Witt Alexander, *A Brief History of the Hawaiian People* (New York: American Book Company, 1891), 249–250.

17 *"the life of the land"*: Kuykendall, *The Hawai'ian Kingdom: Vol. I, 1778–1854*, 220.

17 *Restoration Day celebration*: Thomas G. Thrum, *Hawaiian Almanac and Annual for 1891* (Honolulu: Black & Auld, Printers, 1890), 70.

17 *just over five months*: For years afterwards, Lili'u and other royal children took part in "Restoration Day" celebrations which were often tied to the temperance movement. The first anniversary, on July 31, 1844, included the young chiefs singing a "temperance glee," and when a Reverand asked all the children if they were going to keep the pledge to refrain from drinking alcohol, they rose en masse and shouted "Ae!", the Hawaiian word for "yes," Despite this youthful outpouring, the port town of Honolulu, with its rollicking grog shops, never became a stronghold for the temperance movement's "Cold Water Army" and alcoholism would become a recurring problem for the Hawaiian people.

Chapter 2: Progress and Liberty

18 *newfangled "electrical machine"*: Cooke, Cooke, and Richards, *The Hawaiian Chiefs' Children's School*, 251.

19 *Declaration of Rights*: Allen, *Betrayal*, 55.

19 *down to the sea*: Van Dyke, *Who Owns the Crown Lands of Hawai'i?*, 13.

19 *"the dignity of the Hawaiian crown"*: Ibid., 55.

19 *1.6 million acres*: Ibid., 42.

19 *"one-third or at least one-fourth" of the lands*: Ibid., 44.

19 *a word in their language for it*: McGregor, *Nā Kua'āina*, 38.

20 *effectively became homeless:* Van Dyke, *Who Owns the Crown Lands of Hawai'i?*, 45.

20 *went to the commoners:* Ibid., 48.

20 *another for $8,000:* Bob Krauss, *Grove Farm Plantation: The Biography of a Hawaiian Sugar Plantation* (Palo Alto, Calif.: Pacific Books, 1976), 152.

21 *"the evil that afterwards crept in":* Kuykendall, *The Hawaiian Kingdom: Vol. I, 1778–1854*, 293.

21 *neighboring relation's home:* Lili'uokalani, *Hawaii's Story*, 8.

21 *to King Kamehameha III:* Ibid., 8, and Allen, *Betrayal*, 53.

21 *hasten their deaths:* "Weekly Gossip," *Polynesian* (Honolulu, October 28, 1848).

21 *from the foreign community:* "Editorial," *Polynesian* (Honolulu, January 13, 1849).

21 *at night to carouse:* Gavan Daws, *Honolulu: The First Century* (Honolulu: Mutual Publishing, 2006), 148–50. Moses was finally dismissed from the school after impregnating one of the other pupils, a transgression for which he was rebuked by the kingdom's Privy Council.

21 *"will be a beacon . . .":* Cooke, Cooke, and Richards, *The Hawaiian Chiefs' Children's School*, 318.

21 *"on that of the others":* Lili'uokalani, *Hawai'i's Story*, 8–9.

22 *a service for him was held:* Cooke, Cooke, and Richards, *The Hawaiian Chiefs' Children's School*, 321.

22 *entire native population:* William De Witt Alexander, *A Brief History of the Hawaiian People* (New York: American Book Company, 1891), 260 footnote.

22 *in the year 1930:* "Editorial on population," *Polynesian* (Honolulu, January 26, 1850).

22 *becoming more common:* Kuykendall, *The Hawaiian Kingdom: Vol. I, 1778–1854*, 387.

22 *grandson of Kamehameha I:* Bishop and Krout, *Memoirs*, 83.

23 *June 4 of 1850:* Cooke, Cooke, and Richards, *The Hawaiian Chiefs' Children's School*, 344.

23 *for all her pono:* Ibid.

23 *a Dalmatian:* Ante Kovacevic, "On the Descent of John Owen Dominis, Prince Consort of Queen Liliuokalani," *Hawaiian Journal of History* 10 (1976): 1–24.

23 *a year later:* From the official Washington Place pamphlet, http://
Hawaii.gov/gov/washington_place/WPBrochure.pdf.

23 *known as "Washington Place":* From the Washington Place Web site,
http://Hawai'i.gov/gov/washington_place/Rooms/WP%20Rooms.

24 *by his widowed mother:* As noted throughout Allen, *Betrayal*, the mother-
son bond was particularly strong. Also see Lili'uokalani, *Hawaii's Story*,
p. 23: "[Mrs. Dominis] clung with tenacity to the affection and constant
attentions of her son, and no man could be more devoted than was General Dominis to his mother."

24 *despite his mother's protests:* Cooke, Cooke, and Richards, *The Hawaiian
Chiefs' Children's School*, 184, notes that upon John Dominis' entry into
the school, Amos Cooke wrote, "I called on his mother & she said she
wished John to go ahead as fast as possible. I told her we could not push
him forward very fast & no faster than our own scholars."

24 *a private academy:* Date of retirement confirmed in Ibid., 347–48.

24 *Commissioners for Foreign Missions:* Ibid., xvii–xx.

24 *in 1851:* Ibid., 349.

24 *tools, sewing equipment, and medicine:* According to the Castle & Cooke
corporate site, http://www.castlecooke.net/about/history.aspx.

24 *"they came to do good and did well":* John Garrett, *To Live Among the
Stars: Christian Origins in Oceania* (Suva, Fiji: Institute of Pacific Studies, 1982), 58.

24 *also run by American missionaries:* Lili'uokalani, *Hawaii's Story*, 9.

24 *two-storied home named Haleakalā:* Ibid., 110.

24 *impromptu dances:* Allen, *Betrayal*, 72–73.

25 *"go & come at an Americans bidding":* Jacob Adler, ed., *The Journal of
Prince Alexander Liholiho: The Voyages Made to the United States, England and France in 1849-1850* (Honolulu: University of Hawai'i Press
for the Hawaiian Historical Society, 1967), 107–08, journal entry of
6/5/1850.

26 *"crime and corruption, vigilantes, and lynch laws":* Allen, *Betrayal*, 78.
Kuykendall, *The Hawaiian Kingdom: Vol. I, 1778–1854*, 424, also notes
that 'I'i, Pākī and Liholiho objected to annexation.

26 *depression in 1851 and 1852:* Kuykendall, *The Hawaiian Kingdom: Vol. I,
1778–1854*, 324.

26 *the Americans who lived in the islands:* Ibid., 402–27.

26 *all chewing sugar-cane:* Laura Fish Judd, *Honolulu: Sketches of Life* (New York: Anson D. F. Randolph, 1880), 227.

26 *in the palace for two weeks:* The nineteenth-century Hawaiian historian David Malo notes that the long period of mourning is traditionally Hawaiian, saying that an ali'i might lie in state for ten days or more. The bodies were considered tabu and mourners were considered unclean, unable to leave the house of mourning, for the period that the body lay in state (134–36).

26 *the teenaged Lili'u:* Allen, *Betrayal,* 79.

26 *anywhere in Honolulu:* Riánna M. Williams, *Deaths and Funerals of Major Hawaiian Ali'i* (R. M. Williams, 2000), 31.

26 *"brilliant talents and winning manners":* Alexander, *A Brief History of the Hawaiian People,* 280.

26 *laid to rest:* Allen, *Betrayal,* 79, details how the funeral was moved to January 10 due to storms. The funeral closed the two-week mourning period.

27 *"the age for which he was born":* Kuykendall, *The Hawaiian Kingdom: Vol. I, 1778–1854,* 427–28, quoting the *Polynesian,* January 13, 1855.

27 *loaded with American coins:* Allen, *Betrayal,* 79.

28 *soon become obsolete:* Kanahele, *Emma,* 61.

28 *some native chiefs:* Allen, *Betrayal,* 81–82, makes it seem as though Lili'u was the traditional choice, but Ralph S. Kuykendall, *The Hawaiian Kingdom: Vol. II, 1854–1874,* 78, states that petitioners for Lili'u to be the bride were in the minority.

28 *Lili'u's biological father:* Kanahele, *Emma,* 60.

29 *his stamina and conditioning:* Kuykendall, *The Hawaiian Kingdom: Vol. II, 1854–1874,* 34.

29 *gold lace and a plumed hat:* Kanahele, *Emma,* 61.

29 *to get it for him:* Historian David Forbes says this omission was discussed in a letter from Queen Emma to Flora Jones. Letter at the State Archives of Hawai'i.

29 *a British doctor:* Kanahele, *Emma,* 17.

29 *Bernice Pauahi Bishop:* Allen, *Betrayal,* 82.

29 *Konia and the Bishops:* Lili'uokalani, *Hawaii's Story,* 10–11.

30 *the ali'i towards the commoners:* Bishop and Krout, *Memoirs,* 104–105.

30 *"even the Chinese":* Lili'uokalani, *Hawaii's Story,* 13.

30 *seeing as a child:* Ibid., 12.

30   *"curious urchins"*: Ibid., 11.

30   *the new king shortly after*: Allen, *Betrayal*, 90, states only the date of 1856. Lili'uokalani, *Hawaii's Story*, 13, recounts it as occurring after the wedding.

30   *confined to his home at length*: Lili'uokalani, *Hawaii's Story*, 13.

31   *the Bishops' home*: Alfons L. Korn, *The Victorian Visitors: An Account of the Hawaiian Kingdom, 1861–1866* (Honolulu: University of Hawai'i Press, 1958), 160–61.

31   *less than perfect manners*: Korn, *Victorian Visitors*, 113, bill of fare is reprinted in whole.

32   *travelers to the islands*: Mark Twain and Lady Franklin were early visitors, and Lorrin Thurston campaigned vigorously to make it a park as well as being one of the early backers of the Volcano House hotel.

32   *"lighthearted, merry, and happy . . ."*: Lili'uokalani, *Hawaii's Story*, 17.

32   *750,238 pounds in 1850*: Kuykendall, *The Hawaiian Kingdom: Vol. I, 1778–1854*, 315.

33   *a mere 21,000 pounds*: Ibid., 323–324.

33   *land in Kaua'i in 1835*: Ibid., 175.

33   *multiplied to thirty-two*: Kuykendall, *The Hawaiian Kingdom: Vol. II, 1854–1874*, 142–143.

33   *multiplied more than ten-fold*: Jacob Adler, *Claus Spreckels: The Sugar King in Hawai'i* (Honolulu: University of Hawai'i Press, 1966), 10.

33   *costing more than twice as much*: Alexander, *A Brief History of the Hawaiian People*, 284–85.

34   *the toes of their bare feet*: Krauss, *Grove Farm Plantation*,147.

34   *neared its peak*: Dolin, *Leviathan*, 106. The U.S. whaling fleet reached its height in terms of number of ships in 1846, with 735 out of a total of 900 whaleships worldwide. The most profitable year was 1853.

34   *Hawaiian males of working age*: Gary Y. Okihiro, *Island World: A History of Hawai'i and the United States* (Berkeley, Calif.: University of California Press, 2008), 143.

34   *certain specified reasons*: Kuykendall, *The Hawaiian Kingdom: Vol. I, 1778–1854*, 329.

35   *"a relic of barbarism"*: From George Chaplin, *Presstime in Paradise: The Life and Times of the Honolulu Advertiser, 1856-1995* (Honolulu: University of Hawai'i Press, 1998), 55–56.

35   *part-Hawaiians and Caucasians:* As extrapolated from Kuykendall, *The Hawaiian Kingdom: Vol. II, 1854–1874,* 177 among others.

35   *in other parts of the world:* Elizabeth Abbott, *Sugar: A Bittersweet History* (New York: Overlook Press, 2010), 336.

35   *carried whips:* Takaki, *Raising Cane,* 33

35   *25 cents a day:* Alexander, *A Brief History of the Hawaiian People,* 259.

36   *in 1858:* Adler, *Claus Spreckels,* 8–9.

36   *sugar from molasses:* Kuykendall, *The Hawaiian Kingdom: Vol. I, 1778–1854,* 326.

36   *sustained Native Hawaiians:* Abbott, *Sugar,* 336. For further discussion of the environmental consequences of large irrigation projects, see pp. 379–82 of the same book, citing the World Wildlife Fund's reporting that sugarcane has likely "caused a greater loss of biodiversity on the planet than any other single crop, due to its destruction of habitat to make way for plantations, its intensive use of water for irrigation, its heavy use of industrial chemicals, and the polluted wastewater that is routinely discharged in the sugar production process."

37   *"for miles around":* Gary Y. Okihiro, *Cane Fires: The Anti-Japanese Movement in Hawaii, 1865–1945* (Philadelphia: Temple University Press, 1992), 39. The *Planters Monthly* published this in an 1886 issue.

3: Aloha

38   *unmarried women in the land:* Allen, *Betrayal,* 89.

38   *the reign of Kamehameha I:* Allen, *Betrayal,* 92. Kuykendall, *The Hawaiian Kingdom: Vol. I, 1778–1854,* 78, details how Kamehameha II designated his nine-year-old brother, Kamehameha III, as his successor before leaving for Britain, where he died. Kuykendall, 136n, noted that Kamehameha III adopted Alexander as his son and designated him heir. The young Albert, meanwhile, was a sickly child who nonetheless enjoyed the pleasures of childhood with royal privileges. For his fourth birthday, he toured the Honolulu Fire Department, where, the *Advertiser* reported, he was made an honorary member. In a parade honoring his father the king's birthday, Albert rode on Engine No. 1, carrying a miniature silver trumpet.

39   *Queen Victoria's consort:* Kanahele, *Emma,* 135.

39   *benevolent societies*: Judd, *Honolulu: Sketches of Life*, 233–36.

39   *"their habits and tastes"*: Korn, *Victorian Visitors*, 86.

39   *"their odious intonation . . ."*: Ibid. 34.

39   *the Times, the Edinburgh Review, and Punch*: Ibid., 16.

40   *in the United States*: That may explain why, although Kamehameha IV also received American newspapers, they "disgusted him so much" that "before the King had read them half through . . . he threw them out the window." Ibid., 16.

40   *"so lucky with the ladies . . ."*: Letter from G. Poki Kealoha to Kalākaua, 3 April 1860, David W. Forbes Collection, Kalākaua Letters Part 1, State Archives of Hawai'i.

40   *"a perfect gentleman"*: Korn, *Victorian Visitors*, 32.

41   *Lunalilo's increasing intemperance*: According to her autobiography, Lili'u's brief engagement was a tangled affair. Embarking on a trip to Maui by schooner, Lili'u encountered Prince William Lunalilo, who happened to be on the same boat, and who insisted gallantly that she take his cabin. As Lili'u wrote many years later, "He then asked me in the presence of my attendants why we shouldn't get married. There was an aged native preacher on board, Pikanele by name, who at once offered to perform the ceremony. But having heard the prince was engaged to his cousin Victoria, I did not consider it right to marry him on the impulse of the moment." After Prince William asked her again, Lili'u promised to think it over. Perhaps eager to leave Haleakalā, where she was increasingly under the charge of the Bishops, she agreed, despite the early warning signs of his impetuousness. Although the Bishops did not approve of the match, it was Lili'u, herself, who broke it off after learning more about William's character. Lili'uokalani, *Hawaii's Story*, 14–15.

41   *"you will show them to me"*: Among the most charming glimpses of Lili'u as a young ali'i at this time come from a letter in which she describes a mishap involving an overloaded canoe. She and four others had climbed into the small boat to go fishing. They paddled out into deep water and the waves soon started lapping over the sides. They tried bailing out the water but it didn't work, and several of Lili'u's companions jumped out to swim for help. When a nearby fisherman learned from them that an ali'i was in danger, he came to rescue her. "I could have put my arms around his neck and kissed him, as ugly as he was—for he is very old

and wrinkled," Lili'u wrote, "but could not have done it without danger of upsetting (him), then again he would not have understood any kindly feelings towards him in the way that I intended he should." Her sense of propriety, and a growing awareness of her station as an ali'i, had prevented her making this warm and seemingly harmless gesture. Lili'uokalani to Dominis, 1859, State Archives of Hawai'i.

41 *"but probably appendicitis"*: "The Death of the Prince of Hawai'i: A Retrospective Diagnosis." *The Hawaiian Journal of History, Vol. 28 : 29*.

42 *"the Hawaiian islands"*: Lili'uokalani, *Hawaii's Story*, 23.

43 *in wooden bunks*: Krauss, *Grove Farm Plantation*, 54.

43 *three tons each*: Kuykendall, *The Hawaiian Kingdom: Vol. I, 1778–1854*, 325.

44 *"the boiling juice"*: Krauss, *Grove Farm Plantation*, 58–59.

45 *the larger master suite*: Information on the bedroom arrangements comes from Corinne Fujimoto-Chun, Washington Place's curator.

45 *"his mother's feelings"*: Lili'uokalani, *Hawaii's Story*, 23. An early disagreement between the newlyweds occurred soon after they were married, when Lili'u ignored John's request that she say good-bye to his mother before leaving on a trip to Hilo on Hawai'i Island. Her husband seemed to have been so upset by this slight that he did not go to the wharf to see his bride off on her journey. In a letter afterward, she abjectly begs her husband: "I must ask you again to forgive me John, forgive me for not complying with your last request to go & bid your mother good bye. I will make no excuses in my own favor I merely say forgive me and let me know in your first letter after receiving this that you have forgiven me. It pains me, and it grieves me much that I should give you any pain it was . . . the hardest request you ever made and the saddest parting I ever made from you. Will you forgive me?" It is not clear whether he did: few of John's personal letters have survived. But, for whatever reason, Lili'u soon found reasons to spend time away from Washington Place and the stern gaze of the widow Dominis, perhaps realizing that the gulf between she and her husband was far wider than she had during their courtship imagined.

45 *"so heartbroken a man"*: Korn, *Victorian Visitors*, 98.

46 *"chief of the olden type"*: Kuykendall, *The Hawaiian Kingdom: Vol. II, 1854–1874*, 125.

46 *"on his own authority"*: Alexander, *A Brief History of the Hawaiian People*, 289–290.

46   *a single assembly*: Kuykendall, *The Hawaiian Kingdom: Vol. II, 1854–1874*, 127, 133.

46   *Ko kākou kumukānāwai*: Lili'uokalani, Dorothy K. Gillett, and Barbara Barnard Smith, *The Queen's Songbook* (Honolulu: Hui Hānai, 1999), 7.

47   *"I see but a few . . .":* Kalākaua to Robert C. Wyllie, 12 February 1864, David W. Forbes Collection, Kalākaua Letters Part 1, State Archives of Hawai'i.

47   *for the next two years*: Wyllie to Kalākaua, 13 April 1864, David W. Forbes Collection, Kalākaua Letters Part 1, State Archives of Hawaii.

47   *his parents and sisters*: Kalākaua to Kamehameha V, 13 December 1863, General Letters Box, Bishop Museum. Kalākaua offered an explanation to the king as to why he secretly wed her in an eloquent letter he wrote to the king in English: "I only wish to say that I feel myself in honour bound to make Kapiolani my wife, because I had asked her to marry and be my wife and my feelings as well as my sense of what is due to society urged me not to deceive her. I married her because I liked her, and I hope that in the happenings of our married life your Majesty will find and excuse for my seemingly want of respect."

48   *"connections of his whatever . . .":* Lili'uokalani to Likelike, 22 March 1869, David W. Forbes Collection, Cleghorn Letters Part I, State Archives of Hawai'i.

48   *an avid sportsman*: U.S. House of Representatives, *House Executive Documents. 53rd Congress, 3rd Session. No. 47. Affairs in Hawai'i (The Blount Report)* (Washington: U.S. House of Representatives., 1895), 556, testimony of Frank Wunderberg.

48   *Barack Obama attended*: According to the Punahou Web site, http://www.punahou.edu/page.cfm?p=12.

49   *"flashing black eyes"*: Julius Auboineau Palmer, *Memories of Hawai'i and Hawaiian Correspondence* (Boston: Lee and Shepard, 1894), 7.

49   *"duty before pleasure"*: Lili'uokalani to Likelike, 1865–1869, and undated letters, Cleghorn Collection, State Archives of Hawai'i.

49   *"you controled yourself"*: Lili'uokalani to Likelike, 7 September 1865, David W. Forbes Collection, Cleghorn Letters Part 1, State Archives of Hawai'i.

50   *metaphors and secret meanings*: Lili'uokalani, Gillet, and Smith, *The Queen's Songbook*, 8.

50 *hula kuʻi music*: Julie Anne Sadie and Rhian Samuel, *The Norton/Grove Dictionary of Women Composers* (New York: W. W. Norton, 1994), 282. Also Liliʻuokalani, Gillet, and Smith, *The Queen's Songbook*, 309.

50 *"He Mele Lahui Hawaiʻi"*: Liliʻuokalani, Gillet, and Smith, *The Queen's Songbook*, 43. This was Liliʻu's first published song—or the earliest yet discovered.

50 *E mau ke ea o ka ʻāina*: Ibid., 42.

51 *"all these matters"*: John Dominis to "My Dear Sir," 7 January 1873, General Letters Box, Bishop Museum.

51 *"I do not need it"*: Ibid.

52 *he had already died*: Liliʻuokalani, *Hawaii's Story*, 41.

52 *tuberculosis and alcoholism*: Kuykendall, *The Hawaiian Kingdom: Vol. II, 1854–1874*, 259, quotes the physician saying, "He cannot live very much longer, unless he totally abstains from the use of intoxicating drinks." On p. 246, Kuykendall notes that Lunalilo's appetite for alcohol was a "fatal weakness."

4: High Chiefs of Sugardom

53 *vote in parliament*: Sanford Dole, *Memoirs of the Hawaiian Revolution*, ed. Andrew Farrell, vol 1 (Honolulu: Book Company Publishing, 2008), 24.

54 *the official government newspaper*: Kuykendall, *The Hawaiian Kingdom: Vol. II, 1854–1874*, 184–85 and 213, refers to the *Gazette* as the official government paper.

54 *"kicking people around"*: Allen, *Kalakaua: Renaissance King*, 52.

54 *Dafydd for David*: The origin of the nickname "Taffy" is suggested by bibliographer David Forbes.

55 *reciprocity deal for the U.S.*: Kuykendall, *The Hawaiian Kingdom: Vol. II, 1854–1874 *, 248–51.

55 *issue remained unresolved*: Ibid., 249–257.

55 *as one later put it*: Lorrin Thurston, ed. Andrew Farrell, *Memoirs of the Hawaiian Revolution*, vol. 2 (Honolulu: Book Company Publishing, 2008) 16.

55 *as if it were theirs*: Allen, *Kalakaua: Renaissance King*, 44.

55 *"but Hawaiian milk"*: Helena Allen, *Sanford Ballard Dole: Hawaii's Only President* (Glendale: Arthur H. Clarke, 1988), 19.

56 *members of the Hawaiian Club:* Allen, *Dole*, 5 for taffy pulling, and 48–50 for the Hawaiian Club.

56 *roommate Thomas Walker:* Allen, *Dole*, 67.

56 *advanced by so doing:* Ibid., 68.

56 *raise his young children:* Ibid., 80.

57 *objections of his spouse:* Ibid., 158.

57 *in his memoirs:* Thurston, *Memoirs of the Hawaiian Revolution*, ed. Andrew Farrell, vol. 3 (Honolulu: Book Company Publishing, 2008), 43.

57 *dipping coins in it:* Ibid.

58 *mostly native supporters:* According to a letter from Dole's wife, Anna, who, it should be noted, didn't witness the riot herself. Allen, *Dole*, 98.

58 *"bones of their flesh":* Kanahele, *Emma*, 288.

58 *the crowd outside:* Ibid., 288–89.

58 *liquor-fueled supporters:* Lili'uokalani, *Hawaii's Story*, 45.

59 *Sanford Dole:* Anna Dole to "Mother Dole", Honolulu, 10 February 1874, Hawaiian Mission Children's Society Archive.

59 *"interfered with their work":* Ibid.

59 *"no concern of hers":* Kanahele, *Emma*, 290.

59 *an audience with her:* Ibid.

59 *"hurrahing and making speeches":* Ibid., 292.

59 *the American minister:* Ralph S. Kuykendall, *The Hawaiian Kingdom: Vol. III, 1874–1893* (Honolulu: University of Hawai'i Press, 1967), 10.

60 *landed from the Tenedos:* Ibid.

60 *put the rioters down:* Kuykendall, *The Hawaiian Kingdom: Vol. I, 1778–1854*, 10.

60 *munitions repositories:* Kanahele, *Emma*, 292.

60 *a twenty-one gun salute:* William De Witt Alexander, *A Brief History of the Hawaiian People* (New York: American Book Company, 1891), 337; "Papers of the Hawaiian Historical Society," read before the society in 1930; Curtis Pi'ehu Iaukea and Lorna Kahilipuaokalani Iaukea Watson, *By Royal Command* (Honolulu: Hui Hanai, 1988), 20–21.

60 *"that of the Kamehamehas":* Lili'uokalani, *Hawaii's Story*, 49.

61 *thunderclaps:* Thurston, *Memoirs*, vol. 2, 22–23.

62 *"keeps the Hawaiians quiet":* Kuykendall, *The Hawaiian Kingdom: Vol. III, 1874–1893*, 14, citing Wodehouse to Derby, no. 11, political and confidential, May 28, 1874, BPRO, FO.

62 *a trip to the United States:* Declaring his birthday, November 16, a day of public thanksgiving and prayer, Kalākaua made his farewells at a service in Kawaiaha'o church. "It has been the custom of rulers of other countries to go to foreign lands to obtain assistance, and this is what I desire to do," he told the packed congregation. "I am going to visit our great and good friend, the United States. Wise and prudent statesmen think that a treaty can be made with the United States which will benefit both countries. I am going to endeavor to obtain this treaty which, should I succeed in doing, I think will revive the country." Kalākaua, "Kalakaua's speech at Kawaiahao Church, 16 November 1874," David W. Forbes Collection, Kalakaua Letters Part I, State Archives of Hawai'i.

62 *"grandiose move by the King":* Allen, *Dole,* 105.

63 *a cough remedy:* Kalākaua to Lili'uokalani, 29 December 1874, Cleghorn Collection, State Archives of Hawai'i.

63 *an improved bottle stopper:* These drawings are in Kalākaua's scrapbook at the Bishop Museum Archives.

64 *furnished in the same way:* Kalākaua to Lili'uokalani, 29 December 1874, Cleghorn Collection, State Archives of Hawai'i.

64 *from San Francisco to Honolulu:* Thomas G. Thrum, *Hawaiian Almanac and Annual for 1896* (Honolulu: Black & Auld, 1895), 89, says the *Ajax* was the first steamer to make the San Francisco-Honolulu route. *Mark Twain Himself: A Pictorial Biography* (University of Missouri Press, 2002), 76, notes Twain was aboard the *Ajax* on her maiden voyage to Honolulu.

64 *"Our Fellow Savages of the Sandwich Islands":* Mark Twain, *Mark Twain in Hawai'i* (Honolulu: Mutual Publishing, 1994), xxiii.

64 *almost a hundred times:* Shelley Fisher Fishkin, *A Historical Guide to Mark Twain* (New York: Oxford University Press, 2002), 230.

65 *"play 'empire'":* Twain, *Mark Twain in Hawaii,* 31.

65 *"sceptered savages":* Mark Twain, *The Complete Essays of Mark Twain: Now Collected for the First Time* (Garden City, N.Y.: Doubleday, 1963), 20.

65 *"The High Chief of Sugardom":* Mark Twain, ed. A. Grove Day, *Mark Twain's Letters from Hawai'i* (Honolulu: University of Hawai'i Press, 1975), 257.

65 *1.5 tons per acre:* William H. Dorrance, *Sugar Islands: The 165-Year Story of Sugar in Hawai'i* (Honolulu: Mutual Publishing, 2000), chart on page 6.

65   *"surpasses them all"* Twain and Day, *Mark Twain's Letters from Hawaii*, 257.

65   *". . . whale-ship officers, and missionaries"*: Twain, *The Complete Essays of Mark Twain*, 18.

66   *as its "lawful heirs"*: Fishkin, *A Historical Guide to Mark Twain*, 231–32. Indeed, in a letter to *The New York Tribune* published in early 1873, Twain wrote satirically, "We *must* annex these people. We can afflict them with our wise and beneficent government."

66   *"to any other power"*: Kuykendall, *The Hawaiian Kingdom: Vol. III, 1874–1893*, 27.

67   *second-grade "coffee sugar"*: Jacob Adler, *Claus Spreckels*, 14.

67   *"first used the term "Manifest Destiny"* O'Sullivan, John L. (July–August 1845). Annexation. *States Magazine and Democratic Review* **17** (1): 5–10. See also "The Origin of "Manifest Destiny," Julius W. Pratt, *The American Historical Review*, Vol. 32, No. 4 (Jul., 1927), pp. 795–798.

67   *. . . through large acquisitions of territory*: Ferguson, *Colossus: The Price of America's Empire*, 40.

67   *Just as America's fears*: Ibid., 38.

68   *"the power of the foreigner"*: Lili'uokalani, *Hawaii's Story*, 54–55.

68   *"always held as fundamental"*: J.G.M. Sheldon, "The Biography of Joseph K. Nawahi," trans. M. Puakea Nogelmeier (Honolulu, 1908), 78, Hawaiian Historical Society.

68   *"from bowsprit to spanker boom"*: Adler, *Claus Spreckels*, 3.

68   *Emma on the throne*: Kalākaua, undated memo, David W. Forbes Collection, Kalākaua Letters Part 1, State Archives of Hawai'i.

69   *mandatory military service*: William Woodrow Cordray, "Claus Spreckels of California," thesis dissertation, University of Southern California, 1955, 4.

69   *dodging the draft*: Victor O'Brien, "Claus Spreckels: The Sugar King," *Ainslee's Magazine*, February, 1901, 518.

69   *"Red-face"*: Ibid.

69   *a sugar producer himself*: This family story was related to me by Lyn Wilson, a great-granddaughter of Claus Spreckels.

70   *back into the business*: Cordray, "Claus Spreckels of California," 223.

70   *run out uncaptured*: Henry Austin Adams, *The Man, John D. Spreckels* (Press of Frye & Smith, 1924), 37.

70   *the war that was raging:* Cordray, "Claus Spreckels of California," 230.

70   *thrown out by his partners:* O'Brien, "Claus Spreckels." The writer states that Spreckels "went out unwillingly" from the Bay Sugar Refinery.

70   *a large profit for himself:* Cordray, "Claus Spreckels of California," 10–11.

71   *a German beet sugar refinery:* Adler, *Claus Spreckels,* 22. Adler draws much of his account of Spreckels's early life from Cordray's unpublished dissertation.

71   *speed up its processing:* Cordray, "Claus Spreckels of California," 15.

71   *48 pounds per person:* Henry A. Brown, *Analysis of the Sugar Question* (Saxonville, Mass., 1879), 6.

71   *12,500 pounds of sugar an hour:* Cordray, "Claus Spreckels of California," 16.

71   *Eighth and Brannan Streets:* Ibid., 18. Description of the California Sugar Refinery is based on an undated photo of the plant in Cordray's thesis, which notes that it was located at Eighth and Brannan streets, south of Market Street in San Francisco.

71   *his health restored, in 1871:* Claus Spreckels, "Dictation and biographical sketch," undated sketch by Alfred Bates based on dictation recorded by Spreckels for H. H. Bancroft (Berkeley, Calif.: Hubert Howe Bancroft Collection, Bancroft Library, University of California). The original Bates handwritten document reads (including words crossed out): "The ceaseless strain on his faculties, inseparable from such a career, produced, however, a serious malady, which was at first considered dangerous, & by the advice of his physician Mr. Spreckels again set sail for Europe, returning in 1871 after eighteen months of travel & residence among the health-resorts of Germany, with his health completely restored & his system renovated."

72   *crop for the following year:* Adler, *Claus Spreckels,* 3.

72   *at the original price he'd first offered them:* Charles Hastings Judd, "Interview with Charles Hastings Judd, 1882–: Affairs in Hawaii: San Francisco, 1882," 17 December 1882 (Berkeley, Calif.: Hubert Howe Bancroft Collection, Bancroft Library, University of California).

72   *"the largest sugar raiser there":* O'Brien, "Claus Spreckels," 520.

73   *"an authoritarian Prussian manner":* Cordray, "Claus Spreckels of California," 232, citing the *San Francisco Chronicle* of April 16, 1951.

73   *new rooms before bedtime:* Adams, *The Man, John D. Spreckels,* 50.

5: Pele's Wrath

75 *"the only direct heir by birth"*: Liliʻuokalani, *Hawaii's Story*, 55.

75 *"it sounded more royal"*: Allen, *Betrayal*, 147, citing diary of January 19, 1891.

76 *he silenced any doubters*: Estate of James Campbell, "James Campbell, Esq." (Kapolei, Hawaii: 1978), revised 2003, 2–3 and 14.

76 *"an ovation in every way worthy"*: Liliʻuokalani, *Hawaii's Story*, 59.

77 *They squabbled over money*: As early as 1874, Cleghorn wrote to Likelike about the signs of marital disharmony between his sister-in-law and her husband. "[Lydia] has moved all her things from the mauka (inland) house at Waikiki to the servants house. John will not build a house or give her any money to repair the old House. . . . Lydia and John have had a row about bills." By the following spring, Cleghorn was reporting that the pair was "getting on better than they have for a long time," as evidenced by John Dominis telling him that Liliʻu had begun having her supper with him. Still, there was continuing talk in 1878 of the couple's troubles, including Dominis's jealousy of Liliʻu's friendship with a female friend and his suspicion that she had composed a song for another man.

77 *other women's beds*: "John was, to use a euphemism, rather irregular as a husband—as many husbands in my experience are. He was fond of society, sometimes took more liquor than was good for him, and occasionally (although he never kept a regular mistress) had some love adventures." Report of G. Trousseau, contained in the Blount Report, 996. Allen, *Betrayal*, 159, reports that by 1882 Dominis had fathered a child by another woman who was in Liliʻu's retinue, Mary Hale Purdy Pahau. She doesn't mention infidelity before this point.

77 *she might adopt this infant*: Allen, *Betrayal*, 149.

77 *seminary in the Oakland foothills*: Liliʻu would later assume the duty of a schoolteacher herself, instructing a handful of girls through the Kawaiahaʻo seminary. Liliʻuokalani, *Hawaii's Story*, 117.

78 *her own Christian name, Lydia*: Allen, *Betrayal*, 151. Along with a cluster of songs dedicated to her young niece Kaʻiulani from the same time period, the compositions suggest Liliʻu was enchanted with the children that surrounded her and inspired to celebrate the continuation of the royal line. Also, Liliʻuokalani, Gillett, and Smith, *The Queen's Songbook*, 233–34.

78   *its sweet, tangy fruit:* Darlene E. Kelley, "Queen Liliuokalani and her
      Music—Part 3," 2007, http://files.usgwarchives.org/hi/keepers/qlili03.
      txt. Lili'uokalani, Gillett, and Smith, *The Queen's Songbook*, 233.

78   *the lover was Lili'u's own sister:* Allen, *Betrayal*, 148.

78   *the wistful "Aloha Oe":* Leslie Ann Hayashi and Kathleen Wong Bishop,
      Aloha Oe: The Song Heard Around the World (Honolulu: Mutual Pub-
      lishing, 2004), 21, notes that two songs may have influenced the tune—
      Charles Crozat Converse's "Rock Beside the Sea" or "Lone Rock by the
      Sea," published in the 1850s, and George Frederick Root's composi-
      tion "There's Music in the Air." Page 38 of the songbook says four mea-
      sures of "Aloha Oe" are borrowed from Converse's song. Lili'uokalani,
      Dorothy K. Gillett, and Barbara Barnard Smith, *The Queen's Songbook*,
      notes that four measures of "Aloha Oe" are adapted from Converse's
      song.

79   *"a high state of cultivation":* Adler, *Claus Spreckels*, 37, quoting the petition
      from Spreckels to Kalākaua, filed in "Water-Maui-Moloka'i -Sundries,
      1866–1885," State Archives of Hawai'i.

79   *similar to that for water, wai:* Ibid., 38-39.

79   *a private room at the Hawaian Hotel:* Kuykendall, *The Hawaiian King-
      dom: Vol. III, 1874–1893*, 201–02.

79   *"Cabinet pudding" and "Windsor soup":* Menu from the Hawaiian Hotel,
      1874, State Archives of Hawai'i.

79   *into the early hours:* Adler, *Claus Spreckels*, 40.

80   *"injured our pride & done damage":* Ibid.

80   *many times the King's total annual income:* A review of the king's cash
      book from March 1874–July 1878 suggests his income from land rents
      and other sources was vastly smaller than his borrowings from Spreckels.

80   *income from the crown lands:* Adler, *Claus Spreckels*, 39.

80   *a puppet ruler:* San Francisco's satirical newspaper the *Wasp* published
      a memorable cartoon a few years later reflecting the close relationship
      between Hawai'i's King and the San Francisco-based sugar magnate.
      In it, Kalākaua and Spreckels are standing arm and arm at the corner
      of Bush and Kearney streets, an area at the center of San Francisco's
      business district. A raggedy-looking man armed with a big-barreled gun
      labeled "blackmailing" accosts them. But the pair does not seem overly
      concerned. Perhaps that is because in Spreckels's pocket is a paper la-
      beled "Libel." "Don't Scare Worth a Cent," cartoon, chromolith, n.p. (San

Francisco, CA) *Wasp*, October 28, 1881. State Archives of Hawai'i, Kahn Collection (via library.kccc.hawaii.edu).

80 *E mahalo I ka ona miliona*: Adler, *Claus Spreckels*, 38, citing a letter to the editor signed "Hawai'i" in the Hawaiian *Gazette*, July 17, 1878. See also the Hawaiian-language newspaper *Ko Hawai'i Pae Aina* of July 13, 1878, for a full report of the meeting, and *Ka Nupepa Kuoka* of July 13, 1878, for an editorial supportive of Spreckels.

81 *a murky family history*: Gibson claimed to have been born at sea, baptized in England, and moved with his farm family first to Canada, then to New York City, and then finally, as a young man on his own, to South Carolina. His book is entitled *The Prisoner of Weltevreden: And a Glance at the East Indian Archipelago*

81 *offered the church 10,000 acres*: Paul Bailey, *Hawaii's Royal Prime Minister: The Life and Times of Walter Murray Gibson* (New York: Hastings House Publishers, 1980), 119–20.

81 *the name of Walter M. Gibson*: Ibid., 126.

82 *"The Shepherd Saint of Lanai"*: Thomas Thrum, *The Shepherd Saint of Lanai* (Honolulu: Thos. G. Thrum, 1887), front cover.

82 *a mortgage from Spreckels*: Spreckels held a $35,000 loan, according to Adler, *Claus Spreckels*, 183. See also Daws, *Shoal of Time*, 231. The vast majority of Spreckels' papers were destroyed in the 1906 earthquake and fire in San Francisco, according to his descendants.

82 *"You need not preach to me"*: Kalākaua to Cleghorn, 1880, Cleghorn Collection, State Archives of Hawai'i.

83 *"The king has completely forgotten the facts"*: George Trousseau to Archibald Cleghorn, 3 September 1880, David W. Forbes Collection, Cleghorn Letters Part 1, State Archives of Hawai'i.

83 *she might have died*: Kalākaua wrote to his sister, "It was something quite serious, had it not been for the prompt action of the physician . . . and the untiring watchfulness, care and attention of those in attendance, she would have died. . . . The Queen and I and the Governess has been out here ever since the Child has been ill and do not intend to leave until your return. . . . I have been amusing the baby by buying curiosities for her and to keep her from dispondency. At present she is comparatively very well but there is no knowing at any time she may have a relapse." Kalākaua to Likelike, 21 September 1880, David W. Forbes Collection, Cleghorn Letters Part 1, State Archives of Hawai'i.

83   *"I would rather die myself"*: Cleghorn to Likelike, 21 September 1880, David W. Forbes Collection, Cleghorn Letters Part 1, State Archives of Hawai'i.

84   *"a precious set of fools"*: This conversation between Kalākaua and Spreckels is relayed in a letter from C. C. Harris to E. H. Allen, September 27, 1880, Allen papers, as cited in Kuykendall, *The Hawaiian Kingdom: Vol. III, 1874–1893*, 223.

84   *the moral life of his plantation workers*: According to a privately published biography of Samuel Northrup Castle written by his grandson, William Richards Castle Jr., discussions among shareholders of a sugar plantation that Castle & Cooke invested in included such questions as "Shall we insert in the contracts of laborers a clause compelling them to attend Church once every Sunday on pain of dismissal from service?" (The answer was no.) And "Shall religious meetings be held on the plantation after working hours?" (The answer was yes.) William Richards Castle, *Life of Samuel Northrup Castle: Written by his Grandson* (Honolulu: Samuel N. and Mary Castle Foundation, in cooperation with the Hawaiian Historical Society), 1960, 125.

84   *one of the fastest recorded passages*: Adler, *Claus Spreckels*, 105.

85   *more than other mills were producing*: Cordray, "Claus Spreckels of California," 39–40, describes the mill at Spreckelsville and details how it achieved this higher production.

85   *invested more than $500,000*: Ibid., 52.

85   *in today's dollars*: Modern equivalent values provided by http://www.measuringworth.com/ppowerus/result.php.

85   *an agreement in 1880*: Cordray, "Claus Spreckels of California," 40.

87   *ingratiating themselves into royal favor*: Lili'uokalani, *Hawaii's Story*, 65.

87   *"I ought to be the sole regent"*: Ibid., 76.

87   *played by the military band*: William Nevins Armstrong, *Around the World with a King* (New York: Frederick A. Stokes, 1904), 8.

88   *lit by exploding fireworks*: Takaki, *Raising Cane*, 83.

88   *only 66 were non-Hawaiians*: Kuykendall, *The Hawaiian Kingdom: Vol. III, 1874–1893*, 137.

88   *"like a fire"*: Ibid., 136, Green to Allen.

88   *"sufficient care and medical attendance"*: "Resolutions passed at mass meeting at Kaumakapili Church, presented to HRH Princess Regent by Committee of Thirteen. S.K. Kaai Chairman," 7 February 1881,

David W. Forbes Collection, Liliʻuokalani Letters Part I, State Archives of Hawaiʻi.

89   "*her accessibility to the people*": Liliʻuokalani, Gillett, and Smith, *The Queen's Songbook*, 13.

89   "*I see by the papers*": Kalākaua to Liliʻuokalani, 21 June 1881, David W. Forbes Collection, Kalākaua Letters Part II, State Archives of Hawaiʻi.

90   *an editorial in the New York Times*: "Kingdom for Sale," *New York Times*, July 13, 1881, p. 4.

90   "*You ought to hear Strauss's Band in Vienna*": In another letter to Liliʻu, Kalākaua reflected upon the gaiety and order he witnessed in Vienna on the Sabbath, contrasting it with his experience of that day under the missionaries in his own country. "Can it possibly be that these light hearted happy people are all going to H-ll?" he wondered. "Surely not! But what a contrast to our miserable bigoted community . . . with such rubbish trash that we have so long been lead to believe, it is a wonder that we have not risen any higher than the common brute." Kalākaua to Liliʻuokalani, 10 August 1881, David W. Forbes Collection, Kalākaua Letters Part II, State Archives of Hawaiʻi.

90   "*the old relics that this ancient and noble pile contains*": Kalākaua to Liliʻuokalani, 12 July 1881, David W. Forbes Collection, Kalākaua Letters Part II, State Archives of Hawaiʻi.

90   *lent him a carriage*: William Nevins Armstrong to William L. Green, 12 July 1881, David W. Forbes Collection, Kalākaua Letters Part II, State Archives of Hawaiʻi.

91   "*nature's gorgeous fireworks*": Liliʻuokalani, *Hawaii's Story*, 71.

91   *ditches to divert the flow*: George Kanahele, *Pauahi: The Kamehameha Legacy* (Honolulu: Kamehameha Schools Press, 1986), 159, cites such a meeting occurring August 4, 1881.

91   "*the danger that threatens us all*": Liliʻuokalani's Hilo Address, 13 August 1881, David W. Forbes Collection, Liliʻuokalani Letters Part I, State Archives of Hawaiʻi.

91   *the flow had stopped right there*: Not everyone expressed unreserved gratitude and delight during Liliʻu's tour of Hawaiʻi Island. The ever-watchful Archibald Cleghorn reported to his wife, who was traveling with Liliʻu, that an article in the *Saturday Press* had appeared criticizing the royal retinue for intermperance. "The article did not refer to either her [Liliʻu] or you [Likelike], but some of the party—[who] acted disgracefully and

they can *prove* it, if required," referring to Queen Kapiʻolani's sister and Princess Ruth as being "*drunk* several times on the trip and it is not the 1st, 2nd, 3rd or 4th time she has been *drunk* . . . It is all over the *town*. She gets *drunk*, when ever she has a chance." Cleghorn to Likelike, 10 September 1881, David W. Forbes Collection, Cleghorn Letters Part I, State Archives of Hawaiʻi.

92 *shunned Western ways:* Kanahele, *Pauahi*, 160.

92 *she still couldn't sit up:* Liliʻuokalani, *Hawaii's Story*, 91.

92 "*It is home! It is Hawaiʻi nei!*": Armstrong, *Around the World with a King*, 280.

6: Merrie Monarch

98 *It was the controversial Gibson:* Bailey, *Hawaii's Royal Prime Minister*, 179.

98 *a red, white and blue feather plume:* Gazette, February 14, 1883, and Allen, *Kalakaua* , 143–145.

99 "*productions of Parisian art*": Liliʻuokalani, *Hawaii's Story*, 101.

99 *gown with a 10-foot train:* Kanahele, *Pauahi*, 163.

99 *an active rivalry:* Pacific Commercial Advertiser, February 10, 1883, 2.

99 *no interruption to the church service:* Williams, *Deaths and Funerals of Major Hawaiian Aliʻi*, 62.

100 *coat of arms inlaid in gold:* Allen, *Kalakaua*, 145. Kapiʻolani's sister also presented Kalākaua with more traditional symbols: a *pūloʻuloʻu*, a staff carried by Hawaiian rulers, as well as a *lei palaoa*, a whale's-tooth pendant, according to the *Gazette*, February 17, 1883, 6, and *Advertiser*, February 17, 1883, 2.

100 *swore his oath:* Allen, *Kalakaua*, 145.

100 "*In vain! The crown would not fit*": M. Forsyth Grant, *Scenes in Hawaii; or, Life in the Sandwich Islands* (Toronto: Hart & Company, 1888), 122.

101 *Episcopalian chaplain, who was also the rector:* Kuykendall, *The Hawaiian Kingdom: Vol. III, 1874–1893*, mentions the name of the chaplain, Alexander Mackintosh, on page 263. Mackintosh was the rector of St. Andrew's, according to Grant, *Scenes in Hawaii*, 121.

101 *playing the "Coronation March":* Kuykendall *The Hawaiian Kingdom: Vol. III, 1874–1893*, 262–63.

101 "*the effect was rather comical . . .*" Liliʻuokalani, *Hawaii's Story*, 101. One biographer of Kalākaua later suggested the king crowned himself so the

chancellor would not cast a shadow on him, thus respecting the ancient Hawaiian belief that no one should cast a shadow on the king. But an undated letter to Lili'u from before the coronation provides an answer. In it, Kalākaua explains, "The great difficulty has been is to settle the Question of who is to crown me. And the matter was only set at rest yesterday. I had to change the whole thing and took the responsibility upon myself so as not to cause friction." Presumably various other members of his family and inner circle felt they were due the honor. As for Hawaiian-language newspapers' coverage of the coronation, Professor Noenoe Silva notes that very few such newspapers from this period have survived.

101 *highly amused by this account:* Emma to to Flora Jones, State Archives of Hawai'i, David W. Forbes collection.

101 *the guests resumed their dancing:* Grant, *Scenes in Hawaii,* 126–27.

101 *more than three times as much:* Thurston, *Memoirs of the Hawaiian Revolution,* vol. 2, 64.

102 *his unchecked spending:* Others, somewhat pettily, criticized it for not looking regal enough. A reporter for the *Gazette,* a daily English-language newspaper opposed to the monarchy, wrote that "The Pavilion and Amphitheater looked very tawdry, with a lot of cheap flags showing very plainly the effects of Sunday's heavy rain . . . Of the foreigners present it was noticeable that very few of our citizens could be seen, save those who are in government employ. The effect looking from the Palace veranda was anything but impressive." *Gazette,* February 14, 1883.

102 *a costume ball for 1,000 people:* DK Publishing, *Chronicle of America* (New York: DK Publishing, 1995), 458.

102 *not to count pennies:* In the pages of the *Advertiser,* Gibson himself glibly held forth: "Shall we, upholders of a monarchy with the example of enlightened monarchical Europe, attach no importance to such a ceremonial? Shall we not, rather . . . strengthen the Hawaiian throne by taking measures to provide for a crowning consummation?" The opposition that so vocally critiqued the coronation was supportive of the earlier appropriation of more than $160,000 for construction of the palace, the *Advertiser* noted, surmising, "Possibly they enjoyed immense profit from the expenditure of that . . . some through contracts which they then held from the Government." *Pacific Commercial Advertiser,* February 17, 1883, 4.

102 *"renewed sense of the dignity and honor"*: Lili'uokalani, *Hawaii's Story*, 104.

102 *"The life of my noble wife"*: Kalākaua to William L. Moehonua, 24 March 1876, originally in Hawaiian and translated by Arthur Keawe, David W. Forbes Collection, Kalākaua Letters Part I, State Archives of Hawai'i.

103 *just over 34,000 square feet*: Reference manual, *The Friends of 'Iolani Palace*, 9.

103 *a luxury seen only among the elite*: Ibid., 7. Toilets became fairly common in European urban centers after the mid-nineteenth century purely because of necessity driven by population density. Flushing "water closets" were first manufactured as early as 1861, but obviously it would have taken a while for the technology to filter down beyond the very rich. In America, outhouses or chamber pots were the norm.

103 *six times as much as legislators had appropriated*: Friends of 'Iolani Palace, 5, and Alexander, *A Brief History of the Hawaiian People*, 310.

103 *$7 million in today's dollars*: Calculation based on relative value of dollar amount based on U.S. consumer price index between 1883 and 2009. See www.measuringworth.com/calculators.

103 *"His Majesty listened"*: "King Kalakaua's Movements; He Examines the Electric Light," *New York Times*, September 26, 1881.

103 *"As we stepped into the ballroom we gave a sudden gasp"*: Isobel Strong Field, *This Life I've Loved* (New York: Longmans, Green, 1937), 150 and 162–163. Isobel Strong Field was mistaken that the lights were introduced at the coronation ball. It was more likely at a later royal ball.

104 *four years before the White House*: http://www.whitehousehistory.org/whha_timelines/timelines_workers-02.html.

104 *the Hawaiian Bell Telephone company*: Robert C. Schmitt, "Some Transportation and Communication Firsts in Hawai'i," *The Hawaiian Journal of History*, 12 (1979): 99–119.

104 *each course accompanied*: "Dinner at 'Iolani Palace ," February 24, 1883, State Archives of Hawai'i, reprinted by *Friends of 'Iolani Palace*.

105 *80 selections listed*: David W. Forbes, ed., *Hawaiian National Bibliography*, *1780–1900*, vol. 4 (Honolulu: University of Hawai'i Press, 2003), 77.

105 *the performances known as hula ma'i*: Noenoe K. Silva, *"He Kanawai E Ho'opau I Na Hula Kuolo Hawai'i:* The Political Economy of Banning the Hula," *Hawaiian Journal of History* 34 (2000): 29–48.

105   *a new style of hula:* Noenoe K. Silva, *Aloha Betrayed: Native Hawaiian Resistance to American Colonialism* (Durham, N.C.: Duke University Press, 2004), 108.

105   *"characterized by those who profess to understand":* Forbes, 77–78, citing *Papa Kuhikuhi o na Hula Poni Moi,* February 12, 1883.

105   *apparently written in his own hand:* Thurston, *Memoirs,* vol. 2, 35.

105   *"a retrograde step of heathenism":* Kuykendall, *The Hawaiian Kingdom: Vol. III, 1874–1893,* citing various Hawaiian newspaper accounts in endnotes 52 and 53, 691.

105   *planted the seeds for a rebirth:* Silva, *Aloha Betrayed,* 110.

106   George Chaplin, *Presstime in Paradise: The Life and Times of The Honolulu Advertiser, 1856-1995* (Honolulu: University of Hawai'i Press, 1998), 112.

107   *"Liquid refreshments were freely on tap":* Thurston, *Memoirs,* vol. 2, 29–30.

107   *a ship steaming into Honolulu's port:* "The Mariposa," *Pacific Commercial Advertiser,* August 4, 1883, 2.

108   *a profit estimated at around $150,000:* Adler, *Claus Spreckels,* 131–135.

108   *"His Extravagancy Palaver":* Allen, *Dole,* 114.

109   *"Hail to the Chief":* Adler, *Claus Spreckels,* 109–10.

109   *a "sugar-coated candidate":* Kuykendall, *The Hawaiian Kingdom: Vol. III, 1874–1893,* 267.

109   *an advisor and companion:* Ibid., 268.

110   *the 200% increase in the national debt:* Ibid., 258–259.

110   *"guilty of gross extravagance":* Ibid., 272.

110   *"a man of unusual enterprise":* Ibid., 275, citing *Daily Bulletin,* July 21, 1884.

111   *"Sir Claus":* San Francisco Chronicle, November 23, 1884, 8A.

111   *violence sometimes erupted:* For more background on the violence that sometimes erupted in San Francisco's newsrooms in the nineteenth century, a good source is *War of Words: A True Tale of Newsprint and Murder,* by Simon Read.

111   *dragging the would-be assassin:* "'Mike' De Young Shot; Attempt at Murder by a Man who Didn't Like Criticism," *New York Times,* November 20, 1884.

112   *The Chronicle did not end its campaign:* Bernice Scharlach, *Big Alma: San Francisoc's Alma Spreckels* (San Francisco: Scottwall Associates, 1990), 20. Ms. Scharlach noted in her book that the *Chronicle* published stories

alleging that Spreckels used slave labor on his Maui plantation, used lepers to work in the fields, and had even procured women from the mainland for the king in exchange for his plantation lands.

112 *sales of $50,000 a month*: Adler, *Claus Spreckels*, 72.

112 *the steamer carried good news*: San Francisco Chronicle, July 2, 1885, 2.

7: To England

113 *"tonsorial departments"*: "The Mariposa," *Pacific Commercial Advertiser*, August 11, 1883, 7.

113 *Andrew Carnegie's newly published book*: Andrew Carnegie, *Triumphant Democracy* (Cosimo Classics, 2005). First published in 1886.

114 *a $35,000 mortgage*: Adler, *Claus Spreckels*, 183.

114 *poor financial management*: An ongoing project to translate more nineteenth century Hawaiian-language newspapers into English will shed more light on such issues as the government's alleged financial mismanagement. A Hawaiian language newspaper, for instance, published an overview of the kingdom's financial position, quantifying its debts, receipts, and expenses for the year ended April 30, 1887. It reported that the kingdom's receipts were significantly greater than its outlays or debts, but also that there were some concerns about a road construction project that was reported as having been paid by the government but which had not, in fact, occurred. (Thanks to University of Hawai'i's Puakea Nogelmeier for providing and translating this news article.)

114 *"I would rather see him going barefoot"*: Kuykendall, *The Hawaiian Kingdom: Vol. III, 1874–1893*, 292, citing an article originally printed in the *San Francisco Call* of October 31, 1886.

115 *Spreckels held five cards*: The account of the card game between the king and Spreckels is based on Adler, *Claus Spreckels*, 30. There are many other retellings of this story, but Adler's account is the most comprehensive. For background on the London loan, I relied largely on Kuykendall, *The Hawaiian Kingdom: Vol. III, 1874–1893*, 291–299.

116 *"offensive dictatorial manner"*: "Mr. Spreckels on one or two occasions, and especially at my residence on Octr. 13th ventured to express himself in such a dictatorial manner to His Majesty in the presence of several members of the Assembly—saying that his views must be carried out or he would 'fight' and explaining that this meant a withholding of

financial accommodation and an immediate demand for what was owing to him—that he aroused then and there a determination on the part of the native members present to resist the dictation of 'ona miliona' (Mr. Spreckels), and as they present themselves avowed, to see whether their chief Kalākaua or Mr. Spreckels were king." Kuykendall, *The Hawaiian Kingdom: Vol. III, 1874–1893*, 298, citing Gibson to Carter, no. 25, confidential, October 22, 1886.

116 *Lili'uokalani Educational Society:* Lili'uokalani, *Hawaii's Story*, 114.

116 *the Hale Nauā society:* Hale Nauā, "Constitution and by-laws of the Hale Naua or Temple of Science" (San Francisco: Bancroft Company, 1890), Berkeley, Calif., Bancroft Library.

116 *a feathered cape:* Allen, *Kalakaua*, 199.

117 *"pandering to vice":* Thurston, *Memoirs*, vol. 2, 24.

117 *"mean and little minds":* Lili'uokalani, *Hawaii's Story*, 114-15.

117 *"I am sure":* Diary of Lili'uokalani, 1886, entry for January 31, Bishop Museum Archives.

117 *"I can vouch to how she suffered":* "I have known the Queen intimately for over twenty years. When I arrived here she had not been married long, and her husband, John O. Dominis, an American, and an intimate friend of mine, was fondly beloved by her. John Dominis's character was unimpeachable—ask any one who knew him—Mr. C. R. Bishop, Mr. W. F. Allen, and others. I am now speaking from a physician's point of view. John was, to use a euphemism, rather irregular as a husband-as many husbands in my experience are. He was fond of society, sometimes took more liquor than was good for him, and occasionally (although he never kept a regular mistress) had some love adventures. In this small community they were reported to his wife, and I can vouch to how she suffered by it. She was exceedingly fond and jealous of him." U.S. House of Representatives, *House Executive Documents, 53rd Congress, 3rd Session. No. 47, Affairs in Hawaii*, herein after called "The Blount Report" (Washington: U.S. House of Representatives, 1895), 996.

117 *living in separate homes:* Lili'uokalani, Gillett, and Smith, *The Queen's Songbook*, 14.

118 *before the coronation:* Kanahele, *Pauahi*, 163–64.

118 *in the annex of the Palace Hotel:* Bishop and Krout, *Memoirs*, 221.

118 *she moved to her seaside home:* Kanahele, *Pauahi*, 185–186.

118 *constant doses of morphine:* Ibid., 189.

118   *Pauahi's bier:* Ibid., 190.

119   *"We have heard a good deal":* Pacific Commercial Advertiser, October 21, 1884, 6.

119   *"They smoked, feasted, and sang songs":* Lili'uokalani, *Hawaii's Story,* 109.

120   *the streets of Honolulu:* Pacific Commercial Advertiser, May 11, 1884, 2–3.

120   *she had also inherited lands:* Van Dyke, *Who Owns the Crown Lands of Hawai'i?,* 53.

120   *more than 350,000 acres:* Kanahele, *Pauahi,* 166.

120   *establishment of the Kamehameha schools:* Van Dyke, *Who Owns the Crown Lands of Hawai'i?,* 307–08.

120   *the "self-abnegation of her husband":* "The Kamehameha Schools (editorial)," Pacific Commercial Advertiser, November 11, 1884.

120   *funding operations at Queen's Hospital:* Van Dyke, *Who Owns the Crown Lands of Hawai'i?,* 331–32.

121   *"The wish of my heart":* Lili'uokalani, *Hawaii's Story,* 110.

121   *"Glad to get him to sleep":* Diary of Lili'uokalani, 1885, entry from March 19, 1885, Bishop Museum Archives.

121   *Davies helped Cleghorn pay:* Edwin Palmer Hoyt, *Davies: The Inside Story of a British-American Family in the Pacific and its Business Enterprises* (Honolulu: Topgallant Publishing Co., 1983), 130.

122   *"a piece of superstition":* Diary of Lili'uokalani, 1887, entry for January 27, 1887, State Archives of Hawai'i.

122   *she would never marry:* Sharon Linnea, *Princess Ka'iulani: Hope of a Nation, Heart of a People* (Grand Rapids, Mich.: Erdmans Books for Young Readers, 1999), 53.

123   *"I was tenderly attached to my sister":* Lili'uokalani, *Hawaii's Story,* 116.

124   *Britain and Germany had divided . . .* Evelyn Speyer Colbert, *The Pacific Islands: paths to the present* (Westview Press, 1997), 19–21.

124   *aggressive moves by American businesses:* Ernest R. May, *Imperial Democracy: The Emergence of America as a Great Power* (New York: Harper & Row, 1973), 8. One such proponent of this creed was the Congregationalist minister Josiah Strong, who argued that America would take the lead from Britain in expanding the Anglo-Saxon race, with its "genius for colonizing."

124   *He sought to unite the people of Polynesia:* The idea of creating such an empire had its roots in the reign of Kamehameha III, who appointed an Australian journalist named Charles St. Julian in 1853 to the grandly

titled but unpaid position of "His Majesty's Commissioner, and Political and Commercial Agent to the Kings, Chiefs and Rulers of the Islands in the Pacific Ocean, not under the protection or sovereignty of any European Government." Neither Kamehameha IV nor Kamehameha V took up the crusade, but the vision of uniting the island nations of the Pacific into a confederation found fertile ground in the court of King Kalākaua. First, the Italian adventurer Celso Moreno promoted it, referring in one letter to the king "the grand, humane, and generous idea of uniting under your scepter the whole Polynesian race and make Honolulu a monarchical Washington, where the representatives of all the islands would convene in Congress." Kuykendall, *The Hawaiian Kingdom: Vol. III, 1874–1893*, 311, citing Celso Caesar Moreno, "The Position of Men and Affairs in Hawai'i, Open Letter to His Majesty King Kalakaua," August 7, 1886, Post Scriptum, April 7, 1887 (Washington D.C.).

124   *the great powers:* Contrary to the idea that the division of the Pacific took place under some form of political design on the part of the great powers, the historian Steven Roger Fischer argues against the notion that there was "a nineteenth-century European and American 'land-grab' in Pacific Islands. Britain, seemingly forever dedicated to the principle of insular indifference, found itself time and again drawn into political conflicts necessitating ever greater commitments which, in the end, saw Britain as the nation with the largest colonial encumbrance in the Pacific. France experienced separate Polynesian and Melanesian phases which, once its possessions were secured, at length simply wilted into administrative ennui. Germany's aggressive Pacific policy after national unification in the 1870s forced rivals to chase after what they otherwise might have ignored. This, in turn, drew in those final nations who shared the last slices of the 'Pacific pie.'" Steven Roger Fischer, *A History of the Pacific Islands* (New York: Palgrave, 2002), 166–68.

124   *Tahiti became a colony of France:* Ibid., 134.

124   *Germany had declared the Marshall Islands:* Ibid., 165.

125   *seven attempts to establish governments:* I. C. Campbell, *A History of the Pacific Islands* (Berkeley, Calif.: University of California Press, 1989), 99.

125   *"a mere piece of fussy impertinence":* Kuykendall, *The Hawaiian Kingdom: Vol. III, 1874–1893*, 323, citing L. S. Sackville-West to Rosebery, telegram no. 5 and dispatch no 155, dated June 24, 1886.

125 *John E. Bush, a part-Hawaiian:* Van Dyke, *Who Owns the Crown Lands of Hawai'i?,* 207.

125 *"all decency appears to have been forgotten":* Robert Louis Stevenson, *A Footnote to History: Eight Years of Trouble in Samoa* (New York: Charles Scribner's Sons, 1895), 59–60.

126 *"obviously absurd for the King":* Kuykendall *The Hawaiian Kingdom: Vol. III, 1874–1893,* 333, citing Carter to Bayard, November 3, 1885.

126 *"the 'Kaimiloa' finally became a disgrace":* Ibid., 336, citing Brown to Poor, July 7, 1887.

127 *"Our Mission was simply a Mission":* Ibid., citing Kalākaua to D. McKinley, April 12, 1889.

127 *1,100 or so copies:* Kuykendall estimates the number of pamphlets in circulation as 900 and suggests it was written by Atkinson or Edward William Purvis, who was vice-chamberlain of the royal household until mid-1886. Ibid., 346.

127 *his satirical pamphlets:* The *Gazette,* the by-then vehemently anti-Kalākaua English-language opposition paper noted in its May 24th issue, "The Gynberg Ballads have gone off like hot cakes. Nearly every one not feeling right till he had a copy in his possession, and then retired to a quiet nook to have a good read and a hearty laugh." Forbes, *Bibliography,* vol. 4, 224.

128 *the sheer novelty of the experience:* Lili'uokalani, *Hawaii's Story,* 119.

128 *"I am overcome with awe":* Office of Hawaiian Affairs, *Ali'i Diplomatic Missions and Other Business Travel to Washington, D.C:. Phase 2* (Washington, D.C.: 2009), 53.

128 *"Scottish Rite":* Jasper Ridley, *The Freemasons: A History of the World's Most Powerful Secret Society* (New York: Arcade Publishing, 2002), 170, 267. Pike's system delineated each member's rank into thirty-three degrees and John Dominis had become a master mason of the 33rd degree by the time of their visit to Washington, D.C.

128 *the assistance of the Freemasons:* Always acutely sensitive to rank, Lili'u perhaps made too much of this honor in a letter she wrote to one of her servants. "In my opinion," wrote Lili'u in a letter back to Honolulu, "this is of great importance, because this man has tremendous power, exceeding perhaps the power of every Monarch on earth, intermingled with a humble heart and true Christianity. Furthermore, what makes it so interesting, we are the only ones who have been bestowed with this honor,

and we are the first women same has been awarded, none since the first ancient history of the masons," adding that while the honor was ostensibly for acts of mercy and assistance given to our own nation, "Brother [David Kalākaua, also a mason] is really the true cause of these honors." Liliʻuokalani to Joe, 15 June 1887, Foreign Office & Executive File, State Archives of Hawaiʻi.

128 *an exhibition of Indian warriors:* James W. L. McGuire, "A Short Description of Queen Kapiolani's Voyage to England to Attend the Jubilee Celebration of Queen Victoria of England in the Year 1887," 1887, 9–10, State Archives of Hawaiʻi.

128 *The parcels would be held in "severalty":* Chronicle of America, 475.

129 *"are very dear (at) 25 cents a bud":* McGuire, "Queen Kapiolani's Voyage," entry of May 8, 1887, 11.

129 *the museum's growing collection:* Calvin Tompkins, *Merchants and Masterpieces: The Story of the Metropolitan Museum of Art* (New York: E. P. Dutton, 1970), 60–61.

129 *"it spoke too plainly of death and burial":* Liliʻuokalani, *Hawaii's Story,* 131.

129 *more than two thousand passengers:* George Henry Preble, *A Chronological History of the Origin and Development of Steam Navigation* (Philadelphia: L.R. Hamersly, 1895), 354.

129 *A school of porpoises:* McGuire, "Queen Kapiolani's Voyage," entries of May 26–29, 1887, 23–24.

8: Bayonet Constitution

131 *"the peculiar atmosphere of the city":* Liliʻuokalani, *Hawaii's Story,* 138.

131 *a dozen families might share:* According to http://www.liverpoolhistory-society.org.uk and *A History of Liverpool* by Ramsay Muir.

132 *welcoming her to England:* A letter to Liliʻu from Honolulu may also have reached her at that point, describing her mother-in-law's health: "["Mother Dominis"] has been very sick—was taken with vomiting and great prostration nearly two weks ago and is still in bed, but improving every day . . . I do hope she will be spared until you and John return. One day when she was very sick she said, 'Oh I wish John was here,' and the tears came into her eyes. I thnk she expected to die for she asked Mrs. Damon to lay her out." Liliʻu did not take the report seriously

enough to make efforts to return home ahead of schedule. Cordelia Allen to Lili'uokalani, 2 June 1887, David W. Forbes Collection, Lili'uokalani Letters Part I, State Archives of Hawai'i.

132   *years of secluded mourning:* Christopher Hibbert, *Queen Victoria: A Personal History* (New York: Basic Books, 2000), 285.

132   *the death of her consort:* Ibid., 379.

133   *"human nature is about the same":* Lili'uokalani, *Hawaii's Story*, 143.

133   *rose to kiss Kap'iolani:* McGuire, "Queen Kapiolani's Voyage," 34, says Victoria rose to greet Kapi'olani. *Hawaii's Story*, 145, doesn't specify who rose to greet whom.

133   *turned to Lili'u:* Diary of Lili'uokalani, entry of June 20, 1887, 16, says Queen Victoria shook hands with her; years later, writing *Hawaii's Story*, Lili'u amends the scene to say that Victoria kissed her forehead, 144.

133   *having met Kalākaua:* Allen, *Kalakaua*, 127.

133   *"I want to introduce you":* Lili'uokalani, *Hawaii's Story*, 145.

133   *"The princess possessed a strong will":* Curtis Pi'ehu Iaukea and Lorna Kahilipuaokalani Iaukea Watson, *By Royal Command* (Honolulu: Hui Hanai, 1988), 116.

134   *avoid such embarrassment:* Lili'uokalani to Cleghorn, 15 May 1887, Cleghorn Collection, State Archives of Hawai'i.

134   *It contained a half dozen coachman's uniforms:* Lili'uokalani to friend and coachman Joe, Foreign Office and Executive File, 1887, State Archives of Hawai'i.

135   *population of 5.5 million:* "Her Majesty's Jubilee: The Celebration in London," *Times* (London), June 22, 1887.

135   *the uneaten portions of their sandwiches:* Hibbert, *Queen Victoria: A Personal History*, 381.

135   *"Here she is!":* Emily Warinner, *A Royal Journey to London* (Honolulu: Topgallant Publishing Co., 1975), 40.

135   *crowned since 1066:* According to http://www.westminster-abbey.org/our-history/royals.

135   *9,000 people rose as one:* Warinner, *A Royal Journey to London*, 40.

135   *an extraordinary blue velvet gown:* A photograph of Queen Kapi'olani in the dress can today be seen on display on the second floor of 'Iolani Palace and the remnants of the dress itself are stored in the Bishop Museum's warehouse, now deemed too fragile for public display.

136   *Britons lit beacon fires:* "The Bonfires and Beacons," *Times* (London), June 22, 1887, 8, A section, as well as Warinner, *A Royal Journey to London,* 37, citing the *Illustrated London News.*

136   *"I am tired, but very happy"*: Lytton Strachey, *Queen Victoria* (New York: Harcourt, Brace and Company, 1921), 384,

136   *"excitement and possible revolution"*: Foreign dispatches, *Times* (London), June 29,1887, and June 27, 1887, as well as Kuykendall, *The Hawaiian Kingdom: Vol. III, 1874–1893,* 343, footnote. Also, on June 17, days before the Jubilee, the *New York Times* had published a story headlined "Trouble in Honolulu: A Revolution Threatened in the Sandwich Islands," June 17, 1887. Reporting that the Hawaiian government had been seizing arms to quell unrest, "J. D. Spreckels, Claus's eldest son, told the *Times,* 'Affairs are almost in a revolutionary stage on the islands. The extravagance and mismanagement of the Kingdom of Kalakaua have created a feeling of great dissatisfaction among the foreign residents . . .' As instances of the extravagance there, Mr. Spreckels stated that $40,000 had been expended on the funeral of the King's sister and $80,000 in fitting out as a man-of-war a tub of a steamer . . . He said that in case of a revolution a republic would probably be set up." The palace, Spreckels went on to tell the *Times,* "had been barricaded and supplied with arms and ammunition, and citizens of other countries have gone so far as to call on their home Governments to send men-of-war for their protection."

136   *"only long enough"*: Lili'uokalani, *Hawaii's Story,* 173–74.

137   *"We are just passing through"*: Kalākaua to Lili'uokalani, 5 July 1887, State Archives of Hawai'i. The word *Kunane* (according to the dictionaries at wehewehe.org) means "Brother or male cousin of a female, usually used only as term of address or as an affectionate variation of kaikunāne."

137   *"Since my last, everywhing was peaceable"*: Charles B. Wilson to Lili'uokalani, July 5, 1887, State Archives of Hawai'i.

138   *"My poor brother!"*: Diary of Lili'uokalani, 1887, entries for July 7, July 23, July 24, 1887, State Archives of Hawai'i.

138   *"a crowd of young hoodlums"*: *Pacific Commercial Advertiser,* June 21, 1887, 3.

138   *various chest and stomach ailments:* Walter Murray Gibson, *The Diaries of Walter Murray Gibson, 1886, 1887,* ed. Jacob Adler and Gwynn Barrett (Honolulu: University of Hawai'i Press, 1973), 156, entry from Saturday, June 4, 1887.

139   *broken his promise to marry her:* Flora Howard St. Clair to Gibson, 29 April 1887, State Archives of Hawaiʻi.

139   *a potentially lucrative opium license:* Jonathan K. Osorio, a professor at the Kamakakuokalani Center for Hawaiian Studies at the University of Hawaiʻi, notes that Junius Kaʻae, whom Kalākaua had appointed as registrar of conveyances, had actually received the money from Aki. Professor Osorio believes there has never been a satisfactory link proving that Kalākaua had, in fact, accepted a bribe, adding that the king himself denied the allegations.

139   *"Of late I have heard it remarked":* Kuykendall, *The Hawaiian Kingdom: Vol. III, 1874–1893,* 354, citing G. W. Merrill to T. F. Bayard, May 31, 1887, USDS Dispatches, Hawaii, Vol. XXIV.

139   *"the end must come to the present era":* Ibid.,355, citing the *Gazette,* April 5, 1887.

139   *Dole hosted the first meeting:* Dole, *Memoirs,* vol. 1, 33.

140   *shooting him in cold blood:* Lorrin Thurston, *Memoirs,* vol. 2, 86. In his memoir, Thurston refers to the Hawaiian League member who suggested this, V. V. Ashford, as "one of the knottiest problems in the formative stages of the league," desribing him as "thoroughly vicious" and an "evil genius."

140   *"I am weary, languid, listless":* Kuykendall, *The Hawaiian Kingdom: Vol. III, 1874–1893,* 356, citing Kathleen D. Mellen, *An Island Kingdom Passes: Hawaiʻi Becomes American* (New York, 1958), 193–94.

140   *buying rifles and ammunition:* Dole, *Memoirs,* vol. 1, 55.

140   *"for several hours a regular run":* Kuykendall, *The Hawaiian Kingdom: Vol. III, 1874–1893,* 359, citing the *Daily Bulletin,* June 29, 1887.

141   *Kalākaua himself called out the Rifles:* Ibid., 359.

141   *at the front entrance to the armory:* W. D. Alexander to Arthur, 25 July 1887, folder 203 of Alexander, Wm. DeWitt, in the Alexander & Baldwin Collection, Hawaiian Mission Children's Society.

141   *uniforms that bore a close resemblance:* Neil Bernard Dukas, *A Military History of Sovereign Hawaiʻi* (Honolulu: Mutual Publishing, 2004), 156.

141   *Thurston mounted the podium:* Paul Bailey, *Hawaii's Royal Prime Minister: The Life and Times of Walter Murray Gibson* (New York: Hastings House Publishers, 1980), 254.

141   *In a booming voice:* Dole, *Memoirs,* vol. 1, 33.

141   *resident aliens who wanted to vote:* Iaukea and Watson, *By Royal Command,*

127. This is a point made in a footnote by the editor of this book, Iaukea's daughter Lorna Kahilipuakalani Iaukea Watson, who wrote in his chapter on the Bayonet Constitution that "Many of these people were not citizens, but, rather, resident aliens who claimed 'denizen' status, i.e. they wanted to vote and be elected into office even though they had not become naturalized. The constitution of 1887 gave them this right."

142 *"We have just seen the Jubilee"*: Kuykendall, *The Hawaiian Kingdom: Vol. III, 1874–1893*, 362, citing Cecil Brown. Thurston in his *Memoirs* also relates this meeting in detail.

142 *a resounding chorus of "ayes"*: Kuykendall, *The Hawaiian Kingdom: Vol. III, 1874–1893*, 362.

142 *"Threats of violence"*: Gibson, *The Diaries of Walter Murray Gibson, 1886, 1887*, 161.

143 *"Hang them! Hang them!"*: Lili'uokalani, *Hawaii's Story*, 183. Thurston, in his reminiscences, noted that he was present on this occasion and that no man from a missionary background shouted to have them hanged, nor was any noose suspended in the building.

143 *It was Talula*: Bailey, *Hawaii's Royal Prime Minister*, 259–61.

143 *his drooping mustache and his daily walks*: Iaukea and Watson, *By royal command*, 107.

143 *This was enough to halt the hanging*: Bailey, *Hawaii's Royal Prime Minister*, 262.

143 *"they crossed their rifles before me"*: Field, *This Life*, 209.

144 *"Not while I live"*: Ibid., 213–14. While this exchange with the king as recorded by Field may have been embroidered in light of later events, Field did indeed receive the Star of Oceania from the king. It and the accompanying letters are in the Robert Louis Stevenson Silverado Museum in St. Helena, California.

144 *the Order of the Star of Oceania*: Ibid., 208–10.

145 *prepared to defend their king*: "The Hawaiian revolution. The King expected to ask British protection.," *New York Times*, July 15, 1887.

145 *"for considerable periods appeared to be gazing"*: Kuykendall, *The Hawaiian Kingdom: Vol. III, 1874–1893*, 367, citing C. W. Ashford, "Last Days of the Hawaiian Monarchy," 24–25, and a speech by Ashford on the constitution reported in the *Pacific Commercial Advertiser*, December 16, 1891.

145 *"the document was not in accordance"*: Thurston, *Memoirs*, vol. 2, 93.

146 *no less than governance gridlock*: David William Earles "Coalition Politics in Hawaii, 1887–1890," thesis dissertation.

146 *"it will not be long"*: *Pacific Commercial Advertiser*, July 26,1887, 3.

146 *the jutting promontory of Diamond Head*: McGuire, "Queen Kapiolani's Voyage," entries for Monday, 25 July 1887, and Tuesday, 26 July 1887, 47.

147 *The mournful expressions on the faces*: As Lili'u later wrote, "Mingled with the all the joy felt at our safe return, there was an undercurrent of sadness, as of a people who had known with us a crushing sorrow. There were traces of tears on the cheeks of many of our faithful retainers, which we noticed, and of which we knew the meaning, as we passed by. They knew, and we know, although no word was spoken, the changes which had taken place while we had been away, and which had been forced upon the king." Lili'uokalani, *Hawaii's Story*, 175.

147 *the king's sister seemed to make no attempt*: Iaukea and Watson, *By Royal Command*, 141.

147 *"We could see on his countenance"*: Lili'uokalani, *Hawaii's Story*, 176.

9: Be Not Deceived

148 *"it would form a most excellent harbor"*: http://www.history.navy.mil/docs/wwii/pearl/hawaii-2.htm, citing Andrew Bloxom's report of May 17, 1825.

149 *a military commission*: Van Dyke, *Who Owns the Crown Lands of Hawai'i?*, 125.

149 *"I am a messenger forbidding you"*: Daws, *Shoal of Time*, 192, citing "I am a messenger," *Nuhou*, November 18, 1873.

150 *renewed it on a year-to-year basis*: Kuykendall, *The Hawaiian Kingdom: Vol. III, 1874–1893*, 381, citing Mott Smith to Gibson, March 29, 1883.

150 *"inspired with the idea"*: Ibid., 387.

150 *News of the secret amendment*: Ibid., 392, citing the *Daily Bulletin, Hawaiian Hansard*.

150 *the surrounding lands*: Ibid., 435, citing Testimony of Minister of Foreign Affairs Jona and Austin to Carter, personal, April 10, 1889, in the H.A.P. Carter Collection in State Archives of Hawai'i.

151   *"the acquisition by the United States"*: Ibid., 398.

151   *Hawaiian sovereignty and jurisdiction*: Ibid., 397.

151   *"would be the first step of annexation"*: Sheldon, "The Biography of Joseph K. Nawahi," 78.

151   *objected to the cession*: Van Dyke, *Who Owns the Crown Lands of Hawai'i?*, 128, citing Kuykendall, who in turn cites the *Advertiser* and and the *Bulletin* of July 13, 1892.

152   *"The new Constitution"*: "Signing away his powers; King Kalakaua agrees to the constitution.," *New York Times*, August 7, 1887.

152   *he collapsed on the bed*: Gibson, *The Diaries of Walter Murray Gibson, 1886, 1887*, 164.

152   *where he had stored the manuscript* Ibid., 174.

153   *his last word was "Hawai'i"*: Ibid., 179, citing "Coast Jottings," *Daily Bulletin*, Feb. 8, 1888; *Daily Alta California*, Jan. 23, 1888; *Pacific Commercial Advertiser*, Feb. 7, 1888.

153   *"the color of his soul"*: Thurston, *Memoirs*, vol. 2, 53.

153   *she began to question her teachers*: She wrote in her memoir, "Could it be possible, I thought, that a son of one of my early instructors, the child of such a lovely and amiable Christian mother, could so far forget the spirit of that religion his parents taught, and be so carried away with political passion, as to be guilty of murder?" Liliuokalani, *Hawaii's Story*, 183.

154   *How—laughable"*: Diary of Lili'uokalani, 1887, entry for November 14, 1887, State Archives of Hawai'i.

154   *A three-person commission*: Van Dyke, *Who Owns the Crown Lands of Hawai'i?*, 90.

154   *the income previously spent*: A document to this effect from Hawai'i's supreme court described the king's predicament: "Whereas the Grantor is owing certain sums of money which he is unable immediately to pay in full and it hath been agreed between himself and his creditors or the majority of them that all his real estate and certain of his personal property hereinafter mentioned and all the revenues from the Crown Lands be conveyed and assigned or otherwise as hereinafter expressed assured unto the Trustees for the uses and purposes and with the powers and subject to the conditions hereinafter." Kalākaua Deed of Trust, November 1887, First Circuit Court, Equity 611, State Archives of Hawai'i.

154   *Kalākaua's lavish spending*: Forbes, *Bibliography*, vol. 4, 290.

154   *"It is true that I have been humbled"*: The king continued, ". . . but water

is the power which will wash away all filth; water is the force which will quench fire of the white-hot heat; water is the source which will bring forth good deeds; and water is the element which will sustain life. It was your group and their group which ignited the fire; and mine, is to pour water upon it." Kalākaua to Robert Wilcox, 9 April 1888, original in Hawaiian, trans. Jack Matthews, David W. Forbes Collection, Kalākaua Letters Part III, State Archives of Hawai'i.

155 *"very curious, & new"*: Forbes, *Bibliography*, vol. 4. The publisher was Charles L. Webster, which was part-owned by Mark Twain.

155 *a partner-swapping game*: The definition of 'ume is "a sexual game; to draw, pull, attract." Mary Kawena Pukui and Samuel H. Elbert, *New Pocket Hawaiian Dictionary* (Honolulu: University of Hawai'i Press, 1992), 139.

155 *a ball of twine was rolled*: Robert Louis Stevenson, *Travels in Hawai'i* (Honolulu: University of Hawai'i Press, 1991), xx, from an introduction to the book by A. Grove Day. It may also have been a game known as *kilu*, in which a player chants as he tosses a small gourd or a coconut shell, known as the kilu, toward an object placed in front of one of the opposite sex; if he hit the goal he claimed a kiss, according to David Malo, chapter 42, cited by Ulukau, the Hawaiian Electronic Library.

155 *"The full dress is believed"*: Kathleen Dickenson Mellen, *An Island Kingdom Passes: Hawai'i Becomes American* (New York: Hastings House, 1958), 218.

155 *"I can get my poi"*: Allen, *Kalakaua*, 210.

156 *"How sorry I am"*: Diary of Lili'uokalani, 1887, entry for November 20, 1887, State Archives of Hawai'i.

156 *Hawaiians also began seeking her out*: Kuykendall, *The Hawaiian Kingdom: Vol. III, 1874–1893*, 415.

156 *two Hawaiian loyalists paid her a visit*: "I advise them to use only respectful words and no threats but to explain the situation to him (Kalākaua) how everything & the state of the Country might be changed should he abdicate if only for a year. Then he should take the reigns again and reign peaceably the rest of his life." Ibid., 415. Kuykendall notes that the two W's in Liliu's diary entry for that day are believed to stand for Robert W. Wilcox and Charles B. Wilson.

156 *she would rule until he returned*: Diary of Lili'uokalani, 1888, entry for January 16, 1888, State Archives of Hawai'i.

157   *again called her kipi*: Ibid., entry for January 21, 1888.

157   *"what he said on Wednesday was a threat"*: Ibid., entry for January 21. It is not clear whether Lili'u is referring to Spreckels, but he was called by that nickname in Hawaii.

157   *"the strange life of the Pacific whites"*: Claire Harman, *Myself and the Other Fellow: A Life of Robert Louis Stevenson* (HarperCollins, 2005), 355.

158   *a private corporation*: Robert Weyeneth, *Kapi'olani Park: A History* (Honolulu: Native Books, 2002).

158   *decorated with such "South Sea curiosities"*: Stevenson, *Travels in Hawaii*, 119–20, letter from Robert Louis Stevenson to Adelaide Boodle, April 6, 1889.

158   *one of the king's favorite dishes*: Stevenson, *Travels in Hawaii*, xix, written by A. Grove Day.

158   *"The ocean jewel to the island king"*: Robert Louis Stevenson, *The Works of Robert Louis Stevenson* (W. Heinemann in association with Chatto and Windus, Cassell and Longmans, Green, 1922), vol. 8, 218.

159   *"a very fine, intelligent fellow"*: Stevenson, *Travels in Hawaii*, 94, citing Robert Louis Stevenson's letter to Charles Baxter, February 8, 1889.

159   *The huge tree in front of the main house*: Linnea, *Princess Ka'iulani*, 19–20.

160   *Forth from her land to mine she goes*: Stevenson, *The Works of Robert Louis Stevenson*, Vol. 8, 218. He added a postscript: "Written in April to Kaiulani in the April of her age and at Waikiki within easy walk of Kaiulani's Banyan, When she comes to my land and her father's and the rain beats upon the window (as I fear it will), let her look at this page; it will be like a weed gathered and preserved at home; and she will remember her own Islands and the shadow of the mighty tree, and she will hear the peacocks screaming in the dusk and the wind blowing in the palms and she will think of her father sitting there alone."

160   *no more than a year or so*: James W. Robertson to H.A.P. Carter, 28 March 1889, David W. Forbes Collection, Kalākaua Letters Part III, State Archives of Hawai'i.

160   *"I have just been a week away alone"*: Stevenson, *Travels in Hawaii*, 127–29, Letter from Robert Louis Stevenson to Charles Baxter, May 10, 1889.

161   *"They are true Hawaiians"*: Lili'uokalani, *Hawaii's Story*, 196.

162   *a copy from his studies abroad*: The king had already read Machiavelli's masterwork, but he urged Wilcox to do so, saying, "The book is suitable for all of you, the Politicians of the days to come, to read." Kalākaua

to Robert Wilcox, 9 April 1883, David W. Forbes Collection, Kalākaua Letters Part III, State Archives of Hawai'i.

162 "... her brother whose weakness and lack of capacity she understands": Gina Sobrero Wilcox, An Italian Baroness in Hawai'i: The Travel Diary of Gina Sobrero, Bride of Robert Wilcox, 1887, trans. Edgar Knowlton (Honolulu: Hawaiian Historical Society, 1991), 112–23.

163 Kalākaua spent the night at his boathouse: Iaukea and Watson, By Royal Command, 130.

163 troops running toward the Armory: Lili'uokalani, Hawaii's Story, 200.

163 "riding around that day covered in leis": W. D. Alexander to Arthur Alexander, 1 August 1889, Alexander & Baldwin Collection, Hawaiian Mission Children's Society, Folder 204.

164 Six of Wilcox's men died: Kuykendall, The Hawaiian Kingdom: Vol. III, 1874–1893, 424–29.

164 cut the size of the King's Guard: Ibid., 431–32.

164 "His enthusiasm was great": Lili'uokalani, Hawaii's Story, 201.

164 "Today our homeland is being run": Mellen, An Island Kingdom Passes, 240–41.

164 a three-to-one margin: Thrum, Hawaiian Almanac and Annual for 1891, 56.

165 bills amending the 1887 constitution: Kuykendall, The Hawaiian Kingdom: Vol. III, 1874–1893, 464–65.

165 "ought to be torn limb from limb": Ibid., 464, citing the Daily Bulletin and Pacific Commercial Advertiser, September 10, 1890.

165 production had quadrupled: Thrum, Hawaiian Almanac and Annual for 1894, 19.

166 $12.16 million of Hawai'i's total exports: Ibid., 28.

166 a tiny fraction of the value: Hoyt, Davies, 130.

166 By far the largest producer: Thrum, Hawaiian Almanac and Annual for 1891, 61.

166 Lili'u was one of those shareholders: Diary of Lili'uokalani, 1888, cash accounts for 1888 noting Waimanalo Stock Certificates, State Archives of Hawai'i.

166 weariness had come over him: Iaukea and Watson, By Royal Command, 132.

167 illness prevented him: On the twenty-second, Kalākaua wrote to a dignitary apologizing for not being present at a dinner. David W. Forbes Collection, Kalākaua Letters Part III, Kalākaua to William H. Cornwell, 22

November 1890—"I had eaten something . . . that disagreed with me, and made me very sick and [I] vomited [sic] severely and [it] made dizzy. In that mood I laid down intending to dress soon as the dizziness passed over, but it hung on [and] I even feel it now. . . . I render due apologies for my conduct and feel very sorry, for I have never in my life lost an engagement."

167   *"those of native birth"*: Liliʻuokalani, *Hawaii's Story*, 205.

167   *O wai keia?"*: Iaukea and Watson, *By Royal Command*, 132.

168   *one of the largest and most luxurious hotels*: As described in http://www.sfgate.com/cgi-bin/article.cgi?f=/c/a/2009/08/22/MNB919BDP8.DTL.

168   *an exhausting round of social engagements*: John E. Baur, "When Royalty Came to California," *California History* 67, no. 4 (December 1988): 254.

168   *"His Majesty turned to our President"*: Henry Heyman to George MacFarlane, 26 January 1891, David W. Forbes Collection, Liliʻuokalani Letters Part II, State Archives of Hawaiʻi.

169   *"My last groggy memory"*: Kristin Zambucka, *Kalakaua* (Honolulu: Mana Publishing, 1983), 100–02.

169   *"A spontaneous ovation"*: Kalākaua to (James W. Robertson), 1 January 1891, David W. Forbes Collection, Kalākaua Letters Part III, State Archives of Hawaiʻi.

170   *cirrhosis of the liver*: Williams, *Deaths and Funerals of Major Hawaiian Aliʻi*, 81–82.

170   *"Greetings to you"*: Zambucka, *Kalakaua*, 98-99, citing an eyewitness account by George MacFarlane, first published in the *Paradise of the Pacific*, February 1891.

171   *huge headlines updating the king's condition*: "King Kalākaua Dead: The Kingdom's Sad Bereavement," *Pacific Commercial Advertiser*, January 30, 1891, 2.

171   *"Oh Lord! Oh Jesus Christ"*: "Kalākaua Dead: Last Hours of the Hawaiʻian Monarch," *San Francisco Chronicle*, January 21, 1891.

171   *"both soothing and comforting in the highest degree"*: George W. Woods to John A. Cummins, 26 January 1891, David W. Forbes Collection, Kalākaua Letters Part III, State Archives of Hawaiʻi.

172   *"I honestly hope that there will be no need"*: Davies to Cleghorn, 21 January 1891, David W. Forbes Collection, Cleghorn Letter Part I, State Archives of Hawaiʻi.

173 *"I solemnly swear"*: Minutes of the Privy Council, January 29, 1891, Foreign and Executive Office. State Archives of Hawai'i

173 *"Say yes"*: Lili'uokalani, *Hawaii's Story*, 210.

174 *"I was so overcome by the death"*: Ibid., 209.

175 *she wept and clasped her hands*: "Joy Changed to Grief," *New York Times*, reprinting a story that appeared in the *San Francisco Post*, February 23, 1891.

175 *"When the stricken woman leaned forward"*: "Kalakaua Dead," *Bulletin Publishing Company*, 1891, special section on death of Kalākaua, pages not numbered.

175 *The plaintive cries of the mourners*: "Joy Changed to Grief," *New York Times*, reprinting a story that appeared in the *San Francisco Post*, February 23, 1891.

175 *"The King went cheerfully and patiently to work"*: Lili'uokalani, *Hawaii's Story*, 206–07.

10: Enemies in the Household

177 *the atonal dirges*: Iaukea and Watson, *By Royal Command*, 135. Curtis Iaukea, who attended Kapi'olani in the first moments of her grief and who also attended the late king's funeral, discussed the art of wailing in his memoir.

177 *"senseless wailing"*: *Pacific Commercial Advertiser*, February 16, 1891.

178 *six torchbearers on each side*: "This service, so far from being, as has been alleged, idolatrous, had no more suggestion of paganism than can be found in the Masonic or other worship," Lili'u later wrote, defending the ritual. Lili'uokalani, *Hawaii's Story*, 215.

178 *Robert Louis Stevenson, living in Samoa*: Robert Louis Stevenson and Mehew Ernest, *Selected Letters of Robert Louis Stevenson* (New Haven, Conn.: Yale University Press, 2001), x.

179 *"The occasion is a sad one"*: Stevenson to Lili'u okalani, March 1891, State Archives of Hawai'i .

179 *nearing the height of his literary fame*: Harman, *Myself and the Other Fellow*, 424.

179 *"Her gentle and gracious demeanor"*: Kuykendall, *The Hawaiian Kingdom: Vol. III, 1874–1893*, 481, citing *The Friend*, March 1891.

179 *"correct what I consider corrupt practices"*: Lili'u okalani to A.F. Judd, 16

February 1891, David W. Forbes Collection, Lili'u okalani Letters Part II, State Archives of Hawai'i.

180 *Wilcox appealed to her:* Wilcox to Lili'uokalani, 24 February 1889, David W. Forbes Collection, Lili'uokalani Letters Part II, State Archives of Hawai'i.

180 *the queen's supposed love affair:* There was no convincing evidence of this alleged affair between Lili'u and Wilson.

180 *"smash his printing materials":* The chamberlain believed that it was Lili'u's head of the household guards who had first suggested to her the ill-advised idea of smashing the presses. Robertson to Cleghorn, 21 September 1891, David W. Forbes Collection, Cleghorn Letters Part I, State Archives of Hawai'i.

181 *"not trying to do too much":* Bishop to Lili'uokalani, 5 March 1891, David W. Forbes Collection, Lili'uokalani Letters Part II, State Archives of Hawai'i.

181 *"no likelihood":* Kuykendall, *The Hawaiian Kingdom: Vol. III, 1874–1893*, 481, citing the *San Francisco Examiner*, January 25, 1891.

182 *"No one could be more opposed":* Claus Spreckels, "The Future of the Sandwich Islands," *North American Review*, March 1891, 287–91.

182 *the publication of Alfred T. Mahan's book:* Alfred Thayer Mahan, *The Influence of Sea Power Upon History, 1660–1783* (New York: Little, Brown, 1918), originally published in 1890.

182 *Britain would formalize its relationship:* I. C. Campbell, *A History of the Pacific Islands* (Berkeley, Calif.: University of California Press, 1989), 147.

183 *"there are only three places":* Michael J. Devine, "John W. Foster and the Struggle for the Annexation of Hawaii," *Pacific Historical Review* 46, no. 1 (February 1977): 29, citing Blaine to Harrison, August 10, 1891, in *The Correspondence between Benjamin Harrison and James G. Blaine, 1882–1893*, Albert T. Volwiler, ed. (Philadelphia, 1940), 174.

183 *he had it translated and placed:* May, *Imperial Democracy*, 8.

184 *a mutton lunch and a reviving sea-bath:* Lili'uokalani, *Hawaii's Story*, 221–22.

184 *she joined her husband:* Robertson to Cleghorn, 21 September 1891.

184 *"Madam, I believe your husband is dying":* Robertson to Parker, 27 August 1891, David W. Forbes Collection, Lili'uokalani Letters Part II, State Archives of Hawai'i, and *Daily Bulletin* account of John Dominis's death and funeral, undated, Cleghorn scrapbook, State Archives of Hawai'i.

185   *"that larger and grander brotherhood"*: Liliʻuokalani , *Hawaii's Story*, 224.

185   *"You and papa"*: Liliʻuokalani to Kaʻiulani, 18 September 1891, David W. Forbes Collection, Cleghorn Letters Part I, State Archives of Hawaiʻi.

185   *it had become so lonesome*: Rose Robertson to Cleghorn, 21 September 1891, David W. Forbes Collection, Cleghorn Letters Part I, State Archives of Hawaiʻi.

185   *"it was always a sad day to me"*: Liliʻuokalani to Kaʻiulani, 21 October 1891, David W. Forbes Collection, Cleghorn Letters Part I, State Archives of Hawaiʻi.

186   *"I will have to look to your Father"*: Liliʻuokalani to Kaʻiulani, 11 November 1891, David W. Forbes Collection, Cleghorn Letters Part I, State Archives of Hawaiʻi.

186   *Lilʻiu forbade the removal*: George Trousseau to Frank P. Hastings, 10 October 1891, David W. Forbes Collection, Kalākaua Letters Part III, State Archives of Hawaiʻi.

186   *He became convinced*: "Thurston I met in San Francisco, and I was sorry to see how his patriotic enthusiasm for Hawaiʻi had changed into a sort of hopelessness; he said that, with the large majority of 14,000 voters blind enough to be beguiled by Wilcox and Bush, whom neither monarch nor ministry could suppress, he did not see much future for Hawaiian Independence, which he thought depended upon the commercial credit of the country. As I have said, I was sorry to learn that he took this view; for a few years ago I thought him one of the most hopeful and patriotic sons of Hawaii." Walker to Cleghorn, 21 September 1891, David W. Forbes Collection, Cleghorn Letters Part I, State Archives of Hawaiʻi.

187   *"The poor Queen has not had an easy task"*: Ibid.

187   *"My poor John"*: Diary of Liliʻuokalani, 1892, entry for January 1, 1892, Bishop Museum Archives.

187   *"every inch a queen"*: Allen, *Betrayal*, 268, citing *Paradise of the Pacific*, June 1892.

188   *they decided to form a group*: Thurston, *Memoirs*, vol. 2, 134.

188   *the secret Committee of Thirteen*: Kuykendall, *The Hawaiian Kingdom: Vol. III, 1874–1893*, 347–48. Kuykendall says the Committee of Thirteen from 1887 was so top secret its members weren't definitively known, but he speculates the list included Ashford, Atkinson, Major Benson, Castle, and Dole.

188 *He had $9,200 invested in sugar:* Richard D. Weigle, "Sugar and the Hawaiian Revolution," *Pacific Historical Review* 16, no. 1 (February 1947): 54, citing the Blount Report.

189 *fifty cents for admission:* Moses Handy, ed., *The Official Directory of the World's Columbian Exposition, May 1st to October 30th, 1893* (Chicago: W. B. Conkey Company, 1893), 195.

189 *a private concession:* Neil Thomas Proto, *The Rights of My People: Liliuokalani's Enduring Battle with the United States 1893–1917* (Algora Publishing, 2009), 39.

189 *two years at Columbia University:* Ibid., 39.

189 *"an exceedingly sympathetic administration here":* Thurston, *Memoirs*, vol. 2, 136.

190 *he'd prepared for a riot:* Lili'u recounted that there were 300 strong men, most of whom had little money or property and earned their livings as common day laborers. She described them as "roughs" under the direction of Wilcox and Bush, whom she called "two soreheads who are *huhu* (angry) because I did not make them Ministers as the commencement of my reign." She ended her diary entry that day with a question, "Will they fire the town?" Diary of Lili'uokalani, 1892, entry for February 3, 1892, Bishop Museum Archive.

190 *the costumed sprites marched:* Else Waldron, *Honolulu 100 Years Ago* (Honolulu: Fisher Print. Co., 1967), 80-81.

190 *"Dream that a dead man wanted to strangle me":* Diary of Lili'uokalani, 1892, entry for February 14, 1892, Bishop Museum Archives.

191 *"governed by dolls":* Kuykendall, *The Hawaiian Kingdom: Vol. III, 1874–1893*, 528.

191 *Their dollar value had dropped:* Thrum, *Hawaiian Almanac and Manual for 1893*, 28; Thrum, *Hawaiian Almanac and Manual for 1894*, 24.

191 *the ceremony lacked the "elegance":* Allen, *Betrayal*, 262.

191 *"a disagreeable day":* Diary of Lili'uokalani, 1892, entry for January 28, 1892, Bishop Museum Archives.

192 *"It is a shame to cut down":* Cleghorn to Ka'iulani, 15 August 1892, David W. Forbes Collection, Cleghorn Letters Part II, State Archives of Hawai'i.

192 *"My health is very good":* Lili'uokalani to Ka'iulani, 7 June 1892, State Archives of Hawai'i.

193 *"how strange she should have told me"*: Diary of Lili'uokalani, 1892, entry for July 8, 1892, Bishop Museum Archives.

193 *"pocket money"*: Diary of Lili'uokalani, 1892, entry for August 16, 1892, Bishop Museum Archives.

194 *"The country is on the verge"*: *The Golden Era*, vol. I, no. 1, September 1, 1892, State Archives of Hawai'i.

194 *her German soothsayer*: The Fräulein married Charles D. Chase, who was the vice president of the Island Realty Co. as well as a notary public, in Honolulu in 1894 and died two years later, on May 24, 1896.

194 *a $100,000 loan from W.G. Irwin*: "Hawai'i Should be Annexed; That Is the Belief of William G. Irwin, Spreckels' Business Partner," *New York Times*, January 29, 1893. Adler, *Claus Spreckels*, on page 236 notes that Spreckels called in debts incurred during Lili'u's reign.

195 *a tutorial on geopolitics*: Hoyt, *Davies*, 159–60.

195 *requesting aid from a U.S. warship*: It is not clear from the letters and records that still exist how seriously she took this chilling and prescient information. Wodehouse, however, took it very seriously: He fired off a telegram to his superiors in Whitehall requesting an additional British warship be sent to Honolulu to protect British interests, but the Foreign Secretary turned him down unequivocally. There is no indication that Wodehouse directly told Lili'u that she should not expect help from the British. Kuykendall, *The Hawaiian Kingdom: Vol. III, 1874–1893*, 573–74.

195 *"the enemy is in the household"*: Anonymous to Liliuokalani, Honolulu December 17, 1892, David W. Forbes Collection, Liliuokalani Letters, State Archives of Hawaii. Mr. Forbes was unable to locate the original letter or identify the author, but it is reprinted in Liliuokalani's statement to U. S. Commissioner Blount (p. 397), wherein the Queen says: "The above was written by a gentleman in whose word I have great confidence as a man who had the best interest of Hawai'i at heart."

11: Pious Adventurers

199 *two-thirds of the kingdom's registered voters*: Lili'uokalani, *Hawaii's Story*, 231. A slightly higher number of 8,000 signatures comes from *Onipa'a: Five Days in the History of the Hawaiian Nation* (Office of Hawaiian

Affairs, 1994), 38, citing finance minister William Cornwell. However, the number of formal petitions lodged with the legislature and entered into the record by a noble or representative in 1892 is lower than either of these estimates, numbering a few thousand.

199 *she asked her brother-in-law*: Cleghorn to Ka'iulani, 28 January 1893, David W. Forbes Collection, Cleghorn Letters Part II, State Archives of Hawai'i.

200 *"The haole Members of the House"*: "Ka Hookuu Ana O Ka Ahaolelo," or "The Queen's Speech for the Closure of the 1892 Legislature," from the *Hawai'i Holumua*, January 18, 1893, 2, columns 2 and 3, as translated and reprinted in *Mai Poina, Visitor's Guide 2010*.

202 *Lili'u had arranged with the society*: William De Witt Alexander, *History of Later Years of the Hawaiian Monarchy, and the Revolution of 1893* (Honolulu: Hawaiian Gazette Company, 1896), 30–31.

202 *the role as Lili'u's protector*: Blount Report, 512.

202 *"You will have to be brave today"*: Ibid.

203 *their president held the speech*: Alexander, *History of Later Years of the Hawaiian Monarchy*, 32.

203 *"I was requested by my people"*: Blount Report, 907–10.

203 *The four cabinet members*: Ibid.

203 *"Gentlemen, I do not wish to hear any more advice"*: *Pacific Commercial Advertiser*, January 16, 1893.

204 *"How dare you say that"*: W. D. Alexander to Arthur Alexander, 19 January 1893, folder 207, Alexander & Baldwin Collection, Hawaaian Children's Mission Society.

204 *Lili'u threatened to go out*: Alexander, *History of Later Years of the Hawaiian Monarchy*, 32. Thurston corroborates the part about the ministers fearing violence, saying that they left the palace by the rear way.

204– *mortgage their ranch to William G. Irwin*: Bernard Brian Wellmon, *The*
205 *Parker Ranch: A History* (Fort Worth, Texas: Texas Christian University, 1969), 138, citing a trust deed enacted in 1887, Parker Ranch Files, Kamuela, Hawai'i.

205 *"The whole thing was a roller coaster ride"*: Joseph Brennan, *The Parker Ranch of Hawaii: The Saga of a Ranch and a Dynasty* (New York: John Day, 1974), 113–14.

205 *"declare the throne vacant"*: Thurston, *Memoirs*, vol. 2, 153.

205 *waiting for close to four hours*: Diary of A. F. Judd, entry for January 14,

1893; he wrote that he had "waited + waited" in the palace's throne room. Judd Collection, Bishop Museum Archives.

206 *slipping drafts of the proposed constitution:* Lili'uokalani, *Hawaii's Story,* 230.

206 *Return to your homes and keep the peace:* W. D. Alexander to Arthur Alexander, 19 January 1893, folder 207, Alexander & Baldwin Collection, Hawaiian Children's Mission Society.

206 *"She was under great emotion":* Onipa'a, 39.

207 *"to preserve peace in the realm":* Ibid.

207 *the Hui Kālai'āina in their formal black frock coats:* Alexander, *History of Later Years of the Hawaiian Monarchy,* 35.

207– *"enough arms and ammunition":* "Notes," *Hawaiian Gazette,* January 24,
208 1893, 7.

208 *"The legislature will prorogue on Saturday":* Sanford Dole to George Dole, 12 January 1893, Hawaiian Children's Mission Society.

208 *he took a group of school boys:* Dole, *Memoirs,* vol. 1, 73.

209 *"to carry out her scheme":* Ibid.

209 *one of the sons of Lili'u's teachers:* Family lineage according to http://files. usgwarchives.org/hi/statewide/newspapers/importan31nnw.txt.

209 *strong ties to the sugar industry:* Sumner J. La Croix and Christopher Grandy, "The Political Instability of Reciprocal Trade and the Overthrow of the Hawaiian Kingdom," *Journal of Economic History* 57, no. 1 (March 1997): 161–89. Also, Richard D. Weigle, "Sugar and the Hawaiian Revolution," *Pacific Historical Review* 16, no. 1 (February 1947): 57.

209 *no skaters allowed without masks: Pacific Commercial Advertiser,* January 13, 1893, advertisement.

209 *preparing for a provisional government:* Albertine Loomis, *For Whom Are the Stars?* (Honolulu: University of Hawai'i Press, 1977), 9.

209 *the queen would be forced to abdicate:* Diary of A. F. Judd, entry for January 15, 1893, Judd Collection, Bishop Museum Archives.

210 *"We will not take any further chances":* Thurston, *Memoirs,* vol. 2, 253–54.

210 *Those "damned cowards":* Ibid.

210 *"Her Majesty's Ministers desire":* "Notice," 16 January 1893, David W. Forbes Collection, Lili'uokalani Letters Part II, State Archives of Hawai'i.

211 *The Committee of Safety (all haole):* Six were Hawaiian citizens by birth or naturalization, five Americans, one Englishman, and one German,

according to Kuykendall, *The Hawaiian Kingdom: Vol. III, 1874-1893,* 587.

211 *Lili'u was surrounded by corrupt advisers:* Blount Report, 208.

211 *totaling many millions of dollars:* An unsigned paper discussing economic interests in the islands for 1893 states "American property interests in Hawai'i have become so great that it is no longer a simple question of political advantage to the United States, or of charity or justice to a weak neighbor, which the authorities at Washington have to deal with; but in addition thereto, it is a question involving the fortunes of thousands of their own flesh and blood, and millions of dollars worth of American property." Dole Collection, Box 1, Papers 1893, State Archives of Hawai'i.

211 *an earlier attack of grippe:* Thurston wrote, "I had had a rather severe attack of grippe during December, and had been living strenuously since Saturday morning, having been under pressure almost continuously, night and day. When I got home [from the Armory meeting and ensuing meetings with individuals], I collapsed; a doctor, being called, ordered me to go to bed and stay there, which I did. Owing to my physical condition, I did not attend the meeting at the home of H.Waterhouse that evening; and I knew nothing, until later, of what occurredthere or that leadership had been tendered Sanford B. Dole." *Memoirs,* vol. 2, 159.

212 *a "revolutionary" act:* Ibid., 152.

212 *"Nothing! Nothing!":* Pacific Commercial Advertiser, January 16, 1893.

212 *"wants us to sleep on a slumbering volcano":* Thurston, *Memoirs,* vol. 2, 154.

212 *the crowd shouted Baldwin down:* Onipa'a, 64.

212 *The city was eerily quiet:* Blount Report, 1034.

212 *the life and property of American residents:* May, *Imperial Democracy,* 13. According to the 1894 Thrum's *Almanac,* as of the 1890 census there were 1,928 Americans out of a total population of 89,990. Thrum classified Americans separately in the census from haole, whose population in 1890 was reported at 7,495.

213 *J. B. Atherton: New York Times,* April 9, 1903, obituary of J. B. Atherton.

213 *urged him to use his influence:* Testimony of J. B. Atherton, *Reports of Committee on Foreign Relations 1789–1901 Volume 6* (hereafter called "The Morgan Report"), U.S. Senate, 1894, 954–955.

213 *"the existing critical circumstances":* Blount Report, 208.

213   *the Boston's walrus-mustachioed captain:* It is unclear what orders the commander of the USS *Boston* reviewed before deciding to land troops. See page 736 of the Morgan Report.

213   *"My desire is that you remain neutral":* At least according to Lieutenant Laird, who testified at the Morgan Commission: "The CHAIRMAN. Was there anything in the orders or instructions you received that looked to the establishment of any government different from that of the Queen? Mr. LAIRD. None. The burden of the orders was to look out for the lives and property of American citizens." Morgan Report, 732–45.

215   *Henry Berger's band:* Item on public concert by the Royal Hawaiian Military Band (under the direction of Professor H. Berger), *Pacific Commercial Advertiser*, January 16, 1893.

215   *Speaking with difficulty:* Blount Report, 907–10.

216   *a room dominated by tall bookshelves:* Based on a photograph taken during the evening hours of January 16, 1893, of the four newly named members of the executive council of the Provisional Government, from the Bishop Museum and reprinted in *Onipaʻa*, 65.

216   *"passed a very unpleasant night":* Kuykendall, *The Hawaiian Kingdom: Vol. III, 1874–1893*, 597.

217   *"you have a great opportunity":* Dole, *Memoirs*, vol. 1, 78.

217   *headed as a group down Merchant Street:* Ibid., 56–57.

217   *an employee of Castle & Cooke:* Frost & Frost, AIA, *Aliʻiolani Hale: A Century of Growth and Change, 1872–1977* (Honolulu: Department of Accounting and General Services, State of Hawaii, 1979), 65.

218   *"Her Majesty proceeded on the last day":* Dole, *Memoirs*, vol. 1, 62–63.

219   *Wearing an all-white suit and a straw boater:* Based on a photograph taken on January 17, 1893, from the State Archives of Hawaiʻi and reprinted in *Onipa ʻa*, 86.

Chapter 12: Crime of the Century

220   *Marshal Wilson had asked the cabinet:* Statement of Charles B. Wilson, Blount Report, 1037.

220   *272 household guards . . . :* Onipaʻa, 92.

221   *less than fifty men:* Blount Report, 1037.

221   *an exaggerated idea of the force:* Alexander, *A Brief History of the Hawaiian People*, 55. As to the ministers' reluctance to fight back, Alexander

wrote: "To judge from their conduct, the Queen's Cabinet were over-awed by the unanimity and determination of the foreign community, and probably bad an exaggerated idea of the force at the command of the Committee of Safety. They shrank from the responsibility of causing fruitless bloodshed, and sought a valid excuse for inaction, which they thought they found in the presence of the United States troops on shore, and in the well known sympathy of the American Minister with the opposition."

221 *"I, Liliuokalani, by the Grace of God"*: Lili'uokalani to S. B. Dole, Esq., Forbes Collection. Mr. Forbes notes that this document was received by Mr. Dole on behalf of the provisional government and endorsed as follows: "Received by the hands of the late cabinet this 17th day of January, 1893. Sanford B. Dole, Chairman of Executive Council of Provisional Government."

222 *they worked at the back of the building*: Frost & Frost, AIA, *Ali'iolani Hale*, 1872–1977, 66.

222 *"Things turned out better than I expected"*: Diary of Lili'uokalani, 1893, entry for Tuesday, January 17, 1893, State Archives of Hawai'i.

222 *she looked forward to the bouquet*: Bernice Pi'ilani Cook Irwin, *I Knew Queen Liliuokalani*, 98.

223 *Perhaps Lili'u heard*: Albert P. Taylor, "The Loot of the Coral Throne," *Paradise of the Pacific*, December 1925.

223 *Clerks hurried in and out*: Ibid.

223 *she reluctantly agreed*: Diary of Lili'uokalani, 1893, entry for January 18, 1893, State Archives of Hawai'i.

223 *"remain perfectly passive"*: Diary of Lili'uokalani, 1893, entry for March 20, 1893, State Archives of Hawai'i.

223 *"How I have regretted this whole affair"*: The Hawaiian Mission Children's Society, Honolulu, has a copy of this letter, which is in a private collection.

224 *he ordered the disbanding*: James W. Robertson to Executive Council, 19 January, 1893, David W. Forbes Collection, Lili'uokalani Letters Part II, State Archives of Hawai'i.

224 *the new government specially chartered a steamer*: Sanford B. Dole to Lili'uokalani, 18 January 1893, David W. Forbes Collection, Lili'uokalani Letters Part II, State Archives of Hawai'i.

224 *an itemized list of the late king's belongings*: Cecil Brown to Sanford B.

Dole, 20 January 1893, David W. Forbes Collection, Lili'uokalani Letters Part II, State Archives of Hawai'i.

224 *Mounted troops patrolled the streets:* Loomis, *For Whom Are the Stars?*, 41.

225 *The troops nicknamed it "Camp Boston":* Frost & Frost, AIA, *Ali'iolani Hale, 1872–1977,* 67.

225 *he moved into a small room:* Allen, *Dole,* 199, citing interview of Dole by A. P. Taylor.

225 *the "glorious sight" of the "ensign of Freedom":* Kuykendall, *The Hawaiian Kingdom: Vol. III, 1874–1893,* 608.

225 *"Quos dues vult perdere":* W. D. Alexander to Arthur Alexander, 19 January 1893, Alexander & Baldwin Collection, Hawaiian Mission Children's Society.

225 *"Drove by the Palace":* Diary of Lili'uokalani, 1893, entry for February 8, 1893, State Archives of Hawai'i.

226 *she was being privately tutored:* Ka'iulani to Lili'uokalani, 25 September 1892, David W. Forbes Collection, Cleghorn Letters Part II, State Archives of Hawai'i.

226 *missing "Fairy," her white pony:* Ka'iulani to Lili'uokalani, 18 May 1892, David W. Forbes Collection, Cleghorn Letters Part II, State Archives of Hawai'i.

226 *"I have never given the Queen anything":* Archibald Cleghorn to Ka'iulani, 28 January 1893, David W. Forbes Collection, Cleghorn Letters Part II, State Archives of Hawai'i.

227 *the first read "Queen Deposed":* Nancy Webb, *Kaiulani: Crown Princess of Hawai'i* (Honolulu: Mutual Publishing, 1998), 99.

227 *it was better to try and fail:* She wrote, "Perhaps some day the Hawaiians will say, Kaiulani, you could have saved us and you did not try. I will go with you," according to Kuykendall, *The Hawaiian Kingdom: Vol. III, 1874–1893,* 619, and Webb, *Kaiulani,* 100.

227 *"The Hawaiian pear is now fully ripe":* Blount Report, 400. Letter from J. L. Stevens to Secretary of State Foster reprinted in the report.

227 *She talks in a very simple, dignified way:* "Princess Kaiulani Here," *New York Times,* March 2, 1893.

228 *all stamped with the initials VK:* Webb, *Kaiulani,* 111. The young princess's full name was Victoria Kawekiu Lunalilo Kalaninuiahilapalapa Ka'iulani—thus her initials VK.

228– *"The revolution was not a movement of the people"*: Mellen, *An Island King-*
229 *dom Passes*, 275–76.

229 *"The Political Crime of the Century"*: "A Shameful Conspiracy; In Which
the United States Was Made to Play a Part. Queen Liliuokalani's Dethronement.," *New York Times*, November 20, 1893.

229 *"The Hawaiians have 'revoluted'"*: Kuykendall, *The Hawaiian Kingdom:
Vol. III, 1874–1893*, 632, citing the *Fresno Daily Evening Expositor* of
January 28, 1893, and Feburary 1, 1893.

229 *a sophisticated long-sleeved gown*: Webb, *Kaiulani*, 114.

230 *She cashed in the postal savings accounts*: Diary of Liliʻuokalani, 1893,
entry for February 17, 1893, State Archives of Hawaiʻi.

230 *"It is a gloomy day and it rains, rains, rains"*: Diary of Liliʻuokalani, 1893,
entry for February 5, 1893, State Archives of Hawaiʻi.

230 *They were kāhuna*: The word *kahuna* originally meant an expert in any
field. But, with the arrival of foreigners, the meaning narrowed to priest,
sorcerer, magician, wizard, or minister.

230 *offering themselves as sacrifices*: Allen, *Betrayal*, 299. Allen cites the unpublished papers of a Daddy Bray, in a private collection.

230 *"I wish they would not come here"*: Diary of Liliʻuokalani, 1893, entry for
February 13, 1893, State Archives of Hawaiʻi.

231 *Tears filled the eyes of some*: Diary of Liliʻuokalani, 1893, entry for February 17, 1893, State Archives of Hawaiʻi.

231 *"Kaiulani's appearance upon the scene"*: T. E. Evans to Liliʻuokalani,
25 February 1893, David W. Forbes Collection, Liliʻuokalani Letters
Part II, State Archives of Hawaiʻi.

231 *Blount politely declined*: Diary of Liliʻuokalani, 1893, entry for March 29,
1893, State Archives of Hawaiʻi.

232 *"I am more tired from thinking"*: Diary of Liliʻuokalani, 1893, entry for
April 1, 1893, State Archives of Hawaiʻi.

232 *Several hundred spent the evening*: Diary of Liliʻuokalani, 1893, entry for
April 4, 1893, State Archives of Hawaiʻi.

232 *The pro-government Advertiser*: *Pacific Commercial Advertiser*, April 5
and April 6, 1894.

232 *he was arrested, found guilty, and sentenced*: *Pacific Commercial Advertiser*,
June 14, August 23, and August 24, 1893.

232– *Others called him "Paramount Blount"*: Kuykendall, *The Hawaiian King-*
233 *dom: Vol. III, 1874–1893*, 622–24.

233 *"May he be made to suffer"*: Diary of Lili'uokalani, 1893, entry for May 25, 1893, State Archives of Hawai'i.

233 *he turned his attention back*: Cordray, "Claus Spreckels of California," 98–99.

233 *he briefly seemed to favor*: May, *Imperial Democracy*, 14.

234 *"We could get along"*: Blount Report, 975. Interview with Claus Spreckels: "Q. Would you have been willing to have invested your money in that way [to build the ditch on Maui] but for the reciprocity treaty? A. No, sir; I would not. Q. Has most of the irrigation been brought about under the influence of the reciprocity treaty? A. Yes. Q. And the profits, then, have largely come from reciprocity and cheap labor. A. Yes. Q. If both of these were abandoned, what would be the material prospects of the islands? A. There would be no prospects at all. We could get along—the majority of the plantations—without any subsidy if we had labor, but without labor we could not get along at all. Q. You would have to go out into the world and get cheap labor? A. Yes, sir."

234 *"I can't see why"*: Adler, *Claus Spreckels*, 236–37.

235 *"the means of putting me back on the throne"*: Diary of Lili'uokalani, 1893, entry for May 29, 1893, State Archives of Hawai'i.

235 *"Since the days of Shakespeare"*: Adler, *Claus Spreckels*, 237, citing the *Hawaiian Gazette*, October 3, 1893.

235 *"Herr Rothschild von Katzenjammer"*: Ibid., 238, citing the *Hawaiian Star*, June 9, 1893.

235 *"Gold and Silver will not stop lead"*: Adler, 239.

236 *16 men with masks and guns*: Diary of Lili'uokalani, 1893, entry for June 7, 1893, State Archives of Hawai'i.

236 *explosives were planted*: Diary of Lili'uokalani, 1893, entry for August 16, 1893, and August 19, 1893, State Archives of Hawai'i.

236 *Lili'u balked at making him any promises*: "I do not see why I should prevent the working classes from having or making money for themselves," she wrote in her diary, showing a new skepticism toward advisers sympathetic to her. "To watch for Mr. Spreckles interest if it keeps within the pale of the law is all he ought to expect and not more than the law provides for. I said nothing. I never like to make promises." Diary of Lili'uokalani, 1893, entry for July 18, 1893, State Archives of Hawai'i.

237 *"That a deep wrong has been done"*: Blount Report, 595–99.

238 *express to the queen "sincere regret"*: Blount Report, 1190–91.

239 *Willis began by sending greetings*: This dialogue is reconstructed from Lili'u's unusually long diary entry from the day as well as a memorandum signed by Lili'uokalani recounting the interview. Diary of Lili'uokalani, 1893, entry for November 13, 1893, State Archives of Hawai'i; Memorandum, December 16, 1893, MS, National Archives, Diplomatic Posts, Hawai'i, vol. 30, State Archives of Hawai'i. Direct quotes are from these primary sources; otherwise I have paraphrased the dialogue.

240 *"My decision would be, as the law directs"*: Memorandum, December 16, 1893, MS, National Archives, Diplomatic Posts, Hawai'i, vol. 30, State Archives of Hawai'i.

240 *"The brevity and uncertainty"*: Blount Report, 1191.

241 *"Should the Queen ask"*: Ibid., 1191–92.

241 *Perhaps she didn't read the document*: Lili'uokalani, *Hawaii's Story*, 247.

242 *"dangerous for the community and the people"*: National Archives, RG 84, Diplomatic Posts, Hawai'i, vol. 30.

242 *the financial obligations of the provisional government*: Lili'uokalani to Albert Willis, 18 December 1893, David W. Forbes Collection, Lili'uokalani Letters Part II, State Archives of Hawai'i.

243 *"We do not recognize the right"*: Blount Report, 1276.

244 *she mistook the fireworks*: Diary of Lili'uokalani, 1893, entry for December 31, 1893, State Archives of Hawai'i.

Chapter 13: Secrets of the Flower Beds

245 *"Blount's instruments"*: Blount Report, 1195, citing coverage of the event in the *Pacific Commercial Advertiser*, January 18, 1894.

246 *who had sought to relieve the stress*: N. L. Evenhuis, *Barefoot on Lava: The Journals and Correspondence of Naturalist R.C.L. Perkins in Hawai'i, 1892–1901* (Honolulu: Bishop Museum Press, 2007), 23.

246 *"there was no stiffness"*: Blount Report, 1195.

246 *"Annexation is manifest destiny"*: Ibid., 1199.

246 *he sketched a picture*: "We have a party at home devoted to the lost cause and a moneyed influence abroad conspiring for control. We are in the midst of alien races and more alien creeds. There is a clamor of many tongues within our gates; the pressure of foreign governments at the outer walls. Our enemies are powerful and insidious, and though some

work secretly and others openly all are united to defeat the objects of the January revolution . . . There is but one political goal and watchword for us all and that is annexation. It is the beginning and end of our political alphabet." Ibid., 1201.

247 *the entire cache of fireworks:* "It was hard on the boys," the *Advertiser* reported, "but it was a beautiful sight while it lasted." Ibid., 1202.

247 *"One year ago I signed away"*: Diary of Lili'uokalani, 1894, entries for January 17 and January 18, State Archives of Hawai'i.

247 *"A great deal of indignation is felt"*: Blount Report, 1202, citing the *Pacific Commercial Advertiser*, January 18, 1894.

247 *"Kaulana na pua o Hawai'i"*: "Kaulana na pua o Hawai'i" was composed by Ellen Wright Prendergast (Kekoaohiwaikalani) in 1893, after the overthrow, and is performed to this day by the Royal Hawaiian Band on Fridays on the lawn of Iolani Palace. Eleanor Nordyce and Martha Noyes, "'Kaulana Na Pua': A Voice for Sovereignty," *Hawaiian Journal of History* 27 (1993): 27–42.

247 *"evil-hearted messenger"*: Elbert and Māhoe, *Nā Mele o Hawai'i Nei*, 64.

247 *the song was as electrifying*: Loomis, *For Whom Are the Stars?*, 85–86.

248 *The garden that her mother-in-law had first planted*: Description based on "The Trees and Plants of Washington Place," Lili'uokalani Collection, #153, 2, State Archives of Hawai'i.

248 *Lili'u's supporters expressed their opposition*: Helen Geracimos Chapin, *Shaping History: The Role of Newspapers in Hawai'i* (Honolulu: University of Hawai'i Press, 1996), 93.

249 *they began arresting editors for libel*: Chapin, 102.

249 *It metaphorically suggested*: Mellen, *An Island Kingdom Passes*, 298–99.

249 *"Mahope makou o Lili'u-lani"*: Elbert and Māhoe, *Nā Mele o Hawai'i Nei*, 63–64.

250 *"delight[ed]" in orgies, as did her late brother*: "Heathenism in Hawaii," *San Francisco Chronicle*, March 13, 1893.

250 *"The Queen Wanted to Behead"*: "Minister Willis's Mission," *New York Times*, January 14, 1894, 13.

250 *A cartoon from the December 2, 1893 issue of the Judge*: Victor Gillam, "We Draw the Line at This," color lithograph cartoon, *Judge* 25, 6331, December 2, 1893, Bishop Museum Archives, Drawer Ills. press 1–2, Negative no. CP103.862, slide no. XS 30.786.

250 *"Lili to Grover"*: Victor Gillam, "Lili to Grover: 'You listened to my

DOLE-ful tale . . . ' '", color lithograph cartoon, *Judge* 26, 644, February 17, 1894, Bishop Museum Archive, Box: Ga-Gz, Acc. no. 1991.0386.0002.

250   *"They talk of offering me $20,000"*: Diary of Lili'uokalani, 1894, entry for June 16, 1894, State Archives of Hawai'i.

251   *"At all times, day or night"*: Thurston, *Memoirs*, vol. 2, 295.

251   *"Thurston, I have a suggestion"*: Ibid., 288.

251   *"whether any, and if so, what irregularities"*: The Morgan Report, 363, as found on morganreport.org, http://morganreport.org/.

252   *"Hawai'i is an American state"*: Ibid., 364–67.

252   *he decided that proceeding unilaterally*: Whereas in 1874 and 1889, troops had been called into the streets of Honolulu to keep the peace, in 1893 their purpose was ambiguous and their location just a few blocks away from the palace suggests their presence was meant to intimidate the queen rather than protect American interests in the event of civil unrest. Thus, Cleveland was faced with whether to exercise his executive prerogative to command them to attack, and decided not to do so.

252   *Congress did not take the next step*: Kuykendall, *The Hawaiian Kingdom: Vol. III, 1874–1893*, 648.

253   *the "safety valve" that Western expansion had provided*: Frederick Jackson Turner, *The Frontier in American History* (H. Holt, 1921), 280.

253   *"It is certainly a novelty"*: Tom Coffman, *Nation Within: The Story of America's Annexation of the Nation of Hawai'i* (Epicenter, 2003), 161.

254   *feared for their safety*: Dole, *Memoirs*, vol. 1, 157.

254   *"The recognition and the attitude of the Congress"*: Grover Cleveland to H. Widemann, J. Cummins, and S. Parker, 15 August 1894, David W. Forbes Collection, Lili'uokalani Collection, Part II, State Archives of Hawai'i.

255   *a cent of income*: Lili'uokalani, *Hawaii's Story*, 260–61. Several years after her autobiography was published, Lili'u filed suit against the U.S. It was unsuccessful, but she did get a minor payout. For the the last six years of her life, the territorial government paid her $12,000 per year, totaling $72,000.

255   *"For two years I had borne"*: Lili'uokalani, *Hawaii's Story*, 263–64.

255   *"nervous prostration"—a weakness of the nervous system*: Frank Savary Pearce, *A Practical Treatise on Nervous Diseases for the Medical Student and General Practitioner* (D. Appleton, 1904), 295–302.

255   *"contractions" followed by a "delicious slumber"*: Pearce, 102–03.

255   *these increasingly popular pleasure-producing devices:* One such model, the
      Butler Electro-massage Machine of 1888, consisted of a box attached by
      cords to a roller massage tool shaped like a horseshoe that delivered a
      mild electrical shock. Indications were to use it "over the lower abdomen,
      from 10 to 15 minutes. Change the treatment every other day, using the
      vaginal sponge-electrode, and applying roller over lower abdomen ten
      minutes, and lower spine five minutes." The device could be used by pa-
      tients at home "after a lesson or two." Rachel P. Maines, *The Technology of
      Orgasm: "Hysteria," the Vibrator, and Women's Sexual Satisfaction* (Balti-
      more: Johns Hopkins University Press, 2001), 85.

256   *she signed eleven commissions:* Diary of Lili'uokalani, 1894, entry for De-
      cember 29, 1894, State Archives of Hawai'i.

256   *they hid about 300 rifles:* Loomis, *For Whom Are the Stars?*, 124–69. Al-
      though the author of this narrative account of the counterrevolution did
      not provide endnotes to source her materials, this book was the result of
      many years of careful research by the author and her use of an extensive
      collection of papers and notes of N. B. Emerson, who interviewed the par-
      ticipants in the 1895 counterrevolutionary attempt. The Emerson Collec-
      tion is now in the Huntington Library and *For Whom Are the Stars?* is the
      most detailed account in print of the counterrevolution and highly reliable.

256   *he said from Rudolph Spreckels: Trial of a Queen: 1895 Military Tribunal*
      (Honolulu: Judiciary History Center, 1996), 21.

256   *The plan was for the Hawaiians to gather:* Mellen, *An Island Kingdom
      Passes*, 304.

257   *who later received a "gift":* Loomis, *For Whom Are the Stars?*, 147.

257   *"Overthrow to take place tonight":* Ibid., 114.

257   *By Wednesday, the government had imprisoned:* Ibid., 170–171.

258   *"Sugar mills grinding":* Ibid., 169.

258   *protected by her normal guard:* Transcript of the Proceedings of the Mili-
      tary Commission, February 16, 1895, 148, seventeenth day, testimony of
      Lili'uokalani, State Archives of Hawai'i.

258   *"All right; I will go":* Hawaiian Star, January 16,1895.

258   *"Were they crocodile tears?":* Lili'uokalani, private memorandum, March 4,
      1895, MS KC 3/6, Bishop Museum Archives.

259   *she glanced at a stately, life-sized oil portrait:* Rhoda E. A. Hackler and
      Michael D. Horikawa, *'Iolani Palace* (Friends of 'Iolani Palace, 1995), 23.
      This portrait was painted by William Cogswell in 1891.

259 *"Iolani Palace. Jan 16th 1895"*: Lili'uokalani, private memorandum, January 16, 1895, MS MC 2.9 1985.415, Bishop Museum Archives.

260 *"The sound of their never-ceasing footsteps"*: Lili'uokalani, *Hawaii's Story*, 270.

Chapter 14: Kingdom Come

261 *they found a rusty but usable cache:* "Deadly Dynamite Unearthed," *Pacific Commercial Advertiser*, January 17, 1895, 1.

261 *"Course to pursue":* The State Archives of Hawai'i has a guide to its very large Lili'uokalani Collection (M-93) including a subgroup referred to as "seized documents." These papers were "seized" by Judd on January 16, 1895, after Lili'u was arrested. Judd inventoried and numbered the documents.

262 *He also confiscated:* Diary of A. F. Judd, January 17, 1895, Bishop Museum Archives.

262 *Judd swept up her personal and official documents:* Loomis, *For Whom Are the Stars?*, 183.

262 *Lili'u faced her first full day:* The bedroom where Lili'u was imprisoned had been, until a few days earlier, the office of the republic's auditor general. *Hawaiian Star*, January 16, 1895.

262 *a 21-gun salute at noon:* Transcript of the Proceedings of the Military Commission, February 17, 1895, 148, testimony of Robert Parker, State Archives of Hawai'i, 5, 19–23; also "Our Second Anniversary," *Pacific Commercial Advertiser*, January 17, 1895, 7.

262 *the woman's husband was imprisoned:* Lili'uokalani, private memorandum, March 4, 1895, MS KC 3/6, Bishop Museum Archives.

262 *her "particular personal friend":* Blount Report, 556.

262 *guards even searched the bundles:* Lili'uokalani, private memorandum, March 4,1895, MS KC 3/6, Bishop Museum Archives.

263 *he was "stripped of all his clothing":* Lili'uokalani, *Hawaii's Story*, 270–271.

263 *gowns from fabric of dark blue and white stripes:* Irwin, *I Knew Queen Liliuokalani*, 53.

263 *"The wailing and crying":* *Trial of a Queen*, 11.

263 *"I was very weak":* Lili'uokalani, private memorandum, March 4,1895, MS KC 3/6, Bishop Museum Archives.

264 *"after free and full consultation":* Lili'uokalani to Dole, Documents of

Abdication, 24 January1895, David W. Forbes Collection, Liliʻuokalani Letters III, State Archives of Hawaiʻi.

264   *"For myself, I would have chosen death"*: Liliʻuokalani, *Hawaii's Story*, 274.

265   *As spare as a New England church*: Loomis, *For Whom Are the Stars?*, 187. This nicely turned description comes from Ms. Loomis.

265   *"misled into rebellion"*: Ibid., 191.

265   *"The planning of a new government"*: Ibid., 195–201.

266   *"The question of fixing the punishment"*: Sanford B. Dole to George Dole, 30 January 1895, Kahn Collection 35/50, State Archives of Hawaiʻi.

266   *"This country must be purified"*: Mrs. H.A.P. Carter to Sanford B. Dole, 10 January 1895, Foreign Office and Executive Branch, 1895, Miscellaneous Local (Letters to President) Jan.–June, State Archives of Hawaiʻi.

266   *"The execution of the ex-queen"*: Rev. Orramel H. Gulick to Sanford B. Dole, 11 January1895, Foreign Office and Executive Branch, 1895, Miscellaneous Local (Letters to President) Jan.–June, State Archives of Hawaiʻi.

266   *She wore an all-black gown*: Loomis, *For Whom Are the Stars?*, 207.

266   *"I decline to plead"*: Transcript of the Proceedings of the Military Commission, February 16, 1895, 148, State Archives of Hawaiʻi.

267   *"hold Washington Place"*: Testimony of Liliʻuokalani, Transcript of the Proceedings of the Military Commission, February 16, 1895, 148, sixteenth day, State Archives of Hawaiʻi.

267   *The guard said she'd hoped*: Testimony of Joseph Kaauwau, Transcript of the Proceedings of the Military Commission, Feburary 16, 1895, 148, sixteenth day, State Archives of Hawaiʻi.

267   *More damaging was the evidence*: Testimony of William Kaae, Transcript of the Proceedings of the Military Commission, Februaary 16, 1895, 148, sixteenth day, State Archives of Hawaiʻi, 19–23.

267   *burned it in the back yard*: Ibid.

267   *"L. looks pale & angry"*: Diary of A. F. Judd, February 6,1895, Bishop Museum Archives.

267   *"A minority of the foreign population"*: Translation of Statement of Liliuokalani Dominis, Febuary 7, 1895, Exhibit K, Transcript of the Proceedings of the Military Commission, 148, State Archives of Hawaiʻi.

268   *An interpreter for the tribunal*: Liliʻuokalani, Attorney General's File 506-4-15, Insurrection of 1895, State Archives of Hawaiʻi. The original

shows markings that appear to be where the government struck out sections of her statement. It is highly likely her attorney Paul Neumann wrote this document on behalf of his client.

268 *"I have no right to disclose"*: Lili'uokalani, *Hawaii's Story*, 263.

268 *the maximum sentence*: Attorney General, 146 Court Martial Case Files, Court Martial Orders No. 60, February 27, 1895, State Archives of Hawai'i.

268 *"a beautiful day"*: Diary of A. F. Judd, February 27, 1895, Bishop Museum Archives.

268 *The California poet Joaquin Miller*: Lili'uokalani, *Hawaii's Story*, 287.

269 *"There are hundreds of good men"*: New York Times, March 29, 1895.

269 *"each carrying a hookupu for his chief"*: Ethel M. Damon, *Sanford Ballard Dole and His Hawaii: With an Analysis of Justice Dole's Legal Opinions* (Palo Alto, Calif.: Pacific Books, for the Hawaiian Historical Society, 1957), 308, citing a story related by Sereno Bishop to Consul General Gorham D. Gilman.

270 *"All was in great good fun"*: Ibid.

270 *She passed the time quietly*: Lili'uokalani to Ka'iulani, 31 July 1895, Cleghorn Collection, State Archives of Hawai'i.

270 *"Imprisoned at Iolani Palace"*: Rhoda E. A. Hackler, Loretta G. H. Woodard, and Friends of 'Iolani Palace, *The Queen's Quilt* (Honolulu: The Friends of 'Iolani Palace, n.d.), 7.

270 *"after breakfast and for the rest of the day"*: Ibid., citing Lili'uokalani to Ka'iulani, 31 July 1895.

271 *"Ko'u noho mihi 'ana"*: Lyrics from http://www.huapala.org/Q/Queens_Prayer.html.

272 *they express a fiery anger*: In one song, for example, the writer angrily criticized the head of the military tribunal that convicted her, describing him as:

The hot-tempered haole of Waialae,

His act was to lie to his people,

"Tell all so that you will live,"

Do not be deceived by his cajolery,

Say that there is life through Her Majesty,

Who sacrifices her life for the lahui, [nation, race]

So that you patriot[s] may live.

Still another song Lili'u composed mentioned the garden of Uluhai-malama, a symbol of resistance for Hawaiians, as well as her Waikīkī estate known as Paoakalani, which was a mile or so from where the rebellion had begun. Flowers are common stand-ins in Hawaiian songs for people, and in the stone-eating song they represent the rebellious members of the Royal Hawaiian Band. By linking the flowers of her two gardens, Lili'u may have been sending praise to the men who'd fought to try to restore the monarchy following their humiliating defeat. The song's refrain is:

I've often seen those beauteous flowers
That grew at Uluhaimalama
But none of those could be compared
To my flower that blooms in the fields of
Paoakalani

272 *"The mele acted like conversations"*: Silva, *Aloha Betrayed*, 187-91. Silva writes that at the the end of the year the four songs (under the pseudonym "Ha'imoeipo") were included in F. J. Testa's collection *Buke Mele Lahui*, and two years later the queen included them in her own (unpublished) songbook "He Buke Mele Hawaii."

273 *the heaviest rain storm of the year*: Diary of A. F. Judd, September 5, 1895, Bishop Museum Archives.

Chapter 15: Born Under an Unlucky Star

274 *Dole's decision to try civilians*: Trial of a Queen, 7.

274 *"My dear Kaiulani"*: Lili'uokalani to Ka'iulani, 19 March 1896, Cleghorn Collection, State Archives of Hawai'i.

276 *"Speak for me on my behalf"*: Sheldon, "The Biography of Joseph K. Nawahi," 229.

276 *"It gives me very great pleasure"*: New York Times, November 26, 1896, David W. Forbes Collection, Lili'uokalani Letters Part III, State Archives of Hawai'i.

277 *why Americans seemed intent*: She wrote, "And yet this great and powerful nation must go across two thousand miles of sea, and take from the poor Hawaiians their little spots in the broad Pacific, must covet our islands of Hawai'i Nei, and extinguish the nationality of my poor people,

many of whom have now not a foot of land which can be called their own. And for what?" Lili'uokalani, *Hawaii's Story*, 310.

277 *"We cannot therefore be too cautious"*: Cleghorn to Lili'uokalani, 16 December 1896, David W. Forbes Collection, Lili'uokalani Letters Part III, State Archives of Hawai'i.

277 *they were campaigning*: Soon after the new year she wrote to her business agent that Cleghorn ". . . begs of Mr. Palmer to write up the cause of his daughter, if not, to go in person to Hawaii, that he could do more good than to write. I was astonished." Lili'uokalani to J. O. Carter, 2 Janaury 1897, David W. Forbes Collection, Lili'uokalani Letters Part III, State Archives of Hawai'i.

278 *"Fifteen minutes of pleasant conversation"*: Lili'uokalani to J. O. Carter, 27 January 1897, David W. Forbes Collection, Lili'uokalani Letters Part III, State Archives of Hawai'i.

279 *dictating it to him in the morning*: Forbes, *Bibliography*, vol. 4, 707. She also began translating the *Kumulipo*, an ancient Hawaiian creation chant, passed along by memory among her family and said to have been sung to Captain Cook, as well as writing a comic opera under the pseudonym "Madame Aorena" based on her short and tumultuous reign. "Every morning there are callers and some spend the evening in my parlors singing Hawaiian Airs—ladies as well as gentlemen and I am always willing to sing when asked," Lili'u wrote to one of her longtime courtiers in Honolulu. "It astonishes them to see how well I speak English as well as sing and play on the autoharp, which proved to them I am just the opposite of what has been described of me." Lili'uokalani to James W. Robertson, 22 March 1897, David W. Forbes Collection, Lili'uokalani Letters Part III, State Archives of Hawai'i.

279 *"I want to get this work out in good shape"*: Lili'uokalani, Gillett, and Smith, *The Queen's Songbook,*, xii..

279 *a heartfelt correspondence with Emma Nāwahī*: Lili'u's letters to Emma Nāwahī have not survived, but Nāwahī's letters to Lili'u have. In them, Nāwahī refers extensively to what Lili'u wrote to her, including the dates she wrote, and also to her belief that their letters were being opened and read by their enemies.

279 *"I saw your greeting"*: Emma Nāwahī to Lili'uokalani, 31 March 1897, Lili'uokalani Collection, State Archives of Hawai'i.

279   the confiscation of 1.8 million acres: Van Dyke, *Who Owns the Crown Lands of Hawai'i?*, 170, citing the 1993 Apology Resolution.

280   "injudicious as they stood": Letter forwarded from a W.N.M. via William Lee to Lili'uokalani, 25 September 1897, Lili'uokalani Collection, Box 3m Folder 21, State Archives of Hawai'i.

280   the "evil genius" of the missionary party: Original manuscript of *Hawaii's Story* with Lili'u's edits in pencil, Lili'uokalani Collection, State Archives of Hawai'i.

280   a charge that Thurston would make: Thurston, *Memoirs*, vol. 2, 108.

280   "it does cast a serious shadow": *Philadelphia Inquirer*, February 14, 1898.

280   "a character remarkable for probity": *The Watchman*, February 10, 1898, 14.

281   "I must have been born": Ka'iulani to Nevinson William de Courcy, 1897, General Letters file box, Ka'iulani, Bishop Museum Archives.

281   "It made me feel so sad": Ka'iulani to Lili'uokalani, 17 November 1897, David W. Forbes Collection, Cleghorn Letters Part II, State Archives of Hawai'i.

282   "It has been made known to me": Lili'uokalani to Ka'iulani, 26 October 1897, Cleghorn Collection, State Archives of Hawai'i.

282   A nation controlling Hawai'i: Thurston, *Memoirs*, vol. 2, 350.

283   A women's committee prepared the food: Albertine Loomis, "Summer of 1898," *Hawaiian Journal of History* 13 (1979): 95, citing *Pacific Commercial Advertiser*, June 3, 1898.

283   "We have been abused, conquered and finally annexed": Mehmed Ali, "Ho'ohui'aina Palaka Mai'a: Remembering Annexation One Hundred Years Ago," *Hawaiian Journal of History* 32 (1998): 141–54.

284   the fulfillment of American destiny: Devine, "John W. Foster and the Struggle for the Annexation of Hawaii," 49.

284   the first significant example: The first overseas acquisition of the United States was not Hawai'i but the small Pacific island of Midway, which it claimed under the Guano Islands Act of 1856. "Famous are the Flowers: Hawaiian Resistance Then—and Now," Elinor Langer, *Nation*, April 28, 2008, vol. 286, no. 16.

284   Britain stood aside: Walter Lafeber, *The New Empire: An Interpretation of American Expansion, 1860–1898*, 35th ed. (Ithaca, N.Y.: Cornell University Press, 1998), 363–64.

284 *"H.M. Government recognize the annexation"*: Ernest Andrade Jr., "Great Britain and the Hawaiian Revolution," *Hawaiian Journal of History* 24 (1990): 91–116.

284 *a strongly worded protest*: Lafeber, 364.

285 *$75,000 to settle the dispute*: Daws, *Shoal of Time*, 290–91.

285 *"Instantly, a storm of alohas"*: Mabel Clare Craft, *Hawai'i Nei* (San Francisco: William Doxey at the Sign of the Lark, 1899), 93.

286 *"We went to see the ali'i"*: Silva, *Aloha Betrayed*, 200, translation of *Ke Aloha Aina* account of Lili'u's return by Professor Silva.

286 *the fluttering of a wounded bird"*: Loomis, "Summer of 1898," 97.

286 *"caught the breath of a passing breeze"*: Craft, *Hawai'i Nei*, 84–88.

287 *Lili'u's invitation*: Ibid., 64.

Epilogue

292 *The shy Hawaiian o'o*: Craft, *Hawai'i Nei*, 64.

292 *the Hawai'i state library*: Hawai'i State Librarian's Report, February 18, 2010.

292 *Nearby Thomas Square*: "Thomas Square to be Closed for Cleanup; Homeless to be Pushed Out," *Honolulu Star-Bulletin*, August 1, 2007.

294 *supporters heaped her statue*: Onipa'a, 138, photograph by Elizabeth Pa Martin.

295 *the bulk of her estate*: Samuel P. King, Walter M. Heen, and Randall W. Roth, "The Queen's Estate," *Honolulu Star-Bulletin*, May 17, 2009.

295 *6,400 acres of lands*: See http://www.onipaa.org/7.html, which contains a brief description of the trust's assets.

295 *Its mission is to help*: Annual report, Lili'uokalani Trust, 2007, 4.

295 *the new Hawaiian government*: "House Gives Boost to Native Hawaiian Government" by Kevin Freking, Associated Press, February 23, 2010.

296 *an annual festival*: See www.hawaiiforgivenessproject.org.

A Note on Language and Sources

297 *she called herself Lili'u*: At her birth, Lili'u was named Lydia Lili'u Loloku Walania Wewehi Kamaka'eha. In her youth she was called "Lydia" or "Lili'u" and then "Lili'uokalani" when she became heir apparent, according to the Lili'uokalani Trust (www.qlcc.org/queen.htm).

299 *The word pau:* Mary Kawena Pukui and Samuel H. Elbert, "Hawaiian Dictionary at Ulukau," http://ulukau.org.

300 *a "told to" book:* Forbes, *Bibliography,* 707.

Acknowledgments

303 *the Pacific Golden Plover:* Pukui and Elbert, "Hawaiian Dictionary at Ulukau," http://ulukau.org.

INDEX

Āinahau, 159, 281, 283, 293

Aimoku, John Dominis, 117

Akaka bill, 295

Alexander & Baldwin, 290, 291

aliʻi, xx, xxi, 6–7, 19, 25, 28, 30, 32, 42, 167

  landholdings, 120

  Liliʻu and, 18, 31, 49, 51, 74, 161, 238, 275, 286

aliʻi children, 9–13, 15, 28, 30

aliʻi nui, xix–xx

Aliʻiōlani Hale (government building), 220, 225

Allen, Helena G., 300

"Aloha Oe" (song), 78, 129, 168, 271, 294–95

amnesty to those who overthrew Liliʻu, granting, 238–40, 242, 243

Anglican bishop of Honolulu, 74, 123, 178

Anglican Church, 38–40

Anna (sailing ship), 85

Annexation Club, xxviii, 188, 189, 208

annexation of Hawaiʻi to United States, 26, 83, 124, 126

  Atherton on, 246

  Bayonet Constitution and, 188

  Britain and, 284

  ceremony celebrating, 286

  Claus Spreckels and, 182, 233–34

  Cleghorn on, 83

  Gibson on, 144, 150

  Grover Cleveland and, 229, 238, 243, 285

  Harrison and, 189

  James Blaine and, 189

  Liliʻu and, 187, 194, 210

  Liliʻu on, 282

  Liliʻu's efforts to stave off, 298, 300

  Mark Twain on, 66

  in the media, 90, 229

  Pearl River basin and, 54–55

  popular sentiment regarding, 238

  provisional government, constitution, and, 253

  reciprocity as first step of, 151

annexation of Hawai'i to United States
(*continued*)
Sanford Dole and, 208
sugar industry and, 283
Thurston and, 188, 189, 209, 216,
217, 282
annexation petitions, 285
annexation treaty, 26, 54–55, 229, 243,
279–80
passed by U.S. Congress, 283–84
anthem, 46–47
aqueducts, xxi, xxii
Arnold, Edwin, 187
Ashford, Colonel, 142
Atherton, J. B., 213, 215, 246
Atkinson, A. T., 127
Australia (steamer), 146, 236, 276, 281

Baldwin, Henry P., 212, 258
Bay Sugar Refinery, 70, 116. *See also*
California Sugar Refinery
Bayonet Constitution of 1887, 142,
144–46, 179–80, 242, 248. *See also*
constitutions of Hawai'i
amendments to, 165
Gibson on, 152
Kalākaua and, 145, 162, 163, 199
Lili'u and, 173–74, 180, 181, 188,
189, 194–95, 199–201, 205,
242
upholding, 173, 242
voting rights in, 201
Wilcox and, 162
beet sugar industry, 291
Benicia, USS, 62
Bertelmann, Henry, 257, 258, 265
Betrayal of Lili'uokalani, The (Allen),
300
Big 5 sugar companies, 291

Bingham, Reverend Hiram, 3
Bishop, Bernice Pauahi (Lili'u's sister). *See
also* Bishop, Charles R.: Lili'u and
birth, 24
death from cancer, 118–20, 166,
185–86
inheritances, 29, 120
Kamehameha Schools founded by,
295
Kamehameha V and, 51
Konia and, 29
Lili'u and, 7, 29, 41, 42, 120–21, 181
offered and declined the thrown, 51
pākī and, 29
parties hosted at home of, 30–31, 42
pianoforte playing, 11
William Lunalilo and, 41
Bishop, Charles R., 22–23, 277
Bishop Museum and, 186
Dominis family and, 41
generosity, 120
Konia and, 29
Lili'u and, 29, 41, 42, 118, 121,
180–81, 186, 277
marriage, 22–23, 29, 51
parties hosted at the home of, 30–31,
42
in San Francisco, 180
William Lunalilo and, 41
Bishop, Reverend Sereno E., 179
Bishop Museum, 186, 224, 293, 298,
301
Bishop Museum Archives, 298, 301, 304
Bismarck, Herbert von, 126, 127
Blaine, James G., 183, 189
Blount, James H. ("Reticent Blount"),
229–31, 245, 251–53
background and overview, 229,
232–33

Claus Spreckels and, 234, 236
Grover Cleveland and, 237, 245, 251
in Honolulu, 231–34, 236–38
Lili'u and, 231, 233
Morgan report and, 252
Bohemian Club, 168
Boston, USS, xxvii, xxviii, xxx, 212–14, 232
bribery, 58, 79–80, 139, 154, 218
Britain, xxii–xxv, xxvii, 14, 17, 115, 123, 135, 284. *See also* Liverpool; Paulet Affair
fear that Hawai'i would go to, 67
Ka'iulani in, 223, 226–27, 230, 277
Kalākaua and, 90, 100, 115
Kapi'olani in, 123, 132–36
Lili'u in, 124, 131–35, 147, 160, 172, 192
national anthem, 130
Pearl River basin and, 148–51
reciprocity treaty and, 67
recognition of Hawai'i's independence, 13, 45
as rival in courtship contest for Hawai'i, xxvii, 14
Samoa and, 124
Tonga Islands and, 126
British influence over Hawai'i, fear of, 67
Buckingham Palace, 132–33, 136
Bush, John E., 186, 187, 189, 191
alcohol use, 126
arrested for sedition, 275
Ka Leo O Ka Lahui and, 180, 207
Kalākaua and, 125, 127
Lili'u and, 180, 186, 191
mission in Samoa, 125–27
parties hosted by, 125
political views, 180, 189

populist appeal, 186
positions held by, 125
Wilcox and, 180

California. *See also* San Francisco
Lili'u in, 77
California Sugar Refinery, 71, 234. *See also* Bay Sugar Refinery
Campbell, James, 75, 278
Cannibals, 56
Carter, Joseph O., 241, 242, 258
Carter, Mary, 287
Carver (U.S. cutter), 241
Castle, Henry, 207
Castle, Samuel Northrup, 37
Castle, William R., 156, 207
Castle & Cooke, 140, 156, 290, 291
C&H Sugar, 291
Charleston, USS, 167–68, 172, 174
Chiefs' Children's School, 9–11, 14, 15, 17, 292
Chinatown, 87–88
Chinese workers, 88
City of Rome (steamer), 129
City of San Francisco (ship), 68, 69
City of Sydney (ship), 87
Claus Spreckels (schooner), 84
Cleghorn, Archibald S., 82, 108, 158, 159, 166, 195
on annexation, 83
fall of monarchy and, 226
finances, 121, 192
as governor of O'ahu, 215
Honolulu home, 75
John Dominis and, 134
Ka'iulani and, 74, 83, 186, 192, 226, 227, 277, 283
Kalākaua and, 82, 83, 87

Cleghorn, Archibald S. (*continued*)
  Lili'u, 134, 186, 192, 199, 277
  Miriam Likelike's death and, 122
  United States and, 160, 283
  Waikīkī estate, 122, 158, 159. *See also*
    Āinahau
Clemens, Samuel Langhorne. *See* Twain,
  Mark
Cleveland, Frances Folsom, 128, 278–79
Cleveland, Grover, 128, 252
  annexation and, 229, 238, 243, 285
  James Blount and, 237, 245, 251
  Lili'u and, 229, 239, 278
  and overthrow of Lili'u, 229, 237–38,
    245, 251
  provisional government and, 251, 253
  and restoring Lili'u to thrown, 237–
    39, 241, 243, 244, 251, 252, 254
  Willis and, 239, 240, 243, 252
Clinton, Bill, 295
Coan, Titus, 5
coinage scheme, 108
coins, mint, 108
colonialism, 124
Committee of Safety, 208–11, 213,
  216–17, 221
Committee of Thirteen, 140–42, 188
constitution of 1887. *See* Bayonet
  Constitution
constitutions of Hawai'i, 46, 253
  Claus Spreckels and, 242
  freedom of speech in, 249
  of Kamehameha V, 46–47
  Lili'u and, xxvii, xxviii, 46–47,
    201–11, 216, 218, 221, 226, 252,
    261, 267
  slavery and, 34
  Thurston and, 145, 202, 204, 208,
    211–12, 218

Conundrum. *See* Kaimiloa
Cook, Captain James, xxii–xxv, 4, 33,
  82, 88
Cooke, Amos Starr, 8–10, 12, 15, 21, 24.
  See also Castle & Cooke
Cooke, Anna Rice, 292
Cooke, Charles M., 209
Cooke, Juliette, 8–10, 21, 23, 24
counterrevolution of 1895, 256–60, 268
Cracroft, Sophia, 39, 40
Craft, Mabel, 285, 286
Cummins, John A., 175, 256

Daily Bulletin (newspaper), 106, 110,
  139, 140
Davies, Theo H., 121, 166, 172, 195,
  227, 228, 291
  Ka'iulani and, 166, 172, 195, 228
Dawes, Henry, 128–29
Dawes Act, 128
de Young, Charles, 112
de Young, Michael, 111, 112
Diamond Head, 113
Diamond Head, Battle of, 256–58
Dimond, W. H., 85
disease, 12, 21–22, 25, 66, 82, 88–90
Dole, Anna Prentice Cate, 56–57,
  245–46, 283
Dole, George, 208
Dole, James, 290
Dole, Sanford Ballard, 59, 66, 208–9,
  217, 290
  Albert Willis and, 243, 246
  background and overview, 55, 270
  birthday celebration, 269
  Claus Spreckels and, 68, 69, 235
  Committee of Safety and, 208,
    216–17
  Committee of Thirteen and, 139–40

criticism of and opposition to, 248,
    253–54
critiques of government, 106, 108, 109
decision to try civilians in military
    court, 274
government of, 228, 231–35, 248, 255,
    257, 262, 269, 275, 280–82, 286
Hawaiian League and, 139–41
idealism, 56
Independents and, 114
John Stevens and, 216–18
land ownership and, 255
Lili'u and, 208–9, 216, 217, 221, 223,
    243, 247, 248, 261, 262, 264–66,
    269, 271, 273, 276
Lorrin Thurston and, 57, 58, 106, 110,
    114, 139–40, 153, 216–17, 224,
    243, 269, 270
marriage to Anna Prentice Cate,
    56–57
martial law declared by, 222–25, 257
in the media, 228, 248
positions held by, 153, 208, 216–19,
    289–90
  governor, 289–90
  judge, 153, 217, 290
  president, 216, 220, 223–25, 228,
    253, 269
prison and death sentences commuted
    by, 266, 269, 271, 273, 274, 276
Punch Bowl and, 56
reception, 245–47
residences, 56
reverence for Hawai'i's landscape, 58
speeches, 141, 286
United States and, 243, 252, 269, 286
Walter Gibson and, 153
writings and critiques of government,
    56, 106, 108–10, 114

Dole Food Company, 290
Dominis, John Owen (Lili'u's husband),
    45, 59, 62, 63, 108, 134, 158
  Bayonet Constitution and, 173
  birth of illegitimate son, 117
  death from pneumonia, 184–86
  family background, 23–24
  furniture brought to Honolulu by, 293
  as governor of Maui, 77
  as governor of O'ahu, 48, 62, 77, 108
  Kamehameha V and, 48, 51
  Lili'u's relationship with, 48, 49, 77,
    92, 117, 121, 134
    courtship, 41
    early encounters, 30
    John's affairs and, 77, 117
    marriage, 41–45
  physical appearance, 41
  in United States, 77, 128–29
Dominis, Mary Jones, 41, 45, 48–49,
    293
  illness and death, 157, 161

Edison, Thomas, 103
Edmunds, George F., 150
election of 1874, 58–60
Emma Rooke, Queen, 31, 58, 99, 118
  birth of son, 38–39
  claim to throne, 53
  conspiracy to put her on throne, 68
  death, 119–20
  death of son, 41–42
  and election of 1874, 58
  English accent, 18
  in Europe, 54
  family background, 29
  Kalākaua and, 54, 55, 58–62, 68,
    101
  land and, 55

Emma Rooke, Queen (*continued*)
  Lili'u and, 38
  popularity and supporters, 53, 55,
    58–60, 62, 68
  residence, 59
  Sanford Dole and, 59
  Sophia Cracroft and, 39
  United States and, 53, 55
England. *See* Britain
euchre, 115
extinct species, 76

"flowers" (Hawaiians loyal to the
  monarchy), 272
Forbes, David W., 300
Foster, John W., 194, 227
France as rival in courtship contest for
  Hawai'i, xxvii, 14
Franklin, Lady Jane, 39, 40

Gazette (newspaper), 106
Germany, 73, 124, 217
  Claus Spreckels and, 71, 73, 235
  Kalākaua and, 126, 127
  Lili'u and, 183
  Samoa and, 124–27
Gibson, Talula, 143
Gibson, Walter Murray, 104
  arrest and imprisonment, 142–44
  characterization of, 81
  Claus Spreckels and, 86, 110, 114, 116
  criticisms of, 109, 110, 114, 119, 139,
    141
  death, 152–54, 163
  departure from the islands, 150
  disregard for native Hawaiians, 81
  finances, 80–82, 98, 108, 114, 139,
    141, 142
  as foreign minister, 125
  greed, 81

Hawaiian League and, 140, 142
health problems, 138, 140
Honolulu Rifles and, 140, 142
imperialism and, 124, 125
Independents and, 114
Isobel Strong and, 143–44
joined Catholic Church, 152
Kaimiloa and, 139
Kalākaua and, 80–82, 98, 124, 138,
  144, 150, 152
land and, 81, 82
legal problems, 138–39
life history and overview, 80–82
Lili'u and, 163
Lorrin Thurston and, 141, 153
in the media, 110, 139, 152, 153
"missionary party" and, 163
Mormonism and, 81–82, 152
on new constitution, 152
Nuhou and, 149
Pearl Harbor and, 149–51
personality, 81
physical appearance, 80, 138, 163
politics and, 82
as prime minister, 86
resignation from cabinet, 151
Sanford Dole and, 109, 153
slogan, 189
United States and, 149–53
Wilcox and, 161, 164
writings, 124
government debt. See Hawai'i: economy
  and finances
Grant, Ulysses S., 63, 68
Gresham, Walter, 240, 241
Gynberg Ballads (Atkinson), 127

hānai, 7, 8, 77
habeas corpus, writ of
  suspension of, 222

Hale Nauā Society, 116–17, 155, 178
Haleakalā (Lili'u's childhood home), 121
haole (Caucasians/whites/foreigners),
    164, 185, 208, 299
  businessmen and merchant class, 27,
    190
  constitution and, 201
  in government, 190, 200
  intermarriage with Hawaiians, 22, 23
  Lili'u and, 161
  revival of native Hawaiian culture and,
    176
  Robert Louis Stevenson on, 160–61
  voting rights and political power, 201
hapa haole (part-Caucasian people), 10,
    23
Harrison, Benjamin, 183, 189
Hawai'i
  Britain, France, and U.S. as rivals in
    courtship contest for, xxvii, 14
  economy and finances, 108–10, 114,
    116, 154, 165, 186, 191, 193,
    289
  independence, 80. *See also specific topics*
  sociodemographics, 65
"Hawai'i for Hawaiians" slogan, 82, 189
Hawai'i Island, 5, 31, 42, 91, 204, 212
Hawaiian Commercial & Sugar
    Company, 85, 109, 110, 166, 237,
    290–92
Hawaiian Gazette (newspaper), 54, 101,
    105, 106, 139, 235
Hawaiian Hotel, 79, 238
Hawaiian Kingdom
  overthrow of, 220–29
    celebration of anniversary of,
      244–47
    granting amnesty to those involved
      in, 238–40, 242, 243
    writings on, 301–2

Hawaiian Kingdom, The (Kuykendall),
    301
Hawaiian language, 297–99
Hawaiian League, 139–42, 144, 145,
    147
Hawaiian national anthem, 50
"Hawaiian Patriot, The." *See Ke Aloha
    'Āina*
Hawaiian patriotic leagues, 248, 253,
    278, 279
  Women's Patriotic League, 275,
    279
Hawaiian revolution of 1993. *See*
    Hawaiian Kingdom: overthrow of
Hawaiian Volunteers, 164
Hawaiians, terminology for, 299
Hawai'i's ports, military and strategic
    value of, 54
Hawaii's Story by Hawaii's Queen (Lili'u),
    268, 279, 280, 300
"He Mele Lahui Hawaii" (Christian
    national), 50
Honolulu
  Anglican bishop of, 74, 123, 178
  city life in, 87–88, 157, 158
  immigration into, 88
  James Blount in, 231–34, 236–38
  Robert Louis Stevenson and, 157–
    58
*Honolulu Advertiser. See Pacific
    Commercial Advertiser*
Honolulu Rifles, 140–42, 154, 209, 217
ho'omalimali, 87
Household Guards. *See* Royal
    Household Guards
Hui Aloha 'Āina (political society),
    248
Hui Hānai Council, 300
Hui Kālai'āina (political society), 201–3,
    206, 207, 248

hula, xxiv, xxv, 46, 87, 105–7, 168, 171
hula ku'i, 50, 105
hula ma'i, 105

'Iaukea, Curtis, 133–34
immigration
  into Hawai'i, 66
  into Honolulu, 88
imperialism. *See* United States:
    expansion and expansionist
    sentiment
Independence Day, America's, 253
Influence of Sea Power Upon History, The
    (Mahan), 182
intermarriage, 22, 23
'Iolani Palace, 31, 97, 147, 157, 214, 270
  building of new, 97, 102–4
  Lili'u at, 185
  march on, 162–63
  as museum/tourist site, 293–94
  Throne Room, 178, 185, 264
irrigation, xxi, xxii, 36, 37, 78–81, 85, 112
Irwin, William G., 85, 166, 194

Japan, 284
Jefferson, Thomas, 182
John D. Spreckels (sailing ship), 85, 152
Judd, Chief Justice Albert Francis, 210,
    268
  background and overview, 206
  Lili'u and, 179, 205–7, 261, 262, 267,
    268
Judd, Gerrit P., 13, 16, 19, 25, 206
July 4, 253

Ka Leo O Ka Lahui (newspaper), 207
Ka Makaainana (newspaper), 272
kāhuna (priests), xix, 46, 122, 230,
    265

Kaimiloa (steamer), 126, 127, 139
Ka'iulani Kalaninuiahilapalapa Kawekiui
    Lunalilo, Princess Victoria, 83, 99,
    250
  birth, 74–75
  in boarding school, 226–27
  Cleghorn and, 74, 83, 186, 192, 226,
    227, 277, 283
  death, 295
  in England, 223, 226–27, 230, 277
  illness, 83
  Kalākaua and, 172
  Lili'u and, 75, 92–93, 185, 186, 192,
    216, 261, 270, 271, 274, 277,
    281
  in the media, 227, 229
  Miriam Likelike and, 74, 122
  name, 74
  physical appearance and, 99, 227, 229,
    281
  return to Hawai'i, 281
  Robert Louis Stevenson and, 159,
    160
  and succession to throne, 75, 83, 180,
    216, 227–31, 281–82
  Theo Davies and, 166, 172, 195, 228
  in United States, 62–64, 160, 227–29,
    277
  Waikīkī estate. See Āinahau
  at Washington Place, 286
Kalākaua, House of. *See also*
    Lili'uokalani, Queen: house arrest
  fall of, 220
  festivities at, 97–102, 246–47
  rise of, 184, 220
    ceremony to herald, 97–102, 104–6
  rivalry with Kamehamehas, 99
  under siege from the start, 60
  women of, 120

Kalākaua, King David (Liliʻu's
  brother), xxviii. *See also specific
  topics*
  Amos Cooke and, 12
  attempts at empire building, 124
  Bayonet Constitution and, 144–46
  birth of daughter, 74–75. *See also*
    Kaʻiulani
  Britain and, 90, 100, 115
  cabinet and ministers, 79, 147
  Celso Moreno and, 84
  choice of advisers, 87
  coronation and celebrations for,
    97–102, 104–6
  corruption, 78–82
  criticisms of, 84, 89–90, 102, 106–7,
    109, 119, 139, 140
  in danger of assassination, 68, 140
  death of brother who he named
    successor, 75
  early life, 12, 61–62
  election to throne, 53–54, 58, 100
  finances, 90, 101, 102, 108, 120, 154,
    155
    promissory notes signed, 79–80
  first appointments in his new
    government, 61–62
  first official act as king-elect, 59
  foreigners and, 83
  Gibson and, 80–82, 98, 124, 138, 144,
    150, 152
  illness and death, 167, 169–78
  John Bush and, 125, 127
  Liliʻu and, 86–87, 89, 100, 102, 147,
    156–57, 167, 172, 173
  marriage to Kapiʻolani, 47
  in the media, 89–90, 139
  as "Merrie Monarch," 106
  and the military, 61–62
  and mission to Samoa, 125–27
  objectives/goals for Hawaiʻi, 62
  overview and characterizations of, 40,
    107, 175–76
  Pearl Harbor and, 149
  personality, 107
  physical description, 40, 61
  political ambitions, 86
  as puppet ruler controlled by U.S.
    businessmen, 79–80, 110
  Queen Emma and, 54, 55, 58–62, 68,
    101
  Queen Victoria and, 90
  reciprocity treaty and, 64, 66, 68, 151,
    175–76
  religion and, 89
  request to step down from throne,
    156–57
  in San Francisco, 62, 64, 87, 167–70,
    172
  Sophia Cracroft on, 40
  sugar planters and, 68
  sworn in as king, 60
  travel
    goodwill tour of islands, 62
    plan to circumnavigate the globe, 86
    trip around world, 90
    to United States, 62–64, 66,
      167–71
  United States and, 47, 53, 55, 59, 62
  unsteady hold on the throne, 83
Kalua, 171
Kamanawa, 12
Kamehameha, Prince Albert, 38–39, 41
Kamehameha dynasty/House of
  Kmehameha, 51–53, 60, 97, 118,
  184
  Americans as threat to, 47
  rivalry with House of Kalākaua, 99

Kamehameha I, King (Kamehameha the
   Great), 7, 15, 22, 28, 92, 202
   death, 4
   early life, xxiii
   statue of, 104
Kamehameha II, King (Liholiho)
   assumption of throne, 4
   became Christian, 5
   radical changes made by, 5
Kamehameha III, King (Kauikeaouli), 7,
   8, 13, 15, 16, 21, 27, 149
   American missionaries, education,
      and, 9
   constitution and Declaration of
      Rights, 13, 19, 26–27
   death, 25, 27
   land ownership and, 19
   marriage laws and, 22
   United States and, 26
   Washington Place named by, 23
Kamehameha IV, King (Alexander
   Liholiho), 28, 31, 53
   accession to throne, 26
   annexation of Hawai'i and, 25–26
   birth of son, 39
   death, 45–47
   death of son, 41–42
   early life, 49–50
   marriage to Emma Rooke, 18, 27–30
   personality, 26
   Sophia Cracroft and, 39
   United States and, 25–26
Kamehameha Schools, 120, 295
Kamehameha V, King (Lot Kapuāiwa),
   46, 47, 49, 85
   annexation of Hawai'i and, 25–26
   ascension to throne, 46
   illness and death, 50–51
   John Dominis and, 48

Lili'u and, 49, 50
new constitution proclaimed by, 46,
   47, 205
United States and, 25–26
Kapi'olani, Queen Esther "Julia"
   (Kalākaua's wife), 89, 138, 285
   in Boston, 129
   dress, 98, 135–36
   in England, 123, 132–36
   goodwill tour of islands, 62
   Kalua and, 175
   Lili'u and, 47, 91, 123, 128, 133, 134,
      146–47, 185, 192
   marriage to Kalākaua, 47
   Queen Victoria and, 133, 135–36
   Sam Parker and, 174–75
   stroke, 185
   in Washington, D.C., 128
Kapi'olani Park, 104, 138, 158, 283
Kapuāiwa, Lot. See Kamehameha V
Kaua'i, 20, 33, 36, 37, 43, 57, 120, 161, 184
Kauikeaouli. See Kamehameha III
Ke Aloha 'Āina (newspaper), 248–49
Ke'elikōlani, Princess Ruth, 85, 86,
   91–92, 100, 101, 118–20
   celebration of the completion of her
      new mansion, 99–100
   Claus Spreckels and, 85–86
   death, 118–20
   heart disease, 99
   Kalākaua and, 86, 100, 101
Kīlauea volcano, 32, 40, 57, 91
"Kingdom Come" government, 265
Konia (Lili'u's foster mother), 7, 8, 23,
   24, 29
Kuykendall, Ralph S., 21, 301

Lāna'i, 81–82, 290
land ownership, 42

languages, 297–99
Lee, Sara, 277, 279–80
Lee, William, 279–80
Legends and Myths of Hawaii, The
    (Twain), 154–55
Liholiho. *See* Kamehameha II
Liholiho, Alexander. *See* Kamehameha
    IV
Līhuʻe mill, 43–44
Līhuʻe plantation, 36, 43
Likelike, Princess Miriam, 78, 83, 101,
    104
  illness and death, 121–23
  Kaʻiulani and, 74, 122
  Liliʻu and, 47–49, 121, 122
"*Lilikoʻi*" (name chant), 78
Liliʻuokalani, Queen ("Liliʻu"), 48–49.
    See also specific topics
  abdication of throne, 264, 265
  adopted children, 77–78, 117
  Albert Judd and, 179, 205–7, 261,
    262, 267, 268
  aliʻi and, 18, 31, 49, 51, 74, 161, 238,
    275, 286
  arrest, 258–64
  assassination
    fear of, 248
    rumored plot of, 230
  Bayonet Constitution and, 173–74,
    180, 181, 188, 189, 194–95,
    199–201, 205, 242
  Bernice Pauahi Bishop and, 7, 29, 41,
    42, 120–21, 181
  birth, 6–7, 292
  birthday celebrations, 184, 293
  in Britain, 124, 131–35, 147, 160,
    172, 192
  carriage accident and injury, 92
  characterizations of, 187, 191

childhood, xxvi, 7–13, 15
Christians and, 243
conspiracy to remove her from throne,
    191, 195
criticisms of, 89, 180–81, 187, 191,
    207, 218
dancing, 48–49
declared national day of prayer, 89
education, xxvi, 11, 12
efforts to restore her to thrown.
    See Cleveland, Grover;
    counterrevolution of 1895
engagements, 41
family background, xxv, 28
family physician, 117
finances, 193–94, 230, 238, 242,
    250–51, 254–55
financial legacy, 295
given authority while Kalākaua was
    away, 86–87
health and illness, 76, 77, 167, 185,
    192, 255, 263
house arrest, 268, 270–74, 276
inherited throne, 173–74, 179–80,
    186–88
intention to be powerful ruler, 179–
    81
John Bush and, 180, 186, 191
Kalākaua and, 86–87, 89, 100,
    102, 147, 156–57, 167, 172,
    173
Kapiʻolani and, 47, 91, 123, 128, 133,
    134, 146–47, 185, 192
language and speech, 31, 297–99
legacy, 294–95
letter of protest, 221
in line to throne, 117, 156
loneliness, 117, 121, 192–93, 231
marriage. *See under* Bishop, Charles R.

Lili'uokalani, Queen ("Lili'u") (*continued*)
music, 46, 50, 78, 109, 138, 222, 231,
270–72, 279, 294–95, 300, 305
names, 24, 75, 297
overthrow of. *See* Hawaiian Kingdom:
overthrow of
Pālama home, 121, 161, 162, 164
personality, 48–49, 87, 89
physical appearance, 24–25, 48–49,
98–99
political cartoons about, 250
politics and, 117
public popularity, 89, 91
on punishment for treason, 239–43
reciprocity treaty and, 67–68, 151–
52
relations with parents, 8
reverence for Hawai'i's landscape, 58
Sam Parker and, 185, 190, 203–5,
209, 214, 235, 254, 261, 264
Sanford Dole and, 208–9, 216, 217,
221, 223, 243, 247, 248, 261, 262,
264–66, 269, 271, 273, 276
song composed by, 46
statue of, 294
on trial for "misprision" of treason,
264–67
in United States, 127–29, 276–82,
285–86, 298
first trip, 76–78
values, 49
Wilcox and, 161–64, 180, 191, 214,
267
Wilcox Rebellion of 1889 and,
161–65
writings about, 300–301
writings of, 300. *See also Hawaii's Story
by Hawaii's Queen*
Lili'uokalani Educational Society, 116

Lili'uokalani Gardens, 293
Lili'uokalani v. the United States, 295
"Lili'uokalani's Prayer" (song), 271
Liverpool, England, 131–32, 136
Loan Act, 116
Lodge, Henry Cabot, 183
Lono, xxii
Loomis, Albertine, 301
Lot Kapuāiwa. See Kamehameha V
lottery bill, 193–94, 200, 208, 211, 224
Lunalilo, King William ("Whiskey Bill"),
51, 61
failure to name an heir, 54
illness and death, 51–53, 55, 60–61
Lili'u and, 41
Pearl Harbor and, 149
personality, 41
sugar trade and, 149
United States and, 149

Mānoa, Battle of, 257–58
Mahan, Alfred T., 182–83
mahele, 19, 20, 25, 35, 42, 120
Malo, David, 16
mamo (bird), 76
"manifest destiny," 67, 246
Mariposa (steamer), 107–8, 112, 127,
142
Marshall, James, 32
martial law, 222–25, 257, 267
"Masquerade on Skates" party, 209
Maui
sugar plantations on, 24, 75, 78, 79,
84, 85, 112, 291–92
water rights on, 79, 84, 85
Mauna Loa, 28, 91, 122
McKinley, William, 278, 279, 282, 284
McKinley Tariff, 165–66, 191
measles epidemic of 1848, 21–22

Melville, Herman, 13–14
Miller, Joaquin, 268–69
mint coins, 108
Missionary Party, 144, 153, 164, 280
molasses, 12, 36, 43, 44
Monroe Doctrine of 1823, 67
Morgan, John Tyler, 251
Morgan report, 252
Mormon Church, 81
Moses (Liliʻu's schoolmate), 21–22, 88

Nāwahī, Emma
   Joseph Nāwahī and, 276
   letters, 298
   Liliʻu and, 279
   positions, 248
Nāwahī, Joseph, 151, 165, 214, 248, 253, 279
   criticism of reciprocity treaty, 68
   death, 275–76
   Liliʻu and, 68, 200, 248, 275, 279, 298
   as martyr, 276
   overview, 68
   reciprocity treaty and, 68
National Memorial Cemetary, 289
Neumann, Paul, 109, 263, 265
Nordhoff, Charles, 234
Nowlein, Samuel, 256, 257, 265–67
Nuhou (newspaper), 149

Oʻahu, 8, 24, 75–76, 215, 292
   governors of. See Cleghorn; Dominis
Oʻahu College, 48, 55
Oceanic Steamship Company, 85
"'Onipaʻa" (song), 46–47
opium bills, 194, 200, 211, 224
opium scandal/opium affair, 139, 141, 154, 156
Otis, James, 62

Pākī (Liliʻu's foster father), 7–8, 23, 24, 29–30
Pākī, Lydia. See Liliʻuokalani, Queen
Pālama, Liliʻu's home in, 121, 161, 162, 164
Paauhau Sugar Plantation Company, 204
Pacific Commercial Advertiser (newspaper), 35, 66, 99, 124, 138, 194, 207–8, 232, 247, 266
   owners of, 54, 207, 290
Pacific Navigation Company, 142–43
Palace Hotel, 168, 169
"palace party," 114
Palmer, Julius A., 277, 279, 300
Palmerston, Lord, 39
Parker, Colonel Sam, 174–75, 185, 190, 203–5, 258, 261
   Claus Spreckels and, 205
   John Stevens and, 214–16
   Liliʻu and, 185, 190, 203–5, 209, 214, 235, 254, 261, 264
   Lorrin Thurston and, 205
Parker, Robert Waipa, 163, 258
Pauahi, Bernice. See Bishop, Bernice Pauahi
Paulet, Lord George, 14, 16. See also Paulet Affair
Paulet Affair, 13, 14, 16, 25, 151, 221, 243
Pearl Harbor, 54
Pearl Harbor amendment to reciprocity treaty, 150–51
Pearl River basin, 54–55, 148–52
Pele, xix, 4
petitions
   anti-annexation, 279, 285
   pro-annexation, 233
Philadelphia, USS, 254

Pike, Albert, 128
Pioneer Mill Company, 75
Poepoe, J. M., 146
Polynesia to become oceanic empire, 124, 127
popular government, 47
population growth, 62
Portsmouth, USS, 54
Preston, Frances Folsom Cleveland, 278–79
prisoners, treatment of, 269
provisional government (P.G.), 224, 228, 230–33, 238, 243, 247–49, 251, 252
  anniversary celebrations, 245–47
  Claus Spreckels and, 234–36
  constitution enacted by, 253. *See also* constitutions of Hawai'i
  declaration of, 218
  Joaquin Miller and, 268–69
  John Stevens and, 209, 216, 218, 221, 225
  Lili'u and, 221, 223, 236, 238, 239, 242, 243, 246, 248, 250, 255, 272
  preparaton for, 209, 216
  Sanford Dole as president of, 216, 218–19
  troops, 221, 224
Punahou school. *See* O'ahu College
Punch Bowl (monthly publication), 56
Punchbowl, 6
Punchbowl Battery, 61, 200, 262
Punchbowl Hill, 30, 60, 87, 138, 292
Punchbowl National Cemetary, 289

quarantines, 88–89
Queen Lili'uokalani Trust, 295
Queen's Songbook, The (Lili'u et al.), 300

race riots, 58–60
racial composition of Hawai'i, 65
Rebellion of 1887, 140–47. *See under* Bayonet Constitution
Reciprocity Treaty of 1875, 54, 69, 72, 150–52, 165, 176
  amendments to, 66, 150–51
  annexation treaty and, 44, 54–55
  approved by U.S. Congress, 66
  Britain and, 67
  Claus Spreckels and, 72, 78
  criticisms of and opposition to, 66–68
  and demand for Hawaiian sugar, 72
  failed attempts to negotiate, 26, 62
  Kalākaua and, 64, 66, 68, 151, 175–76
  Lili'u and, 67–68, 151–52
  McKinley tariff bill and, 165
  in the media, 44, 54, 66
  overview, 44, 66
  passage in 1876, 68, 69, 150
  Pearl Harbor and, 150–51, 182
  Queen Emma on, 55
  renewal, 150
revolution of 1993. *See* Hawaiian Kingdom, overthrow of
Rickard, William, 256
riots during election of 1874, 58–60
Rooke, Emma. *See* Emma Rooke
"Rookery" (cottage), 56
Roosevelt, Theodore, 183, 284
Rosebery, Lord, 125
Royal Hawaiian Agricultural Society, 34, 35
Royal Hawaiian Band, 93, 101, 108, 109, 115, 116, 138, 158, 231, 247, 294
Royal Household Guards, 59, 207, 220, 224, 267, 272. *See also* Washington Place: guards posted at

Royal School, 9, 292. *See also* Chiefs' Children's School
Ruth, Princess. *See* Keʻelikōlani, Princess Ruth

Sacramento Union (newspaper), 64, 65
Safety, Committee of, 208–11, 213, 216–17, 221
Salisbury, Lord, 126, 132
Samoa
  civil war, 124–25
  mission to and alliance with, 125–27
San Francisco, 77, 160, 233, 306
  arms purchased in, 140, 254, 256
  Gibson in, 150–53
  Kalākaua in, 62, 64, 87, 167–70
  Kalākaua's funeral procession in, 172
  Liliʻu in, 77, 127, 136, 276–77
  steamer service between Honolulu and, 85
  sugar trade and, 36, 66–67, 69–72, 78, 84, 85, 109. *See also* Hawaiian Commercial & Sugar Company
San Francisco Chronicle (newspaper), 109, 111–12, 250
San Francisco Examiner (newspaper), 181, 187
San Francisco mint, 108
Sandwich, Earl of, xxiii
Saturday Press (newspaper), 110
Seward, Major William T., 256
Silva, Noenoe, 272
Simpson, Alexander, 14
"Skating Rink," 209, 211
smallpox epidemic, 25, 88–90
Smith, W. O., 188, 208
Snow Cottage, 238
Spain, 282

Spreckels, Adolph B. "A.B." (Claus's son), 111–12, 291
Spreckels, Alma de Bretteville (Adolph's wife), 290
Spreckels, Anna Christina Mangels (Claus's wife), 69, 70, 85
Spreckels, Claus ("Sugar King")
  annexation and, 182, 233–34
  background and life history, 69–73
  Bay Sugar Refinery and, 70, 116
  California Sugar Refinery and, 71, 234
  Celso Moreno and, 84
  criticisms of, 109, 110
  departures from San Francisco, 71, 84, 108, 116
  end of reign in Hawaiʻi, 114
  family lawsuit, 290
  felt no obligation to plantation workers, 84
  finances, 108, 114, 234–35, 237
    bribery, 79–80
  Germany and, 71, 73, 235
  Gibson and, 86, 110, 114, 116
  health problems, 71
  irrigation, water rights, and, 78–80, 84, 85, 292
  James Blount and, 234, 236
  Joe Strong and, 104
  Kalākaua and, 79–80, 84, 114–16
  Kalākaua government and, 86, 110
  Keʻelikōlani and, 85–86
  Liliʻu and, 236, 276
  Lorrin Thurston and, 110, 205, 233
  Mariposa and, 107–8
  marriage, 69
  nervous breakdown, 71
  overview and characterizations of, xxviii, 69, 110, 235–36

Spreckels, Claus ("Sugar King")
(*continued*)
  personality and lifestyle, 79, 85, 116,
    234–36
    Teutonic approach to business and
      parenting, 72–73
  provisional government and, 234–36
  reciprocity treaty and, 72, 78
  relations with Hawaiian royal family, 114
  relations with his children, 70, 72–73,
    108, 111, 237, 290–91
  returns to San Francisco, 71, 116, 236,
    237
  royal decorations, 116
  Sam Parker and, 205
  in San Francisco, 70, 112, 113,
    276–77
  Sanford Dole and, 68, 69, 235
  ships, 84–85, 113
  sugar business and, 69–72, 78, 84,
    85, 112, 233–34, 290–91. *See
    also* Hawaiian Commercial &
    Sugar Company; Spreckelsville
    plantation
  transportation and, 84
  trips to Hawai'i, 72, 113, 233–36
  waning influence in Hawai'i, 116
  writings, 181–82, 235
Spreckels, Gus (Claus's son), 290
Spreckels, John D. (Claus's son), 69,
  70, 72–73, 291. See also John D.
  Spreckels
Spreckels, Rudolph (Claus's son), 73,
  234, 256, 290
Spreckels Sugar Company, 291. See also
  Hawaiian Commercial & Sugar
  Company
Spreckelsville mill, 85
Spreckelsville plantation, 84, 85. *See also*
  Spreckels, Claus

"Stand Firm" (song), 46–47
Stevens, Ashton, 168–69
Stevens, John Leavitt, 194–95, 205, 209,
  215–18, 225, 233, 252
  aboard USS *Boston*, 212–13
  Albert Willis and, 238
  background and overview, 194
  illness, 215, 216
  John Foster and, 227
  Lili'u and, 194, 195, 211, 221, 222,
    233, 237–38
  Lorrin Thurston and, 194, 205, 209,
    216–17
  Sam Parker and, 214–16
  Sanford Dole and, 216–18
  writings, 195
Stevenson, Fanny, 158, 159
Stevenson, Robert Louis, 125, 157–60,
  178–79
  Lili'u and, 158, 161, 178–79
Strong, Isobel, 103–4, 143–44, 157, 158
Strong, Joe, 104, 157, 158
sugar boiling, 43–44
sugar industry, 43–44, 165–67, 290–91.
  See also Hawaiian Commercial &
  Sugar Company
  Mark Twain on, 65
  in U.S. vs. Hawai'i, 66–67
sugar mills, 43–44, 72, 75, 85, 204
"Sugar Palace" (mansion), 291
sugar plantations, xxvii
  James Cook and, xxii
sugar quality, 66–67
sugar trade, xxvii–xxviii, 191. *See also*
  reciprocity treaty
  McKinley Tariff and, 165–66, 191
  San Francisco and, 36, 66, 69–72, 78,
    84, 85, 109. *See also* Hawaiian
    Commercial & Sugar Company
Sugar Trust, 233

sugarcane, methods of hauling, 85
sugarcane fields. *See also* Līhu'e
  plantation
  laborers in, 87

Temple of Science. *See* Hale Nauā
  Society
Tenedos (British gunboat), 54
Teutonic (ship), 227
Texas, annexation of, 67
Thirteen, Committee of, 140–42, 188
Thomas, Admiral Richard, 17, 18
Throne Room, 178, 185, 264
Thurston, Lorrin Andrews, 145,
    208–12, 224
  annexation and, 188, 189, 209, 216,
    217, 282
  Annexation Club and, 188, 189, 208, 209
  background and life history, 57, 106
  business ventures, 188
  Charles Wilson and, 210
  Claus Spreckels and, 110, 205, 233
  Committee of Safety and, 211
  Committee of Thirteen and, 139–40,
    142
  constitution and, 145, 202, 204, 208,
    211–12, 218
  Daily Bulletin and, 110
  death, 290
  expansionism and, 253
  Gibson and, 141, 153
  Hale Nauā Society and, 116–17
  Hawaiian League and, 139–40
  Honolulu Rifles and, 141, 209
  illness, 216–18
  Independents and, 114
  John Bush and, 186
  John Morgan and, 251
  John Stevens and, 194, 205, 209,
    216–17

  Kalākaua and, 106–7, 137, 142
  Kapi'olani and, 147
  Lili'u and, 58, 147, 186, 188, 200, 205,
    209, 212, 280
  in the media, 228, 229
  opium affair and, 141
  overview of, xxviii, 106–7
  Pacific Commercial Advertiser and, 207,
    290
  personality, xxviii
  as P.G.'s minister, 251
  positions
    Minister of Interior, 137
    representative, 188
  reverence for Hawai'i's landscape,
    58
  Robert Wilcox and, 186
  Sanford Dole and, 57, 58, 106, 110,
    114, 139–40, 153, 216–17, 224,
    243, 269, 270
  speeches, xxviii, 141–42
  United States and, 189, 252, 253
  U.S. Congress and, 282
  Volcano House Hotel and, 189
  World's Columbian Exposition and,
    188–89
Thurston, Lorrin P., 290
Thurston, Lucy Goodale, 280
Thurston, Reverend Asa, 3–6, 9, 57
trade, command of the seas and the
    power of, 182–83
transportation between islands and
    mainland, 84
travel ban during smallpox epidemic, 88,
    90
Trousseau, Dr., 184, 214–15
Turner, Frederick Jackson, 253
Tuscarora, USS, 54
Twain, Mark, 64–66, 154–55
Twigg-Smith, Thurston, 290

United States. *See also* annexation; specific topics
  American troops in Hawai'i, 59–60, 214–16, 219. *See also* Hawaiian Kingdom: overthrow of; Wilcox Rebellion of 1889
  Congress, 63
  expansion and expansionist sentiment, 67, 124, 184, 253, 283
  proposed reciprocity treaty with Hawai'i, 44, 54–55
  relations with Hawai'i, 54
  as rival in courtship contest for Hawai'i, xxvii, 14
  threat posed to monarchy by Americans, 47

Victoria, Queen, 38–39
  Charles Bishop on, 181
  Jubilee celebrations, 123, 132–36, 138, 142
  Ka'iulani and, 192
  Kalākaua and, 90
  Kalākaua compared with, 40, 142, 147
  Kapi'olani and, 133, 135–36
  Lili'u and, 123, 124, 133, 147, 223
  Lili'u compared with, 181, 226
  Lorrin Andrews Thurston on, 142
  as model for Hawai'i's monarchs, 18
volcanoes, xviii–xix, 32, 36, 57, 188–89. *See also* Mauna Loa
voting rights, 165, 201

W. G. Irwin (sailing ship), 85
W. H. Dimond (sailing ship), 85
Wailuka, 86
War Between the States, 33, 44

Washington Place, 42, 247, 248, 267
  gardens, 42, 163, 231, 259, 261, 273
  guards posted at, 60, 224, 230–31, 256
  Kamehameha III and, 23
  Lili'u arrested at, 258–59
  Lili'u on house arrest at, 270, 273, 274
  Mary Dominis and, 45
  mortgaged, 230
  naming of, 23
  residents, 256, 258, 285, 286, 293
    Lili'u and John Dominis, 30, 41, 42, 50, 74, 77, 86, 155, 157, 161, 163, 184, 185, 223, 224, 230, 248, 255–56
  tours of, 293, 305
  weapons found at, 259, 267
water rights, 78–80, 85, 292. See also irrigation
Westminster Abbey, 135
Whitney, Henry M., 54–55
Wilcox, Robert William, 180, 187, 189
  in 1895 counterrevolution, 256–58
  background and overview, 161–62
  firearms purchased by, 162
  John Bush and, 180, 191
  Kalākaua and, 154, 161–63
  Lili'u and, 161–64, 180, 191, 214, 267
  populist appeal, 186
  positions held by
    House of Representatives, 164–65
    secretary of foreign affairs, 267
  Sanford Dole and, 265–66
  sentenced to death, 265–66
Wilcox Rebellion of 1889, 161–65, 214
Wilkes, Commodore Charles, 149
William G. Irwin and Company, 205

Willis, Albert S.
  Grover Cleveland and, 239, 240, 243, 252
  on Hawai'i, 253
  Lili'u's interviews with, 238–42, 250
  and the media, 247
  Sanford Dole and, 243, 246
Wilson, Charles Burnett, 180, 185, 210,
    220, 268
  Lili'u and, 136–38, 185, 202, 210,
    262–64
    supposed love affair, 180

Wilson, Eveline "Kitty" Townsend, 262,
    270
Wilson, Marshal, 220
Wodehouse, James, 62, 80, 143, 194,
    205
Wolf, Gertrude, 193–94
Women's Patriotic League, 275, 279

Young, Brigham, 81

Zealandia (ship), 153